D1271373

SPORT IN SOVIET SOCIETY

SOVIET AND EAST EUROPEAN STUDIES

Editorial Board

JOHN BARBER, A. BROWN, R. W. DAVIES, P. HANSON,
DAVID LANE, MARY MCAULEY, A. PRAVDA,
G. H. N. SETON-WATSON, P. WILES

The National Association for Soviet and East European Studies exists for the purpose of promoting study and research on the social sciences as they relate to the Soviet Union and the countries of Eastern Europe. The Monograph Series is intended to promote the publication of works presenting substantial and original research in the economics, politics, sociology and modern history of the USSR and Eastern Europe.

SOVIET AND EAST EUROPEAN STUDIES

Sport in Soviet Society

DEVELOPMENT OF
SPORT AND PHYSICAL EDUCATION
IN RUSSIA AND THE USSR

JAMES RIORDAN
Lecturer in Russian Studies
University of Bradford

CAMBRIDGE UNIVERSITY PRESS

CAMBRIDGE

LONDON · NEW YORK · MELBOURNE

Published by the Syndics of the Cambridge University Press
The Pitt Building, Trumpington Street, Cambridge CB2 1RP
Bentley House, 200 Euston Road, London NW1 2DB
32 East 57th Street, New York, NY 10022, USA
296 Beaconsfield Parade, Middle Park, Melbourne 3206, Australia

© Cambridge University Press 1977

First published 1977

Printed in Great Britain by
Western Printing Services Ltd, Bristol

Library of Congress Cataloguing in Publication Data
Riordan, James.
Sport in Soviet society.
(Soviet and East European studies).
Based on the author's thesis, University of Birmingham.
Bibliography: p.
Includes index.
1. Sports – Russia – History. 2. Physical education and
training – Russia – History. I. Title. II. Series.
GV623.R56   796'.0947   76 9729
ISBN 0 521 21284 7

142244

To my mother

Contents

Contents

Acknowledgements

The basic material for this book was gathered in different parts of the Soviet Union from 1960 to 1975, eventually materialising as a PhD thesis for the University of Birmingham. My thanks are due particularly to my former colleagues and team mates at Progress Publishers, Moscow, Yuri Sdobnikov and Len Stoklitsky, for firing my enthusiasm yet harnessing my energy; they are, of course, not a whit responsible for any of the views I express. I am also indebted to the USSR–Great Britain Society in Moscow for facilitating my sports visits to the Baltic republics and Central Asia, and to Progress Publishers for enabling me to work in sports schools, be an active member of *Spartak*, study in the archives of the Moscow Physical Culture Institute and visit many other Soviet cities.

I owe it to David Lane for initially suggesting this theme to me and to Brian Bicat for his valuable comments on my final draft. Most of all I would like to record my gratitude to two people without whom this study would probably have not been completed, despite their contempt for almost all forms of physical exercise: Geoffrey Barker and my wife, Rashida. As my research superviser, Mr Barker read my numerous drafts so thoroughly that the thesis eventually grew to nearly a thousand pages. But for his criticism and advice, the book would lack much of the analysis, continuity and readability demanded of any book in this series. If it were not for the encouragement, selfless labour and Tatar obduracy of my wife, I should spend all my free hours playing instead of writing about sport. With the greatest respect and affection, I thank them both.

J.R.

Bradford
January 1976

Introduction

My desire to undertake this study springs from a long-standing involvement in sport and a more recent interest in the study of Soviet society. In 1961, I was able to combine the two by going to the USSR, where I lived and worked for five years and had an opportunity to observe and engage in Soviet sport.

In my first period of residence in the USSR, from July 1961 to August 1965, I was initially a postgraduate student (for 18 months) and subsequently an employee of a publishing house in Moscow. While a student, I took an active part in student sporting activities as a member of student football and tennis teams and as a participant in less organised pursuits – e.g. weekend rambles, fishing and skiing excursions. As a Soviet employee and trade union member, I engaged in sporting activities (summer and winter fishing, shooting and chess) organised from my workplace and then became a member of the *Spartak* Sports Society, playing regularly for the Moscow *Spartak* badminton team (1963–1965). I also pursued a wide range of sports activities that included soccer most Sunday mornings in summer at the Lenin Stadium (and often, too, in the yard of my block of flats), tennis, swimming, skiing and chess.

As a spectator, I watched a great variety of sporting contests at levels from backyard to international matches, in Moscow and Leningrad, the Baltic republics, the Transcaucasus and Central Asia.

Finally, as the part-time Moscow correspondent (1961–1965 and 1970–1971) of the journal of the British Olympic Association, I was able to see sports organisations and amenities in different parts of the country, making special sports tours of the three Baltic republics in 1964 and of Central Asia and Kazakhstan in 1965, which afforded an opportunity to discuss sport widely with administrators and athletes and to see sport at various levels: school, children's sports club, trade union society, factory circle and collective farm.

In my second period of residence in the USSR, from October 1970 to March 1971, I was again a resident employee of the same publishing house, though I then had specific research purposes in mind in revisiting Moscow. Largely because I was a Soviet employee, I gained access to primary sources normally inaccessible to Western scholars: materials in the Sports Archives of the Central State Institute of Physical Culture and Sport as well as in sports libraries and museums both at the Central State Institute of Physical Culture and the Lenin Stadium. I became a regular member of a 'Keep Fit' (*Bodrost' i zdorov'ye*) group which met twice weekly at the Lenin Stadium. I also managed to visit, through the good offices of the USSR–Great Britain Society, two sports boarding schools (one in Tallinn and one in Kiev) and other sports complexes and to interview a number of sports officials, sportsmen and physical educationalists. Some of these meetings developed into extensive, less formal contacts. For example, an international sportsman played host at his town and country homes, took me to training sessions and sports events and on a tour of his former institute. Since this second period of residence, I have managed to spend at least a month of each year in the Soviet Union, and I led a sports tour to Moscow and Leningrad during 1975.

This residential and first-hand experience provided me with opportunities for gaining some insight into an area of social activity little known in the West, revealing not only the workings of sports institutions but also something of the motives, attitudes and values of those who work within them. It also led me to the belief that a historical account of sport could contribute to an understanding of the nature of Soviet society – looking at it from a different angle, as it were – and of the place of sport in society in general.

Soviet views on sport and physical culture

In the official Soviet view, sport is considered to be part of physical culture which has four components: (a) organised

physical education; (b) playful activities or games; (c) all forms
of (socially approved) active leisure-pursuits; and, (d) organised
sport.[1] Organised physical education consists of general physical
exercises with a therapeutic motive uppermost, e.g. morning
exercises or physical education in school; physical exercises with
a sporting bias, such as gymnastics and acrobatics; physical
exercises for utilitarian work purposes, e.g. 'production gymnastics';
and physical exercises for mass artistic or aesthetic display. Playful activities may be individual, group or mass games which,
although not as a strictly regulated obligation, are based on
generally accepted rules and relatively stable conditions of conduct. Active leisure pursuits are included in physical culture as
long as they are considered to add to the mental and physical
well-being of the individual or to that of the community in
general. Some pursuits are at times referred to more narrowly as
'tourism' – which consists of a variety of organised outdoor
activities including hiking, camping and rock climbing. Organised
sport is regarded as a playful, competitive physical or mental
activity, based on rules and norms, with the object of achieving a
result.

In Soviet writings, the word 'sport' is sometimes interpreted
differently. As a leading Soviet sport theorist, Professor N. I.
Ponomaryov, has noted, 'some writers take sport as the dominant
form of expression of physical culture; they therefore use the
concept "sport" as a synonym for the concept "physical culture"'.[2] Moreover, the combined expression 'physical culture
and sport' is commonly found in Soviet writings on sport although,
strictly speaking, it is incorrect – since, in terms of the categories
of widely accepted Soviet theory, sport is a component of physical
culture and not something separate.

For some Soviet authors, sport is also a 'societal institution with
a socialising function'.[3] Others see it in an even broader per-

---

[1] These definitions are largely based on those provided in A. D. Novikov
and L. P. Matveyev (eds.), *Teoriya fizicheskovo vospitaniya* (Moscow,
1959), pp. 95–136.
[2] N. I. Ponomaryov, 'K voprosu o predmete marksistkoi sotsiologii
fizicheskoi kul'tury i sporta', *Teoriya i praktika fizicheskoi kul'tury*, 1973,
No. 1, p. 63.
[3] N. I. Ponomaryov, 'Fenomen igry i sporta', *Teoriya i praktika fizicheskoi
kul'tury*, 1972, No. 8, p. 6.

spective. Thus, 'Sport is an important and complex social phenomenon. It may be viewed as *physical exercise* for the purpose of
attaining top results and victories in competition; as a unique
social movement involving millions of people and consistently
confirming lofty human ideals; as the sum total of state and public
institutions that help a vital social sphere to function; and as a
complex and lofty *art form* that inspires sportsmen and provides
spectators with real aesthetic enjoyment.'[4]

The four components in the Soviet framework – organised
physical education, playful activities, active leisure pursuits and
sport – together comprise physical culture which, itself, is
regarded as part of the overall culture of a society. It is 'the sum
total of social achievements connected with man's physical
development and education . . . [it is] part of the overall culture
of society and represents all measures taken to make people
healthy and to improve their physical abilities'.[5] This rather
broad and explicitly instrumental definition, perhaps predictable
in a planned 'conscious' society, implies that sport may be a
separate sector of culture but is regarded as an integral part of a
broadly conceived sphere of cultural life. In terms of its social
significance, it is seen, to use the Marxist terms current in the
USSR, as part of the cultural 'superstructure' of society resting
on the 'base' of the (ownership) relations of production; it is
therefore expected to vary in nature and function in different
types of society.

Figure 1 represents an attempt to portray the Soviet view of
the component parts of physical culture and their inter-relation-
ship.

Given this conceptual framework, sport in the Soviet Union is
by no means a matter of fun and games; it is not the 'garden' of
human activities. Physical culture is on a par with mental culture
and has important functions to discharge: 'The ultimate goal of
physical culture in our state is to prepare the younger generation
for a long and happy life, highly productive labour for the benefit
of society and for defence of their socialist homeland.'[6] Professor

[4] V. B. Kuchevsky, 'Sport kak sovokupnost' obshchestvennykh otnoshenii',
Teoriya i praktika fizicheskoi kul'tury, 1972, No. 9, p. 5.
[5] *Entsiklopedichesky slovar' po fizicheskoi kul'ture i sportu*, Vol. III (Moscow, 1963), p. 226.
[6] V. V. Belorusova, *Pedagogika* (Moscow, 1972), pp. 182–183.

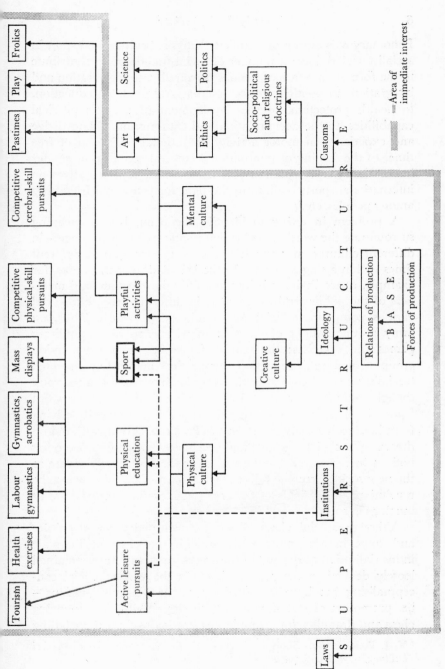

Fig. 1. Sport in society: the Soviet view

Ponomaryov is even more explicit: 'Physical culture and sport in socialist society have a number of social functions: to contribute to the formation of a harmonious personality, to socialisation and integration, to political, moral, mental and aesthetic education, to health protection, to the development of people's physical capabilities, to the accumulation and transmission of knowledge and experience in motor activity, to rational utilisation of free time, to the forging of international cultural contacts, to greater international representation [i.e. more Soviet representatives on international sports bodies], to the fight for peace and friendship among peoples, etc.'[7]

A problem in trying to identify the penumbra of meaning surrounding the word 'sport' is that nuances change in usage – in different cultures, among various social groups, and at different times within a single culture. In the USSR during the 1920s, for example, as we shall see below, not only did the state and members of the public tend to see sport in differing ways, but so did various competing official and semi-official groups. Thus, an army group thought of sport mainly in terms of paramilitary games and exercises; the minds of members of a trade union group turned to 'production gymnastics' and newly invented 'socialist workers' games' in the first place; a strong health group thought only in terms of 'physical culture' and used the word 'sport' itself to denigrate physical competition as an evil deriving from bourgeois society; while to the *Proletkul'tists*, it conjured up dreams of socialist pageants and spectacles. (Of course, diverging notions in the search for the ideal, for the forms appropriate to the new society, emerged, in the years immediately following the revolution, in all fields of culture – in literature and theatre as much as in sport.)

Although official views of what constituted physical culture and sport became more uniform with the onset of full-scale industrialisation at the end of the 1920s, the terms have remained loosely defined to the present day. On the whole, official conceptualising has been governed by normative considerations – i.e. promotion of state-favoured activities. While countenancing chess and draughts, for example, the state stops short of including

[7] N. I. Ponomaryov, 'Sport i obshchestvo', *Teoriya i praktika fizicheskoi kul'tury*, 1973, No. 6, p. 72.

such activities as dominoes and card playing in the Soviet sports movement (see above, p. 202). Sometimes it draws distinctions within a sport: men's soccer and wrestling are included in the sports movement, women's soccer and wrestling are not (see pp. 320–322); body building and boxing are recognised as Soviet 'sports' as long as they keep within certain officially prescribed limits – which are not static. In yet other 'sports', the state appears to be less motivated by functional than by political factors, tolerating activities such as horse racing and folk games, which involve gambling and which imply values that go against the official ethos, as a concession to popular tastes.

For practical reasons, I have, in the body of this book, generally adopted the Soviet interpretation of physical culture and sport.

Social significance of sport in Soviet society

While not wishing to overstate the importance of sport in Soviet society, it is my belief that sport has had particular social significance in the development of the USSR. This is all the more so because the place of sport is evidently more central in the Soviet social system. Suffice it here to make the point that sport is one of the most far-reaching social activities in the USSR; it extends to and unites wider sections of the population than probably any other social activity, transcending nationality, sex, age, social position, rural/urban location and political attitudes. It has proved to be of utility by reason of its inherent qualities of being easily understood and enjoyed, being capable of developing mass enthusiasm, being apolitical (at least superficially), and permitting safe self-expression. It has had an advantage over sex, drinking, religious ritual and other forms of emotional release and companionship formation by being officially approved, and therefore less guilt-inducing, yet being relatively free of rigid official sanctions. It has had an advantage over literature, theatre and other forms of cultural expression in being more readily comprehensible to the mass public as well as less amenable to direct political control over style and content. It has had the advantage over political meetings and parades by being less demanding on intellect and patience.

These advantages have been particularly marked in a society

which has, in a short span of time, lived through such shattering events as three revolutions, a civil war, rapid industrialisation, forced collectivisation of agriculture, purges, mass terror, and two world wars. In such a society, hard work, discipline, self-censorship and periodically necessary acute readjustments seem to have needed a counterpart in sport, which offers a broad channel for the discharge of emotional tensions.

The study of sport in a centrally planned and communist-governed society may therefore be revealing because it deals with such a wide range of social processes and investigable forms of activity, within which a whole nexus of social phenomena has found fairly open expression.

I
The beginnings of
an organised sports movement,
1861–1917

As team sports spread from England throughout Europe and the world, and as the various schools of gymnastics gained in popularity, they gradually made their way into a Russia that, in the 1860s, was becoming more and more receptive to new modes of entertainment and physical education. With serfdom abolished in 1861, the way was open for industrial and urban development at a much higher tempo than hitherto. Members of the well-to-do middle class and liberal noblemen began to organise private clubs in the major cities for the pursuit of such sports as yachting, tennis, skating, fencing, cricket, croquet and gymnastics – even billiards and snooker.[1] For their entertainment as spectators and punters, professionals and promoters were providing horse racing, boxing, cycling, soccer and various displays of strength. In Table 1 are listed the earliest sporting organisations formed in Russia.

This brief sketch of the development of individual sports cannot be taken as presenting a fully balanced picture of sporting life in Russia prior to 1917. It is intended as a source of background information to the Soviet period and, in part, as a corrective to the Soviet tendency to play down the extent and quality of pre-revolutionary participation in sport.

Aquatic sports

The first sports club of a new type was the St Petersburg River Yacht Club, formed in 1860. Its members were not drawn

[1] For example, the 'English Club' in Moscow, founded by Russian and foreign merchants in the 1860s, catered exclusively for billiards and snooker. With the change of political fortunes, it became the Museum of the Revolution, as it is today, on Gorky Street.

TABLE I   *The organisation of Russian sporting activities in the 18th and 19th centuries*

Period	Sport	Earliest organisation set up	Date founded	Class
1700–1799	Yachting	Neva Flotilla	1718	Military
1800–1824	Shooting	Amateur Shooting Society	1800[a]	Aristocracy
1825–1849	Horse racing	St Petersburg Horse Racing Society	1826	Aristocracy
	Swimming	Neva School of Swimming	1834	
	Yachting	Imperial Yacht Club	1846	
1850–1879	Chess	St Petersburg Chess Club	1853	Gentry
	Fencing	Officers' Fencing Gymnasium	1857	
	Boating	St Petersburg River Yacht Club	1860	
	Lawn tennis	Neva Lawn Tennis Circle	1860	
	Gymnastics	Pal'ma Gymnastics Society	1863	
	Ice skating	Amateur Skating Society	1864	
	Cricket	St Petersburg Tennis and Cricket Club	1868	
1880–1889	Cycling	Tsar'skoye Selo Cycling Circle	1880	Middle class
	Heavy athletics[b]	Krayevsky Heavy Athletics Circle	1885	
	Athletics	Petrov Amateur Running Society[c]	1886	
		St Petersburg Circle of Amateur Sportsmen[c]	1888	
1890–1899	Soccer	Victoria Football Club[d]	1894	Middle class
	Boxing	Baron Kister's English Boxing Arena	1895	
	Skiing	Moscow Skiers' Club	1895	
	Ice hockey	St Petersburg Circle of Amateur Sportsmen	1898	

[a] Approximately.

[b] Heavy athletics comprised a wide range of strongman feats and exercises: weightlifting, wrestling, body building and various circus acts. Dr Krayevsky's Circle was followed by *The Hercules Club* in 1896 and *Sanitas* in 1897.

[c] The Petrov Society's members confined themselves to running, mainly cross country; the St Petersburg Circle at first engaged in a number of athletics events, then branched out into other sports, such as soccer, cycling, ice-hockey and lawn tennis.

exclusively from the aristocracy, as had been the case with the famous Imperial Yacht Club, dating from 1846, whose membership had been restricted to 150 noblemen – the Grand Dukes, the high dignitaries of the Court, the Tsar's aides-de-camp and a few foreign diplomats who were granted honorary membership. Although the new club admitted the middle classes, it was still socially exclusive insofar as, like other clubs, it stressed its amateur status and excluded anyone who had ever been employed in manual labour for wages.[2] One novel concession it did make, however, was to admit women (in 1866). Besides yachting, the club also held regular rowing races, the first official tournament being held in 1860. A Scot, MacGregor, set up the first canoeing club in the 1860s. In 1867, a yacht club was opened in Moscow; others were founded along the Volga, Dnieper, the Black Sea and Baltic Sea coasts. By 1898, there were over 40 such clubs in existence to form the All-Russia Association of Rowing and Yachting Clubs. A separate association for rowing was formed in 1908, with national championships held every year from 1896 to 1914 and a total of 24 rowing clubs in existence by 1914.

In 1908, a swimming school opened in Shuvalov, near the capital; in addition to the various styles of swimming, it also gave lessons in diving and water polo. Although no outstanding successes were gained internationally, water sports grew steadily in popularity. In 1912, an Amateur Swimming Society started up in Moscow, which inspired the creation of the *Sanitas* and the *Skhodnya* swimming clubs and the Society for Mountain Skiing and Aquatic Sports in the city. All water sports were pursued outdoors, there being no indoor swimming pools in the country. By 1914, it is estimated that some 1,500 swimmers belonged to the various clubs.[3]

[2] I. A. Tarabrin (ed.), *Pyat'desyat shagov sportivnoi Rossii* (Moscow, 1967), p. 107.
[3] *Sport v SSSR* (1968), No. 6, p. 31.

---

[a] Other clubs had played soccer as a sideline to other sports before 1897, but the *Victoria* (an Anglo-German club) was the first to be exclusively concerned with soccer.

Sources: *Entsiklopedichesky slovar' po fizicheskoi kul'ture i sportu* (*v. 3 tomakh*) (Moscow, 1961): Vol. II, p. 22 (horse racing); p. 252 (swimming); Vol. III, p. 312 (chess). F. Samoukov (ed.), *Istoriya fizicheskoi kul'tury* (Moscow, 1964), pp. 216–222.

Lawn tennis

After its introduction in mid-century, lawn tennis soon attracted a following among the rich. Like its English parent, the Russian offspring gained royal patronage with several of the tsars taking up the game, which of course made it fashionable with both the gentry and the *parvenu* middle class. The Neva Lawn Tennis Circle came into being in St Petersburg in 1860, to be joined, eight years later, by the St Petersburg Tennis and Cricket Club. Both clubs played cricket and croquet, but these games do not appear to have caught on among Russians outside the twin capitals (partly owing to lack of grass). The games imported by foreigners were, of course, not always intended for Russian consumption: although cricket and field hockey were reported as having been played by British residents as far apart as Odessa and St Petersburg between 1870 and 1890, they seem to have made little impact on Russians. Tennis did, however, and courts had been laid in Moscow, Rostov, Taganrog, Kiev, Odessa and Nizhny Novgorod by the end of the century. By 1913, as many as 115 lawn tennis courts had been laid in Moscow and St Petersburg, and the National Association of Lawn Tennis Clubs, formed in 1907, had the large number of 48 member clubs in 1908.

Winter sports

With snow covering European Russia for six or seven months of the year, and parts of Siberia all the year round, winter games naturally played an important part in organised winter recreation.[4] During that part of the year when the rivers were ice-bound, yacht clubs not infrequently turned themselves into ice skating or figure skating organisations. In effect, the first skating club arose in the capital in 1864. Somewhat later, the Society of Amateur Skaters sent its members abroad to take part in competitions and, in 1883, A. P. Lebedev won the unofficial world figure

[4] In the centre of European Russia, in Moscow, the winter snow normally lasts from November to April, with temperatures averaging 10°C below zero in January. In the North-East of Siberia, in the Lena Basin, the average January temperature is −40°C and snow lasts for 200 days a year; in Yakutia, the northern hemisphere's pole of cold, the snow lasts for most of the year.

skating title in Helsinki – the first Russian success in international competition. When the official world championships were inaugurated, Lebedev won the men's title in 1890. A member of the same society, Alexander Panshin, won the Austrian speed skating championships and went on to win the world title in 1889 at the Amsterdam Speed Skating Club; a month later, he won the first ever Russian speed skating tournament, held in Moscow.

In the first decade of the 20th century, the great Russian figure skater Nikolai Panin dominated Russian, European and world figure skating and won a gold medal at the 1908 London Olympic Games. In speed skating, too, Russians continued to do well internationally. In 1910 and 1911, Nikolai Strunnikov won European and world titles and set a world record that remained unsurpassed for 17 years. The following year, however, he left the sport in protest at the parsimonious attitude of the Russian authorities, having been refused financial support for his journeys to compete abroad. His vacant European title was won in 1913 by Vasili Ippolitov.

Moscow became the centre of organised skiing with the establishment in 1895 of the famous Moscow Skiers' Club. In 1910, a league was set up with ten member clubs and a National Skiers' Association founded, so initiating the first national ski championships over 30 versts (32 km). Long distance skiing became very popular: in 1911, four Moscow skiers completed the Moscow–St Petersburg run (a distance of 725 km) in 12 days, 6 hours and 22 minutes. The next year, the first ski jumping contests were held at Pargolovo, near the capital.

Ice hockey was another game cultivated by the St Petersburg Circle of Amateur Sportsmen after 1898, and a city championship was held with eight teams taking part, including *Yusupov Sad*, *Narva* and *Merkur*. *Yusupov Sad* became strong enough to make a successful foreign tour in 1907, winning six of its eight games against Swedish, Norwegian and Berlin teams. In that year, the Petersburg League had 15 clubs which formed the nucleus for an All-Russia Ice Hockey Association of 32 clubs formed in 1914.

Fencing and riding

Another sport at which Russians did well internationally was fencing. It had long had many adherents among the aristocracy but now gained increasing popularity among the middle class, many of whom aspired to the culture of the nobility, skill with the foil being very fashionable. An Officers' Fencing Gymnasium opened in the capital in 1857, to be followed by similar military clubs in other parts of the Empire, notably at Warsaw and Kiev. In 1900, Alexander Zakovorot, a working man by birth, one of the few to break through the social barriers, gained the world épée title in France.

Equestrian sports – particularly as spectacles – were gaining support as the 19th century wore on. Horse racing as an institutionalised sport had begun as far back as 1826, organised by noblemen in the small town of Lebedyan on the River Don. Since then, it had been mainly a sport for cavalry officers but, by the turn of the century, race courses had been laid out – not in the English open grass course style, but more commonly as dirt tracks in the Greek style of 'hippodromes' – which could also be used for other spectator sports, like cycling, athletics, soccer and even motor-cycling. (In fact, after 1890, they were as much the venues for cycling as they were for horse racing, trotting, steeple-chasing and hurdling.) By the end of the century, horse races were attracting crowds of between 10,000 and 20,000, so providing a living for professional jockeys who were engaged by various noblemen's stables. That their skill was relatively high is evident from several notable victories abroad: Konstantin Avalov rode the winner of the British Grand National at Aintree in 1912 – the toughest steeplechase in the world – and a Russian officer won a major hurdles race in Vienna in 1914. Horse racing had long enjoyed royal and noble patronage, the nobility taking a pride in the improvement of horse racing stud and importing bloodstock from areas of the Empire noted for their fine horses – e.g. the Caucasus, Turkestan and Bashkiria. The Orlov stables gained world renown in the late 19th century for their excellent bloodstock. Greyhound and whippet racing, so popular with the English working class, were evidently never introduced into Russia.

The skills of horse riding were by no means confined to the

hippodromes. At the turn of the century, a small band of cavalry officers who had studied horse riding in Italy carried off most of the honours at Russian riding *concours* and also won the King's Cup, awarded to the best horseman at the London Show Jumping Tournament, for three years in succession (1912–1914). The Russian cavalry followed the system of riding taught by an ex-circus rider, James Fillis, an Englishman who had been invited to Russia to teach horsemanship at the Officers' Cavalry School between 1898 and 1909, and who remained the principal influence on the Russian riding style right up to World War I, if not later. Apart from the amateur horse riding societies and the private riding academies in St Petersburg, Moscow, Kiev, Warsaw and Riga, riding of a traditional kind was, of course, extremely popular among the various peoples of the Russian Empire, particularly among the Cossacks, Georgians, Bashkirs and Kirgiz.

Cycling

Cycling gained prominence in the 1880s, both as a participant and as a spectator sport. The first cycling races in Russia were held on the Field of Mars in the centre of St Petersburg in 1882; a year later, the first club was formed – the Tsar'skoye Selo Cycling Circle. From being merely a relaxing novelty for *lycéens*, cycling began to be taken seriously; races were first held along the dirt paths of Yekaterina Park, then a cement track was laid nearby and a stand for spectators built. Several other clubs grew up – so that, by 1892, there were as many as 17 and some other cities had their own tracks and stadiums – even as far away as Tashkent in Central Asia. (The Tashkent Amateur Cycling Society was formed in 1885.) Many of these were constructed and patronised by foreign bicycle firms, who not only saw a profitable outlet for their goods but also the prospect of big money in the first real Russian spectator sport, for cycling was drawing large crowds – on 24 July 1883, some 25,000 spectators watched cycling races at the Moscow Hippodrome. Similarly large crowds attended cycling meetings in St Petersburg's Semyonov Hippodrome.

In winter, racing took place indoors on wooden tracks, the

first ones being laid in Moscow's manège on Manège Square in 1892, in the St Petersburg Riding Academy and in Tula in 1894. The extent of the sport's popularity may be judged by the fact that the manège used by the Petersburg Amateur Cycling Society was open daily from 9 a.m. to 1 a.m. Besides lessons in cycling, the society also provided instruction in a variety of sports – from tennis to tag. Entrance fees were high, but ladies were admitted free, though as spectators only.

The first national champion, in 1893, (over 80 km), was George Davis, an English resident in Moscow. But Russian cyclists were no novices. Internationally, they gained a reputation that they have hardly matched since. In 1896, on the Catford track in London, Mikhail Dyakov won the 25-mile cycle race. He held four world records between 1894 and 1898 while Russian national champion. His compatriot, Nikolai Mal'kevich from Kiev, made the long-distance tours Kiev–Alexandria–Cairo, Chernyayev–Irkutsk–Moscow, and St Petersburg–Paris. In 1895, Mikhail Dzevochko beat the Austrian road champion, Franz Herger, in the Petersburg–Moscow road race (725 km).

Athletics

Athletics was given a boost by the St Petersburg Circle of Amateur Sportsmen, founded at Tyarlevo near the capital in 1888; it had grown out of the Petrov Amateur Running Society, formed a couple of years earlier. By 1893, its athletics programme included jumping, hurdling, running, discus and javelin. The next year it paid 90,000 rubles for a large area of wooded land on Krestovsky Island, which it turned into a sports centre incorporating a soccer pitch, pavilion, shooting gallery, two tennis courts, a running track, jumping pit and an area for field sports. The Circle was financed mainly by subscriptions from members (largely servicemen and foreign residents in the capital) who still numbered only 50 in 1900. By this time, athletics clubs existed in all the major cities: Moscow, St Petersburg, Kiev, Khar'kov, Nizhny Novgorod, Riga, Warsaw and Odessa.

Although no athletes were sent to the 1908 Olympic Games, the first All-Russia athletics championships were held in that year and a National Amateur Athletics Association was formed in

1911, in preparation for the 1912 Olympics. Despite the failure to win any Olympic medals, athletics was popular enough to warrant some 50 athletics clubs in 1913. It is worth noting that none of them accepted women, whose participation in sport in general and athletics in particular was not yet socially acceptable.

Wrestling and weightlifting

Russian strongmen had long had their following among both the populace and the nobility who often sponsored them. Professionals performed mostly in circuses and travelling fairs – of which there were more than 6,500 in the mid-1860s:[5] 'no circus performance was complete without its wrestlers, boxers and weightlifters'.[6] The acts varied from *poses plastiques* and muscle play to weightlifting, wrestling, boxing and feats of strength – all under the general heading of 'heavy athletics'. Members of the gentry and businessmen spent hours watching and betting on wrestlers – many of whose bouts were 'fixed' in the best commercial tradition. Such strongmen as the world-renowned Estonian, Georgi Hakkenschmidt, 'the Russian Lion'; Alexander Zass, 'Sampson', whose finale was to carry on his shoulders from the arena a grand piano and pianist plus a dancer on top of the piano; Yevgeny Sandow, whose speciality was to wrestle with an African lion in the circus ring (he was also author of the first Russian 'body building' book in 1904); and Ivan Lebedev, editor of the journal *Hercules* and the man on whom Anton Chekhov (a great patron of the sport) based his character Uncle Vanya, are still names revered among world strongmen.

One of the most popular circus performers, Ivan Poddubny, was six times world heavyweight wrestling champion up to 1910. The amateur wrestlers, A. Petrov and N. Orlov, won silver medals at the 1908 London Olympics, and M. Klein won a silver medal at the 1912 Stockholm Olympics. At the 1913 world weightlifting contest in Copenhagen, as many as six Russians were placed in the six weight divisions.

[5] P. Lyashchenko, *The History of the National Economy of Russia* (New York, 1949), p. 724.
[6] F. Legostayev, *Fizicheskoye vospitanie i sport v SSSR* (Munich, 1951), p. 8.

Even the 'weaker sex' were allowed to take part in 'heavy athletics' – to attract more paying customers. At the end of the 19th century, 'Madame Atleta' pressed 89.5 kg and raised 52 kg with one hand and a certain Mrs Trefilova-Bubnova, weighing only 52 kg, pressed 57 kg and came third in a (men's) feather-weight contest. Women wrestlers were regular members of circus troupes; the redoubtable Masha Poddubnaya, wife of the great weightlifter, Ivan Poddubny, was women's world heavyweight wrestling champion and would invite all comers to wrestle her in the circus ring after she had disposed of her fellow troupers.

The popularity of weightlifting and wrestling – the Graeco-Roman style, then known as the 'French' style, was employed – may be judged by the existence of two regular journals, *Hercules* and *Stadion* (the only other sporting magazine in existence in the 19th century was *Tsiklist – The Cyclist*); more than ten books were published on 'heavy athletics' before the 1914 war, as compared with one each on soccer, skiing and athletics. In 1885, Dr V. F. Krayevsky set the sport on a 'respectable' footing by founding the first wrestling and weightlifting club and propagand-ising the art and beauty of the sport. In 1896, the professional wrestler Lebedev founded the famous *Hercules* Club; this was quickly followed by the equally famous *Sanitas*, which put out the following advertisement in the press – reminiscent of similar advertisements in the West today, though they no longer appear in Russia:

> *Sanitas* Physical Development Club
> 98, Nevsky Pros., St Petersburg
> Heavy athletics: Wrestling, Gymnastics, Therapeutic Body Building
> with a guarantee of increasing chest measurements by 5–15 cm
> Medical examination
> Special hours for women[7]

Similar clubs sprang up in Kiev and Moscow in 1898 and in Riga and Chernigov in 1899. Despite the success of Russian strongmen and their obvious popularity among the public (and commercial promoters), the social stigma officially attached to 'heavy athletics' prevented the forming of a national association until 1913.

[7] *Stadion*, 1897, No. 9, p. 5.

Boxing

The first boxing manual, *English Boxing*, was published in 1894 by Baron Kister of the First Life Guards Regiment in Moscow; he set up Baron Kister's English Boxing Arena, which held boxing displays and sparring sessions every Saturday evening; he also, in 1895, arranged the first public match between a London professional boxer, Fred Harrison, and a Russian Resident, Hennigsen; this was described in the magazine *Tsiklist*, although the result was not reported.[8] Boxing, however, tended to be regarded as a *muzhik*'s sport, violent and dangerous, devoid of grace and skill – even when confined to the Marquess of Queensberry's Rules (formulated in England in 1866), as it was. As a Guards' officer and a gentleman, Kister was ostracised for his association with the sport, and, even though he transferred the Arena to his wife (it became Baroness Kister's Arena), he was eventually discharged from the army. The club continued successfully, putting on 'athletic' evenings on Saturdays, in which boxing was the highlight, until 1901. Boxing was further boosted by the arrival in 1898 of the famous French pugilist, Erneste Lustalla, who set up another boxing school. It was not until the eve of World War I, however, that the first national boxing championships were held.

Gymnastics

Gymnastics became increasingly popular as the century progressed, partly for political reasons. Russia's defeat in the Crimean War in 1855, like Prussia's defeat by Napoleon, resulted in an examination of ways to enhance national solidarity, morale and preparedness. Just as the German *Turnen* gymnastics societies, the Czech *Sokol* and the Scandinavian gymnastics movements of the 19th century had been attempts to regenerate their peoples after military disasters; so, some Russian officials hoped, the same could be done for Russia.

The first gymnastics club arose in St Petersburg in 1863 (although a Swede, de Pauli, had opened the first Gymnastics Institute in Russia back in 1830) and was followed in the same year by the famous *Pal'ma* Gymnastics Society which soon had

[8] *Tsiklist*, 1895, No. 7, p. 7.

branches in five other cities. In 1868, the Moscow Gymnastics Society was formed and held its meetings in a large hall on Tsvetnoi Boulevard (nowadays the *Dinamo* Club gymnasium). Pyotr Lesgaft, the 'father' of Russian physical education introduced gymnastics on the Prussian model into the army in 1874 and, shortly after, established gymnastics courses for army officers and, in 1896, for civilians. The first national federation for any sport, the Russian Gymnastics Society, was formed in 1883 on the initiative of several social reformers, including the writer (and medical practitioner) Anton Chekhov.

The physical exercises introduced into Russian schools and colleges in the 1870s largely served the interests of the army. Kozlovsky, their most influential exponent, succeeded in 'selling' his proposals to the tsar, Alexander II, by pointing out that gymnastics could be a direct form of military training, permitting a reduction of national service and a great financial saving. So-called 'disciplinary exercises' were designed to produce 'a disciplined subject in peacetime and a fearless fighter in war'.[9] The official school gymnastics manuals of 1872 and 1878, in fact, prescribed exercises modelled on the Prussian military drill regulations of 1847. Marching in ranks and columns, turning on the march, wheeling, forming sections, etc., were to be practised under the command of a gymnastics leader or drill instructor.

Nonetheless, it was the nationalistic Slav *Sokol* school of gymnastics (rather than the Prussian or Swedish) that was mainly assimilated into Russia in the 1880s by the new gymnastics societies. With its narrow base among the aristocracy and spurred on by the rising middle class, gymnastics became popular enough for a team to be sent to the Olympics of 1912 and actually win medals.

Other sports

The American-invented team game of basketball was introduced into Russia at the turn of the century: in 1906, the St Petersburg sports club, *Mayak*, formed several basketball teams that competed with teams from the *Bogatyr'* Society and, in 1909, even defeated a touring side from the USA. Another American inven-

[9] *Pamyati Pyotra Frantsevicha Lesgafta* (St Petersburg, 1912), p. 34.

tion, volleyball, appears not to have penetrated pre-1917 Russia.

Of the cerebral sports, chess has had a long tradition among the aristocracy and intellectuals; the historian, Vasili Klyuchevsky, describes how Ivan the Terrible enjoyed long and frequent games of chess with his favourite opponent and henchman, Malyuta Skuratov, while Peter the Great 'would sit and play chess with simple sailors, drink beer with them and stuff his long Dutch pipe with their makhorka'.[10] It was a popular game among dissident intellectuals and revolutionaries, too; men like Lenin, Gorky, Trotsky, Krylenko and Lunacharsky did much to promote it after the revolution. Even on the eve of war, in 1914, the All-Russia Chess Association is said to have had as many as 5,000 registered members – considerably more than most other sports associations.[11] By contrast, the Russian Tourist Society had only a few hundred members and the Russian Mountaineering Society only 134 members in 1914.

Soccer

The team sport that has the greatest spectator interest today, soccer, began to take on an organised form in the 1890s, partly encouraged by the enormous success of cycling in attracting paying spectators. It is worth describing the development of soccer at some length: first, because it quickly became the most popular organised sport in terms of numbers of both participants and spectators; second, because it mirrored the pattern of development of several other sports, though on a larger scale; and, third, because it showed the rôle played by foreigners in introducing and finally abandoning the sport once it had taken root in Russia.

The most important agents in popularising the game of soccer in Russia were British residents. These British 'ambassadors' were primarily the owners of local factories and mills, their managers and technicians, and the British diplomatic corps. Their dominance over soccer in Russia lasted until about 1908, when Russian

[10] V. Klyuchevsky, *Kurs russkoi istorii*, Part IV, 2nd edn. (Moscow, 1923), p. 42.
[11] *Sport v SSSR*, 1968, No. 6, p. 31.

clubs were numerous and strong enough to beat – and usurp the positions of – their former instructors.

Strangely enough, the first football game started by the British in Russia appears to have been rugby; the bold initiator was a Mr Hopper, a Scotsman who worked in Moscow. His efforts to launch rugby football were soon cut short however. In 1886, the game was stopped by the police, who considered it brutal and liable to incite demonstrations and riots.

In the early days of soccer in Russia, the game was played, first, by the British among themselves and, a little later, by mixed teams of British and Russians, the latter being mainly students, cadets and clerks in business houses. In 1894, however, Harry Charnock, general manager of the vast Morozov mills (and one of four soccer-playing brothers in Moscow), introduced soccer to his workers. This step was said to be an attempt to woo them away from vodka drinking on Sunday, the only free day of the week.

The first recorded soccer match among Russians was played in the interval between cycling races at the Semyonov Hippodrome in St Petersburg in 1892. The rules of this game of kick-and-rush were primitive, and there was no referee – since nobody knew exactly how the game was played. It took a Russian-born Frenchman, Georges Duperont (later to become President of the All-Russia Football Association and, in Soviet times, Chairman of the Petrograd Football League), a member of the St Petersburg Circle of Amateur Sportsmen,[12] to translate literature on the game and to arrange the first Russian match to be played, in 1896, on Krestovsky Island, roughly according to the rules adopted by the Football Association of England. The next year, Duperont's team was challenged by the Petersburg Sports Circle, which played on the Square of the First Cadet Corps; this is regarded as the birth of organised Russian soccer. A section of

[12] The St Petersburg Circle of Amateur Sportsmen was formed in 1888 and popularised a number of organised sports in Russia, including athletics, ice hockey and skiing. The Circle took up soccer in 1897 and entered the St Petersburg Football League under the name *Sport* in 1902 – the first Russian club to do so. It survived the 1917 October Revolution, was renamed *Skoraya pomoshch'* (First-Aid) for one year in 1921, reverted to *Sport* in 1922 and in 1925 became the *Petrogradsky raion* team. It seems to have disappeared in 1927.

the St Petersburg Circle of Amateur Sportsmen branched off to form a soccer club under the name of *Sport* in 1897, but it was two years before a second Russian soccer club was formed.

In the meantime, a number of teams of foreign residents were being formed and were playing friendly matches against one another. The *Victoria* Football Club was formed in 1894 by English and German employees in St Petersburg; they played occasional matches within the club in a reasonably organised way. The first refined game came, as in England and America, from English schools and colleges in the capital which attempted to codify and unify the laws about 1899. The united English college students' team played under the name of *Gloria*; in 1899, it played matches against *Victoria*, the Scottish Circle of Amateur Footballers, the English Football Club and *Germaniya F.C.* (made up of German employees, primarily of the Putilov Factory). The following year, teams of foreign residents played their first games against Russian teams. In the same year, nine new soccer teams appeared, including seven Russian teams – the Yekaterin-hof Circle of Amateur Footballers, the Lakhtinsky, Petrovsky and Krestovsky soccer circles, teams from the *Kolomyagi* and *Staroderevo* Amateur Sports Circles, and the *Rossiya* Circle of Footballers – and two foreign residents' teams – *Prussiya*, attached to the German Football Association, and a team from the British diplomatic corps under the pretentious title of 'The Special Circle of Sportsmen for Playing Football and Lawn Tennis of the Superior Society of the English Colony'. The game had now reached such proportions that a unified code was essential for successful organised competition to take place; a printed code was therefore forthcoming in 1900 and paved the way for the first football-league in Russia, the St Petersburg Football League (the Moscow Football League was not formed until 1910), being formed in 1901 by three foreign residents' clubs – *Nevka*, *Nevsky* and *Victoria*. These three clubs contested the First St Petersburg Football Championship in 1901, to the winners of which an English entrepreneur, T. M. Aspden, awarded a cup, known as the Aspden Cup and contested until 1917. The *Nevka* team (1900–1904) consisted mainly of Scotsmen working at the Sampson Weaving Mill and the *Nevsky* (1900–1912) – of Englishmen employed at the Neva Spinning Mill. A Russian team, *Sport*, entered the league in 1902 but lost all its matches. The next year *Sport* did better and came third in the league, ahead of *Nevka* and *Neva* (the oldest English sports club in St Petersburg, formed in 1860). Russian soccer was improving, with two Russian teams, *Sport* and the Petrovsky Circle, forming second teams in 1903.

But friction was arising between the previously dominant foreign residents' teams and the newer Russian teams. One cause for displeasure among the growing number of Russian soccer players and fans was the fact that soccer administration in the capital was largely in the hands of foreigners – who were accused of showing bias against Russian teams and players. Thus, during 1903, official protests were lodged at the exclusion of all *Sport* players from the St Petersburg combined team to play the league champions *Victoria* and at the sending off of a Russian player, Chirtsov of *Sport*, by an English referee, V. S. Martin, during a match against *Nevsky* and Chirtsov's subsequent banning for one year. The Russians felt that Chirtsov had met with an injustice since he 'had been knocked on to the snow and almost throttled by the English player Sharples' in retaliation for a 'hard but quite legitimate tackle'. Sharples was exonerated by the (English) league officials. In the reaction to this decision by the Russian sports magazine *Sport*, it is not hard to discern elements of the nationalistic feelings that accompanied the rise of Russian soccer:

The League committee's decision is to disqualify Chirtsov for a year and to let off Sharples with a 'caution'! This year we had Sharples the Throttler! In future we shall probably have Jim the Stabber and Jack the Ripper! Match reports will soon be crime reports. Will that gladden the hearts of Russian sportsmen? I don't think so. The English, in their typical high-handed way, with their large voting majority, are banning a Russian who is completely guiltless and leaving a man who is obviously dangerous but is one of their own! Let Russian clubs band together and form their own league. I am sure a great future awaits soccer in Russia, but for that we can do with fewer Sharpleses![13]

This admonishing of English officials and the call to Russian teams to form their own league were also indications of the growing popularity and strength of Russian soccer. The next

[13] *Sport*, 6 October 1903.

year, 1904, for the first time, there were as many Russian teams in the St Petersburg League as foreign teams and, in 1908, a Russian team, *Sport*, became the first to win the League title. This marked the end of foreign residents' teams as significant agents in the development of Russian soccer. All three major teams, *Nevsky*, *Neva* and *Victoria*, left the St Petersburg League in 1909 and formed their own league, calling it the Russian Society of Amateur Footballers. They also competed for a cup awarded annually by the British Ambassador, A. Nicholson, from 1910. In response, the Russian clubs in both St Petersburg and Moscow boycotted the 'foreign' league. Although the two leagues were reconciled in 1911, the foreign residents' teams never regained their former glory and dropped out of competition on the eve of World War I in 1913.

One aspect of the keen Russian–English rivalry was that it was drawing a large number of spectators – especially when there was the prospect of a Russian victory. During the 1908 season, after *Sport* had defeated *Victoria*, an all-time record 'gate' of over 2,000 came to see the big test of Russian–English strength when *Sport* met and beat *Nevsky*. Passions evidently ran high during the match and one English player, Monroe, was sent off the field – which fanned the crowd's divided patriotic loyalties: 'Despite the blatant infringement of the football rules by Monroe and even of the rules of normal civility adhered to by educated people, the English section of the crowd made a terrible din and began to clamour for the return of Monroe, whose departure the Russian section of the crowd accompanied with loud hissing.'[14]

The nationalistic element was not entirely removed by the discontinuation of Russian–English fixtures after 1908, since St Petersburg Russian teams began to make tours within the Russian Empire and other soccer clubs, including foreign teams, visited the capital. At the end of August, 1907, *Sport* met the Finnish team *Unitas* in Helsinki, and a Swedish team in Stockholm. In 1908 *Sport* went to Riga and beat the local team *Union*. *Sport* returned to Helsinki in 1910 and lost to the Finnish team *Kampaterna*. A Russian newspaper, commenting on the defeats, blamed the first on 'the biased referee who made two errors in favour of the Finns' that resulted in two Finnish goals, and the

[14] *Novoye vremya*, 30 September 1908.

second on the Russian players who, 'on the eve of the match, "overindulged" in drinking spirits'.[15]

By this time, the popularity of soccer almost certainly exceeded that of any other sport in terms both of participants and of spectators, it 'was the most widespread of all sports'.[16] The British diplomat, Robert Bruce Lockhart, who played for the Moscow *Morozovsy* team, reports that 'at a league match the average attendance was about twelve thousand people, and the women must have contributed thirty per cent of the total'.[17] The proliferation of teams, the uncertain interpretation of the rules and manner of play, especially between Russian and English residents' teams, along with the desire and need for regular organised competition on a nationwide level led, in January 1912, to the holding of the first conference of the All-Russia Football Association, set up for the purpose 'of uniting all Russian sports organisations playing soccer, working out common laws of play and affiliating to FIFA'.[18] In the autumn of the same year, the first Russian city soccer championship took place, St Petersburg, Moscow, Khar'kov, Kiev and Odessa competing. It is noteworthy that the All-Russia Football Association had forbidden any Russian city team competing in the national championships to contain more than three Englishmen; Odessa, which won the 1913 national championships, was reprimanded for playing four Englishmen.

The game was so widespread that in 1914 at the height of pre-revolutionary football development, 23 teams played in the Petrograd Football League;[19] a total of 19 soccer clubs with 97 teams played 324 matches in the capital, and 34 soccer clubs with 93 teams from seven districts in and around Petrograd played 368 matches for the *Dacha* Cup. In Moscow, 25 teams contested the Moscow League in 1913 and leagues existed in several southern towns, especially in the mining communities of the Donbas. By now, the game was organised and important enough both to warrant the publication of a football periodical,

[15] *Novoye vremya*, 21 May 1910.
[16] V. I. Zholdak, *Stranitsy moskovskovo sporta* (Moscow, 1969), p. 100.
[17] R. B. Lockhart, *Giants Cast Long Shadows* (Putnam, 1958), p. 175.
[18] N. Y. Kiselev (ed.), *70 futbol'nykh let* (Leningrad, 1970), p. 39.
[19] Petrograd was St Petersburg's wartime name.

Vestnik petrogradskoi futbol'noi ligi (The Petrograd Football League Herald), published for the first time on 17 August 1916, and to have a permanent panel of football referees which survived until 1923.

Alongside the official clubs and leagues, however, there existed the unregistered 'outlaw' workers' teams which had been refused entry to the Russian Football Association. They usually played on rough and open ground, watched by fellow workers. The *Murzinka* Football Club,[20] which took its name from the village where a pitch was rented, was formed by employees at the Obukhov Factory in Petrograd. Workers at the giant Putilov munitions plant in the capital hired the premises of the old Yekaterinhof Amateur Sports Circle. Both these workers' soccer clubs, *Murzinka* and *Putilovsky*,[21] when the authorities removed the ban on workers' clubs playing against those of the gentlemen amateurs in 1914, entered teams in the leagues (four and three respectively).

In 1916, two more workers' soccer clubs joined the Petrograd League – *Volga*, a club formed by workers at the Alexandrov, Semyannikov and Atlas factories, and *PTCh*, abbreviated from *Pochtovo-telegrafnye chinovniki* ['Post and Telegraph Clerks']. One reason for permitting workers' soccer clubs to take part in the League was to improve the chances of Russian teams against foreign opposition – since, after 1910, Russian teams were increasingly developing international ties and the government was taking an interest in encouraging Russian success against foreign opposition.

In 1910, the first foreign team, *Corinthians* from Prague, came to Russia and played three matches in St Petersburg, each watched by large crowds of *paying* spectators: 'The three matches with St Petersburgers evoked enormous interest. For the first time, tickets for the matches were sold prior to the games at the Central Ticket Office (23, Nevsky Prospekt). Each match was

---

[20] *Murzinka* has, under different names, survived to this day; in 1924, it was renamed *Volodarsky raion*, then *Bol'shevik* and *Klub imeni Lenina*; today, it has become *Sportivny klub 'Bol'shevik'*

[21] *Putilovsky* is today regarded as the oldest workers' club in the country; after the October Revolution, it became *Krasny Putilovets* ('Red Putilovite'), then *Kirovsky zavod* and, finally, *Kirovets*, which it remains.

watched by 4,000–5,000 spectators.'[22] *Corinthians* won two matches and lost one to a combined city team. The next year, an English professional club, *The Wanderers*, came to St Petersburg and played three days running, thoroughly beating a combined English residents' side, a combined Russian side and a combined Moscow and St Petersburg side. The press commented: 'As expected, we lost these international matches, but, after all, we were playing against the founders of the game, against our teachers.'[23] In 1912, the newly formed Russian F.A. sent the first team of Russian nationals abroad to represent their country in the Olympic Games, held in Stockholm. (The team wore yellow shirts with the national crest on their chests.) It lost to Finland and, disastrously, to Germany (0–16) – a defeat that dented Russian national pride. That was the first and last time a Russian national team competed abroad in tsarist times.

Although all these international fixtures demonstrated the relative weakness of Russian soccer, compared with that of countries in which the game had had a longer history, they did stimulate the game, help to bring in a paying public and attract government attention to a sport that, it was felt, might yet prove to be a successful bearer of Russian patriotic hopes. Given a few more years, Russian soccer might, in fact, have developed the type of structure that prevailed in countries like England with its professional clubs which had, at the turn of the century, become commercial concerns with profit as a major yardstick of success, largely based on working-class participants and spectators.

Popular games

Of course, outside the organised sports movement, popular games went on being enjoyed by the bulk of the population – as long as the authorities did not intervene. Village 'wall-to-wall' fist fights were common even in the 19th century: all adult members of one village would line up and advance against a similar wall of opposing villagers. A foreign traveller writes of the ferocity yet apparent sportsmanship of the combatants: 'What is astonishing is that the Russians engage for their pleasure, and sometimes

22 *Novoye vremya*, 4 October 1910.
23 *Novoye vremya*, 22 August 1911.

without having taken a drop of vodka, with their best friends in fights the like of which would cost professional pugilists dear. To go by the ferocious expression on their faces, it would seem a matter of fighting to the death; yet as soon as the fight is over, off they go to drink together.'[24] Such fights certainly caused some concern to landowners as a possible means of training peasants for battle against their masters and, in 1832, Nicholas I issued a decree banning village fist fights.

The abundance of waterways and their strategic importance encouraged the transportation of cargoes in sailing and rowing boats on rivers and lakes. Fishing and shooting took place from boats, rafts and river banks. Although these were labours of necessity and not of sporting love, the water did provide a playground for rowing races, swimming and diving. On his peregrinations in Russia in the 18th century, the Russian traveller, Glagolev, described the diversions of the people of Tula: 'One can only be amazed at their daring when they throw themselves into the river from a pile, bridge or lock four or five *sazheni* (8.5–10.7 m) high. They are quite agile and use virtually all known swimming styles . . . although one would never even suggest that rules and schools exist.'[25]

In winter, ice skating, cudgelling on ice and the old favourite of a snow fortress siege all had their support among the common people; singing in chorus, hunting and dancing were common to all seasons. Although hygiene was rudimentary, many Russians seemed to attach great importance to bodily cleanliness and physical stamina. The weekly steam bath followed by a dip in the icy river, or sometimes a roll in the snow, was an almost religious duty. Foreign travellers were evidently amazed to see adults at 30 or 40 degrees below zero 'swimming gaily in ice holes and rushing out naked from hot steam baths to roll in the snow . . . mothers rubbing down young children with snow and pouring icy water over them'.[26]

At itinerant fairs, professional entertainers or jesters (*skomorokhi*) treated spectators to displays of fencing with pikes and

[24] C. De Grunwald, *Peter the Great* (MacGibbon and Kee, 1956), p. 14.
[25] I. S. Glagolev, *Razvlecheniya zhitelei Tuly* (Moscow, 1734), p. 78.
[26] N. I. Ponomaryov, *Vozniknovenie i pervonachal'noye razvitie fizicheskovo vospitaniya* (Moscow, 1970), p. 221.

swords, acrobatics and tight-rope walking. And at folk festivals, combatants would measure their strength and skill by tossing and lifting weights, throwing stones at targets or for distance, hurling the javelin and leaping over fires.[27]

Other survivals from earlier times – and ones which still have considerable support among Russians even today – were Russian folk games with various-sized balls, sticks, bones and stones, including the following:

gorodki – a game in which a 50 cm stick is hurled at a square containing wooden pegs, the aim being to knock, successively, various configurations of pegs out of the square;

lapta – a game similar to rounders or baseball;

lunki – a game in which a ball is rolled along the ground to a hole some distance away;

shariki – a game similar to marbles;

babki – a game using bones; one bone is used to knock two or more configurations of bones out of a circle; some 40 versions of the game are currently practised in Russia;

svaika – a game in which a spear is thrown to land in the middle of a metal ring lying on the ground some distance away;

kila (or *shalyga*) – 'on the left-hand side of a yard, 8 or 9 men play *kila*, which is a leather hair-filled ball, the size of a man's head. The two sides come together wall-to-wall; one player kicks the ball and tries not to lose it to the other side . . . the aim being to force the ball into a *gorod* ["town"] marked by a line. Anyone who breaks the rules has his neck "soaped". Players shout *"Kila!"* when the *gorod* is taken.'[28] This game was evidently a primitive version of football; it was played both in summer and in winter (on ice).

None of this implies that life in 'Merrie Rus' was one long round of merrymaking. Far from it. Life was short, perilous and hard, leisure and the material means for it were at a premium and, increasingly from the 16th century, Church and State persecuted the peasants and urban poor for taking part in such 'idle

[27] Ibid., p. 199.
[28] N. G. Pomyalovsky, *Ocherki bursy* (St Petersburg, 1801), p. 102; it is interesting that the shout of disapproval '*na mylo!*' ('have him soaped!') may be heard at Russian soccer grounds today.

pursuits' – a notion not at odds with a Puritan philosophy elsewhere in Europe.

The Olympic Games

Russia was a founding member of the modern Olympic movement and Russian sportsmen first participated in the Olympic Games in 1908 (the Fourth Olympics, held in London). A team of five contestants went to Britain, sponsored by voluntary contributions. It did surprisingly well, winning a gold medal in figure skating, two silvers in wrestling and taking 14th place overall (among 22 nations). For the next Olympic Games, held in Stockholm in 1912, the sports societies were prepared to sponsor a much larger contingent. The government, appreciating the prestige value of sports success, set up a Russian Olympic Committee, headed by Baron F. Meyendorf. With quite generous government backing and organisation, a team of 169 athletes gathered to take part in all 15 sports on the Olympic programme. Whether the prospects of a foreign jaunt were too intoxicating (notably to the army officers who made up over half the party) is uncertain, but many of the team (including Baron Meyendorf) missed the boat altogether and had to stay behind. In the Games, Russia ultimately shared 15th place with Austria, out of 28 countries, and won few medals. The best performance, once again, came from a wrestler, M. Klein, who, breaking his arm in the semi-final and having to lose his chance to wrestle in the final, won a silver medal. The only other medals were one in gymnastics, second place for the Russian team in pistol and revolver shooting and third places in yachting and clay pigeon shooting.[29]

The Olympic setback – referred to in the press as a 'sporting Tsushima'[30] – was largely a reflection of the backward state of Russian sport and Russian society. Stung by the blow to Russian prestige, the government took steps to put sport on a more solid basis. One problem had always been how to bring together the

[29] K. A. Andrianov et al, *Olimpiiskie igry* (Moscow, 1970), p. 231.
[30] On 27 May 1904, during the Russo-Japanese War, virtually the entire Russian fleet was sunk by the Japanese off Tsushima in the Sea of China, thus bringing the war to an end with the victory of an Asiatic power (which had only recently acquired a modern army) and depriving Russia of her ice-free port on the Pacific.

nation's foremost athletes in national teams; given the anarchic organisation of sport and the vast size of the Empire, the task was far from easy. The government now decided to hold national championships, 'Olympiads', on the model of the Olympic programme. This, it was felt, would stimulate the work of the sports societies and prepare athletes properly for international competition. However, it was to be another forty years before Russia participated again in the Olympic Games. It is worthy of note that the idea of holding national 'Olympiads' based on the Olympic Games was a notion taken up again in Soviet times; in 1956, '*spartakiads*' were inaugurated – games to be held in the year preceding each session of Olympics – a sign of the importance in terms of national prestige attached by both the Imperial and the Soviet authorities to international success in sport, particularly at the Olympics.

Sports organisation, 1900–1914

The 20th century opened inauspiciously for the tsarist authorities. An industrial crisis and an accompanying decline in urban living standards caused a rash of strikes, both economic and political, and increasing violence. Mounting unrest affected the countryside, too – where, in many regions, peasants were sacking estates. Attempts to decapitate the absolutist political power resulted in the assassination of Prime Minister Plehve in 1904 and of the tsar's uncle, Grand Duke Sergei in 1905. The immediate official reaction led to over a thousand demonstrators being shot outside the Winter Palace in January 1905 and the inauguration of a period of intense reaction under Prime Minister Stolypin, who took office in 1906. Another blow to the state was the most humiliating military setback (with the possible exception of that in the Crimean War) it had suffered since the days of the Golden Horde: utter defeat at the hands of an oriental power in the 1904–1905 Russo-Japanese War.

One conclusion apparently tacitly drawn by some tsarist officials from these disasters was that sport might be employed as a means of combating the evils that had culminated in the events of 1905. Particularly after the Japanese-inflicted defeat, it was hoped that the participation of the population at large in some form of fitness campaign would improve the country's morale and cohesiveness. Sport was also to divert the workers and students from their revolutionary activity and safeguard young people from the unhealthy influence of the street and political hooliganism. In the words of the Minister of Education, Kasso, sport was to be 'a means of counteracting the moral irresolution of students'.[31] Further, by widening admission to existing clubs and admitting office workers and qualified industrial workers and by setting up new clubs at factories, in army and navy units and even in the countryside, the government intended to neutralise the growing popularity of the 'outlaw' sporting clubs and militant workers' *druzhiny*, which were engaging in workers' military training under the guise of sport. (The *druzhinniki* at the Obukhov Works, for example, would meet on Sundays on the banks of the Neva and row off to a deserted spot where they would practise hand grenade and bomb throwing, unarmed and armed combat, wrestling and fencing, and military drilling.[32] Members of the Workers' Boxing Club in Rostov, formed in 1905, also practised revolver shooting and studied Marxist writings on the side.[33] Similar *druzhiny* existed in factories in Moscow, Khar'kov, Oryol and Ivanovo-Voznesensk. Often they would include folk games like *lapta* and *gorodki* in their physical training.)

The early years of the 20th century were, therefore, a busy time for the organised sports movement, with tentative government backing and overall control. More and more clubs were formed, schools and courses of physical training were established in the larger cities, and leagues and national associations came into being, providing competition in specific sports. In 1909, the first Russian sporting weekly, *Russky sport*, appeared, though typically soccer and racing filled more pages than lawn tennis, gymnastics and wrestling put together.

This upsurge in organisation in the main sports was not too far behind that in other industrialising countries, as Table 2 shows.

According to our early data, there existed 1,266 sports clubs,

[31] *Tsiklist* (1906), No. 7, p. 17.
[32] S. D. Sinitsyn (ed.), *Istoriya fizicheskoi kul'tury narodov SSSR*, Vol. 1 (Moscow, 1953), p. 127.
[33] N. P. Novoselov, 'Fizicheskaya kul'tura v period russkoi revolutsii, 1905–1907', in *Ocherki po istorii fizicheskoi kul'tury* (Moscow, 1950), p. 67.

TABLE 2   *Dates of founding of national sports associations: selected countries,*
1863–1912

Sport	England	USA	Germany	Russia	Russia's lag on Britain (years)
Association football	1863	—a	1900	1912	49
Swimming	1869	1878	1887	—a	–
Cycling	1878	1880	1884	1884	6
Rowing	1879	1872	1883	1898	26
Skating	1879	1888	1888	—a	–
Athletics	1880	1888	1898	1911	31
Lawn tennis	1886	1881	1902	1907	26
Skiing	1903	1904	1904	1910	7

a None formed.
Sources: P. C. McIntosh, *Sport in Society* (Watts, London, 1968), p. 85;
Entsiklopedichesky slovar' po fizicheskoi kul'ture i sportu, Vol. I, pp. 123, 171;
Vol. III, pp. 8, 52, 111, 190, 207.

societies and circles in 1913, with an average membership of
some 60 persons.[34] Although many of these clubs were located in
the major Russian cities, particularly St Petersburg and Moscow,
the relatively industrialised provinces also accounted for a large
number: the Ukraine had 196 sports clubs with 8,000 members
and Belorussia had some 1,000 members in its *Sanitas, Sokol,
Bogatyr'* and *Maccabee*[35] sports clubs.

Many clubs were well-equipped. The *Morozovsy* soccer club,
for example, had an excellent pavilion with its own dressing
rooms, baths, a dining room, a large hall for social gatherings

---

[34] I. G. Chudinov, 'Fizicheskaya kul'tura v gody grazhdanskoi voiny', in
Ocherki po istorii fizicheskoi kul'tury, Vol. III (Moscow, 1948), p. 73.

[35] The world-wide *Maccabee* federation of Jewish gymnastics and sports
associations was founded in 1902 and had organisations in a number of
countries, including Russia, especially Belorussia and the Ukraine, where
there were large concentrations of Jews. It held (and still holds) *Macca-
beeads* once every four years on the Olympic principle, but for Jews
only. The tsarist government appears to have tolerated a number of
Maccabee sports associations – perhaps believing they might deflect
more militant Jews from political action. In any case, Jews were frequently banned from membership of Russian sports organisations – e.g.
the *Sokol* and the *Poteshnye* (see below).

and a cinema – facilities as good as, if not better than, most amateur clubs in Britain had at the time.[36]

The major formal branches of the sports movement were the *Sokol*, the Scouts, the *Poteshnye* and factory, college and, after 1912, the state body for physical education under General Voyeikov.

The Sokol

The *Sokol* gymnastics and sports movement of the Czechs found ready application in Russia, but while the Czech version was distinguished by being a centre for Czech small-nation national- ism and independence aspirations, the Russian *Sokol* had an underlying great-power ideology that was explicitly pan-Slavist (and anti-Semitic – Jews could not become members). Its mem- bers were imbued with the 'patriotic' idea of uniting all Slavs under the aegis of Russia. After the debacle of the Russo-Japanese War, the movement and its ideology found increasing support from the government and from young Russians, especially in the schools and colleges. By 1910, *Sokol* gymnasts were strong enough to form the Union of Russian *Sokols* which united all the pre- viously independent *Sokol* organisations of Russia. The unified movement flourished with government backing: it held congresses regularly, published two magazines – *Sokol* and *The Bulletin of the Russian Sokol* – and Russian members travelled abroad to attend all-*Sokol* gatherings. Activities were by no means confined to gymnastics, members engaging in field and track athletics, outdoor team games and military training.

The Scouts (Skauty)

The Boy Scout movement had, of course, begun at the turn of the century during the Boer War in South Africa. A British officer, Colonel Baden-Powell, who had observed that the Boers used boys for scouting and reconnaissance missions, began to form units of boy scouts in the British army. Shortly after, tsarist army officers who had trained abroad introduced the Scout movement to Russia, forming the first troop in Tsarskoye Selo in 1909. The

[36] Lockhart, *Giants Cast Long Shadows*, p. 175.

Russian Scout Society was set up in 1914 to coordinate activities and, by 1917, there were 50,000 Boy and Girl Scouts in 143 Russian towns.[37]

As with Scout movements elsewhere, most of the activity had a distinctly military–patriotic–religious stamp and was devoted to training of a paramilitary nature (rifle shooting, learning the Morse code, tying knots, camping, parading, etc.), but it did include *Sokol* gymnastics, athletics, team games, skiing, skating and tobogganing. It may be that the authorities saw the Scouts as a means of training an army reserve and a youth group dedicated to the well-known trinity of Autocracy, Orthodoxy and Folkdom – i.e. to Russian absolutist monarchism, obscurantist Russian Christianity and Russian great-power chauvinism.

The Poteshnye

The *Poteshnye*, named after the boys' regiments of Peter I, were first set up in 1908 to train rural and urban youth in military and gymnastic exercises and in sports that had a military application. In January 1908, the War Minister, Suhhomlinov, submitted to the tsar's plans to organise military training for schoolchildren, primarily in the countryside, in out-of-school hours. The next year, the Education Ministry directed all education inspectors to arrange military training at elementary schools in their areas under the supervision of retired or reserve army officers. Although the *Poteshnye* engaged in *Sokol* gymnastics and various sports and games, their main concern was the training of children and students for military parades and public displays. This militarisation of youth in lieu of its physical education brought a great deal of criticism from intellectuals, educationalists and medical people; by early 1914, as a result, the movement had virtually fallen into desuetude.

Factory clubs

After the shock of 1905, a number of factory owners began to set

[37] O. I. Pantyukhov, 'Istoriya russkovo skautskovo dvizheniya. Otdel: Rossiya, 1909–1922 gody', in *Russkie skauty*, Tsentral'ny shtab Natsional'noi Organizatsii russkikh skautov (San Francisco, 1969), pp. 19–20.

up sports clubs for their employees. The giant Morozov mills, for example, created sports clubs for their workers, starting in 1906 with a Workers' Sports Club at Orekhovo-Zuyevo, an industrial settlement about 60 miles east of Moscow. In 1912, the Putilov management provided facilities for and founded a Circle of Amateur Sportsmen for its employees. The Welsh industrialist, Ivor Hughes, sponsored soccer at his steel factories in the town of Yuzovka (named after him). Similar clubs appeared in Khar'kov, Kramatorsk and elsewhere. Since many factory owners, managers and skilled personnel were foreigners, there was an attempt to introduce a foreign pattern of sport on a factory basis, with intra- and inter-factory competitions. Many of the sponsors and a good proportion of the players were, however, foreigners.

The Chief Supervisor of the Physical Development of the Population of the Russian Empire

In 1912, General Voyeikov was appointed 'Chief Supervisor of the Physical Development of the Population of the Russian Empire'. His office was, in effect, a Ministry of Sport. Two years later, with the start of World War I, a Provisional Committee of representatives of various government departments and sports societies was set up to assist the Chief Supervisor, and General Voyeikov had effectual political control over all sports and quasi-sports organisations in Russia. This centralised state control of sport was primarily intended for mobilising the population for the war effort. In 1915, the Committee issued an *Announcement on the Mobilisation of Sport* and created special military sports committees to which were appointed, alongside army repre-sentatives, members of civilian sports organisations. The aim was to generate civic activity which would produce fighting men who were more physically and morally fit. But these efforts were too tentative and too late; the government found it hard to arouse the public enthusiasm that it had dampened down for so many years. Apart from the *Sokol* and one or two other sports societies, the response was minimal: in some areas, like the artillery workshops of the Putilov munitions plant, the mobilisation-for-sport committees were actually run by revolutionary groups. In 1917, the whole organisation was to be taken over by the

Bolsheviks and turned into the military training organisation, *Vsevobuch.*

Conclusions

Within the antiquated social and political structure, it was diffi-cult to progress far with the organisation of any independent activity from below without seeming to call into question the prevailing reactionary ideology and undermine the very founda-tions of the tsarist state. First, sport and physical education implied the cultivation of the body as well as the mind – and this tended to be at odds with the extreme obscurantism of the educational and religious authorities; it smacked not only of the flesh, but of materialism. Second, although the régime was not blind to the importance of sport as a factor promoting military training, what it could not accept was that sports clubs should be given some measure of freedom of action – since this could be utilised for very non-military purposes; it feared that the sports clubs would serve as an excuse for people to meet and exchange ideas un-controlled by the authorities, that they would become centres of revolutionary activity and, in the non-Russian parts of the Empire, of movements for national liberation – just as they had with the Czech *Sokol* movement in Bohemia and Moravia and with the *Turnen* in Germany.

In Western Europe, it had been the industrialists who had inspired a large-scale sports movement based on the growing urban population: thus, in England, it had been the 'philistines' of the Industrial Revolution 'who laid down a pattern of sport for an urban community', as the Dutch sports philosopher Huizinga put it.[38] In Russia, though urbanisation created the needs for an urban pattern of recreation (including sport) that differed radically from the casual, open-air and largely un-organised rural pattern, this did not happen. That is not to say that the development of organised sport was altogether unaffected by the Russian bourgeoisie; in fact, many of the new sports clubs were set up and run by them. But an even bigger influence on the sports movement, as on the economy, was the large foreign com-munity resident in Russia; not only did the majority of sports

[38] J. Huizinga, *Homo Ludens* (Paladin, 1970), p. 32.

then popular in their home countries come to Russia with these foreigners, they also served as a bond between ex-patriates of different nationalities.

In the absence of a forceful pioneering bourgeois drive in Russian sport, the working class might have shown the way. But the outmoded social structure found little room for concessions to working-class pressures for recreational facilities or a pattern of sport that reflected the needs of the urban workers. Moreover, the high entrance and competition fees of existing clubs were often prohibitive for the urban poor, who had better uses for their wages – or so some in authority thought: 'Sport is primarily an expensive pastime and therefore is not for the workers. Their path is the *kabak*. And, in the morning, hunched and scraggy, off they go again to work.'[39] There is more than a hint of contempt here to justify social *apartheid* in sport, which kept the workers out of the middle-class and foreign clubs and contests. Consequently, they tended to organise independently of middle-class and state institutions – as they were to do politically in the Soviets – in factory *druzhiny* (brotherhoods) and *dikie* ('wildcat' or 'outlaw') groups. Often they were refused admission to foreign and middle-class clubs and leagues, since they did not fall in with a definition of 'amateur' required for membership designed to discriminate against manual workers and artisans. There is, however, evidence to show that some outstanding working-class athletes did, in fact, manage to participate in registered clubs and in tournaments, as the following indignant letter, sent to *Russkoye Slovo* in 1911, makes clear: 'It has happened of late that persons we know to be concierges (*dvorniki*), coach drivers (*izvozchiki*) and artisans (*mastera*) have broken into skiing, figure skating and speed skating competitions alongside gentlemen students, government employees and men of respectable society. Is this right? Of course not. Being engaged in manual labour these people consequently have an unfair advantage over gentlemen, just as the professional has over the amateur. We therefore call upon the authorities to put the matter in order.'[40]

[39] *K sportu*, 1912, No. 11, p. 16.
[40] 'N.V.', in *Russkoye Slovo*, 12 December 1911. Social exclusiveness, of course, also characterised sports clubs in England during the development of organised sport. For example, in 1866, the Amateur Athletics Club excluded 'mechanics, artisans and labourers' from membership.

In any case, the prevailing labour legislation made it hard for the industrial workers to take part in sport. Not only was labour in many Russian factories physically exhausting, but few workers had enough time off from work to enable them to spare leisure time for active or spectator sport. The Marxist historian, Pokrovsky, reports that, 'despite the Law of 2 June 1897, restricting the working day to $11\frac{1}{2}$ hours (on Saturdays and the eves of feast days to 10 hours), regulations were often broken and it was not uncommon for a worker to labour for 13 or 14 hours a day, six days a week'.[41]

The inability – and often the unwillingness – of the tsars, the Church and the industrialists to take measures to promote organised sports, to find a balance between the needs of the people and the availability of resources and institutions to meet those needs, tended to widen the gulf between them and the urban workers and only served to create a dual power in the sports movement between the unregistered workers' clubs and the officially recognised sports associations. As a consequence, most workers were not integrated into the system through the medium of games and the workers' unregistered sports clubs developed political overtones as a result of their semi-clandestine nature.

The tsarist régime's failure adequately to meet the mounting needs of the urban populace for appropriate recreation may well, *inter alia*, have contributed a mite to its demise in 1917. The British diplomat, Robert Bruce Lockhart, who was in Russia during World War I, wrote that had British entrepreneurs been able to spread the passion for playing soccer more quickly in Russia, the Whites might have won on the playing fields of Moscow what they lost in the Reading Room of the British Museum. He regarded the introduction of soccer by the British industrialists and workers then resident in Russia as 'an immense step forward in the social life of the Russian worker and, if it had been adopted rapidly for all mills, history might have been changed'.[42]

The Soviet authorities were, then, to inherit from tsarist Russia an incipient sports movement that, although it lacked many of

---

[41] M. N. Pokrovsky, *Russkaya istoriya s drevneishikh vremyon*, Vol. II (Moscow, 1965), p. 568.
[42] Lockhart, *Giants Cast Long Shadows*, pp. 173–174.

the facilities and organisation to be found in most industrial Western states at the time, did have one great advantage for the Bolsheviks: it was largely centrally controlled. In Britain and the USA, on the other hand, the governing bodies of sports were separate from one another and independent of the government, based for purposes of control and largely of finance on their members. As in the economy, the tsarist state had to some extent discouraged Russian individual enterprise; it had established some degree of control over the organisation of sport – in schools, in the army, in the Olympic Committee and even in national sports organisations. It had set up the Office of the Chief Supervisor of Sport, a government body to coordinate the sports movement and thus the pre-revolutionary equivalent of the present All-Union Committee on Physical Culture and Sport attached to the USSR Council of Ministers. Further, largely for historical reasons, most clubs were mixed sport centres, linked to local and central government – a similar structure to that which developed in Eastern Europe, Latin America, Spain and Italy.

The Soviet authorities were thus able to take over a ready-made state organisation of sport, however ramshackle, without having to dismantle a wide-ranging structure of autonomous sports clubs and associations. Some private clubs and sports movements, like *Sanitas*, the Moscow Bank Clerks' Sports Society, the Amateur Skiing Society and Moscow Skiing Club (neither confined to skiing), the *Maccabee* movement and the Scouts did linger on for a while after 1917, but most were engulfed by the ensuing Civil War and others were either taken over or forcibly disbanded in the mid-1920s.

2

The ideological roots of
Soviet physical education and sport

The October revolution brought a rupture with the past in many ways; yet several aspects of Soviet sport, as of other areas of social life (education, for example), still show, if not continuity with the past, at least strong influence by factors having their origins outside the Soviet period. It would certainly be wrong to imagine that a totally new structure, inspired only by new ideas, was erected after 1917. The roots of Soviet sport in part lie deep in Russian history, in the Russian people's habits and traditions, the Russian climate, the Russian state's preoccupation with external and internal enemies, the intellectual ferment of Russian society in the latter part of the 19th and early 20th centuries. It would have been strange had these currents played much less a rôle in shaping the practice of sport in the Soviet Union than the social thought of foreign philosophers – and these, it must be realised, included Locke and Rousseau, as well as Marx and Engels. In addition, foreign practice, in the form of the pattern of organised sport pioneered for industrial society by Britain, by the gymnastics schools of Germany, of the Scandinavian countries and of what is now Czechoslovakia, and Prussian military training all put their imprint on Soviet physical culture and sport. Moreover, individual foreigners were influential both in the practice and in the organisation of specific sports in Russia.

In this chapter, I shall try to identify the key ideas (and their sources) that have affected the development of Soviet physical culture.

Key ideas

The harmonious development of body and mind

Belief in the mutual dependence of mental and physical education is a recurrent theme in the writings of a number of Russian social thinkers prior to the Russian Revolution. Whereas, in other parts of Europe, a philosophical justification for sport as an activity in its own right had been more-or-less officially accepted since the 17th century, the tsarist authorities had clung more firmly to an idealistic dualism of mind and body. In so doing, they unintentionally encouraged a body of 'rational', democratic and progressive opinion which tended firmly to oppose the dualism that prevailed in Russian education, as well as the instrumental approach involved in seeing gymnastics and sport in general only as something to serve military purposes.

The critic and social thinker Vissarion Belinsky (1811–1848), for example, believed that 'the development of mental capacity corresponds to that of the health and strength of the body'[1] and that 'running, jumping, gymnastics and, particularly, Russian folk games encourage more than any other physical activity such traits as will power, initiative and creativity . . . and develop a harmonious personality'.[2] Supporters of Belinsky's educational views, the social thinkers Nikolai Chernyshevsky (1829–1889) and Nikolai Dobrolyubov (1836–1861) regarded games as an essential adjunct to mental development: 'All that is fine and beautiful in a person is unthinkable without attention to the harmonious development of his whole system and his all-round health',[3] wrote Chernyshevsky. 'No system can be completely healthy if one facet of it is developed to the detriment of another',[4] said Dobrolyubov. And for the writer-patriarch Leo

---

[1] V. G. Belinsky, *Polnoye sobranie sochinenii*, Vol. x (Moscow, 1957), p. 127.
[2] V. G. Belinsky, *Izbrannye pedagogicheskie sochineniya*, Vol. ii (Moscow–Leningrad, 1948), p. 76.
[3] N. G. Chernyshevsky, *Polnoye sobranie sochinenii*, Vol. xiii (Moscow, 1951), p. 73.
[4] N. A. Dobrolyubov, *Izbrannye filosofskie proizvedeniya*, Vol. i (Moscow, 1948), p. 119.

Tolstoy (1828–1910), 'only a fully developed individual, equipped with theory and science can change life'.[5]

The concern of such thinkers for the health and physical development of Russian children led to the formulation of theories about harmonious and balanced development of the physical and mental aspects of human life that were to be taken up more fully in Soviet times.

Russian physical culture and sport from Russian soil

Some thinkers, particularly those of Slavophile persuasion, were convinced that the Russian pattern of sport, both in its theory and in its practice, should have deep roots in and grow out of Russian soil. The old feelings of simplicity, naturalness, moral strength and legitimacy that such thinkers perceived in the way of life of the Russian peasant commune should, they felt, be the foundation of a moral code which could be acquired and re-inforced via sports and team games.

The belief in predominantly Russian or, at least, Slav sport had a strong patriotic populist base that was apparent in resistance to the importation from Germanic and Latin Europe of organised games and gymnastics systems; this was manifest, for example, in the ardent propagation by some enthusiasts of *Sokol* gymnastics. In Soviet times, this belief reappeared in the 1920s in the form of a movement in favour of banning 'bourgeois' (Western) sports and gymnastics systems and of encouraging Russian folk games (as well as various 'production gymnastics' and mass physical fitness displays). Just after World War II, when Stalin's xenophobic campaigning was at its most pathological, this was to be reflected, too, in an official drive to purge sporting language of foreign terminology.

Faith in the common people

As we have seen, there were those in pre-revolutionary Russia who believed that if only the Russian people, particularly the 'dark peasant masses', had the opportunity of developing their

[5] L. N. Tolstoy, *Pedagogicheskie sochineniya*, Vol. I, 2nd edn. (Moscow), p. 17.

mental and physical capacities to the full, they would surely lift
the country out of its backwardness. The image of the lumbering
bear would give way to that of the *sokol* – the bright-eyed falcon.
A system of physical culture for the people and the opportunity
for them to join clubs and take part in tournaments at home and
abroad – given shorter working hours, better nutrition and culture
– would, perhaps, open up an era that would put Russia in the
forefront of world achievement. Such were the notions held by
some Russian intellectuals. Anton Chekhov, a founder of the
Russian Gymnastics Society and patron of peasant-strongman
sports as well as a playwright, voiced such thoughts in a speech to
mark the opening of the Society. Referring to its members, he
said, 'These are the people of the morrow. The time will come
when everyone will be as strong and skilful. There lie the nation's
hopes for the future and its happiness.'[6] Chekhov, like his friend
the writer Alexander Kuprin (who was a founding member of the
Kiev Athletics Society, refereed wrestling bouts, was a regular
contributor to the journal *Hercules* and pioneered several new
sports), was a patron of such peasant athletes as Ivan Lebedev
(the prototype for his 'Uncle Vanya') and Ivan Poddubny – both
renowned for their feats of strength.

In Soviet times, the idea of devotion to popular values
(*narodnost'*) was to become a pillar of official Soviet ideology; the
continually reiterated notion that all the sacrifices and efforts,
with little immediate return, were for the sake of 'the toiling
people' helped to sustain the effort. In physical culture and sport,
the related professed ideal of mass participation (*massovos'*) was
to become a persistent ideological theme.

Physical effort as the source of dignity, morality and happiness

In some Russian writings, not only was physical effort something
to be revered for its own sake but man's physical development
through labour and exercise was presented as a cause for pride
and a source of honour – and its cultivation as a duty. Tolstoy,
for example, firmly believed that physical work and exercise were
essential to mental creativity: 'Sedentary mental work without

[6] A. P. Chekhov, '*People of the Future*', in *Gerkules* (*Hercules*), 1898,
No. 11, p. 5.

movement and bodily activity is sheer agony. I am no use for anything by evening if I do not work with my legs and arms during the day.'[7]

The sturdy virility of simple folk was held up against the sybaritic effeminacy of aristocrats – brawn and calloused palms against flabbiness and 'lily-white hands' (*beloruchki*), the industry and hardiness of working people against the contempt for physical exertion of masters and their employment of peasant 'souls' and industrial 'hands' to do manual work, even the menial tasks involved in such sports as hunting and yachting. Even in the opinion of the perhaps most extreme of such writers, the spirit could be tempered by tempering the body.

The contempt for physical exertion rather general among the 19th-century Russian nobility did, in fact, evoke a reaction in their ranks – from some writers as well as the populists. Later, in the 'workers' state', some of the ideas of these aristocratic writers and populists were to be drawn on to express a 'correct' reverence for physical labour and feats of strength by proletarians. During the period of rapid industrialisation, feats of strength and skill in labour and sport were to be elevated to a particularly high status (sometimes not without elements of the demagogic), and rewarded accordingly. The slogan of 'healthy minds in healthy bodies' as a model for all citizens was widely propagated.

The sources of these ideas

If these were some of the key ideas contributing to form Russian attitudes to the cultivation of the physique, from what currents of physical-educational thought did they mainly derive?

The Sokol

Although a school of military drilling and physical training already existed in Russia, mainly based on the Prussian model and the instruction of General Suvorov (1730–1800), the Russian authorities attempted to refashion this at the turn of the century in line with German and Swedish ideas on gymnastics – including the introduction of a variant of the German style of ceremonial

[7] Tolstoy, *Pedagogicheskie sochineniya*, p. 97.

marching ('goosestepping') which remains to this day. As we shall see later, both foreign schools made a lasting impression on Russian – and Soviet – gymnastics, calisthenics and army training.

From the 1860s, however, it was the Czech *Sokol* system that came to dominate in official Russia, largely because of its 'racial' folk associations.

The *Sokol* ('Falcon') movement had grown up in Bohemia and Moravia and some other parts of Austria–Hungary in the 1860s. Initially, it was, in fact, one of the legal forms for nationalism – like the *Turnen* in Germany. The *Sokol* Gymnastics Society, formed in 1862, became one of the principal forms of uniting and organising young Czechs. Its members wore national costumes and called each other 'brother' and 'sister'. Besides holding regular gymnastics meetings, the society also conducted a great deal of cultural work. By 1871, there were 130 *Sokol* societies in the Czech lands, and the movement had its own newspaper. The *Sokol* system of gymnastics, popularised by Miroslav Tyrš (1832–1884), a professor of fine arts at Prague University, was somewhat similar to the German school, inasmuch as it employed a variety of gymnastics equipment and put greater emphasis on the form of movement rather than the effect of exercises on the human organism. It lacked the disciplined repetition of exercises that distinguished the German system; rather, it featured complex and artistic combinations of exercises, giving stress to graceful movement and decorative configurations. To these ends, the gymnasts employed not only parallel bars, the horse and the beam, but also free exercises and exercises performed in time to music, sometimes with scarves, sticks, swords and shields.

The political and cultural overtones of the *Sokol* made it more attractive to Russia – and the Soviet Union – than either German or Swedish physical education, since it implied a panslavism which was by no means alien to the régimes in either tsarist or Stalinist Russia.

Pyotr Lesgaft

The figure who made the most lasting impression on Russian and Soviet physical education was *Pyotr Lesgaft* (1837–1909), biologist, anatomist, educationalist and social reformer – the founder of the new discipline of physical education in tsarist Russia.

Lesgaft started his career in 1861 as a teacher of anatomy at the St Petersburg Academy of Medicine; he was subsequently invited to take up a professorship at the University of Kazan' and went there in 1869, but was soon dismissed for his outspoken criticism of the unscientific methods used. For a while, from 1872, he worked as consultant on therapeutic gymnastics in the private surgery of a Dr Berglindt but, after the publication of several articles and books (including a descriptive history of sport in Europe and ancient Greece and an article, published in 1874, on naturalistic gymnastics), he was put in charge of the physical training of military cadets. The next year, 1875, he was commissioned by the War Ministry to spend two summers in Western Europe studying the systems of physical education current there. Altogether, he visited 26 cities in 13 Western European states. The British system was evidently most to his liking, although he abhorred the 'strict orders, fagging and lording of senior pupils over juniors'[8] that he witnessed in some public schools. He also visited the Central Army Gymnastics School at Aldershot, the Royal Military Academy at Woolwich and Oxford University. What especially took his fancy was the 'English predilection for strict rules of hygiene, competitive games in the open air, long walks and boat trips, swimming and other regular exercises.'[9] On his return, in 1877, he published his *Relationship of Anatomy to Physical Education and the Major Purpose of Physical Education in Schools*, in which he outlined a physical education programme for military colleges. He was, in fact, able to supervise its progress in twelve academies. At the same time, he took a keen interest in organising courses for physical education instructors for the military academies – provision for which, until then, had been non-existent.

While supervising officer training, Lesgaft published his major works, *Family Upbringing* (1884), *Teaching Physical Education to Schoolchildren* (Part 1 in 1888, Part 2 in 1901) and *Fundamentals of Theoretical Anatomy* (1905). His desire to organise

8 See D. Ekonomov, *Strastny uchitel'* (Moscow, 1969), p. 76.
9 Ibid., p. 77.

sport in civilian schools was for some time thwarted by the authorities, who still tended to look on it as frivolous and tending to encourage academic idleness. This led Lesgaft in 1892 to found and become Secretary of the 'Society for the Encouragement of the Physical Development of Student Youth' which quickly spread its branches to Odessa, Kiev and Moscow. Besides encouraging public discussion of children's and young people's physical development both in the home and in school, this philanthropic organisation constructed play areas in a number of towns and provided sports amenities for children of the poor, arranging for them competitive games, camps and excursions as well as boating in summer and ice skating and sledding in winter. The Society finally, in 1896, persuaded the Minister of Education to set up the first civilian physical training courses for men *and* women instructors with Lesgaft in charge. However, Lesgaft was accused of inciting student unrest and the courses were closed down in 1907. After the October Revolution, Lesgaft's 'Courses' were reorganised into the famous Institute of Physical Culture in Leningrad that today bears his name.

The admission of women to training was certainly novel: the official view in Russia had long been that sport was the preserve of men and that women were not suited to it by their social status and anatomical structure. For much of his academic career, Lesgaft espoused the cause of women's sporting rights, giving official physical education and anatomy courses to women students at his home and, after 1896, at the university; 100 women students attended in the first year and 166 in the second. Lesgaft regarded women's participation in sport a means to social liberation: 'Social slavery has left its degrading imprint on women. Our task is to free the maidenly body of its fetters, conventions and drooping posture, and return to our pupils their freedom and suppleness which have been stolen from them. We must develop in them firmness, initiative and independence, teach them to think and take decisions, give them knowledge of life and make physical educationalists out of them.'[10]

Lesgaft's medical studies of the human system led him to the conclusion that it was in constant development and change,

[10] P. F. Lesgaft, *Sobranie pedagogicheskikh sochinenii*, Vol. III (Moscow, 1956), p. 178.

partly under the influence of the social environment; physical exercise was the only means of developing the system overall and in its individual components. It attained optimum development when all bodily organs were exercised in a balanced way. Physical education instructors should, in his opinion, have a knowledge of chemistry and physics, particularly the general laws of mechanics, so as to be able to apply them to the 'human mechanism'.

On the basis of his theory, he elaborated and recommended a system of physical education for the school and the home:

(1) the child starts by simple movements which are explained to him but not demonstrated; he has to analyse them himself and distinguish one from another, then begin to understand them. The movements, recommended for early school classes, consist of normal walking, running, jumping and throwing a ball;

(2) the child then learns to master exercises of gradually increasing complexity in various conditions, after which he can tackle more difficult tasks swiftly and easily. These exercises are designed for the intermediate classes and consist of running against the clock, long and high jumping and distance throwing;

(3) the child then learns to harmonise his movements in time and space and in relation to surrounding objects, already foreseeing the result. By these exercises, he develops muscular control and learns to act in the best possible way in any circumstances. Exercises are for the upper forms and include running at a set speed, target or distance ball throwing, exercises associated with an understanding of spatial relationships and the temporal distribution of effort;

(4) simultaneously with these groups of exercises, the child checks the skills he has acquired and consolidates them by employing difficult actions during games, excursions and work movements.

At each stage of physical education, different, increasingly complicated, pedagogical aims are pursued, the main purpose being to teach the child consciously to master the movements of his body and to attain the best results with the minimum energy and time expenditure. In Lesgaft's opinion, just as in intellectual education, the child should not merely accumulate knowledge but be able to apply it, so in physical education, he should both develop physical skills and be prepared to apply them in the best way possible.

The exercises to be included in this system were mainly gymnastics, team games, expeditions and rambles. Lesgaft, however, opposed the German system and any gymnastics that employed special equipment: 'Exercises employing equipment involve sharp sensations; they therefore blunt the emotions of young people and make them less receptive and impressionable; it is hardly surprising that, when young people go to university, they smoke heavily, drink and challenge one another to duels.'[11] Further, in his opinion, the type of gymnastics in vogue in Germany and Sweden did not correspond to children's anatomical structure and were therefore physically harmful. He favoured the type of free gymnastics that is today known in Russia as 'artistic gymnastics', which would satisfy the children's natural desire for physical movement and achievement, and also encourage such qualities as will power and initiative: 'A person develops in the family, the family gives him affection, warmth, makes him responsive and kind; the school develops his mind, gives him the ability to form his own views, judgments and thoughts; along with an independence of thought the person's moral values are formed. Physical exercises develop activity in a person and he acquires the ability to subordinate all his desires to his will.'[12]

Games were also a means of character training. These did not, however, include (competitive) sport which, he believed, had a bad effect on the moral outlook of young people, encouraged egotism and was educationally harmful inasmuch as it did not develop exercises gradually. Games were to encourage a group spirit, unselfishness, social awareness and devotion to society:

Games arouse and gradually develop social instincts . . . In every school game, the player is a member of a small society, actively participating in it, forgetting about his personal, selfish aims and engrossed exclusively in the attainment of common aims, all the while adhering to all the accepted principles and laws that restrict the right of every individual . . . A sense of justice, of comradeship, of fair play, an acquaintance with public opinion – these are all given

---

[11] *Pamyati Pyotra Frantsevicha Lesgafta*, 'Shkola i Zhizn'' (St Petersburg, 1912), p. 95.
[12] Ibid., p. 98.

us by games. Are not these the feelings we wish our children to possess, both as future citizens and as useful and active members of society?[13]

Nature rambles were to encourage creative thought and action by acquainting the child with nature at first hand rather than through learning to rote. That is why 'excursions should not be spoiled by triumphant marches, military evolutions, flags, badges, prizes, sport [i.e. competitive sport] or the like. One should constantly remember that the fewer the strong diversions, the less the loss from the child's standpoint, the more he will preserve his strength and the better his self-possession. I personally believe that excursions will encourage the child to think, ennoble his feelings and inspire creative thought.'[14] For adults, too, 'there is a very good English custom of taking a walk before breakfast, even if it is only 5–6 versts [5–6 km]. After that, one can tackle any mental or physical activity in a more active frame of mind.'[15]

Lesgaft's ideal child, like Rousseau's *Emile*, was to grow up into the ideal citizen – most able, physically and mentally, to provide the greatest contribution to the common good. Such a person had to be harmoniously developed, both physically and intellectually, and possess the 'ideal' organism: 'Only if all organs are developed harmoniously is the human organism able to improve and produce the greatest effort with the least expenditure of time and energy.'[16]

The implications of Lesgaft's system and views went far beyond what the tsarist authorities were willing to allow. Certain of his views are reminiscent of Rousseau's advice to *Emile* – character training through physical activity, the political and national ends of physical culture and its therapeutic value. Others were clearly inspired by his acquaintance with the British system of physical education, which he lauded, and British public school ideas on the unselfishness and team spirit of the type of games encouraged by the English 'Muscular Christians'.

He himself was no revolutionary; if anything, his educational philosophy reflected the ideology of the small but growing

[13] Ibid., p. 100.
[14] Ibid., pp. 102–103.
[15] P. F. Lesgaft, *Sobranie pedagogicheskikh sochinenii*, Vol. III, p. 299.
[16] *Pamyati Pyotra Frantsevicha Lesgafta*, 'Shkola i Zhizn'', p. 93.

Russian and the large West-European bourgeoisie. It was, though, Lesgaft more than anyone else who was to influence the Soviet system of physical education. Several major tenets of his theory and his system today underlie the physical education system prevailing in the USSR: ideas of 'harmonious development', of social awareness through physical education, of the principle of gradual and consistent training, of belief in a biological justification for exercise and games in general, of women's social emancipation through the bodily liberation of games and physical education, and of the strict observance of age, sex and individual idiosyncrasies of children when playing games and engaging in physical exercise can all be derived from him. Training and teaching in the USSR are still largely guided by Lesgaft's views on mastering bodily movements by stages, starting from the learning of correct forms of movement in the nursery and gradually increasing the load up to the elaboration of spatial and temporal orientation. On the other hand, his hostility to 'sport' – competition and the paraphernalia surrounding it, such as badges, trophies and flags, professionalism, public displays, victory celebrations and similar rituals – while finding ready accord in the 1920s, came to be rejected totally with the onset of full-scale industrialisation and the widespread application of incentives throughout the economy.

Physiologists: Sechyonov and Pavlov

The physiological studies of certain Russian scientists were to have a considerable impact on Soviet physical education and sport, including national fitness programmes, athletics training methods and physical exercises at work. Their ideas are said to form the basis on which the Soviet theory of physical education is constructed: 'The work of the great Russian physiologists, Sechyonov and Pavlov, and their followers forms the basis of the entire system of physical education in the Soviet Union.'[17] Other Soviet sources explicitly acknowledge the debt to Lesgaft: 'Pyotr Frantsevich Lesgaft . . . was the founder of the scientific system of physical education in our country.'[18] The seminal rôle of these

[17] A. Svetov, *No Limits to Strength and Skill* (Novosti Publishing Agency, Moscow, 1965), p. 44.
[18] F. I. Samoukov (ed.), *Istoriya fizicheskoi kul'tury* (Moscow, 1964), p. 230.

men cannot, therefore, be ignored. Their research largely involved the study of the effects of physical exercise on the growth of the human organism and on the mind, the recreative benefits of 'active rest' and the advantages of physical fitness for longevity and self-realisation.

Ivan Sechyonov (1829–1905) referred to by Pavlov as 'the father of Russian physiology', admired Darwin and Chernyshevsky and advanced an essentially materialist conception of psychic and spiritual phenomena. According to his principal theory, mental and bodily activities were two forms of the vital activity of the human organism, of which the physical was primary and psychological secondary. 'Muscle tone serves as the major controller of consciousness in coordinating movement.'[19] Physical education should, therefore, in his view, be an integral part of all-round education as a means of strengthening the material foundation of consciousness.

His study of muscular activities, notably in three works – 'The Part Played by the Nervous System in Man's Working Movements' (1900), 'Essay on Man's Working Movements' (1901) and 'On the Question of the Effect of Stimulation of the Sensory Nerves on Muscular Work' (1903–1904) – brought him to the theory of 'active rest', i.e. that rest in movement is more beneficial than passive rest. An experiment he made with lifting weights by rhythmic motions – first with the right hand, then with the left – forced him to conclude: 'When I first began the experiment, I was very much surprised to find that my left hand worked much more strongly than my right did. My surprise was heightened when it appeared that the work done by the tired right hand after the work of the left became much stronger than in the first period of work.'[20]

The implications of his findings were to have considerable significance for later Soviet studies of fatigue and rest, of the physiology of work and training methods. 'His [Sechyonov's] research is widely applied today for substantiating work-and-leisure régimes and training for a variety of sports.'[21] Sechyonov's work undoubtedly played no small part in justifying and working

[19] *Entsiklopedichesky slovar' po fizicheskoi kul'ture i sportu*, Vol. III, p. 23.
[20] I. M. Sechyonov, *Izbrannye proizvedeniya* (Moscow, 1953), p. 144.
[21] *Entsiklopedichesky slovar'*, Vol. III, p. 23.

out the 'production gymnastics' or physical exercises that are so common a feature of Soviet factory life today.

If Lesgaft was the pioneer of a new discipline, a new theory of physical education, Ivan Pavlov (1849–1936) put it in the context of a general theory of physiology. 'Pavlov's work has immense significance for physical education in that it sets it on a natural-scientific basis.'[22] He was to become for many years the unquestionable authority in the USSR on psychology; virtually all investigations into physical education and training methods were to base their findings on his concepts.

By means of numerous experiments with animals, Pavlov concluded that the human organism and its environment were connected by conditioned reflexes – 'temporary connections of the nervous system that constantly appear, grow strong and then disappear'.[23] According to his theory, 'the conditioned reflex is the basis of all of men's higher nervous activity'.[24] This theory had several implications for Soviet physical education; primarily, it meant that exercise was highly salutary for the central nervous system. Systematic participation in a variety of games, gymnastics and sports improves the general functioning and capacity both of the physical organism and of the mind: hence the need for regular sporting activity by all citizens, for the good of society as well as of the individual.

Pavlov's research affected the Soviet approach to the study of systems of physical education and training. The preoccupation with science and the search for a scientific technique of sports development are conspicuous features of Soviet sports and training methods. Such is the commitment to 'science' that many coaches are expected to be as much scientists as they are athletes: 'The coach must be acquainted with Pavlov's physiology, Soviet educational theory and psychology. To analyse technique, he must also know mechanics, physics and mathematics.'[25]

It is the official Soviet assertion that 'the principles of Pavlov's theory of the nervous system are fundamental to the formation of

[22] Ibid., Vol. II, p. 218.
[23] I. P. Pavlov, *Polnoye sobranie sochinenii*, Vol. II (Kniga' I, Moscow, 1951), p. 245.
[24] Ibid., p. 246.
[25] P. Sobolev, L. Borodina, S. Korobkov, *Sport in the USSR* (FLPH, Moscow, 1958), p. 52.

motor habits, the physical qualities of strength, speed, stamina and skill, improving the functional capacity of the organism – especially for purposes of work – establishing, maintaining and developing sporting form, improving sports achievements, recuperating after strenuous muscle work, tempering the organism, physical exercise at work, training methods and maintaining fitness as people grow old'.[26]

Pavlov remained a strong churchman and was long openly critical of the Soviet régime, yet it supported his work because his theory of conditioned reflexes was regarded as a substantiation of and belief in the plasticity of Nature – including Man. In the last years of Stalin's life, Pavlov's teaching was officially made the obligatory basis of all medical theory.

Marxism–Leninism

Much is made in Soviet literature on physical culture of the debt owed to Marx, Engels and Lenin. Since all three wrote virtually nothing directly on the subject, this may sound a strange debt; it is, however, the implications of their teaching that are generally referred to. The section that follows attempts to examine sport in the light of Marxist–Leninist writing and Soviet interpretations of it.

Marxist philosophy At the time Marx was writing, metaphysics was in the grip of a dualism that separated mind from matter and, under the influence of Christian theology, often exaggerated a distinction into an antagonism; in such a world view, body and soul were seen as warring parties with the body cast as the villain of the piece. Marx rejected the dualist philosophy and stressed that not only was there an intimate relationship between matter and mind, but that the former largely determined the latter. In his view, political and social institutions and the ideas, images and ideologies through which men understand the world in which they live, their place within it and themselves, ultimately derived from the 'economic base' of society. This determined the class relations into which men had to enter with one another in order to produce:

[26] *Entsiklopedichesky slovar' po fizicheskoi kul'ture i sportu*, Vol. II, p. 219.

In the social production which men carry on they enter into definite relations that are indispensable and independent of their wills; these relations of production correspond to a definite stage of development of their material powers of production. The sum total of these relations of production constitutes the economic structure of society – the real foundation, on which rise legal and political superstructures and to which correspond definite forms of social consciousness. The mode of production in material life determines the general character of the social, political and spiritual processes of life. It is not the consciousness of men that determines their existence, but, on the contrary, their social existence that determines their consciousness.[27]

This fundamental Marxist tenet contains certain implications for recreation:

(1) Since the human psychosomatic organism develops and changes under the influence of external conditions including the social environment, subjection to physical exercise not only develops that part of the body to which it is directed but also has an effect on the body as a whole – on the personality. A strong bond exists between social and individual development and between the physical and mental development of the individual. Societies are likely to seek to shape this development.

(2) In liberal capitalist society, whose prevailing ideology is that of 'independent' decision making and 'free' contracting between 'equal' social atoms, sport has normally been regarded as the concern only of the individual, a feature of life unconnected with classes and social values, with economics and society's mode of production; little attention has been paid to it as a social phenomenon. To the Marxist, however, sport is part of the social superstructure and therefore strongly influenced by the prevailing relations of production – not something 'in itself' and so divorced from politics; a society's pattern of sport will ultimately depend on the specifics of that society's socio-economic foundation, its class relationships. Moreover, says Marx, 'with a change in the economic foundation, the entire immense superstructure is more or less rapidly transformed':[28] the nature of sport can therefore be expected to alter with any change to a new socio-economic formation.

[27] K. Marx, *A Contribution to the Critique of Political Economy* (Chicago, 1904), pp. 11–12.
[28] Ibid., p. 13.

(3) The acceptance of a dualist metaphysic, a sharp separation of body and mind, had often led to a concern with things of the mind at the expense of bodily activities. Marx emphasised that practical activities have a decisive influence on all human development in the broadest sense. None more so than work, through which people could change themselves as well as Nature: 'Labour is, in the first place, a process in which both man and Nature participate, and in which man of his own accord starts, regulates, and controls the material reactions between himself and Nature. He opposes himself to Nature as one of her own forces, setting in motion arms and legs, head and hands, the natural forces of his body, in order to appropriate Nature's productions in a form adapted to his own wants. By thus acting on the external world and changing it, he at the same time changes his own nature.'[29]

This proposition implies a strong link between work and such other bodily activities as physical exercise and games playing. It has led some Marxist historians to seek the origin of games and sports in practices in primitive society leading to the improvement of physical dexterity and utilitarian skills vital to working and hunting. In this, they refer to Engels, who wrote: 'The use of various forms of weapons in work and military activity among primitive peoples developed their mental and physical abilities.'[30]

From his studies of early bourgeois society, Marx came to the conclusion that production was actually inhibited by, *inter alia*, the denial to the workers of time for recreation which would help restore their energy for production and make it more efficient. Marx was concerned with civil society's need for workers to obtain more free time – not only for pure leisure but also for recuperating their strength and applying themselves more vigorously to productive work after reasonable rest and recreation. What he saw as the sheer wasteful inefficiency of the capitalist production of his day in neglecting the recreative functions of play agitated him: 'The capitalist mode of production (because it absorbs surplus labour) produces . . . not only the deterioration of human labour power by robbing it of its normal, moral and physical, conditions

---

[29] K. Marx, *Capital* (FLPH, Moscow, 1961), Vol. 1, p. 177.
[30] F. Engels, *The Origin of the Family, Private Property and the State* (FLPH, Moscow, 1958), p. 28.

of development and function. It produces also the premature exhaustion and death of this labour power itself.'[31] In another place, he writes that 'from the point of view of the direct process of production, this saving [of working time] may be considered as the production of *basic capital*; man himself is that basic capital'.[32] Physically fit and mentally alert workers are better able to cope with new industrial skills and increasingly complex technology and to have higher productivity by showing less absenteeism and greater activity on the job.

Modern industry, however, objectively requires more than physically fit workers; it needs versatile, fully developed individuals, healthy in body and in mind. In the education system of the future, therefore, citizens were to be given, Marx advised, the opportunity for balanced all-round education, in which physical education was to be an integral part; the system would consist of three elements combining training of the mind with training of the body:

First, mental education.

Second, bodily education, such as is given in schools of gymnastics, and by military exercise. Third, technological training, which acquaints the pupil with the basic principles of all processes of production and, simultaneously, gives him the habits of handling elementary instruments of all trades.[33]

In the English Factory Acts, Marx had seen the germs of the prototypes of such a system in which mental and physical education would be combined with manual labour to improve social production and to produce all-round individuals: 'From the Factory system budded, as Robert Owen has shown in detail, the germ of the education of the future, an education that will, in the case of every child over a given age, combine productive labour with instruction and gymnastics, not only as one of the methods of adding to the efficiency of production, but as the only method of producing fully developed human beings.'[34]

Whether games playing contained its own justification within

[31] K. Marx, *Capital*, p. 265.
[32] Ibid., p. 332.
[33] K. Marx, 'Instructions for the Delegates of the Provisional General Council. The Different Questions', in K. Marx and F. Engels, *Selected Works* (Progress Publishers, Moscow, 1969), Vol. II, p. 81.
[34] K. Marx, *Capital*, pp. 483–484.

itself or whether its value was to be sought in ulterior ends was not a question specifically raised by Marx. The Marxist vision of the future, however, does seem to imply that work and physical recreation will merge, or that work will be elevated to the plane of recreation by the removal of the yokes of specialisation and compulsion. But Marx evidently did not envisage recreation under communism as simply games – rather as a fusion of work-like activities with play. In this, he affirmed a principal criterion of playful activities, namely, that they are freely chosen and are pursued for their inherent pleasure rather than for practical results.[35]

To sum up, Marx provided few clear-cut guidelines on physical culture. On the one hand, he stressed the interdependence of work and physical recreation and, on the other, he saw the playful use of energy as contributing to the enrichment of the personality, or self-realisation. But, as the American sociologist, C. Wright Mills, once pointed out: 'There is no *one* Marx. The various presentations of his work which we can construct from his books, pamphlets, articles, letters, written at different times in his own development, depend upon our point of interest, and we may not take any one of them to be The Real Marx.'[36] The same might be said of Lenin. That is not to say, of course, that there is no consistency in the writings of Marx or Lenin, no Marx*ism* or Lenin*ism*.

Leninism If Marx made scant direct reference to sport, Lenin was scarcely more prolific on the subject – despite the sixty volumes of his writings in the latest Soviet edition. Unlike Marx, who personally abhorred any physical exercises,[37] Lenin was,

---

[35] This view was later upheld by Trotsky who maintained that, 'The longing for amusement, distraction, sight seeing and laughter is the most legitimate desire of human nature. We are able, and indeed obliged, to give the satisfaction of this desire a higher artistic quality, at the same time making amusement a weapon of collective education, *freed from the guardianship of the pedagogue and the tiresome habit of moralising*' [my italics]. (See L. Trotsky, *Problems of Everyday Life* (Monad Press, New York, 1973), p. 32.)

[36] C. Wright Mills, *The Marxists* (Pelican, London, 1962), p. 42.

[37] Y. Kapp, *Eleanor Marx* (Lawrence and Wishart, London, 1972), Vol. I, p. 193; the only game Marx seemed to enjoy was chess (p. 26); Engels, on the other hand, was 'an enthusiastic rider to hounds, a mighty walker and a deep drinker', ibid., p. 108.

moreover, an active practitioner of physical fitness and sport in his own life. As one observer has put it: 'Of all the prominent Russian revolutionaries, he was the keenest sportsman. From boyhood he had been fond of shooting and skating. Always a great walker, he became a keen mountaineer, a lively cyclist, and an impatient fisherman.'[38] Particularly during his periods of imprisonment and exile, he valued fitness as a stimulant to mental alertness. While in a St Petersburg prison, he wrote that he did 'gymnastics with great pleasure and value *every day*' (Lenin's emphasis).[39] In a letter from Munich to his sister, then in prison in Russia, he urged her 'to do gymnastics and have a good rub-down every day. It is absolutely essential when you are alone . . . force yourself to do several dozen exercises (without stopping!)! That is very important.'[40] Of his personal preferences, his wife recalled that he enjoyed ice skating, shooting, hiking, *gorodki* and cycling – even to the extent of ordering bicycles for his wife and himself from Berlin through the Russian Sports Society *Nadezhda* in 1910.[41] His favourite pastime – like that of several other émigré Russian intellectuals – was chess, which he played regularly (many games by correspondence with Lunacharsky and Gorky). On his return from Russia, however, his wife reports that 'Vladimir Il'yich had to give up chess, his favourite game, because it involved too much of his time'.[42] He did become, nonetheless, honorary president of the Moscow Chess Society in November 1922.

Lenin's sporting activity may seem to have little relevance to an understanding of sport in the Soviet Union. One must bear in mind, however, the Soviet establishment's massive cult of Lenin and penchant for looking to Lenin's personal example when seeking to justify current policies. Official advocacy of daily exercises and such pursuits as chess can thus call on Lenin's own preferences. The desire to promote certain forms of recreation has

[38] R. B. Lockhart, *Giants Cast Long Shadows*, p. 134.
[39] V. I. Lenin, *Polnoye sobranie sochinenii*, Vol. IV, p. 72
[40] Ibid., p. 73.
[41] V. Bonch-Bruyevich, *Nash Il'yich: vospominaniya* (Detgiz, Moscow, 1956), p. 22.
[42] N. K. Krupskaya, *Vospominaniya o V.I. Lenine*, Vol. I (Politizdat, Moscow, 1968), p. 242.

certainly resulted in the highlighting of individual aspects of Lenin's habits and mode of life.

What are clearly more important are his writings on the subject of sport and physical education. Like Marx, Lenin's educational philosophy favoured a combination of the training of the mind and body: 'It is impossible to visualise the ideal of a future society without a combination of instruction and productive labour, nor can productive labour without parallel instruction and physical education be put on a plane required by the modern level of technology and the state of scientific knowledge.'[43] In his article 'Karl Marx', he refers to Marx's appraisal of Owen's school in Lanarkshire – which combined mental and physical education with manual work – as the germ of the education of the future.[44] This model even found some reflection in the decree 'On Compulsory Instruction in the Military Art', passed in the crisis months of 1918, which brought into being the military sports organisation *Vsevobuch*. Its chairman, Nikolai Podvoisky, later described the decree as 'combining gymnastics and all forms of physical development and training with general and military training in our country. By this decree, physical culture was introduced into the working people's common education system, their training for defending their country and for highly productive and varied work.'[45] He went on to stress Lenin's contribution to the decree: 'Vladimir Il'yich often stressed, and the decree established, the correct view of the physical education of the masses as a means of obtaining the harmonious all-round development of the individual.'[46]

Lenin, therefore, derived from and shared with Marx the notion of potential fully developed individuals, of men who could not attain the full measure of their latent abilities under capitalism: 'It is necessary to develop people's abilities, to reveal the talents which are an untapped source in the people and which capitalism has repressed, crushed, stifled in their thousands and

---

[43] V. I. Lenin, *Polnoye sobranie sochinenii*, Vol. II, p. 485.

[44] V. I. Lenin, *Izbrannye proizvedeniya v 3–kh tomakh*, Vol. I, p. 53; see p. 59 above.

[45] N. I. Podvoisky, 'Lenin i fizicheskoye vospitanie', *Krasny Sport*, 1940, No. 4 (831) (21 January), pp. 3–4.

[46] Podvoisky, *Lenin i fizicheskoye vospitanie*, pp. 3–4.

millions.'[47] Under socialism and complete communism, however, everyone would have a chance to choose the physical activity they wanted to pursue and attain complete self-realisation. It would 'not merely satisfy the needs of its members, but ensure *complete* welfare and free *all-round* development of *all* members of society'.[48]

Influenced by his own experience of physical and mental training during periods of privation and confronted by the practical problems of power, Lenin added an emphasis on character training that was absent in Marx. He recognised the effects that sport might have, for instance, upon the development of qualities of character valuable to individuals and society, upon the social behaviour of citizens and upon the promotion of health. In his comments on the advocates of 'free love' and on Leftism in the cultural revolution, Lenin took a position on the moral effects of sport which was not far removed from that of English 'Muscular Christians' like Dr Arnold of Rugby and the novelists, Thomas Hughes and Charles Kingsley: 'Young people especially need to have a zest for living and be in good spirits. Healthy sport – gymnastics, swimming, hiking, all manner of physical exercise – should be combined as much as possible with a variety of intellectual interests, study, analysis and investigation . . . That would give young people more than external theories and discussions about sex . . . Healthy bodies, healthy minds!'[49] Sport would also safeguard clean-limbed youngsters from such vices as drunkenness and smoking – as the decree 'On Curbing Tobacco Smoking' was intended to do in 1919. When asked how young people should spend their spare time, Lenin once replied, 'Young men and women of the Soviet land should live life beautifully and to the full both in public and in private life. Wrestling, work, study, sport, making merry, singing, dreaming – these are things young people should make the most of.'[50] Games playing, then, was, in Lenin's view, conducive to moral as well as physical health; it

[47] V. I. Lenin, *Polnoye sobranie sochinenii*, Vol. II, pp. 85–86.
[48] Ibid., Vol. VI, p. 232.
[49] C. Zetkin, *Vospominaniya o Vladimire Il'yiche Lenine*, Part II (Gospolitizdat, 1955), p. 84.
[50] Quoted in A. Bezymensky, *Vstrecha komsomol'tsev s V.I. Leninom* (Gospolitizdat, 1956), p. 18.

was a valuable ingredient in character training. One can imagine Lenin's ideal young people (not unlike the heroes of Kingsley's *Westward Ho!* and Hughes's *Tom Brown's Schooldays*) drawn in glowing colours, adorned with every sort of athletic accomplishment and displaying the excellence of simple understanding and the urge to serve the proletarian dictatorship. The resolution passed by the Third All-Russia Congress of the Russian Young Communist League (October 1920) – at which Lenin spoke – surely reflected his views on the functions of physical education: 'The physical education of the younger generation is an essential element in the overall system of communist upbringing of young people, aimed at creating harmoniously developed people, creative citizens of communist society. Today, physical education also has direct practical aims: (1) preparing young people for work; and (2) preparing them for military defence of Soviet power.'[51] This, the first clear-cut official statement on the aims of Soviet sport, makes no bones about the rational use of physical education for purposes of work and defence. It does, however, hint that, once the society is on its feet and socialism moving towards communism, utilitarian-instrumental aims will give way to that of self-realisation. Nonetheless, here (some years before Soviet industrialisation commenced) was a commitment to use sport for labour and military purposes.

On another occasion, Lenin indicated the powerful social force that sport might be in contributing to women's emancipation. 'It is our urgent task to draw working women into sport. . . If we can achieve that and get them to make full use of the sun, water and fresh air for fortifying themselves, we shall bring an entire revolution in the Russian way of life.'[52] Furthermore, Podvoisky writes that Lenin stressed to him the 'huge significance of the task of *Vsevobuch*: correctly to train physical educationalists and so to attain through them a cultural, comradely mutual relationship between young men and women'.[53] Lenin, therefore, saw in sport a convenient vehicle for drawing women into public activity and

---

[51] I. D. Chudinov (ed.), *Osnovnye postanovleniya i instruktsii po voprosam fizicheskoi kul'tury i sportu, 1917–1957* (Moscow, 1959), pp. 43–44.

[52] Quoted in N. I. Podvoisky, *Rabotnitsa i fizicheskaya kul'tura* (Moscow, 1938), p. 3.

[53] N. I. Podvoisky, 'Lenin i fizicheskoye vospitanie', p. 3.

an area where they could relatively quickly achieve a measure of equality with men – and be seen to do so.

Marx, as we have seen, spoke of military training as an element in physical education – indeed, in education in general – in his 'Instructions to the Delegates of the Provisional General Council'. Lenin, likewise, pointed to military training as a way to keep youth fit. In a comment on Engels's 'Can Europe Disarm?', he spoke of the 'need for the military training of young people and of gymnastics . . .'.[54] Podvoisky writes that, in his discussions with Lenin on the nature of Soviet sport and physical education, Lenin 'had stressed the importance of cavalry training, skiing, cycling and water sports . . . and [at the height of the Civil War] the need to use pre-military training for labour as well as the aims of war'.[55]

Lenin, therefore, implied that there was more to sport than mere physical enjoyment; it could, and indeed should, contribute to forming the all-round individual of communist society, to character formation, especially among young people, to women's emancipation and to some – not very explicit – labour and military goals. The stress later put on the interdependence of sport and work, rather than on the enrichment of the personality, may well not have been where Lenin would have put it himself had he not had a war on his hands. It is evidently necessary to distinguish the immediately pre-revolutionary Lenin, say, of *State and Revolution* (the work in which he most emphasises free personal development)[56] from the Lenin in power worried about defence and productivity. Similarly, one must distinguish the rather vague forecasts about the future ideal society made by Marx and Engels, Lenin and Trotsky in relation to the second stage of communist society or 'full communism' from their more

---

[54] V. I. Lenin, *Polnoye sobranie sochinenii*, Vol. XXVIII, p. 478.
[55] N. I. Podvoisky, *Rabotnitsa i fizicheskaya kul'tura* (Moscow, 1938), p. 114.
[56] Free personal development will take place, wrote Lenin, as the pressure of work and state coercive functions decrease: 'Socialism will shorten the working day, raise the *people* to a new life, create such conditions for the *majority* of the population as will enable *everybody*, without exception, to perform state functions, and this will lead to the *complete withering away* of every form of state in general.' (See V. I. Lenin, 'State and Revolution', in *Lenin, Selected Works*, Vol. II (Moscow, 1963), p. 397.)

practical remarks about its first or socialist stage. In the later 'interpretations' of Lenin, made during the rapid industrialisation period, the emphasis shifts to what Podvoisky, writing in 1940 on Lenin's views on physical education, calls 'a scientific approach to military and labour methods' by means of sport and physical education, 'making them accessible to the working people so as to attain higher labour productivity'.[57]

To sum up, the amalgam of Russian, foreign 'bourgeois' and Marxist–Leninist ideas and institutions, rather eclectically selected for application in Soviet policy-making, was to depend on short- or middle-term expediency as well as on Marxist ideology, as variously interpreted at different stages of Soviet history. The pattern of physical culture that was to emerge in Soviet times clearly reflected ideas and models deriving from a variety of sources.

The heritage of institutions from tsarist Russia was considerable. The Lesgaft Higher Courses became the Lesgaft Institute of Physical Culture, the Moscow River Yacht Club – the Red Stadium, the Office of the Chief Supervisor of Sport – the sports section of *Vsevobuch*; the All-Russia Football Association and the Moscow Collegium of Referees continued without a change in name; many soccer clubs of the tsarist period continued with the same players, premises, colours and, sometimes, the same name for several years. The Soviet authorities had, however, to discard the Russian Olympic Committee – Soviet foreign policy and the country's weakness militating against participation in the 'bourgeois' Olympics until 1952, the Scouts and the *Sokol* – because of their hostility or lack of political commitment to the Soviet cause, as well as many of the former middle-class sports clubs and their journals.

Foreign gymnastics systems imported into Russia in tsarist times were to come to constitute the basis of the Soviet physical culture drive and of the system of physical education introduced in schools and colleges and in the armed forces.

Bourgeois theorists' ideas about the harmonious and balanced development of body and mind were to become an underlying ideological theme in Soviet physical culture – both because they accorded with socialist ideology and, perhaps more importantly,

[57] N. I. Podvoisky, 'Lenin i fizcheskoye vospitanie', p. 121.

because they matched the technical and cultural needs of an industrialising society being built mainly by peasant labour.

The notions of such scientists as Sechyonov and Pavlov, which provided a scientific basis for rationalising physical recreation and employing 'active rest' to improve productivity, were to find a ready response in a state eager to use all possible means to industrialise rapidly. The extensive application of science, particularly knowledge of physiology and biomechanics, to training methods for various competitive sports (especially once the Soviet Union began to compete internationally after World War II) owed much to the early work and traditions of people like Lesgaft and Pavlov.

A Marxist–Leninist interpretation of culture, mental and physical, including a belief in the interdependence of the mental and physical states of human beings, provides the general framework within which physical and mental recreation is viewed in the USSR (as in all communist-governed states). It should, however, be noted that aphorisms drawn from and myths about Lenin in regard to physical culture have been taken up to justify Soviet policies at particular stages of development and need not necessarily be taken as creative Marxist thinking. (Indeed, they have sometimes replaced it.) As Marx and Lenin would readily have admitted, it is the socio-economic processes that largely fashion patterns of sport, not the prescriptions of philosophers who, to paraphrase Marx, only interpret the world.

3
Militarisation of sport, 1917–1920

When the Bolsheviks seized power, they found a country on the verge of economic collapse. Civil war and foreign intervention accelerated and intensified radical transformations in the economy and politics. The Bolsheviks were at war, and centralised control in the interests of war production was an obvious recourse. At the end of June 1918 came a decree on general nationalisation which heralded the period of ruthless centralisation now known as *War Communism*.[1]

Theorising and experimenting

It was against the background, then, of war and cataclysmic events that the new, universal system of physical education that Bolshevik educationalists had been advocating before the Revolution had to be introduced. The first steps to be taken were by no means obvious, for there was no pattern to follow; the change-over from criticism of capitalist institutions and the sports structure of industrial states to practical action in an eighty per cent peasant society in the throes of civil war, however, presented huge problems. What of the past was valid and useful? What had to be discarded? Were the schools of gymnastics and the organised sports utterly bourgeois and unworthy of a place in a new prole-tarian culture? Could Russian middle-class societies and sports movements like the Scouts and the *Sokol* be used and adapted – or should they be disbanded and a fresh start made? Was the bourgeois legacy a cancer that had to be cut out of the Russian

[1] For an authoritative treatment of the period 1917–1923, see E. H. Carr, *A History of Soviet Russia* (Penguin Books, 1970), Vols. 1–3: *The Bolshevik Revolution*.

body to make it healthy or could the best of bourgeois practice be adapted to serve the needs of the struggling proletarian state? Was there any social value in attempts to achieve top-class results, to break records, and so on? These were the types of questions that were being debated, often furiously, in educational circles during this initial period.

The first few years were, naturally, a period of improvisation and experiment, with the many left groups eager to implement their theories. The régime was to take some measures (like, for example, the banning of the Scout, *Sokol* and *Maccabee* organisations and a number of bourgeois sports clubs) that were later to be revoked or regretted, but which, at the time, were mainly dictated by the chaos and uncertainty and the 'besieged military camp' atmosphere. It was also to pass a number of decrees that, because of the conditions then obtaining, turned out to be little more than declarative. Essentially, however, physical education during the period of War Communism came to be geared to the needs of the war effort, as a Soviet historian admits: 'During the Civil War and foreign intervention, physical culture and sport were put to the service of universal military training and preparation for the fight against the enemies of the young Soviet Republic. Because of this, the administration of physical culture throughout the country was the responsibility of a military department.'[2]

Vsevobuch and the militarisation of sport

Compulsory military service to the new régime had been decreed on 22 April 1918; on 7 May, by a decree of the All-Russia Central Executive Committee of the Soviets of Workers', Soldiers' and Peasants' Deputies, a new government agency was set up: the Central Board of Universal Military Training (*vseobshcheye voyennoye obuchenie*) attached to the All-Russia *GHQ* (*Glavny shtab*); sections of *Vsevobuch* were also created in military committees, the sections being responsible for coordinating work according to an overall programme. Understandably, given the period, it received a relatively high level of publicity and priority. The principal aim of *Vsevobuch* was 'to supply the Red Army

[2] F. I. Samoukov (ed.), *Istoriya fizicheskoi kul'tury* (Moscow, 1964), p. 266.

with contingents of trained conscripts as quickly as possible'.[3] One means of achieving this was to carry out a crash programme for physical fitness; accordingly, *Vsevobuch* was given control of all sports clubs and societies and made responsible for the physical training of all people of recruitable (18–40) and pre-recruitment (16–18) age. Only schoolchildren were outside its scope: their physical training was the responsibility of the People's Commissariat of Education.

To implement its programme, therefore, *Vsevobuch* set up military committees wherever the Bolsheviks were in sufficient control. Given the uncertain conditions of the time and the reluctance with which war weary – and sometimes politically hostile – citizens greeted new military appeals, it is not certain to what extent the local committees were effective. Certainly, they lacked qualified instructors, sports equipment and facilities. For its programme to be realised, *Vsevobuch* had to provide facilities and attract (as well as compel by way of military service) young people to engage in physical exercise. Therefore, the Central Board of *Vsevobuch* decreed that: 'for the purpose of the swiftest broad involvement of the working population in physical, general culture and political development which is being held back by the lack of clubs and gymnastics facilities and by equipment inadequate for its great educative and formative mission, we order chiefs of local *Vsevobuch* organs to fit out clubs, gymnastics and sports installations by *subbotniki*[4] of young men shortly due for military service and all sporting forces, and also to use local resources in building and equipping clubs by means of mandatory labour'.[5]

An inventory and report from the Driss *uyezd* (county) section of *Vsevobuch* in Belorussia runs: 'Sports grounds 1, tennis rackets 2, old balls 5, new balls 4, foils 2, masks 1, javelins 1, discuses 1. Pre-military training is conducted 4 times a week.'[6]

[3] N. I. Podvoisky, *Kakaya fizicheskaya kul'tura nuzhna proletariatu i kem ona dolzhna sozdavat'sa?* (Moscow, 1923), p. 26.
[4] *Subbotniki*: days of unpaid voluntary work on social jobs carried out after normal paid work or on a rest day – originally on Saturday (hence the derivation from the Russian word for Saturday – *subbota*).
[5] *K novoi armii* (*organ TsU Vsevobucha*), 1920, Nos. 17–18, pp. 27–28.
[6] K. A. Kulinkovich, 'Razvitie fizicheskoi kul'tury i sporta v Belorusskoi SSR', in *Ocherki po istorii fizicheskoi kul'tury* (Moscow, 1964), p. 39.

The 'militarisation' of sport led to the requisitioning of sports equipment from the existing sports clubs; the Belorussian report quoted mentions the requisitioning of equipment from the *Sokol, Maccabee* and *Shevardeniya* sports clubs and from the Scouts.[7] This inevitably led to clashes with the club organisers and members, many of whom maintained that sport should be apolitical, and not a political or military weapon. As a result, many clubs were looked upon as pockets of potential or actual counter-revolution, were assimilated (e.g. often the *Sokol*) or forcibly disbanded (e.g. often the Scouts clubs). It is asserted that 'during the Civil War, in several regions temporarily under White Guard control, the Scouts and *Sokol* members are actively supporting the enemies of the Soviet republic'.[8] Consequently, *Vsevobuch* was given the task, 'relying on the active assistance of the *Komsomol*',[9] of conducting 'a resolute fight for the complete elimination of bourgeois sports organisations and of purging the sports and gymnastics clubs of all class enemies'.[10] Military sports clubs were formed at factories, railway depots and mines all over the country – such clubs as *Klub Oktyabrskoi Revolutsii, Raikomvod, Goznak, Pishcheviki, Burevestnik, Stroiteli* and *OPPV* (*Opytno-Pokazatel'naya Ploshchadka Vsevobucha*). The *Komsomol* played a prominent part in the requisitioning, the forming of cells at pre-military training centres and the conducting of political instruction. Its Second Congress, in October 1919, passed a special resolution pledging an all-out attack on the Boy Scout movement and urging the government to disband the Scouts: 'The Congress considers the Scouts a purely bourgeois system of spiritual and physical indoctrination of young people in

---

[7] Ibid., p. 37.
[8] *Vestnik militsionnoi armii*, 1920, No. 10.
[9] The *Komsomol* (Russian abbreviation of 'Communist Youth League') is a youth organisation set up in 1918 to assist the Communist Party; membership is now for young people between 15 and 26 years of age.
[10] *Vestnik militsionnoi armii*, 1920, No. 10. That not all bourgeois clubs succumbed at once is evident from a record of the Petrograd soccer championships and cup competitions. A total of 14 teams contested the 13th Spring Cup in 1920, all of them having been formed prior to 1917; they included *Merkur, Sport, Unitas, Tosmen, Kolomyagi* and *Tsar'skoye Selo* (which soon became *Detskoye Selo* after the killing of the royal family).

an imperialistic spirit, and calls for the immediate dissolution of all extant Scout organisations in Soviet Russia.'[11]

The importance of political education in sports groups was heightened by the presence of sports instructors, on whom the régime had to depend, who were tsarist-trained and politically suspect. Most *Vsevobuch* instructors were, in fact, former 'bourgeois' sports and physical training specialists. During 1918, there were 17,428 ex-NCOs of the tsarist army working as instructors in *Vsevobuch*.[12] It was feared that 'hostile elements had penetrated into the organs of *Vsevobuch* and had tried to conduct counter-revolutionary work against the Soviet physical culture movement'.[13] On 24 September 1919 the government passed a resolution obliging *Vsevobuch* to broaden its work, improve its quality and pay more serious attention to sport 'as an important element in the military training of the working people'.[14] An experienced political leader, Nikolai Podvoisky (who had been chairman of the Military Revolutionary Committee in Petrograd during the October Revolution), was put in charge of *Vsevobuch* and the formation of Red Army reserves. Podvoisky immediately formulated new aims: 'First, purge the *Vsevobuch* instructors of hostile, alien elements; second, make physical education and military training compulsory and universal and involve as many young workers and peasants as possible in physical education and shooting practice; third, link physical and military training with communist education and directly involve the local Soviets, *Komsomol* and trade unions in the military training of workers.'[15]

At the end of 1918, according to *Vsevobuch*'s own estimates, it had trained some 2 million people and formed 350 sports groups in workplaces. To mark its first anniversary, on 25 May 1919, it held a gigantic parade on the Red Square in Moscow, reviewed by Lenin and Trotsky that is today regarded as the

[11] I. D. Chudinov (ed.), *Osnovnye postanovleniya, prikazy i instruktsii po voprosam fizicheskoi kul'tury i sporta, 1917–1957* (Moscow, 1959), p. 24.
[12] Z. Starovoitova, *Polpred zdorov'ya* (Moscow, 1969), p. 40.
[13] F. I. Samoukov (ed.), *Istoriya fizicheskoi kul'tury* (Moscow, 1956), p. 84.
[14] Ibid., p. 85.
[15] N. I. Podvoisky, *O militsionnoi organizatsii vooruzhyonnykh sil Rossiiskoi Sovetskoi Federativnoi Sotsialisticheskoi Respubliki* (Moscow, 1919), p. 9.

forerunner of the great sporting parades that have become characteristic of Soviet festivals. After the military-sports parade, sports meetings were held in other parts of Moscow: at the *Sokol* Sports Club, the *Zamoskvorech'ye* Sports Club (the former Imperial Yacht Club on the then Sparrow Hills, later to become a Red Army sports centre) and the Hippodrome (race course).

In line with the policy of combining military drill and weapon handling with political and general education and instruction in elementary hygiene, it was decided to coordinate the activities of *Vsevobuch* with those of the Commissariats of Education and of Health. In Podvoisky's opinion, it was impossible to bring the Civil War to a successful conclusion or to build socialism without a large-scale campaign to improve physical fitness and health.

Having inherited a country with an inclement climate, whose population was overwhelmingly illiterate, where vital statistics tended to be considerably worse than those of industrial states of Europe in 1900, where disease and starvation were common, and where most people had only the most rudimentary knowledge of hygiene, the Soviet leaders appreciated that it would take a radical economic and social transformation to alter the situation substantially. But time was short, and able-bodied and disciplined men were vital, first for the country's survival, then for its recovery from the ravages of war and revolution, for industrial recovery and defence against further likely attacks.

Regular participation in physical exercise was to be one – relatively inexpensive but effective – means of improving health standards rapidly and a channel by which to educate people in hygiene, nutrition and exercise. One indication of the health policy being pursued was the campaign during the Civil War under the slogans 'Help the Country with a Toothbrush', 'Help the Country by Washing in Cold Water', 'Help the Country by Observing the Dry [i.e. prohibition] Law', and 'Physical Culture 24 Hours a Day'. With the influx of peasants into the cities (bringing with them rural habits), the significance of health through exercise took on a new dimension.

The ignorance which was the cause of so much disease, starvation and misery – and which hampered both military effectiveness and labour productivity – was to be combated by a far-reaching programme of physical exercise and sport. If the material facilities were lacking, then people were urged to make full use of 'the sun, air, water and natural movement – the best proletarian doctors'.[16] The campaign could only catch on, in Podvoisky's opinion, if the emotional attraction of *competitive* sport were to be utilised to the utmost – this at a time when 'competition' and 'sport' had become rather 'dirty' words; certainly, a number of educational-ists regarded competitive sport as debasing physical culture and inculcating a bourgeois ethos. This was a view held, for example, by Lunacharsky, the Commissar of Education; it had (as we have seen) been subscribed to previously by Lesgaft. Nonetheless, competitive sport and contests began to be organised from the lowest level upwards, culminating in the All-Russia Pre-Olympiads of 1920. Physical culture, including sport, therefore, was to be a significant means of dispersing ignorance and encouraging civic responsibility.

The existing *Vsevobuch* training programme was extended from 96 hours to 576 hours in urban areas and to 436 hours in rural localities, spread over two years. The increase in hours was to be entirely devoted to sport: swimming, fencing, skiing, ice skating and a variety of team sports, particularly soccer, alongside gymnastics and athletics. The new programme also made pro-vision for lectures in hygiene, anatomy and physiology.

The First All-Union Congress of Physical Culture, Sport and Pre-Military Training opened in Moscow on 3 April 1919. Discussion at the congress centred on four main problems: the physical education of young people; the organisation of military training; the training of instructors; and the creation of sports clubs. The congress adopted a resolution on the establishment of a Supreme Council of Physical Culture, attached to *Vsevobuch*, which should be in charge of all matters associated with recrea-tion. The Supreme Council came into being in October 1920 as an advisory body to the Central Board of *Vsevobuch*. These were the first steps leading to a coordination of work in the field of sport which, up to then, had been divided between the Commis-sariats for Health and for Education, *Vsevobuch* and a variety of public organisations, particularly the *Komsomol*. In addition, 12 *oblast'* (regional) and 52 *guberniya*[17] (provincial) physical

[16] Ibid., p. 41.
[17] During the 1920s, the former tsarist territorial administrative units such

culture councils were set up; they were to be staffed by representatives from all bodies concerned with physical culture. Their duties were to supervise the fulfilment of directives from the Supreme Council, to provide physical education in schools and sports clubs and to organise medical services for those participating in sport. The ambitious programme of the Congress was in few places, however, in those uncertain times, carried out to the full.

According to the official figures of the Central Board of *Vsevobuch*, on 1 January 1921, there were 1,419 physical culture groups with 143,563 members, of whom 5,500 (4 per cent) were women. In addition, there existed 151 sports clubs.[18] The total number of people trained by *Vsevobuch* over the three years 1917–1920 amounted to 4,475,000, the majority of whom were sent to join the Red Army; it also trained some 6,000 physical education instructors, the nucleus of the new grade of specialists who were gradually to oust the old tsarist-trained personnel.[19] Physical culture parades and mass contests were inaugurated and new facilities (some 2,000 sports grounds by 1921) constructed, often with assistance from *Komsomol* members. A start was made by Muscovites, for example, armed with picks, shovels and simply their bare hands, on the construction of a grand new sports stadium at the foot of Sparrow Hills – to be named the International Red Stadium (eventually materialising, much later, in 1956, as the Lenin Stadium). Podvoisky struck the keynote at the foundation-laying ceremony when he said, 'The Civil War fronts are still ablaze, starvation and ruin hold the young Soviet republic in a vice, yet we are today starting our campaign for mass physical culture.'[20]

as *guberniya* (province), *uyezd* (county) and *volost'* (parish) were abolished and new units such as *okrug* (area), *oblast'* (region) and *raion* (district) took their place.

[18] The sports clubs were mainly formed before the revolution and were organised on a territorial basis, whereas the physical culture groups were post-revolutionary organisations based on workplaces.

[19] *Vestnik militsionnoi armii*, 1921, No. 9.

[20] Podvoisky, *O militsionnoi organizatsii vooruzhyonnykhsil*, p. 9.

Physical education in school and college

Despite preoccupation with the war and the 'militarisation' of sport, a great deal of discussion was taking place among educationalists about the place of sport in Soviet education and socialist life. Furthermore, many principles of the desired organisation of work and life were being enunciated in the form of decrees, as earnests of intention, though the poverty, disorganisation and lack of authority to enforce them made their immediate implementation impossible; among these, relevant here, were the introduction of the 8-hour day, the limiting of teenagers' working time to 6 hours a day, and the banning of child employment. Clearly, it was felt, without free time, workers and their children could not take part in any form of recreation. The first steps were, nevertheless, being taken to make physical culture an essential part of the school curriculum and to work towards the principle of the fully developed individual.

An important landmark in education was a government declaration of 16 October 1918 on the 'Unified Labour School' – the creation of a uniform school system for the whole country, which was to be free, comprehensive, co-educational and separated from the Church. It was to be some time before all the stipulations of the new decree could be put into effect, but the principle had been defined: that all children were educable and should be educated. Without this, it was felt, no significant social progress could be made.

If all children were now to go to school, they were also to be given compulsory physical education. Already on 7 December 1917 the Medical and Hygiene Department of the new Education Commission,[21] headed by Lunacharsky, recommended that 'all schools should be concerned with the physical as well as the mental development of children and should introduce gymnastics, games, swimming and excursions'.[22] The 'Fundamental Prin-

---

[21] The Education Commission and the People's Commissariat of Education of the Russian Federation both came into being in November 1917, the former being concerned largely with administrative, the latter – with executive matters. On 10 July 1918, administration of education passed to the People's Commissariat of Education and the Commission was disbanded.

[22] Chudinov, *Osnovnye postanovleniya*, p. 41.

ciples' of the Unified Labour School stated quite categorically that 'gymnastics and sport develop feelings of responsible collective action and a spirit of mutual assistance as well as strength and skill'.[23]

In the spring of 1918, on the initiative of the Medical and Hygiene Department referred to above, a campaign was launched to improve the physical fitness of children and students by providing summer holiday camps – often on estates sequestered from the nobility. After the absorption of the Education Commission by the People's Commissariat of Education, the Medical and Hygiene Department was renamed the Department of School Hygiene, in which a number of leading doctors and teachers were to work under the supervision of Dr Vera Bonch-Bruyevich. (She died suddenly in the influenza epidemic of November 1918.) The Department began to prepare detailed recommendations on hygiene and physical education in schools, published regular bulletins (*Byulleteni shkol'no-sanitarnovo otdela pri kommissariate narodnovo prosveshcheniya*), and formulated the basic principles of the rôle of physical education in schools: 'Physical education must create healthy, properly developed citizens who are capable of performing any task and defending themselves and others . . . It must promote initiative in young people and teach them to take the path of creative endeavour in life.'[24]

The Department also started work on the training of physical education instructors. In June 1918, six-month courses were instituted for physical education instructors in Moscow (at the Military Gymnastics and Fencing School), in Yaroslavl', Perm', Smolensk, and Simbirsk. Soon after, the first institutes of physical education were established on the basis of these courses, and suitable (confiscated) buildings allotted them: the sizeable town estate of Count Razumovsky (who had fled the country) was handed over, in December 1919, to the new Moscow Institute of Physical Culture; earlier, in October, Lesgaft's Higher Courses for Physical Education Instructors in Petrograd had become the basis for the country's first Institute of Physical Culture, named after Lesgaft and, like the Moscow Institute, accorded higher

[23] *Izvestiya VTsIK*, 16 October 1918.
[24] *Byulleten' shkol'no-sanitarnovo otdela pri kommissariate narodnovo prosveshcheniya*, 1918, No. 2, p. 4.

school status. A third higher educational institution concerned with courses for physical education instructors was the Moscow Military School of Physical Education for Working People, which was formed in 1920 with a staff of over 200, principally to train instructors on 2-year courses for the army – but also as an important centre of research into sport and physical education.

Competitive sport

Although competitive sport was naturally curtailed during the war years, it did exist – and was actively encouraged by *Vsevobuch* and other bodies – as a means of attracting people to physical culture and better health, arousing their identification with a local club or town and encouraging the collective spirit that was felt to be part of the new ideology. Soccer and other team games were especially encouraged, soccer being included in the programme at the pre-military training centres and recommended for all sports clubs. City soccer championships continued, as before the revolution, between 1918 and 1920 – despite the chaotic conditions.

Other sports, particularly those with a military bias – skiing, boxing, wrestling and fencing – were included in the *Vsevobuch* programme. *Skiing* was given special priority, and a battalion of skiers – the Northern Expeditionary Ski Battalion – was despatched to fight on the Eastern Front against Admiral Kolchak, the self-styled 'Supreme Ruler of Russia', and commander of the White Guard Army. Subsequently, between 1919 and 1920, as many as 75 ski companies and reconnaissance groups were formed; their reported military successes did much to boost the sport at home. In the winter of 1919–1920, despite the desperate conditions of Civil War, 60 people took part in the Petrograd city championships, and, a year later, the first national ski championships were held in Moscow. Skiing, of course, had been widely popular before the revolution, two of the country's leading multi-sport clubs being the Moscow Ski Club (founded in 1895) and the Society for Amateur Skiers (founded in 1901). They were both permitted to continue as semi-independent organisations until the late 1920s.

Speed skating, too, had had many followers before the revolution and still maintained its popularity. Even during hostilities, on 20–21 January 1918, 21 speed skaters contested the championship of the Russian Soviet Federative Socialist Republic on Moscow's Maiden's Field. All four distances were won by Yakov Mel'nikov, one of the most renowned speed skaters in the history of the sport: his time for the 10,000 metres (17 minutes 48.7 seconds) recorded in the 1919 national championships stood for the next 20 years.

Moscow also held city boxing, weightlifting and French wrestling championships in November 1918. Despite the starvation, the cold, a typhoid outbreak and the Civil War, the championships attracted a large crowd. As a newspaper of the time reported, 'The success of the contest exceeded all expectations; the public thronged into the Blue Hall of Union House, and those too late to secure themselves entry tickets formed a great crowd around the door of the overcrowded hall.'[25]

It is sometimes claimed that 7 May 1918 is the date of birth of Soviet athletics, when the first post-revolutionary sports event took place: a cross country run (4,500 metres) in Petrovsky Park, Moscow, won by Nikolai Bocharov of the Moscow Ski Club. If athletes had the advantage of pre-revolutionary stadiums and grounds, other sportsmen were not so fortunate. Moscow swimmers, for example, had to make do with the small swimming pool at the Sandunov Steam Baths for their contests.

Other sports competitions of this time included the first motor-bike race – Moscow to Klin and back – which took place in 1918, and the first national chess championship, in 1920.

Apart from the competitions in individual sports, the authorities were preparing for massive physical culture festivals throughout the country, to which they gave the grand name of 'Pre-Olympiads'. These were to set the stage for a national festival of physical culture timed to coincide with the Second Congress of the Third International (19 July to 7 August 1920). In honour of the latter event, some 18,000 people participated in a huge gymnastics and sports display at the new Red Stadium (formerly the Moscow River Yacht Club). The star feature of the programme was an 'international' soccer match between a Russian team and foreign delegates at the Congress. Podvoisky is

[25] *Russky sport*, 10 November 1918.

said to have approached a young Scottish Temperance Society delegate, William Gallagher (later to become Chairman of the British Communist Party) and asked him to pick a team among the foreign delegates. The 'International XI' included a Canadian, Dick Beech; an Irishman, Paddy Murphy; an Englishman, Tom Quelch; five Americans, Joe Chaplin, Joe Fineberg, Eddie McAlpine, David Ramsey and the writer (and ex-Harvard soccer player) John Reed (of *Ten Days That Shook the World* fame), and two Dutch delegates. The captain was William Gallagher. Understandably, the International XI lost by a heavy margin to a representative Moscow team.[26] The winners received the valuable prizes of one jar of fruit and one bag of flour each.

Pre-Olympiads were held simultaneously in Omsk, Tashkent and Yekaterinburg (now Sverdlovsk). The Tashkent games, which were given the prestigious title of the 'First Central Asian Olympics', lasted for 10 days early in October 1920. As many as 3,000 people took part, mostly natives of Turkestan. The games included a variety of sports but, since the organised sports of Europe were mostly unknown, the participants largely confined themselves to their own national games, such as the equestrian games *poiga*, *ulak*, *kyz-ku* and *ogdarysh* and the local form of wrestling, *kurash*. At the final ceremony, 1,500 athletes put on a display of gymnastics and folk dancing.[27] The significance of this sports festival in Turkestan for the Soviet nationalities policy of the time may be judged by the fact that this was the first time in the history of Central Asia that Uzbeks, Kazakhs, Turkmenians, Kirgiz and other local peoples, as well as Russians, had competed in any sports event together. As was made clear later, the authorities regarded sport as an important means of integrating the diverse peoples of the old Russian Empire in the new Soviet state: 'The integrative functions of sport are great. This has immense importance for our multi-national state. Sports contests,

[26] Starovoitova, *Polpred zdorovya*, pp. 91–94; the composition of the team was provided by the veteran American communist Joe Fineberg (who played in the match and subsequently settled in the Soviet Union), with whom, just before his death in 1963, I worked in Moscow.
[27] Y. Sholomitsky, 'Fizicheskaya kul'tura i sport v sovetskom Uzbekistane', in *Ocherki po istorii fizicheskoi kul'tury* (Moscow, 1964), p. 90.

festivals, *spartakiads* and other types of sporting competition have played an important part in cementing the friendship of Soviet peoples.'[28]

Practically speaking, the Civil War and foreign intervention were over by November 1920. The new state was now to enter a period of restoration and reconstruction. The end of the period of hostilities also signified the demise of *Vsevobuch*, since it had served its purpose. The military organisation of sporting activity was no longer necessary in peacetime, and new methods had to be found which would be more in tune with the new social conditions. *Vsevobuch* was finally disbanded in 1923 (although it was to re-appear in September 1941 and exist for the duration of World War II).

[28] *Sport v SSSR*, 1973, No. 5, p. 9.

4
Years of physical culture,
1921–1929

The effects of the policy of 'War Communism' combined with the destruction and chaos of seven years of war soon showed themselves in every aspect of life. Late in February 1921, Lenin submitted to the Party Central Committee a project for a new economic policy, later to be known as NEP. NEP signified, in essence, a major concession to the vast peasant majority as the price of retaining power. The State retained what Lenin called the 'commanding heights' of the economy, primarily the largest industrial installations, but permitted private trade and some private production. Until 1928, by which time the economy was more or less back on its feet, there was no basic change in this mixture of competing economies. The nationalised sector operated to a system that Lenin termed 'state capitalism'.[1]

Physical culture: background to the controversy

Just as in other fields of endeavour, in sport this was a time of constant discussion. Controversy raged over its rôle in a workers' state and its organisational structure, with various groups contending for influence. The NEP period was to see a completely new structure, the involvement of trade unions in organisation, disputes over theory and practice involving the *Komsomol*, the Party, trade unions, the old *Vsevobuch* leaders, the 'hygienists', *Proletkul'tists* and other groups, and the promotion of international (largely 'proletarian') sporting contacts.

Basically, these were the years of *physical culture* rather than sport, the dividing line between the two being the presence of an

[1] For a thorough historian's analysis of the NEP period, see E. H. Carr, *A History of Soviet Russia* (Penguin Books, 1970), Vols. 4–7.

element of competition: 'Sport begins where the struggle for victory begins.'[2] Competitive sport bred, in some people's minds, attitudes alien to socialist society. They frowned upon the 'record-breaking mania' of contemporary sport in the West, and they favoured non-commercialised forms of recreation that dispensed with grandstands and spectators. Doubts were cast on the social value of competitive sport – above all, on attempts to attain top-class results, which were considered an unjustified drive to break records based on false ambitions. They charged that competitive sport distorted the 'eternal ideals' of physical education, that, instead of being universal, it led to narrow specialisation and was detrimental to health; it encouraged commercialism, demoralisation and professionalism. Competitive sport, it was alleged, diverted attention from the basic aim of providing recreation for the masses; it turned them into passive spectators. Such were the views of those, often influential, persons who dominated the thinking on physical education and sport during the 1920s. In some ways, the antagonism toward competitive sport was a curious feature, since in economics, this was an era of competition. Economic competition, however, was more or less forced on the Bolsheviks by the circumstances, while in certain social fields (e.g. education and sport) they were able to try to implement their collectivist ideas.

One notion that all those working within a Marxian approach agreed upon, however, was acceptance of the view that all work in this, as in other fields, should be subordinate to the goal of the ultimate achievement of a communist society. The question posed was: 'How can physical culture be organised and employed most effectively to help secure the goals of the proletarian state?' It was on the answers to this question that opinions differed.

Organisation

When the Civil War ended, a number of different administrative futures were open to sport: it could remain under the aegis of *Vsevobuch* and retain a quasi-military rôle; it could be supervised by a civilian agency – a government body, *Komsomol* or

[2] *Fizkul'tura i sport*, 1971, No. 1, p. 1.

trade unions; workers' clubs or other cultural organisations could take over responsibility for sport; it could have either a central agency or several autonomous regional centres. Because of the lack of clear guidance from the Party, the immediate result was, by today's standards, rather anarchic, with various groups jostling for position. We consider them in turn.

Vsevobuch

The paramilitary organisation set up in wartime had given sport considerable impetus. Being vested with mandatory powers, it had accumulated the best resources and human reserves for the popularisation of sport, which had become a national issue with relatively high priority consideration. With the onset of NEP, however, the reconstruction of the economy began to push aside matters which, during the Civil War, had had special attention – and these included sport.

In an attempt to preserve the network of sports clubs and groups which it had established during the Civil War, *Vsevobuch* at first tried to combine them into local sports centres. By the end of 1921, it had 325 *raion* (district) and 975 *uchastok* (sector) sports centres and 188 separate sports clubs.[3] These ran into trouble with the authorities, however, because 'they were not firmly enough associated with trade union, *Komsomol* and Party organisations, and rarely conducted educational work among their members. . .'.[4] Being relatively untutored politically by the standards now obtaining, they were unable to cope with 'members of pre-revolutionary sports societies who were creeping in and hampering the development of Soviet physical culture'.[5] Without financial backing from the government to maintain such a large number of sports centres and clubs, the leaders of *Vsevobuch* were forced to abandon the project and, instead, put forward the idea, in mid-1922, of a new, all-embracing, independent sports organisation – a Russian Association of Red Physical-Culture Organisations. The project envisaged the formation, under a RARPCO umbrella, of sports clubs by individual sports on a territorial

[3] Z. Starovoitova, *Polpred zdorov'ya* (Moscow, 1969), p 33.
[4] F. I. Samoukov (ed.), *Istoriya fizicheskoi kul'tury* (Moscow, 1956), p. 96.
[5] Ibid., p. 96.

principle. This was opposed most vigorously by the *Komsomol* on the grounds that '(a) it was inexpedient to create at this time a new youth organisation parallel to the *Komsomol*, and (b) the former bourgeois club athletes, antipathetic to the Soviet régime, might infiltrate the sports clubs'.[6] Nonetheless, RARPCO did come into being, but had a short life, being dissolved in March 1923 along with *Vsevobuch*.

Vsevobuch was, in fact, reorganised into a sports organisation for the armed forces; in the spring of 1923, it became the *Vsevobuch Experimental and Display Centre (Opytno-pokazatel'-naya ploshchadka Vsevobucha)*. Its influence in Moscow, the capital, may be judged from an article in *Krasny Sport*: 'In a purely sporting sense, VEDC is undoubtedly the strongest of all Moscow's sports organisations; regular planning, from the lack of which other clubs usually suffer, and good team-work have enabled VEDC model teams to attain exceptional success in every sport they take up.'[7] For its headquarters it was given the premises of the Moscow Ski Club. In 1928, it was renamed the Central House of the Red Army (*TsDKA*, later *TsDSA* – the Central House of the Soviet Army – and today *TsSKA* – the Central Sports Club of the Army).

It is, nonetheless, probably true to say that in the 'breathing space' between the Civil War and the industrialisation drive, between *Vsevobuch* during 'War Communism' and the start of the *GTO* fitness campaign in 1931, sport had less association with the military than at any other time in Soviet history. The dismantling of the *Vsevobuch* apparatus and the handing of the administration of sport over to 'civilian' bodies were, perhaps, accompanied (and partly motivated) by a certain anti-militarising feeling both among ordinary people and among many leaders, particularly those influential in social policy – people like Lunacharsky, Semashko, Krupskaya, Zigmund and Bonch-Bruyevich.

[6] *Izvestiya fizicheskoi kul'tury*, 1922, No. 8, pp. 11–12.
[7] *Krasny sport*, 1923, No. 1, p. 3.

The Komsomol

The Communist Youth League had been concerned with sport during the Civil War and considered it one of the main spheres of its activity. In fact, its members had been responsible for much of the work done under *Vsevobuch* authority: they had set up clubs, got sport going at factories, built sports installations, themselves provided much of the grass-roots enthusiasm for sports participation, and spearheaded the political campaign against the old 'bourgeois' sports societies and movements – often with as much undiscriminating and destructive passion as the Puritans during the English Civil War. At its Third Congress, in October 1920, the *Komsomol* passed a resolution 'On the Militia Army and the Physical Education of Young People' which was the most clear-cut document yet on the socialist principles of physical education and sport. Besides making it obligatory on all of its members to assist in the work of *Vsevobuch*, the *Komsomol* laid down the following principles: 'The physical education of the younger generation is a necessary element in the overall communist upbringing of young people, intended to create a harmoniously developed person, a creative citizen of communist society. . . It serves also the direct practical aims of (1) training young people for work, and (2) preparing people for the armed defence of their country.'[8]

How important the *Komsomol* was to *Vsevobuch*'s work may be appreciated from the fact that, at the end of 1920, some 30,000 *Komsomol* members were acting as sports instructors under *Vsevobuch* authority in the Ukraine, and 'constituted virtually 100 per cent of Ukrainian *Komsomol* membership'. A further 153,318 *Komsomol* members, including 17,546 girls, completed *Vsevobuch* courses.[9]

At its Fouth Congress, in the autumn of 1921, the *Komsomol* called once more for an all-out attack on the 'bourgeois' sports societies that were now reappearing in the more relaxed atmosphere of NEP: 'They are harmful to Soviet power and divert

[8] I. D. Chudinov (ed.), *Osnovnye postanovleniya, prikazy i instruktsii po voprosam fizicheskoi kul'tury i sporta, 1917–1957* (Moscow, 1959), pp. 43–44.
[9] *Vestnik fizicheskoi kul'tury*, 1923, Nos. 8–9, p. 2.

young people from socio-political life.' A study of the state of sport in Belorussia at this time, stated that,

in the town of Velizh, a branch of the *Sokol* sports society has been set up with 83 schoolchildren among its members. . . In Gorodok, a branch of *Bogatyr'* has started up. In Orsha, Bobruisk, Borisov and Slutsk, branches of the Jewish nationalist society *Maccabee* have become extremely active. The branches of this last-named society indoctrinate young people in a nationalistic spirit, propagate notions of cultural-national autonomy, and sow bourgeois habits. The Russian Association of Red Physical-Culture Organisations, which has begun to operate in Belorussia on the order of *Vsevobuch*, acts as a screen for the activity of these bourgeois societies.[10]

At the Fourth Congress, therefore, the *Komsomol* attacked the *Vsevobuch*-sponsored Association and called for a government sports council. It subsequently seized the initiative by forming its own sports societies open to all young people – but excluding members of the bourgeoisie. In Moscow, Kaluga, Vladimir and elsewhere, it formed the *Muravei* ('Ant') Sports Society, in Petrograd, Novgorod and the Ukraine it set up *Spartak* ('Spartacist') – not to be confused with the present *Spartak*, which did not come into being until 1935 – and, in Belorussia, the *Krasny Molodnyak* ('Red Youth') society. These sports organisations were responsible to the various committees of the *Komsomol*. In a relatively short time, they gained a substantial membership: in Moscow, *Muravei*, at the end of 1923, had 180 groups embracing 10,000 members. By early 1923, Vitebsk province in Belorussia had 19 youth groups run by the *Komsomol* with a membership of 1,230 (including 423 girls) employing 23 permanent instructors.

As at its previous (Second and Third) congresses, the *Komsomol* also attacked the Boy Scout organisations. For their unqualified condemnation of everything connected with the Scout movement, however, they were taken to task by Nadezhda Krupskaya who, besides being Lenin's widow, commanded much authority in Soviet education. She advised the *Komsomol* to learn from the Scouts, 'Scouting has something that irresistibly attracts young people, gives them satisfaction, binds them to the organisation.

[10] K. A. Kulinkovich, 'Razvitie fizicheskoi kul'tury i sporta v Belorusskoi SSR', in *Ocherki po istorii fizicheskoi kul'tury* (Moscow, 1964), pp. 41–42.

This something is to be found in the way it treats adolescents.'[11] She listed its attributes as a careful study of young people's psychology, interests and needs; a utilisation of children's initiative, colourfulness; the attraction of ceremony and ritual; the clever use of children's group feelings; and the employment of lively forms of activity and, especially, games. 'The *RKSM*, if it seriously intends to educate the younger generation and is to have even the slightest appreciation of the colossal tasks which confront this generation, and if it is not to confine itself to childish aping of grown-ups, must, as soon as possible, incorporate these methods into its own practice.'[12]

Although the Boy Scout movement was to be banned, the *Komsomol* did heed Krupskaya's advice and, when forming the first Pioneer detachments (for children between 8 and 15), engaged former Scoutmasters 'who accepted the principles of work of the Pioneer organisations'.[13]

It must be borne in mind that, at this time, during the initial NEP period, the *Komsomol* was still relatively independent of Party control, particularly since the Party leadership was largely preoccupied with economic matters and internal dissentions of its own.

The Party

A new direction to the controversy over sports organisation came with the findings of a special commission of the Central Committee of the Russian Communist Party (Bolsheviks) made known in March 1923. A month later, the Twelfth Party Congress advocated that local sports clubs should be the responsibility of factories, farms, offices, colleges, etc. Either they were to be run like other workers' clubs for the benefit of the local community (but under trade union control) or confined to the workers of a particular workplace and their families. This put an end to any schemes for organisational autonomy such as the *RARPCO*,

[11] N. K. Krupskaya, *RKSM i boiskautizm* (Moscow, 1923), p. 17.
[12] Ibid., p. 42.
[13] *Pedagogicheskaya entsiklopediya* (Moscow, 1968), Vol. III, p. 853. The Young Pioneers also took over from the Scouts both their motto 'Be Prepared' and their emblem – the *fleur de lys* – which has now evolved into three flames.

since, the Party averred, this could lead to the isolation of sport from other social activities and would restrict its cultural side. This was in line with the Party's overall policy on independent centres at the time; the general rôle accorded such potentially autonomous interest groups like the trade unions, collective farms and sports clubs was one of overall subordination to central goals defined by the Party. They were, therefore, submitted to Party control, which gradually eroded their independent power.

The Party believed that it could best realise its objectives in sport if the sports groups were organised from workplaces, where it and its auxiliary organisations – the trade unions and the *Komsomol* – were strongest, and not through independent sports societies. At the same time, the Party could not concur with the idea that sport should be the exclusive domain of young people and the *Komsomol*. It maintained that, in a State that enforced the dictatorship of the proletariat, the trade unions were the broadest 'transmission belt' from the Party to the working people and that it was one of their fundamental duties to educate their members, to take care of their recreational needs and to develop their many-sided interests. It was therefore decided to hand over local sports organisations to the trade unions, including the recently formed *Komsomol* societies (*Muravei, Spartak*, etc.), urging, at the same time, that the *Komsomol* should cooperate with the unions and marshal young workers at factories into sports sections so as to capitalise on their interest in sport and 'strengthen the ties of the *Komsomol* with the mass of young people'.

The Supreme Council of Physical Culture, which had been attached to the now defunct *Vsevobuch*, was transferred, in June 1923, to the All-Russia Central Executive Committee (*VTsIK*). It became a permanent coordinating body and its new and extensive duties were 'to harmonise and coordinate the research, studies and organisational work in physical education and sport of the various government departments and organisations in the Russian Republic'.[14] Similar councils were to be created in each republic, *guberniya* and *uyezd*; they were to supervise sport throughout the country, direct and approve physical education programmes for students and members of sports groups, ratify the regulations of sports organisations, draw up a calendar of

[14] Chudinov, *Osnovnye postanovleniya*, p. 71.

sporting events and see that they were carried out, and direct research and the publication of sports literature.

Since the bulk of sports groups were now to be organised not independently, but under the trade unions, the sports administration was to work directly with all ministries, government agencies and non-government bodies active in sport. This policy was apparent in the composition of the Supreme Council, which consisted of a chairman and a vice-chairman appointed by *VTsIK* and one representative each from the People's Commissariats for Defence, Education, Health, Internal Affairs and Labour, plus one each from the *Komsomol* Central Committee, the Trade Union Central Council and the Moscow City Soviet. The chairman of the Supreme Council was to be Nikolai Semashko, the incumbent People's Commissar for Health; he was to combine the two posts until 1930.

Concerned at the continuing bickering and ambiguity in organisation, however, the Party issued its first authoritative resolution on sport and physical culture on 13 July 1925: 'On the Tasks of the Party in Physical Culture'. From the point of view of organisation, the Central Committee instructed all Party organisations to ensure that its directives were followed. Their major tasks were three-fold:

(1) politicisation – to ensure political leadership of the sports movement, to make sure it combined political education with sport and to prevent it being cut off from the mass trade union and political organisations;

(2) leadership – to ensure that all sports groups were effectively under some sort of Party guidance and that no independent clubs should continue to exist; all sports associations, leagues and clubs that remained from before the revolution were to be disbanded;

(3) ally-creating – to make it a mass movement that embraced peasants and industrial workers, old and young, men and women, Russians and members of other ethnic groups.

Trade unions

After the 1923 Party Congress, the trade unions, by virtue of their being the largest mass workers' organisation, had to consider the organisation of workers' recreation an integral part of their work.

They began to form sports clubs at workplaces and were authorised to take over all the *Komsomol* societies. Through their ability to enrol non-Party employers in their clubs, they had, by 1925, taken over from the *Komsomol* as principal organisers of sport. In that year, some 350,000 union members were enrolled in sports clubs, and 450,000 by 1928. By contrast, whereas, in October 1924, 31 per cent of all sports participants were *Komsomol* members, in 1926, only just over 10 per cent were, although 97 per cent (2,500,000) of those engaged in sport were young people.[15]

There is little doubt that friction existed between the unions and the *Komsomol* over the organisation and functions of sport – particularly when it came to handing over *Komsomol* sports societies to local union bodies. Neither the *Komsomol* nor the Party was entirely happy with this situation, and accused the unions of being '*Proletkul'tist*',[16] ignoring Party directives (particularly the major one of 1925 on the aims of sport), and concentrating on the therapeutic side of physical education to the detriment of its recreative functions. 'In many union organisations, the directives of the Party Central Committee are not being carried out satisfactorily. Certain union leaders, underestimating the educative significance of physical culture, continue to regard it merely as a means to better health. Sports groups continue to be subordinated to union club boards and are put on the same level as drama, music and other club groups.'[17]

At the Fifteenth Party Congress in November 1926, the trade unions came in for more criticism over their handling of sport: 'The Congress condemns the bookish, utilitarian approach to physical culture (equating it merely with hygiene and physical jerks) and the scornful attitude of a substantial part of club

---

[15] *Fizicheskoye dvizhenie v SSSR* (Vysshii sovet fizicheskoi kul'tury pri VTsSPS) (Moscow, 1925), p. 5.

[16] The *Proletkul't* (abbreviation for 'Proletarian Cultural and Educational Organisation') was formed after the February 1917 Revolution with the intention of producing a proletarian culture as an indispensable part of a socialist revolution. It became widely influential after the October Revolution and, until 1919, remained independent of the Party; it was then subordinated to the Commissariat of Education, transferred to the unions in 1925, and eventually abolished in 1932.

[17] *Vestnik fizicheskoi kul'tury*, 1926, No. 5, p. 13.

leaders towards competitive sport. The Congress points out that
it is impermissable to impose upon workers the desires and values
of the club leaders.'[18]

The resolution would seem to be a concession to and reflection
of popular taste. Although the organisation of sport at the lower
levels was to remain on a 'production basis' (i.e. in union hands),
the Congress resolved that, henceforth, sport at factory level
should be reorganised: sports sections were to be established that
would concentrate on particular sports. It was felt that this would
generate more popular interest and enable instructors to conduct
more specialised work instead of the general 'labour gymnastics' or physical education lessons they had mostly given up to
then.

But the reorganisation brought a new problem in its wake, for
the unions now came under mounting attack both from the
Komsomol and the Party for a sin of which they have been inter-
mittently accused ever since, right up to the present day: 'In a
number of trade union sports organisations, now that sections for
individual sports have been set up, all attention is being concentrated on a leading group of athletes who show top-class results;
the physical education of the vast mass of young people is becoming secondary. Many athletes who have practical experience and
some technical knowledge of training methods are being allotted
to special small groups and kept away from the rank-and-file
young sports enthusiasts.'[19]

Signs of 'professionalism' were already apparent in soccer: in
1925, a 'Disqualification Commission' was formed with the task
of 'preventing dirty play', and player transfers were prohibited;
the first footballer popularity poll was held in 1926 (won by a
goalkeeper, N. Sokolov, of Leningrad). This 'élitism' incensed the
Komsomol and led it to appeal, at its Eighth Congress in 1928,
for an overhaul of the whole organisational structure of sport and
the institution of a single national voluntary sports society. It
pointed out that the Supreme Council and its various sports
councils were quite incapable of establishing much order in the
sports movement because they lacked the power to enforce
directives.

[18] Chudinov, *Osnovnye postanovleniya*, p. 112.
[19] *Vestnik fizicheskoi kul'tury*, 1927, No. 3, p. 7.

The Party Central Committee recognised these shortcomings and passed a resolution, on 23 September 1929, calling for a radical change in this unsatisfactory state of affairs. The movement suffered from 'a lack of scope in involving the vast mass of working people, a bias towards record breakers, a lack of departmental coordination, an overlapping of functions and poor organisation in the countryside'.[20] It therefore directed that the whole sports movement should come more under centralised state control; all the local sports councils were to be reorganised into direct state administered bodies and the Supreme Council of Physical Culture attached to the All-Russia Central Executive Committee was to be replaced by a more powerful state controlled body, the All-Union Council of Physical Culture.

The tightening-up and greater centralised control were, of course, features of overall Party policy at the end of the 1920s as the industrialisation programme, with its First Five-Year Plan and collectivisation campaign, got underway. During the NEP period, trade union leaders, like those of the *Komsomol*, had had some degree of independence of Party control – even though most were Party members. In fact, because the state had had to make substantial concessions to the peasants early in NEP and because many union leaders disagreed with Stalin over the method of capital accumulation for the country's industrial development, the trade unions had had considerable freedom of action to pursue their own organisational interests. This continued until 1929, when a number of prominent trade unionists were moved to minor posts.

Dinamo Sports Club

The only two large sports societies beyond the direct supervision of the Supreme Council of Physical Culture were *Dinamo* and the Red Army Club, both of which are products of this period. *Dinamo* was set up on 24 June 1923 on the initiative of Felix Dzerzhinsky, then head of the internal security agency. It was initially confined to the staff of the All-Russia Extraordinary Commission for Combatting Counter-Revolution and Sabotage (the *Cheka*), which had been established immediately after the

[20] Chudinov, *Osnovnye postanovleniya*, p. 123.

Revolution to look after internal security (in 1922, this became the *GPU*, and, in 1924, the *OGPU*). As such, it had a specially strict training programme for service personnel. Dzerzhinsky, who became *Dinamo*'s first honorary president, insisted that sport was absolutely essential to develop 'strength, dexterity, courage and endurance' among his men. The word '*dinamo*' was significant, as the writer Maxim Gorky suggested, in expressing 'energy, motion and force'.[21] In addition to training service personnel, *Dinamo* gradually began to function as a normal sports society open to all service personnel of the internal security agency, border guards and 'gendarmerie', members of their families and auxiliary staff.

In a relatively short time, the society had sections in almost every large town in the country. By October 1923, it had as many as 36 sections with over 3,000 members in the capital alone. Its sports groups cultivated gymnastics, shooting, boxing, wrestling, ju-jitsu, fencing, basketball and soccer.[22] Being the first of the great Soviet sports societies and having the security agency's resources behind it, it was able to command substantial sports facilities, including the first big sports centre to be built in Moscow, the *Dinamo* Stadium (which was the capital's biggest until the opening of the Lenin Stadium in 1956) and the *Dinamo* Stadium in Leningrad, built in 1929 (the city's first stadium to have stands).

The rôle of physical culture

A controversy even greater than that about organisation continued throughout the 1920s over the rôle physical culture, including sport, was to play in socialist society. *Vsevobuch* had turned sport into a means of producing physically fit men and women for the war effort; however, it had come to the conclusion that competition was valuable in that it rallied popular support and

[21] Quoted in V. Verkholashin, 'Dinamo – eto sila v dvizhenii', in *Sport i vek* (Moscow, 1967), p. 136.

[22] Ibid., p. 124. The first shooting gallery for *Dinamo* club members was, in fact, located at 13 Bol'shaya Lyubyanka in Moscow – the present headquarters of the *KGB* (see documents in Sports Museum of Lenin Stadium)

excited interest in physical education as a whole. Towards the end of its existence, *Vsevobuch* came under mounting criticism for its alleged 'politicisation' and 'militarisation' of sport, and a neglect of its other functions. Its chairman, Podvoisky, conceded the one-sidedness of his organisation's approach to sport, pointed out that it had been due to the 'besieged camp' situation, and that *Vsevobuch* would alter its orientation: 'Physical culture changes its essence depending on the aims of the class controlling that culture for its own benefit, and the nature of that class. . . There is no need to tie politics to sports–gymnastics, nor to pursue political aims under the guise of sports–gymnastics. For the proletariat, the aims, tasks and direction of sports–gymnastics depend on the aims, tasks and condition of the class struggle.'[23]

But the rôle of physical culture continued to be hotly debated by a variety of 'schools' and interest groups, all with their own theories and practical solutions. Some of the main ones that exerted an influence on the Soviet sports movement during the 1920s and beyond are described below.

The 'hygienists'

Some of *Vsevobuch*'s keenest critics – for its alleged 'sportisation' (i.e. emphasis on competition in physical activity) and 'militarisation' of physical culture – were to be found among the scientists and medical personnel who had gathered round it and were later to work for the Scientific and Technical Committee attached to the Supreme Council of Physical Culture. They were mainly medical people – physiologists, anatomists, hygienists and health workers who were concerned about the need to improve health standards, eliminate disease and epidemics, reduce infantile mortality and the overall mortality rate. One means they saw to make people aware of personal hygiene and bodily fitness was physical culture – which many of them contrasted sharply with 'sport'; to their minds, sport implied competition, games that were potentially injurious to mental and physical health. Such pursuits as weightlifting, boxing and gymnastics were, in their opinion, irrational and dangerous, and encouraged individualist

---

[23] N. I. Podvoisky, *Kakaya fizicheskaya kul'tura nuzhna proletariatu i kem ona dolzhna sozdavat'sya?* (Moscow, 1923), p. 16.

rather than collectivist attitudes and values – and, as such, were contrary to the desired socialist ethic.

The 'hygienists' could certainly call on influential support; the chairman of the government-sponsored Supreme Council of Physical Culture, Nikolai Semashko, who was himself a doctor and concurrently also Commissar for Health, was in some ways sympathetic towards the 'hygienists', as too was the Commissar for Education, Lunacharsky. Semashko made his immediate aim explicit: 'The fight to make the proletariat healthy must be the immediate task not merely of the worker–peasant state, but of each worker separately. On its success depend the solution of the economic tasks of the country's restoration (for human beings are a productive force), the organisation of the republic's defence and the development of proletarian culture.'[24] By his widely-publicised slogan 'Physical culture – 24 hours a day!', he meant that 'people should work, rest and sleep properly, observe the rules of hygiene and strengthen their organisms'.[25] To the accusations that he was bringing a 'narrow medical approach to physical culture and sport' and that he was causing the 'hygienisation of physical culture', he insisted that: 'One should not contrast physical culture to a "medical approach" since it is a means to better health, just as one should not contrast hygiene to health, inasmuch as these are different names for one and the same thing.'[26]

Semashko was opposed, though, to restricting physical education to narrow medical confines and to banning competitive games: 'If you keep the populace on the semolina pudding of hygienic gymnastics, physical culture will not gain very wide publicity.'[27] Competitive sport was, he believed, 'the open gate to physical culture... It not only strengthens various organs, it helps man's mental development, teaches him attentiveness, punctuality and precision of movement, it develops grace of movement, and inculcates the will power, strength and skill that distinguish Soviet

[24] N. A. Semashko, *Puti sovetski fizkul'tury* (Moscow, Fizkul'turizdat, 1926), p. 14.

[25] Ibid., p. 59.

[26] *Teoriya i praktika fizicheskoi kul'tury*, 1927, No. 5, p. 6.

[27] N. A. Semashko, 'Fizicheskaya kul'tura i zdravookhranenie v SSSR', in *Izbrannye proizvedeniya* (Medgiz, Moscow, 1954), p. 264.

people.'[28] Moreover, although he wrote the following words in 1926 – i.e. before the full-scale campaign for 'socialist emulation' had been started to accompany the industrialisation campaign – he clearly anticipated the régime's support for competition: 'Competition should serve, ultimately, as a means of involving the masses in the building of socialism. That is how I look upon competitive sport and competition generally.'[29]

All the same, there were others of the 'hygienist' school who did not share his 'broad' views. Several members of his staff at the Health Commissariat and lecturers at the institutes of physical education, including the Principal of the State Institute of Physical Culture in Moscow, A. A. Zigmund, were firmly opposed to a whole number of sports and competitive games. Zigmund, who favoured the banning of such sports as soccer, athletics and boxing was also Chairman of the Scientific and Technical Committee attached to the Supreme Council of Physical Culture, and therefore carried a good deal of influence. The Committee was responsible for physical education syllabuses in primary and secondary schools. As a specific subject, physical education was excluded from many schools, since it was felt that it should be 'an integral part of the educational process and not something tacked on superficially to the curriculum'.[30] Zigmund wrote that the 'existence of physical education instructors is a sign of pedagogical illiteracy'.[31]

'Hygienists' dominated the teaching of physical education at the Petrograd and Moscow physical education institutes; in 1924, in fact, the Moscow Institute was, for a period, renamed the Central State Institute of Physical Culture and Curative Pedology[32] in order to bring it more in line with the 'hygienists''

[28] Ibid., p. 267.
[29] N. A. Semashko, *Puti sovetskoi fizkul'tury*, p. 22.
[30] *Vestnik fizicheskoi kul'tury*, 1925, No. 3, p. 2.
[31] *Fizkul'tura i sport*, 1925, No. 2, p. 17.
[32] Pedology, which was widely practised in Russia in the 1920s and early thirties, was considered to be the science of child development, using experimental and observational techniques and taking into account both hereditary and environmental factors. Some pedologists saw it as 'a scientific synthesis of all that comprises the essentials of individual disciplines concerned with the developing human being' (M. Y. Basov, *Obshchie osnovy pedologii* (Moscow, 1931), p. 18). Pedologists published an influential magazine *Pedologiya* (1928–1932). In their published views

notion of the rôle of physical culture in Soviet society. The curriculum contained exclusively medical subjects and 'hygienic gymnastics', while games and sport were ignored.

One result of pressure from the 'hygienists' was the reduction in the number of contests that took place in the first half of the 1920s and the exclusion of certain 'harmful' sports from those sports contests that did take place. The First Trade-Union Games, in 1925, for example, excluded soccer, boxing, weightlifting and gymnastics from its programme, even though these were four of the most popular sporting pursuits in the country at the time. Boxing was outlawed in the same year in the Leningrad *Uyezd* by order of the Leningrad *Guberniya* Physical Culture Council.

One of the channels largely controlled by the 'hygienists' was the sporting press. As Figure 2 shows, sports publishing in the late 1920s and early 1930s involved fairly frequent name changings and broken publication histories; these were partly a reflection of battles for influence within the physical-culture movement. The stress on physical culture and the secondary rôle of 'sport' – sometimes even avoidance of the word – are a typical feature of the 1920s and to a large degree reflect the influence of the 'hygienists'. In the 1930s, 'sport' came back into official grace – note the change, for example, of *The Ukrainian Physical Culturist* to *Sport* in 1935.

A change in the fortunes of the 'hygienist' school came with Party intervention in sport in an elaborate declaration of 1925, which effectively rejected the 'hygienists'. Their prominence in trade union sports clubs had, in the past, been more than once criticised in government documents, but the Party had never before put its considerable weight behind opposition to them. Their downfall was partly due to the changing political climate in the mid-1920s and the alleged connection of some of their leading exponents with Trotsky – whose star had been on the wane since 1924. In the 'witch hunt' of 'Trotskyists' that occurred

on sport, some pedologists claimed that certain sports were harmful, physically and mentally, and encouraged selfish habits. The Party in 1936 declared pedology a 'pseudo-science' and proscribed its practice and teaching; its chief exponents, like those of the 'hygienist' and *Proletkul't* movements, disappeared during the great purge of 1936–1938.

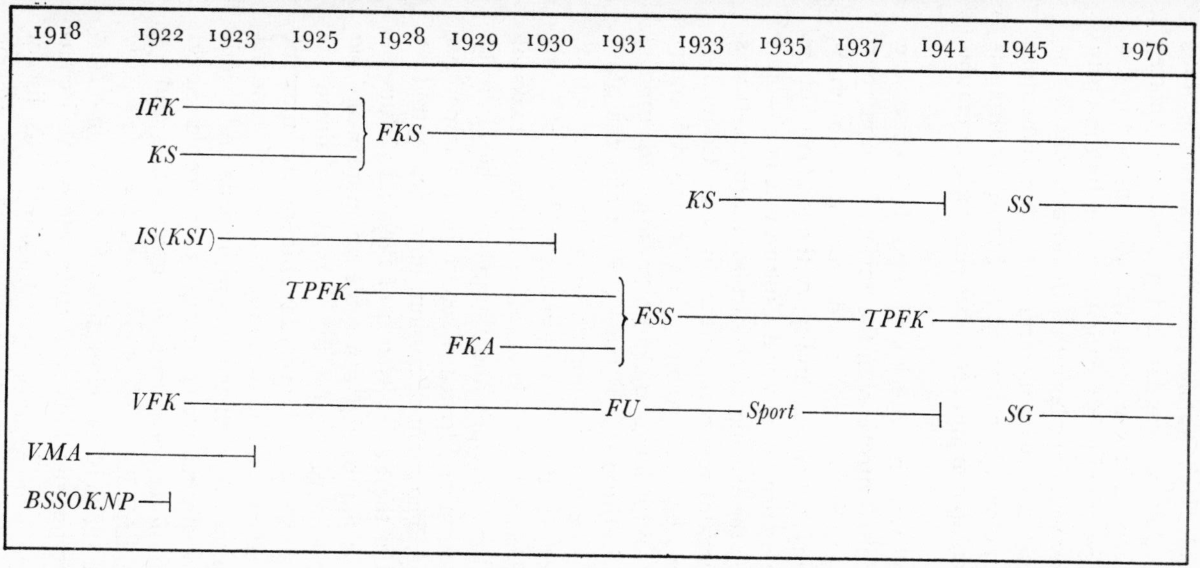

Fig. 2. Main sports periodicals, 1918–1976

BSSOKNP Byulleten' shkol'no-sanitarnova otdela pri Kommissariate narodnvo prosveshcheniya (Bulletin of the School Sanitary Section of the People's Commissariat of Education): weekly.
FKA Fizkul'taktivist (Physical Culture Activist): monthly journal.
FKS Fizkul'tura i sport (Physical Culture and Sport): monthly journal.
FSS Fizkul'tura i sotsialisticheskoye stroitel'stvo (Physical Culture and Socialist Construction): monthly journal.
FU Fizkul'turnik Ukrainy (The Ukrainian Physical Culturist): monthly journal published in the Ukraine.
IFK Izvestiya fizicheskoi kul'tury (Physical Culture News): monthly journal.
IS (KSI) Izvestiya sporta (Sports News): monthly journal published by Krasny Sport International (Red Sport International).
KS Krasny Sport (Red Sport): daily newspaper.
SG Sportivnaya gazeta (Sporting Gazette): weekly journal published in the Ukraine.
Sport Sport (Sport): monthly journal published in the Ukraine.
SS Sovetsky Sport (Soviet Sport): daily newspaper.
TPFK Teoriya i praktika fizicheskoi kul'tury (Theory and Practice of Physical Culture): monthly magazine published jointly by the Supreme Councils of Physical Culture of the USSR and RSFSR and the RSFSR Commissariat of Health.
VFK Vestnik fizicheskoi kul'tury (Physical Culture Herald): monthly journal published in the Ukraine.
VMA Vestnik militsionoi armii (Militia-Army Herald): weekly journal published by Vsevobuch.

at the end of the decade, Dr Zigmund (the Principal of the State Institute of Physical Culture) was labelled a Trotsky supporter and removed from his post. (He subsequently disappeared in the purges.) A more immediate reason for the demotion by the Party of the 'hygienists' may well have been that the former was beginning to see competitive sport (with its record breaking, individual heroes and spectator potential) as a useful adjunct to its impending industrialisation campaign and accompanying socialist emulation movement.

But the 'hygienists' were not quickly silenced. It is a measure of the openness of some controversy in the Soviet Union in 1925 that, just four months after the Party had issued its pronouncement on the rôle of physical culture and sport, the First All-Union Methodological Conference on Physical Culture was held – and provided a forum for the voicing of 'hygienist' attitudes. It was attended by 306 delegates representing the Supreme Council of Physical Culture and its local councils, the Red Sport International, the Health and Education Commissariats, trade unions, the Red Army, the institutes of physical culture and the State Academic Council. The major reports give some indication of trends at the conference: 'Physical Culture as a Means of Combatting Industrial Disease' (Nenukov), 'The Military Tasks of Soviet Physical Culture' (Kalpus and Baranov), 'The Harmful Effects on the Organism of Physical Exercise of a Competitive Nature' (Gorinevsky). The main discussion, however, centred on Zigmund's report 'On the Soviet System of Physical Culture' – which the conference approved (with some amendments). The report urged that Soviet physical culture should be aimed 'at making the personal work and everyday life of the mass of workers and peasants healthy, and at raising the general standard of culture of the masses'. As well as personal hygiene and health measures at work, Zigmund recommended that people should make full use of 'the forces of nature' for good health and for tempering the organism. He stressed the need for a 'properly structured system of physical exercises that would take into consideration the socio-economic, biological and professional circumstances of those engaging in physical education'. His list of 'approved' sports included athletics, swimming and rowing (against oneself and the clock, not against opponents); 'non-approved' sports included boxing, wrestling, soccer and fencing – all of which, by their very nature, implied competition. Furthermore, he rejected the 'use of physical exercise as spectacles for mercenary ends, narrow specialisation and professional *"rekordsmenstvo"* [indulgence in record setting and record breaking].'[33] It was predominantly on the basis of these views that the final conference resolution read: 'Scientific work should primarily illumine and substantiate the principles of making the younger generation healthy, strengthening Pioneer detachments and trade union members and revealing the most correct methods of training young people for labour and defence.'[34] These principles were re-affirmed at the Second and Third conferences in 1927 and 1929 – which provides further evidence that the 'hygienists' had managed to stand their ground at least until the end of the decade.

The strong link, however, between physical culture and hygiene has remained to this day. It is aptly expressed in another of Semashko's slogans of the early 1920s: 'Without medical supervision there can be no Soviet physical culture!' The call in the First Methodological Conference's resolution for 'correct methods of training young people for labour and defence' actually anticipated by six years the introduction of the 'Ready for Labour and Defence' national fitness programme – which was, in fact, henceforth, to underlie the Soviet sports movement.

Proletarian physical culture: 'theatricalisation' of sport

In the sphere of sport, the 'Proletkul'tists' demanded the rejection of competitive sport and all organised sports that derived from bourgeois society, as remnants of the decadent past and emanations of degenerate bourgeois culture. A fresh start had to be made through the 'revolutionary innovation of proletarian physical culture', which would take the form of 'labour gymnastics' and mass displays, pageants and excursions. Gymnasiums and their 'bourgeois' equipment would be replaced by various pieces of apparatus on which young proletarians could practise their 'labour movements'.

[33] *Izvestiya fizicheskoi kul'tury*, 1925, No. 22, p. 2.
[34] *Pervaya vsesoyuznaya konferentsia nauchnykh rabotnikov po fizicheskoi kul'ture* (Moscow, 1926), p. 7.

The 'Proletkul'tists' therefore, went much further than the 'hygienists' in condemning all manner of games, sports and gymnastics 'tainted' by bourgeois society. In a book called *New Games for New Children* which they had published, the 'Proletkul'tists' advocated such new games as 'Swelling the Ranks of Children's Communists Groups', 'Rescue from the Fascists', 'Agitators', 'Helping the Proletarians', and 'Smuggling Revolutionary Literature across the Frontier'.[35]

One such novel proletarian 'game' was played on Sparrow Hills in Moscow in the summer of 1924, with 6,000 participants. The game was called simply 'Indians, British and Reds', the Indians being led by a plumed chieftain, the British by 'Joseph Chamberlain' and the Reds by the 'Chairman of the Revolutionary Military Council' (Trotsky). The plan of events was as follows:

(1) life goes on peacefully in all countries, with people engaging in games and sports: Indians in primitive games, hunting, dancing and fighting; the British pursuing sports [note the negative connotation] and carrying out punitive expeditions; and the Reds simulating work in factories, engaging in proletarian recreation and workers' outdoor fêtes;

(2) the British suddenly attack the Indians and conquer them;

(3) the Reds receive an appeal for help, cross the sea [the Moscow River] and join the struggle;

(4) the Indians join the Reds and, together, attack the British and defeat them;

(5) victory festivals take place in a new communist world.[36]

Many other such theatrical spectacles were presented; the Sparrow Hills became a favourite site for proletarian pageants and mock battles. The Proletkul't was, in fact, accused by some of a 'theatricalisation of sport'. Another 'proletarian event' took place in 1927 to mark the Tenth Anniversary of the Revolution; it was entitled 'The Pageant of Universal October' and was intended to portray pictures of world revolution. It was a strict rule that everyone should join in – as British miners, American cowboys, turbaned Indians, Polish cavalry, a religious procession of émigres, huge Chinese dragons pulling rickshaws, Red Army

---

[35] M. A. Kornil'eva-Radina and Y. P. Radin, *Novym detyam – novye igry* (Moscow, Narkomzdrav RSFSR, 1927), p. 37.

[36] Starovoitova, *Istoriya fizicheskoi kul'tury*, pp. 139–140.

men, workers and peasants of the USSR – some 7,000 'performers' in all. 'The two sides, capitalists and workers, suddenly clash and a radio appeal is made to the workers of the world to come to the class front. Universal October is approaching; one final onslaught on the citadels of capital and the announcement is made: "Now the red banner is flying over the entire world. Salute the *GHQ* of world revolution, the Communist International".'[37]

While the 'hygienists' admitted the possibility of the usefulness of some 'bourgeois' sports, the 'Proletkul'tists' made no such concessions. Thus, the 'hygienist' and ex-student of Lesgaft, V. V. Gorinevsky, described the game of lawn tennis as 'ideal from the biological standpoint in encouraging harmonious development; I find it hard to say what organs and muscles are not in use in tennis'.[38] The 'Proletkul'tist', S. Sysoyev, on the other hand, maintained that this game 'for the white-pants brigade and the bourgeoisie exhibits no comradeship or teamwork – the very qualities that the Russian needs. Tennis is also an expensive summer game. . . It should not and cannot receive as much support in the USSR as other, mass games.'[39]

Other 'Proletkul'tists' were particularly vociferous in their condemnation of competitive sport for the 'champion mania' it bred; it was suited only to the 'record-chasing' bourgeois and the professionals.

The 'Proletkul't' movement had earlier been admonished by Lenin, who pointed out the need to draw on the cultural heritage of the past and to base further development on everything valuable that had been accumulated by mankind up to the Revolution: 'What is important is not the *invention* of a new proletarian culture, but the *development* of the best forms, traditions and results of *existing* culture from the viewpoint of Marxist philosophy, and the living conditions and struggle of the proletariat in the epoch of its dictatorship.'[40] Other critics maintained that there were no such separate entities as bourgeois and proletarian sports; there was, rather, a bourgeois and a proletarian *attitude* to sport, a bourgeois and proletarian *spirit* of competition. Sporting

[37] Ibid., p. 142.
[38] 'Diskussiya o laun-tennise', in *Krasny Sport*, 21 January 1924.
[39] Ibid., 21 January 1924.
[40] *Leninsky sbornik*, xxxv (Moscow, Partizdat, 1945), p. 148.

attainments were, they asserted, necessary for inspiring young people to fresh successes in sport – which were, in some way, a measure of the country's cultural and technical development. Lunacharsky called for a careful study of foreign sporting experience and the inclusion of everything worthwhile into Soviet sport, particularly boxing and rugby. In an open letter to the press, he wrote that: 'Training for boxing involves the entire organism, the nervous system, heart, blood circulation, the respiratory system and, in every way, the muscles of the upper part of the body and the legs; it develops inventiveness and accuracy . . . stamina, self-control, fearlessness and courage more than any other sport. Even the fiercest bout teaches one to regard one's opponent as a comrade with whom one has common cause.'[41] Further, in his book *Thoughts On Sport*, he lauded rugby as a *'dzhentel'mensky boi* ["a gentlemanly battle"] that encourages courageous qualities; it is a sport that should be widely practised'.[42]

To many 'Proletkul'tists', the recourse to 'bourgeois' institutions such as sports seemed a compromise, a withdrawal from already conquered positions. They might have exerted more influence over the movement, however, if they had had a better-defined programme of proletarian physical culture to take the place of organised sports. As it was, a number of factories introduced 'production gymnastics' for their workers and some trade union clubs confined their activities to 'regenerative exercises', which tended to turn people, especially the young, away from sport and came in for increasing criticism from the *Komsomol* and the Party.

Subsequently, several 'Proletkul'tist' notions were taken up and incorporated in Soviet sport, while their originators were rejected (and mostly liquidated after 1934). 'Production gymnastics' were, for example, to be taken up on a mass scale with the onset of the First Five-Year Plan and are, today, a distinctive feature of Soviet physical education – though their purpose is more utilitarian than aesthetic, more geared to higher productivity than the proletarian bodily perfection that the 'Proletkul'tists' advocated. Nonetheless, the attempted portrayal of proletarian

[41] *Fizkul'tura i sport*, 1929, No. 17, p. 18.
[42] A. V. Lunacharsky, *Mysli o sporte* (Moscow, 1930), p. 72.

grandeur and the Soviet messianic mission in sporting displays, pageants, children's games and even art forms, so favoured by the 'Proletkul'tists', is as strong today as it ever was.

Foreign systems

Now that the cobwebs of tsarist obscurantism had been swept away, some felt it possible to introduce into Russia some of the models for games that had been advocated by the leading thinkers of the bourgeois industrial revolutions. After all, they reasoned, if Russia was to be an industrialised urban society, she would need a pattern of physical culture befitting such a society – and ready-made models already existed in the West. The former secretary of the Russian Olympic Committee, Georges Duperont, a former Frenchman who had taken Soviet nationality, advocated the French 'dynamic' system of gymnastics of Georges Demenie. Others favoured the 'natural method of physical education' of another Frenchman – Jacques Ebert, who opposed specialisation and favoured the cultivation of several games in order to achieve all-round development.[43] Others favoured the calisthenics schools of François Dellsarte and its contemporary exponent, Isadora Duncan. In fact, Lunacharsky invited Miss Duncan to Soviet Russia in 1921 and the *Vsevobuch* chief, Podvoisky, helped her to set up her own academy in Moscow. She took Soviet citizenship, married the poet Sergei Yesenin and undoubtedly had an influence on the formation of the Soviet calisthenics movement. She left the country, however, in 1923 and, although she returned briefly in 1924, found little further support for the educational principles incorporated in her own calisthenics method.

The Party intervention of 1925

The search for new solutions and new paths of development was apparent in all spheres of Soviet life. In sport, the lack of an agreed policy on its rôle in society had been obvious for several years and was beginning to have a stultifying effect on the rate of growth of the movement in general. The situation altered, how-

[43] A translation of his book *Sport Versus Physical Culture* was published in Moscow in 1926.

ever, with the intervention of the Party in its historic document issued on 13 July 1925. Conscious of the growing importance of the sports movement, and the confusion about the functions of sport in Soviet society, the Party made clear its views on physical culture, including sport; the resolution stressed that:

Physical culture must be considered not simply from the standpoint of public health and physical education, not only as an aspect of the cultural, economic and military training of young people (rifle shooting, etc.). It should also be seen as a method of educating the masses (inasmuch as it develops will power and builds up team work, endurance, resourcefulness and other valuable qualities). It must be regarded, moreover, as a means of rallying the bulk of the workers and peasants to the various Party, Soviet and trade union organisations, through which they can be drawn into social and political activity. . . Physical culture must be an inseparable part of overall political and cultural upbringing and education, and of public health.[44]

Sport, then, was to be a means for achieving: better health and physical fitness; character-formation, as part of general education in producing a harmonious personality; military training; the identification of individuals with groups (Party, Soviet, trade union) and their encouragement to be active socially and politically.

We have already seen that sport, having become the responsibility of the health commissariat, was employed as a means of inculcating standards of hygiene and regular exercise in a predominantly socially backward peasant population. Its therapeutic value was, for example, widely advertised in the intermittent three-day anti-TB campaigns of the late 1920s. It was not thought incongruous to put out a poster, ostensibly advertising sports, yet featuring a young man with a rifle and toothbrush above the slogan 'Clean Your Teeth! Clean Your Rifle!' But sport was not confined to improving physical health; it was regarded as important in combating anti-social and anti-Soviet behaviour in town and country. If urban young people, especially, could be persuaded to take up sport and engage in regular physical exercise, they might develop healthy bodies *and* minds. Thus, the Ukrainian Party Central Committee issued a joint

[44] *Izvestiya tsentral'novo komiteta RKP* (b), 20 July 1925.

resolution (with the *Komsomol*) 'On Intensifying Physical Culture Work' on 16 February 1926 expressing the hope that 'physical culture would become a vehicle of the new life . . . a means of isolating young people from the bad influence of the street, home-made liquor and prostitution'.[45] The rôle assigned to sport in the countryside was even more ambitious; it was 'to play a consider-able part in the campaign against drunkenness and uncivilised behaviour by attracting village youth to more sensible and cultured activities. . . In the fight to transform the village, physical culture was to be a vehicle of the new way of life in all measures undertaken by the Soviet authorities – in the fight against religion and natural calamities.'[46] Sport, therefore, stood for 'clean living', progress, good health and rationality and was regarded by the Party as one of the most suitable and effective instruments for implementing its social policies.

The far-reaching aims envisaged by the Party for sport may be illustrated by its early concern that physical culture should make some contribution to the social emancipation of women – an aim that had been taken up immediately after the Revolution by *Vsevobuch*. In a letter to Podvoisky through the medium of *Pravda*, the first women graduates from the Central Military School of Workers' Physical Culture showed that they were quite aware of the social significance of sport for them:

Your lectures encouraged and helped us to overcome our passivity and prejudices. We saw in you a sincere defender and supporter of equal rights for women. You spoke to us as comrades and you stressed that above all we should develop our personalities, that baubles and bangles have no value in life, that it is a person's inner qualities, creative force, the ability to act sensibly that really count. Your talks inspired us to criticise the bread-and-butter miss. You understood how important physical culture is for women and you tried to impress its importance upon us women, among whom there is so much passivity and conservatism, the results of age-old servi-tude, both economic and social.[47]

[45] A. M. Landar', 'Fizicheskaya kul'tura-sostavnaya chast' kul'turnoi revolyutsii na Ukraine', *Teoriya i praktika fizicheskoi kul'tury*, 1972, No. 12, p. 13.

[46] Ibid., p. 13.

[47] *Pravda*, 22 June 1922.

Next, the Party defined the forms of physical education; they were to include 'physical exercise in the form of sport, games, gymnastics, public and personal hygiene in work and everyday life, the use of natural forces (sun, air, water), and correct régimes of work and relaxation'. Moreover, properly controlled by medical and educational personnel, competitive activities could be valuable in drawing more people into sport; it could also be used to raise levels of skill. Sporting achievements were, the Party asserted, an attractive inducement to others to raise their standards; furthermore, if the Soviet Union were to take part in international sport – and the resolution stated that 'sporting contacts between worker-athletes of the Soviet Union and other countries help to fortify the international workers' front' – it required a mass basis on which to draw for its resources to attain a high level of performance. This aspect of the 1925 resolution was a rebuff to the 'hygienists', most of whom, as we have seen, opposed competitive sport.

This resolution, and the follow-up resolutions at the next Party conference in 1926 on deficiencies in trade union sports work, illustrate two important factors of the NEP period. First, it had evidently taken the Party some eight years to get round to dealing with sport and working out a coordinated policy on it – as it had in literature and the arts, too. Second, control over sport was still by no means 'monolithic' and dominated by the Party; the 1925 resolution was essentially a consolidation period measure intended to clarify and improve Party guidance over the sports movement. Rigid control by the Party was yet to come, organisationally. It was, however, now possible to develop sport, no longer based on compulsion of the *Vsevobuch* type, but based more on a voluntary desire for recreation.

In concentrating one's attention on the development of physical education and sport, there is an obvious danger of exaggerating their relative importance in society – and in Soviet policy making. As an adjunct of overall culture, particularly health and education, and as an instrument of socialisation, sport was certainly assigned a specific social rôle in the Soviet scheme of reconstruction during the 1920s. It was neither ignored nor allowed to develop haphazardly (as had occurred in most other industrialising states) in the hands of individual enthusiasts, who often made the playing of their sport exclusive to a particular social group, stratum, class or sex. On the other hand, Soviet sport (like other, perhaps more crucial, elements of the cultural revolution) because of the backward state of the economy and more pressing productive priority goals was by no means in the forefront of official thinking. (It was not until the USSR entered international competitions in the 1950s and set itself the goal of using world sports supremacy to demonstrate the advantages of the Soviet state-socialist way of development that sport came to occupy a position of any significance in Soviet social policies.)[48] An idea of the relative importance ascribed to physical culture by the state in the 1920s may be gleaned from the fact that only three books and brochures were on physical culture out of every five hundred published and only one five-hundredth of the paper used in non-periodical publishing between 1918 and 1928 went on sport.[49] Moreover, in not one year between 1924 and 1929 did the percentage of budgetary expenditure on physical culture reach one-twentieth of one per cent. Thus, *as far as state resources were concerned*, the relative priority assigned to sport was very low. (Sport has, of course, a powerful impact on the public mind yet costs *very little*; it is therefore good value in public relations.)

Competitive sport

Despite experimental false starts and shortcomings in the NEP period, the amount of actual sports activity was rapidly increasing. By 1925, the number of registered sports club members in the country had increased five-fold compared with 1913 – from 50,000 (0.04 per cent of the population) to 250,000 (0.2 per cent) – and, by 1929, over 15-fold – to 759,000 (0.5 per cent). What is more, over half the organised sports for men and just less than half for women that are today popular in the USSR had had their first national championships by 1929 (see Appendix II).

---

[48] Soviet sportsmen competed in no 'bourgeois' sports tournaments, except chess and speed skating, prior to 1945.

[49] M. V. Shishigin, 'Sportivnaya pechat' – aktivnoye sredstvo propagandy fizicheskoi kul'tury i sporta', *Teoriya i praktika fizicheskoi kul'tury*, 1973, No. 5, p. 13.

The First Workers' Spartakiad

The great sporting event of the decade was the First Workers' *Spartakiad* in 1928, dedicated to the inception of the First Five-Year Plan and the tenth anniversary of the Soviet sports movement. At the opening ceremony, a Party official explained its name and world-wide significance: 'We take the word *"Spartakiad"* from Spartacus – the hero of the ancient world and leader of the insurgent slaves. . . Both the Comintern Congress and the *Spartakiad* unite the working people fighting for socialism and communism. They are inseparable in the common struggle for revolution – classical physical culture and the revolutionary militant culture of Marxism–Leninism.'[50]

The *Spartakiad* was held in Moscow during a fortnight in the summer; it was launched on 12 August by an impressive sports parade of 30,000 banner-carrying athletes marching in colourful formation through the Red Square to the strains of the 'Internationale', on their way to *Dinamo* Stadium, where the games were to be held. As a popular spectacle for recruiting enthusiasts to the sports movement, it must have created a big impression. It is not entirely clear exactly how many athletes took part, because some reports at the time put the figure at 4,000,[51] and more recent descriptions claim a variety of figures in the region of 7,000.[52]

Besides being a national sports festival, the games were intended to be a universal workers' Olympics, as their name implied. Due to the strained relations between the Comintern sports organisation and the social democratic Socialist Workers' Sport International – and the ban by the latter on its members taking part in the *Spartakiad* – the games were largely dominated by Soviet athletes. Nevertheless, a substantial foreign contingent did take

---

[50] *Pravda*, 14 August 1928.
[51] *Pravda*, 13 August 1928; *Fizicheskaya kul'tura i sport*, 1928, No. 33, p. 32.
[52] *Entsiklopedichesky slovar' po fizicheskoi kul'ture i sportu* (Moscow, 1961), Vol. 1, p. 171, gives 7,125, as does Y. S. Sholomitsky, 'Fizicheskaya kul'tura i sport v sovetskom Uzbekistane', in *Ocherki po istorii fizicheskoi kul'tury* (Moscow, 1964), p. 95; but F. I. Samoukov (ed.), *Istoriya fizicheskoi kul'tury* (Moscow, 1964), p. 276, and V. V. Stolbov and I. G. Chudinov, *Istoriya fizicheskoi kul'tury* (Moscow, 1970), p. 165, give the figure of 7,225.

part: some 600 foreign athletes from 12 or 14 countries[53] – i.e. some 15 per cent of the total entry of 4,000.

The comprehensive sports programme of 21 sports (the 1928 'bourgeois' Olympics in Amsterdam included only 17 sports) covered athletics, gymnastics, swimming, diving, rowing, wrestling, boxing, weightlifting, fencing, cycling, soccer, basketball and shooting. Although most standards of performance were not yet up to world class, the games were a signal indication of how far the Soviet sports movement had come in a relatively short time.

Though standards at the *Spartakiad* were not as high as those at the Amsterdam Olympic Games, it is claimed that 'in virtually all events, the *Spartakiad* winners exceeded the records set at the 1925 Workers' Olympics held in Frankfurt',[54] sponsored by the Socialist Workers' Sport International – from which Soviet athletes were barred. Due to the lack of proper training, sports facilities and qualified instructors, it would, indeed, have been surprising if the *Spartakiad* results had set world records. Yet the scope of the programme (of the Amsterdam Olympics programme, only the marathon and the 3,000 metres steeplechase were missing) and participation led at least one foreign (communist) journalist to prophesy that 'in a few years from now, there will remain only two great sporting nations: one bourgeois, the other proletarian – America and the USSR. And I am quite certain the time will come when America will have to give way'.[55]

The winter counterpart to the *Spartakiad* took place at the end of 1928, with 638 participants in skiing, speed skating (men and women), biathlon and special ski contests for border guards, rural sportsmen and postmen. In some of these events, the Soviet Union did, in fact, have world-class performers: Yakov Mel'nikov, for example, had won the 5,000 metres speed skating event at the Stockholm world championships in February 1923.

---

[53] *Pravda*, 13 August 1928, gives 12 nations: Austria, Britain, Czechoslovakia, Estonia, Finland, France, Germany, Latvia, Norway, Sweden, Switzerland and Uruguay; *Fizicheskaya kul'tura i sport*, No. 33, 1928, adds Algeria and Argentina.
[54] V. P. Koz'mina, 'Mezhdunarodnoye sportivnoye dvizhenie', in *Ocherki po istorii fizicheskoi kul'tury* (Moscow, 1967), p. 197.
[55] *Folkets Dagblad*, 28 August 1928.

Gymnastics, soccer, basketball

The most popular sports between 1921 and 1929 were evidently gymnastics, soccer, basketball, athletics, skiing and speed skating.[56] Gymnastics suffered in the early 1920s, through *Proletkul't* influence, largely because it was associated with certain foreign sports movements. Before 1925, it had largely been confined to the Ukraine and Georgia and the military academies. However, after the Scientific and Technical Committee of the Supreme Council of Physical Culture had put its weight behind the gymnastics movement at its 1925 conference, the sport began to take root in schools and trade union sports groups. Regular gymnastics championships, however, were not conducted until after 1933.

Soccer retained its place as the country's most popular sport in the summer months. The game spread from the towns to the countryside (just the opposite trend to that in England) encouraged by state-directed tours of small towns and villages by established teams – mainly from Moscow and Leningrad – giving exhibition matches; regular inter-city tournaments commenced. Although only four cities entered teams in the first soccer championships of 1922, the number rose to 16 in the following year.

That factory workers' teams were not yet up to the standard of the old clubs is evident from the fact that *Detskoye Selo* won 22:0 against *Petrovat* (a team from Petrograd Military Motorised Transport); the old Petrograd clubs also provided eight of the Russian team that successfully toured Finland, Sweden, Norway, Germany and Estonia that year. The following year, 1924, most of the 'bourgeois' clubs were renamed, though retaining their premises, teams and colours; the league championships were contested on a district basis, with the former *Sport* club representing Petrograd District and *Kolomyagi* – Leningrad *uyezd*. In 1925, the process of renaming the old clubs was complete: *Sport* now became Petrograd District 'A', Kolomyagi – Petrograd District 'B', *Unitas* – Vyborg District 'A', *Merkur* – Central District 'A', and *Krechet* – Central District 'B'; these district teams contested the 1925 and 1926 league championships with such recently-formed 'Soviet' clubs as *Krasny Putilovets, Dinamo*,

[56] I. A. Tarabrin (ed.), *Pyat'desyat shagov sportivnoi Rossii* (Moscow, 1967), p. 187.

Bol'shevik and the Miners' Association Team. By 1927, however, the old 'bourgeois' clubs had served their purpose in popularising the game and their district teams disappeared from the league; nonetheless, the players, equipment, club colours and premises of some pre-revolutionary clubs were simply transferred to the 'new' Soviet proletarian clubs – e.g. *Putilovsky* became *Krasny Putilovsky, Kolomyagi – Stadion imeni V.I. Lenina* and *Unitas – Pishchevkus.*[57] In international competition, soccer was the only sport in which games took place between Soviet and other national teams; it provided by far the greatest number of international sporting contacts for the USSR.

Another team game, basketball, received encouragement from an unexpected quarter: S. Sysoyev, the *proletkul'tist*, who was on the staff of the State Military Academy, was responsible for unifying and codifying the rules of this American-invented game. It was the women's basketball championship which was inaugurated first – in 1923, a year before the men's.

The impact of organised sports on the national republics

The value both of competitive sport and of grand sports festivals was appreciated, it would seem, in rallying support for the Party and in striving to unite the various nationalities in the republics. Tashkent, for example, was the venue of a second Central Asian Olympiad in 1921 with a considerably bigger programme than the First Games, held in October 1920, which had been mainly confined to local folk games. On this occasion, the sports included athletics, weightlifting, wrestling, basketball, gymnastics, soccer and chess. The athletics events even included the modern pentathlon and decathlon. To popularise organised sports, a Russian team was sent to give displays; an American immigrant, S. L. Jackson (who later became a Merited Boxing Coach of the USSR), gave demonstrations of boxing. This Olympiad was later followed by an All-Turkestan Olympiad (in 1924) and a First All-Uzbekistan *Spartakiad* (in 1927).

Some 26,000 people were said to be members of the various sports clubs of Uzbekistan by the end of 1926. In Azerbaidzhan,

[57] N. Y. Kiselev (ed.), *70 futbol'nykh let* (Lenizdat, 1970), pp. 89–114.

by the end of 1929, there were over 600 sports sections with 15,000 members, of whom just less than half were from the native population.

It was later recognised that, in their haste to use organised sport as a cohesive agent to bring peoples together, some officials had tried to import into Central Asia European games for which there existed no real popular (even urban) basis. 'In the late 1920s and early 1930s, there were many attempts in Tadzhikistan to make tennis popular. Due to lack of consideration for national characteristics (and even ignoring national folk games) only a few city people took up the game.'[58] The propagation of soccer occasionally had quite the opposite effect to that desired (i.e. identifying the people with the political system and integrating them into the Soviet 'commonwealth of nations'). It was used as anti-Russian propaganda by local religious leaders: 'Addressing the local population, the mullahs used to say, "See, the Russians have brought you the head of the devil; see how it jumps and brings you misfortune".'[59] It is perhaps natural that the primitive origins of the game should have been harked back to by pre-industrial people unaccustomed to games that were highly controlled and circumscribed by rules which ensured that the excitement of the struggle did not carry the players too far. All the same, these sporting initiatives should be seen as a highly principled aspect of the general revolutionary liberation of what were formerly subject peoples.

Sport and education

Like other areas of social action in the 1920s, education went through a period of experimentation, principally with progressive educational theories. In many schools, physical education was replaced by a study of hygiene and health, seen in their relation to a factory, a market, a bakery, and so on. Such was the school physical education syllabus drawn up by the Educational Research Section of the State Academic Council that was in operation in schools between 1923 and 1927 (it was known as the

---

[58] D. Yeshchin and A. Pustovalov, *Natsional'ny vopros v fizkul'turnom dvizhenii* (Moscow–Leningrad, 1938), p. 12.
[59] Ibid., p. 76.

'*GUS* Syllabus'). 'This was a complex syllabus, not one by subject, in which various subjects, including physical education, were combined.'[60]

Physical education, as a separate subject in its own right, received little encouragement from the new syllabus covering the years 1927–1929 ('Syllabus of Physical Exercises for Labour Schools'). Although this was supposed to be a unified, compulsory syllabus for all the schools in the country, it did not meet with much success. Despite a number of resolutions and programmes, it was not until 1929 that physical education actually became a compulsory subject in schools and colleges, with an allotted weekly quota of two hours.

As industrialisation got underway, a strict regimen was evolved for all Soviet schools, and a full programme of compulsory physical education for primary and secondary schools was introduced in 1933. What was often lacking in the 1920s were the material resources for pursuing any sports activity at school: a lack of playing fields, gymnasiums, equipment, clothing – which often prevented the implementation of directives to include physical education and games in the school timetable.

Nonetheless, the 1923 *GUS* syllabus and the 1927 physical education syllabus did lay a basis for school physical education, particularly the preparation of detailed plans of each lesson by doctors and educationalists in a central research institute; during the 1930s, these were passed on to every school for compulsory application. The instructions given to physical education teachers in the 1927 syllabus included the following aims for school physical education: 'To fortify and maintain health, to enhance the organism's resistance to illness, to counteract the "industrial diseases" of school life, to cultivate dexterity, suppleness, speed, coordination, precision, the ability to use one's strength rationally, to develop a sense of balance, rhythm and attentiveness, to inculcate moral values and form good social habits.'[61] These aims were to be pursued by employing 'natural forms of movement which man has used throughout his evolution: walking, running, throwing, balancing, skiing, swimming, skating, sledding, elements of classical and folk dancing, climbing, excursions and nature

[60] F. I. Samoukov (ed.), *Istoriya fizicheskoi kul'tury* (Moscow, 1964), p. 284.
[61] Quoted in *Fizicheskaya kul'tura v shkole*, 1967, No. 9, p. 4.

rambles'.[62] Little mention was made of using equipment, since hardly any existed. Besides physical education lessons, exercises were recommended for out-of-school time, particularly early morning exercises. In 1929, a daily morning broadcast began (and has continued to the present day) with 'keep fit' lessons for the population at large, attempting to get people into the habit of doing at least a quarter of an hour's physical education every morning before breakfast.

No mention was made in either of the two physical education syllabuses produced in the 1920s of team and combat sports like soccer, rugby, basketball, boxing and wrestling – partly because facilities were lacking, but mainly because the educational body concerned with physical education in schools and colleges was preoccupied with the bodily functions of games for improving health and opposed team and combat sports as potentially deleterious to mental and physical health.

Conclusions

To sum up, this was a decisive period for the future of Soviet society, with the death of Lenin and the acute struggle in many spheres of life, culminating in the defeat of the Trotskyite tendency, bureaucratisation, the decision on forcible collectivisation and the start of 'revolution from above' and open 'class war' in the countryside. By the end of the period, Stalin's pre-eminence was unchallenged and the whole country may be described as having been thrust into the straightjacket of industrialisation.

The years of experimenting and searching in sport reflect a contradiction fundamental to the period: that between the subjective desires of the authorities to shape society according to ideological preconceptions and the objective lack of the material conditions for the implementation of ideals. There can be little doubt that, because they were not based on the reality of Russia's situation, some immediate aspirations for sport were utopian and unrealistic.

Despite acceptance of the most advanced ideas and the passing of resolutions and directives by responsible assemblages, despite

[62] Ibid., p. 5.

the enormous sacrifices and efforts made by some, Russia remained a backward country economically and culturally – a predominantly illiterate peasant nation. That, to some extent at least, explains the apparent hesitations, the disputes and controversies in many fields, including that of culture. The search for a way forward in sport was accompanied by conflict over its basic rôle and functions which, in turn, reflected deeper-going political and social conflicts.

There existed during the NEP period a widespread idealistic adherence to the notion of a 'healthy mind in a healthy body', a feeling that physical culture could somehow be used, along with other policies, to combat socially and politically undesirable phenomena such as prostitution, drunkenness and delinquency. In one simplistic formulation of the sort rather popular at the time, physical culture stood for progress, good personal and social health and rationality; it was therefore a useful instrument for combating all anti-social and anti-Soviet phenomena (including religion). The importance assigned to this manifest function of sport was evident in the battle for influence waged by such groups as the 'hygienists' and 'pedologists'. The former waged a successful struggle to obtain control of the sporting press, institutes of physical culture and school physical education and managed to impose restrictions on certain competitive sports, as well as to secure a close official administrative link between health protection and physical culture.

In a country that had made a sharp break with its past and was proceeding to tear down many of the previously revered trappings associated with its old nationalism and to eradicate the values that went with them, it was inevitably going to take time for new norms and values to fill the void. Further, in a deeply divided multinational state, the new régime, in attempting social transformations that required both personal sacrifice and popular initiative, urgently needed to establish national – or, rather, supra-national – unity and community spirit. Sports festivals, as we have seen, were held in the 1920s in non-Russian areas like the Transcaucasus and Central Asia, often with the explicit political purpose of bringing the various nationalities of the region together with sportsmen from Russia, the Ukraine and Belorussia, of breaking down mutual distrust and hostility, and of rallying support for the Party and its policies – indirectly through sport and directly by including in the festivals, banners, parades and political speeches.

Two of the Party's policies of which sport was intended to be an agent were: (1) the promotion of the emancipation and mass employment of women – particularly in Moslem areas (where women had been virtually excluded from all public life before 1920); and (2) the countering of religion, particularly all-embracing faiths like Islam that impinged upon large areas of social life – including sporting activities (which were often regarded by religious leaders as interfering with work and distracting men from serious spiritual concerns). Any enticement of Central Asian youth, particularly young women, into the sports activities organised by the Soviet authorities was regarded as a breach in the 'feudal-bey' and religious order, as an encouragement of the progressive values supposedly imparted by sport that were seen as confronting the 'irrational', 'superstitious', 'mystical' and 'sub-servient' aspects of religion.

As the political realities in the aftermath of revolution and, increasingly, official policy began to conflict with the aspirations in regard to socialist culture of certain revolutionary Marxist and health-oriented professional circles, the Party leadership seems initially to have regarded sport as a relatively harmless area for concessions – and even to have tolerated open conflicts. Insofar as sport could provide an aesthetically satisfying, emotionally excit-ing and revolutionary stirring area for participation and spectacle, the Party evidently felt it preferable to have real or potential oppositionists concentrating some of their energies in mass sports pageants and displays rather than in more 'intellectual' spheres of political and economic import. Nonetheless, towards the end of the 1920s, as the Party established full and undisputed control over sports policy (as over every significant area of policy), it subordinated all organised sporting activities to its own utilitarian requirements – to training the population for labour and warfare and to bearing the rigours and inequalities of emergent Soviet society. At this stage, all opposition to Party policy in sport was stifled.

Other non-Party individuals and groups who found it difficult to find niches for themselves under the new régime may well have discovered in sport an area of interest that they could share with fellow 'misfits'. This applied to foreigners who had stayed on in Russia (many of whom became instrumental in popularising 'new' sports like boxing, soccer and calisthenics) and former functionaries of the tsarist régime (some of whom moved into the administration of sports groups – like the former scout masters who became Young Pioneer leaders). Tsarist-trained intellectuals, too, uncertain about their status under and attitude to the Soviet régime could find in games like chess or, say, Isadora Duncan's calisthenics studio a personally rewarding outlet for self-expression and creativity in a society which was becoming highly disciplined. For the time being, while not countenancing opposition from such quarters to its policies, the Party seemed, with some exceptions, willing to tolerate and use such people to popularise and administer sporting activities throughout the USSR and to provide skilled entertainment in the major industrial centres.

5
Industrialisation and competitive sport, 1929–1941

Industrialisation, collectivisation and mass repression

Towards the end of the NEP period, the economy was getting back on its feet: in the economic year 1925–1926, industrial production had reached ninety per cent of its 1913 level.[1] By the end of 1925, a policy of industrialisation which emphasised the importance of the production of the means of production had been sanctioned by the fourteenth Party congress. Smilga, the deputy president of Gosplan, made a firm declaration of principle in May 1926: 'We must orient ourselves on our own resources; we must act like a country which does not wish to turn into a colony; we must force the industrialisation of the economy. Because we are behind Europe and have started to re-equip later, we must firmly state that the path of increased development of industry is the shortest and the only path to the improvement of our national well-being.'[2] The scene was thus set for the implementation of an industrialisation programme that was forcibly to hurl the whole of the country into a gigantic campaign to 'build socialism', then to lead to the forcible collectivisation of agriculture and transform the USSR from a backward agricultural into an advanced industrial, if unbalanced, economy. The first Five-Year Plan went into operation on 1 October 1928 on a scale and with planning that more resembled a military campaign than peacetime construction.

If the country was to industrialise rapidly, the Party leadership believed, it would have to collectivise its agriculture. In the autumn

---

[1] See E. H. Carr and R. W. Davies, *Foundations of a Planned Economy, 1926–1929* (Macmillan, London, 1969), p. 271. This book gives a detailed background to the industrialisation controversy.

[2] Quoted in ibid., p. 277.

of 1929, the 'Party leadership came to the abrupt conclusion that the *kolkhozes* were the only viable solution, and one that must therefore at all costs be implemented on a national scale. . . . The régime then entered upon a trial of strength with the peasants, which was known as the period of "mass collectivisation", and which was to last for nearly four years. This was a veritable civil war, fought by both sides with unyielding obduracy.'[3]

The fear of military defeat – which had precipitated this industrial and agricultural revolution – helped to create a society that became more and more totalitarian. By the early 1930s, the first members of a new Soviet-trained class of specialists had been educated: this was to replace the old, non-proletarian 'intelligentsia' and was 'uncontaminated' by tsarist or bourgeois-liberal ideas. Stalin's rise to supreme power came to a climax with the great purges of the second half of the 1930s, which carried off most of the policy makers of the first decade of Soviet power: all the members of Lenin's Politburo, the top leadership of the Red Army and the upper and middle levels of the Communist Party. In this period of mass repression, 'millions perished and every member of the population was held under immediate threat'.[4]

A social phenomenon that accompanied this repression was the growing portrayal of Stalin as a 'superman': 'In the final stages of the "cult of personality", he was built up with the most astonishing adulation as a genius not only in politics, but also in strategy, the sciences, philosophy and almost every field. His picture looked down from every hoarding, his bust was carried by Soviet alpinists to the top of every Soviet peak, he was elevated to be, with Marx, Engels and Lenin, the fourth of the great political geniuses of the epoch.'[5] This 'cult of Stalin's personality' was reflected throughout Soviet society in many 'mini-cults' of leaders in all walks of life, by the development of 'stars' and even 'superstars' whom ordinary men and women could look upon from afar and on whose achievements they might dwell as they

---

[3] M. Lewin, *Russian Peasants and Soviet Power* (Allen and Unwin, London, 1968), p. 19. This book is an authoritative study of collectivisation.
[4] R. Conquest, *The Great Terror* (Pelican, London, 1968), p. 11. This book is a detailed study of the period of mass repression.
[5] Ibid., pp. 106–107.

took part in the universal campaigns of 'socialist competition' or emulation at their ordinary jobs.

The implications for the sports movement of these socio-economic processes were extremely important, for it was in the 1930s that the pattern of Soviet sport as we know it today was principally formed and its main rôle and explicit functions in society were set. If the previous decade may be described as having been dominated by *physical culture*, the 1930s were to be a decade of competitive *sport*.

The organisation of sport

The Party Central Committee adopted a resolution on 23 September 1929 criticising the lack of coordination in the sports movement. It called for more centralised and direct government control. To these ends, two steps were taken.

An All-Union Physical Culture Council

The first step was to set up, on 3 April 1930, the All-Union Physical Culture Council attached to the Central Executive Committee of the USSR. The Council was, in fact, to have executive powers to decide all issues connected with the organisation of sport and to make proposals of a legislative nature to All-Union and Republican government bodies. In other words, the Council was really to be a Ministry for Sport. How powerful it was may be judged from its proposed functions (as listed in the Party resolution): 'administration and control over the activity of Republican sports councils, all government and independent organisations (government departments, trade unions, cooperatives and voluntary societies [i.e. societies whose membership was open to the public at large] that are responsible for organising sports activities; control over construction of major sports sites, research and study in training physical education and sports specialists; command of all production activity concerned with sport; responsibility for popularising and propagandising sport, including the control of all sports publications and the organisation and conduct of congresses, festivals, and national and international competitions'.[6]

Unified coordination of the sports movement was completed with the transfer to the new Council of all local sports councils – from Republican down to district levels. From being mere consultative bodies since their inception in 1923, they were now to become executive government agencies.

Primary sports clubs based on workplaces

The second step taken by the Party was to transfer all primary sports clubs to local workplaces. In the future, all local sports clubs were to be organised on a production basis, all the people belonging to a particular factory, office or college (and members of their families) being eligible for membership of the sports 'collective' at their place of work. In fact, this arrangement was already in operation throughout most of the country: in 1928, sports circles (*kruzhki*) at workplaces had some 258,000 members, while clubs (*kluby*) organised on a territorial basis had a membership of only 127,000. Now the latter clubs were to be abolished, membership of the sports groups was to be solely on a production – as opposed to territorial – basis, and the factory circles were to be renamed sports collectives (*kollektivy*).

Sport, therefore, now had, first, a powerful central organisational nucleus in the form of the All-Union Council – which was to exist with only relatively minor changes until 1959 – and, second, at the other end of the scale, active and politically controllable sports groups directly at places of work and cultural and educational centres. Sport was brought into line with the standard Stalin pattern for all activities, becoming a hierarchical State functional organisation.

Purges

As in other areas of activity during the 1930s, the old sports administration was, however, under constant attack from the sporting press; apparently, the transfer from Republican consultative councils to a centralised system with greatly enlarged

---

[6] I. D. Chudinov (ed.), *Osnovnye postanovleniya, prikazy i instruktsii po voprosam fizicheskoi kul'tury i sporta, 1917–1957* (Moscow, 1959), pp. 124–125.

powers had not removed all the defects, as perceived by the Party. Inept leadership at lower levels, poor planning, lack of coordination (once more), wasteful expenditure, and concentration on small groups of proficient athletes at the expense of the masses were just some of the accusations made in the press. The Chairman of the All-Union Council, Nikolai Antipov, and his successor, Vasily Mantsev, constantly urged modifications in organisation and tried various permutations in the composition and structure of the Council to meet the criticism, which was mainly inspired by the difficult political period the country was going through. Both Antipov and Mantsev disappeared in the great purge of 1936–1938 – as, too, did Mantsev's successor, I. I. Kharchenko, who became Chairman when the Council was renamed the All-Union Committee on Physical Culture and Sport Affairs in June 1936. Among other notables in the field of physical education and sport to be purged was Professor S. M. Frumin, Principal of the Central State Institute of Physical Culture which, only a year before Frumin's fall from grace, had been given the honour of being named after Stalin.[7] Sport was, of course, no exception to the general purge which affected leaders in all walks of life.

Voluntary sports societies

Despite the problems in administration, the trade union primary sports collectives involved more and more workers in sport – and sportsmen in work. The First Trade-Union Sports Conference, in November 1930, called on members to subordinate sport to socialist construction. In factories, one of the most common wall slogans was 'Every Sportsman Should Be A Shock-Worker, Every Shock-Worker – a Sportsman'. 'Production gymnastics' was introduced and, between 1931 and 1933, the sports collectives claimed an increase in membership of up to 2 million. In the subsequent years, up to the end of the decade, the number of registered athletes is claimed to have increased to nearly five and a half million, or over three per cent of the population. How reliable

---

[7] On a visit to the Central Institute in early 1971, I was told that Professor Frumin had, in fact, been rehabilitated; his name now appears on the honours board of the Museum within the Institute.

the data are is hard to say, statistics of the purge period being necessarily suspect.

By the mid-1930s, the sports movement had become more complex, especially at workplace level; this was, of course, part of a general process of institutional bureaucratisation typical of the period. It was one thing getting employees to join trade union sports collectives, but it was quite another sustaining their interest by arranging contests with other workplace teams. There was the problem, too, of what to do about (and even how to discover) proficient athletes: how best to train them and arrange top-flight competition for them. Most of these issues did not fall adequately within the competence of the individual union sports collective, yet they were mostly outside the responsibility of the government sports councils. It was therefore decided in 1935 to set up trade-union-based voluntary sports societies (*dobrovol'nye sportivnye obshchestva*). The enterprise collectives were to remain at work-place level as the primary links in the sports movement, but now they were to come under a specific trade union sports society. In March 1935, the first society, *Spartak*, was formed, representing members of producers' cooperatives. Shortly after, sports societies of particular trade unions in the Moscow Region were formed: *Lokomotiv* (representing railway workers), *Burevestnik* (*Stormy Petrel*, representing workers in state trade), *Krasnoye Znamya* (*Red Banner*, representing cotton-textile workers) and several others. Having decided that the Moscow experiment was worth extending to the country as a whole – like that of the *Dinamo* Society, which had been established by the security services in 1923 – the authorities began to set up sports societies throughout the country. By 1 January 1937, they numbered 69 and, by late 1938, 99.

The formation of the sports societies – which were to be an important link in the whole sports movement right up to the present – confirmed the production principle of primary organisa-tion in that, since Soviet trade unions are organised on an industry-by-industry basis, so too are the sports societies. Thus, a railway-man and any member of his family can join *Lokomotiv*, an automobile worker and his family can join *Torpedo* and a con-struction worker and his family can join *Stroitel'* (*Builder*) if they want to engage in sport. The primary sports collective remained at the workplace, but it was no longer to stand alone. Instead, it was to serve as a basis from which district, regional, Republican and All-Union competitions were to draw participants to form top teams – a form of 'democratic centralist' hierarchy in sport.

Every society was to have its own rules, membership cards, banner, badge and colours. It was to be financed out of trade-union dues and other funds and given the responsibility for building large sports amenities, acquiring equipment and sports clothing for its members and maintaining a permanent staff of coaches, instructors and medical personnel. It was to have an organisation at each administrative level and be run at the top by a sports section of the All-Union Central Council of Trade Unions. The sports societies were termed 'voluntary' in the sense that membership of them was open to any member of the appropriate trade union either on the basis of individual membership or via membership of a sports collective (unlike the sports collectives, whose membership was confined to employees at a particular workplace). They were not voluntary in the sense that their formation was a matter of choice, that staff were only unpaid, part-time volunteers or that they were run without government supervision. Members had the right to use the club's equipment and facilities free of charge, elect and be elected to its steering bodies.

All-Union Committee on Physical Culture and Sports Affairs

To mark the fact that 1936 was the year of the new Constitution, the year in which 'socialism' was proclaimed, the Party called for yet another organisational restructuring in sport. This came on 21 June 1936 when the Party announced that 'in the interests of better satisfying the ever-growing demands of workers for sport and physical culture', it would 'improve state control and supervision over activities in physical culture and sport'.[8] It therefore altered the name of the All-Union Physical Culture Council to the All-Union Committee on Physical Culture and Sports Affairs and put it under the direct authority of the Council of People's Commissars – i.e. it brought sport under the closer scrutiny of government leaders. Apart from raising the official standing of

[8] Chudinov, *Osnovnye postanovleniya*, p. 155.

sport, the new nomenclature indicated a shift of emphasis from pure physical culture to physical culture combined with competitive sport as a means of politically socialising the population to the new prevailing norms, with emphasis on its utilitarian, 'applied' functions in preparing people for labour and defence. The cloud that had hung over the word 'sport' (implying competition) since the early 1920s was now officially lifted.

All-Union League and Cup competition

One of the principal tasks of the sports societies was to act as a catalyst in raising standards through more rational organisation and competition: they were more direct 'transmission belts' to sportsmen than had previously existed and could control local activity. Contests were to be conducted on an intra- and inter-society and territorial basis. Each society had its local, regional, Republican, and All-Union championships for each sport it practised. The selection of sport society teams at all levels was based on these competitions. This system of contests led to the creation of nation-wide sports leagues and cup competitions for such popular games as soccer, basketball and ice hockey. Until 1935, All-Union championships (e.g. in soccer) had been contested by city teams; in 1936, however, the All-Union Football League and Cup competition were both instituted. Societies such as *Dinamo*, *Spartak*, *Torpedo*, *Lokomotiv* and *Burevestnik* had so-called 'teams of masters' in every major town, some of which competed in one of the various leagues. These leagues created new interest and mass appeal, especially in the most popular male team game, soccer, and drew many thousands of spectators to view important matches. In soccer, there were four national divisions in 1936 and 1937, with 7–8 teams in each division; in 1938, the first division was enlarged to include 26 teams. The next year it was reduced to 14, at which it has more or less remained to this day.[9] Big city and security police teams, with their massive resources, tended to dominate the leagues, especially the First Division. In the Division 1 table of the Fourth USSR Championship in 1938, Moscow teams occupied six, and *Dinamo*

[9] In 1974, there were three divisions: Division 1 had 16 teams, Division 2 had 22, and Division 3 had 125 teams divided into 6 geographical zones.

teams five, of the top ten places. Moscow *Spartak* also won the Third USSR Cup Competition of 1938, competed for by 296 teams.[10]

Acknowledgement of the importance of the *Dinamo* and *Spartak* sports societies – and of competitive sport in general – came with a government decision in June 1937 to award them the country's top distinction, the Order of Lenin. The previous year, some fifty athletes and sports workers had been awarded medals and various orders. This was the first time that individual sportsmen had featured in the 'honours list', which was some indication of the official 'solicitude' (and public adulation) that heroes and shock-workers in sport – like individuals who excelled in other spheres – were accorded in the 'cult' period.

The GTO badge and the uniform rankings system

The formation of the voluntary sports societies and the increasing numbers of participants led to a review of the motivational provisions in sport. Thus, two important elements in the Soviet sports system to give people clear-cut targets of achievement were instituted in the 1930s. The first, the 'Ready for Labour and Defence' *(Gotov k trudu i oborone (GTO))* programme, was intended to achieve two aims.

One was to extend the scope of sports participation, give everyone something to aim for – i.e. set modest targets whose attainment brought some official honorific recognition – and start to make regular participation in sport a normal feature of 'the

---

[10] *Division 1 of the Fourth USSR Football Championships: 1938*

1	Spartak (Moscow)	14	Stalinets (Leningrad)
2	TsDKA (Moscow)	15	Sel'mash (Khar'kov)
3	Metallurg (Moscow)	16	Stalinets (Moscow)
4	Dinamo (Kiev)	17	Lokomotiv (Kiev)
5	Dinamo (Moscow)	18	Dinamo (Rostov)
6	Dinamo (Tbilisi)	19	Temp (Baku)
7	Dinamo (Leningrad)	20	Spartak (Leningrad)
8	Lokomotiv (Moscow)	21	Spartak (Khar'kov)
9	Torpedo (Moscow)	22	Zenit (Leningrad)
10	Dinamo (Odessa)	23	Pishchevik (Moscow)
11	Stakhanovets (Stalino)	24	Lokomotiv (Tbilisi)
12	Traktor (Stalingrad)	25	Kryl'ya Sovetov (Moscow)
13	Elektrik (Leningrad)	26	Burevestnik (Moscow)

Source: N. A. Kiselev (ed.), *70 futbol'nykh let* (Lenizdat, 1970), p. 144.

socialist way of life'. The targets were to be not for a single sport, or even for sporting ability alone, but for all-round ability in a number of sports and knowledge of the rudiments of hygiene, first-aid and civil defence.

The second aim was to establish a mass base from which potential 'stars' could be drawn. Once the 'stars' were discovered, it was necessary to categorise them according to their level of ability in a particular sport and to give them the incentive and amenities to realise their potential. For this purpose, a second element was introduced into the system: a uniform rankings system for individual sports, setting four levels of superior achievement.

The GTO badge for general physical competence. In March 1931, acting on a proposal from the *Komsomol*, the All-Union Physical Culture Council resolved: 'With the aim of stimulating independent activity among Soviet people, the Council is establishing an award for all-round physical ability . . . [it is to take] the form of a "Ready for Labour and Defence" badge and a certificate from the All-Union Physical Culture Council . . . By all-round physical ability, the Council has in mind the completion of a set programme of practical and theoretical tests.'[11]

How broad the sports activity had to be may be judged from the number of separate activities and theoretical subjects included in the test: 15 events – including running, jumping, grenade throwing, skiing and swimming – and 6 subjects, including a knowledge of the Soviet sports movement, military affairs, first-aid and hygiene. Recipients had further to be members of a shock-brigade in industry or agriculture.

The inclusion of theoretical subjects and the stipulation of active participation in shock-work are typical of the industrialisation period, and the overt military bias was an indication of the Soviet preoccupation with defence at a time when an attack from the imperialists – who were, as was consistently and correctly stressed, implacably hostile to the Soviet régime – was presented as imminent.

Shortly after the *GTO* scheme was launched, it was decided that greater differentiation in the mass of sporting achievement was needed – so, from 1 January 1933, a second and higher level

[11] Chudinov, *Osnovnye postanovleniya*, p. 137.

of the *GTO* was set, covering 22 sports activities (2 for women) and 3 theoretical requirements. This became known as Stage 2 of the *GTO* system and was a much stiffer test than Stage 1, being already on the way to singling out proficiency, inasmuch as Stage 2 implied a certain amount of systematic training and necessitated use of facilities to do so. It is hardly surprising that the first holders of the *GTO* Stage 2 badge were officers of the Frunze Military Academy in Moscow.

The BGTO badge. Insofar as the *Komsomol* was responsible for involving young people in the *GTO* system and, in fact, had initiated the whole movement, it was natural that it should suggest a third element in the system – this time for schoolchildren. Early in 1934, the 'Be Ready for Labour and Defence' (*BGTO*) badge was instituted for schoolchildren by the All-Union Physical Culture Council to cover 16 sports and theoretical subjects.

The introduction of the *BGTO* stage completed the system which now stretched in natural succession, with increasing difficulty, from the *BGTO*, taken while at school, to the *GTO* Stage 1 and *GTO* Stage 2. This comprehensive sports programme, which was to become the basis of a movement for national fitness and pre-military training, was designed to involve millions of young men and women in 'sport in general' – i.e. to persuade them to make sport and some form of exercise a regular feature of their everyday lives. It was arranged to develop and test their speed, agility, strength, endurance and general military aptitude. Although the prize was no more than a silver lapel badge, it is apparent that many young people were drawn into more than a passing acquaintance with sport.

The uniform rankings system for individual sports. In order to give some recognition to superior sporting achievement (the yardstick of foreign competition being largely unavailable) the All-Union Physical Culture Council in 1935 created a uniform system of classification of sports achievements. This, it hoped, would help coaches to spot gifted athletes and train them with specific targets in mind and would stimulate the best performers to aim for certain set superior standards in a particular sport. There were to be four rankings decided by times recorded in a particular event and/or success in competition, both national and international.

The idea of a ranking system was not entirely new. Four All-Russia rankings had been established for track and field athletes back in 1918, for cyclists in 1924, swimmers in 1927 and gymnasts in 1934. An even higher honorary title, Merited Master of Sport of the USSR, had been decreed by the *TsIK* on 27 May 1934.[12] *Pravda* reported at the time that a major purpose of the new title was to stimulate better results, but that the ultimate intention was to use 'stars' to inspire the masses: 'The Soviet government has instituted the title of Merited Master of Sport. There can be no doubt that this will play an exceptional part in lifting the sports movement to an even higher level. It is the task of sports groups to surround the Master with care and attention, and to create conditions for him constantly to grow and improve himself, thus being able to impart his experience and knowledge to the millions of sportsmen.'[13]

It was only in 1935, however, that the All-Union Physical Culture Council ratified a new project instituting uniform Master, First, Second and Third rankings in a range of sports. Over the next two years, the standards for the First, Second and Third rankings were drawn up and were put into operation in 1937 for the following ten sports: athletics, boxing, fencing, gymnastics, shooting, speed skating, swimming, tennis, weightlifting and wrestling. The Master of Sport title was to be awarded to athletes setting *good* All-Union records, winning a Soviet championship or gaining the First ranking in a few sports.

Although the rankings system did not have long to prove itself before war came, it did show that a steadily increasing number of proficient athletes was emerging – e.g. 884 Masters in 1940.

Massovost' and masterstvo and abuses of amateur status

The decision taken in the mid-1930s to stratify in sport, to distinguish a more or less professional group of sportsmen from the

---

[12] This paralleled the introduction of the 'Merited' title in other fields: 'Merited Artist' and 'Merited Teacher' were both introduced in 1936. Along with the the titles went an increment in the recipient's monthly salary – 10 rubles in the case of teachers, and 20 rubles in the case of sportsmen. See *Pedagogicheskaya entsiklopediya*, Vol. II (Moscow, 1965), p. 103.

[13] *Pravda*, 29 May 1934.

main body, was in keeping with the country's social development and its concomitant official values: in industry and agriculture, reward and prestige went to the *peredoviki*, the workers and teams that attained the best results. The individual, whether factory manager, collective farm chairman or Party leader, rose high or fell low on the basis of performance, of results shown. The ordinary people were to be inspired by the efforts of persons with whom they could identify, whose faces could be seen in the newspapers, on street hoardings and on factory and farm boards of honour. These were men and women not greatly different from themselves in looks, speech, dress and manners.

Yet, to produce the most talented athletes with the paucity of sports facilities available, it was necessary to give them intensive coaching and reward them accordingly. This, inevitably, has resulted ever since in disputes within the sports movement as to the right balance between *massovost'* (mass participation) and *masterstvo* (mastery). Just how much special treatment should the master sportsmen get? Should they be given time off from work for training? How should they be rewarded? In a socialist state that declared itself free of the commercialism and professionalism of capitalist societies, there inevitably arose the dilemma for Party and government of wanting to see excellence in sport and the prestige that winning or doing well internationally brought to the country; yet, on the other hand, there is evidence of a desire to curb the excesses that tend to go hand in hand with professionalism, particularly exacerbated by the 'natural' striving of workplaces, societies, clubs and individuals to sponsor their own teams by all possible means in order to bring glory and rewards to their own particular association.

The warning signals were hoisted high from the very start. On 27 October 1935 the authoritative newspaper *Krasny sport* warned: 'We are not against prize-giving as such, but we are against abuses and perversions. . . We have definitely established the importance of certificates and medals, and they should be the major, if not the only, proper sports honours and awards.'[14]

Yet, with the putting into operation of the ranking system in 1937 and the call, in the same year, for the formation of select teams in various parts of the country for the new (1936) leagues

[14] *Krasny sport*, 27 October 1935.

in such sports as soccer, boxing, shooting and wrestling, it was, perhaps, inevitable that these sportsmen should be taken out of production and permitted virtually full-time training facilities. Nonetheless, a resolution by the Moscow Committee on Physical Culture and Sports Affairs, issued in January 1937, specifically prohibited payments to athletes. Officially, only coaches, sports officials and other such paid administrators were to make sport their full-time vocation. Yet, despite frequent warnings and the adoption of new regulations to guide sports societies in the distribution of funds, illegal assistance to athletes persisted. Two years later, *Krasny sport* once more condemned the practice: 'Half-trained sportsmen should not receive extra money for fictional "work", they should not receive subsidies and all manner of gifts for success in competition. That is a bourgeois practice that has crept into Soviet sport.'[15]

With so much stress on records and winning, other abuses began to creep in. The pressures for winning sometimes resulted in attempts to win at all costs. In a Division 1 'derby' match in Leningrad on 24 July 1937 between Leningrad *Dinamo* and Moscow *Dinamo*, three Leningrad players were seriously injured and the fans rioted. The match has gone down as one of the roughest in Soviet soccer history. Since then, every major soccer match has had a 'wall' of soldiers ringing the ground between the fans and the pitch. Sports societies not infrequently competed with one another for top talent and even 'bought' and transferred the best players in blatant disregard of the transfer regulations – which do not appear ever to have been rigorously enforced. The authorities did something to punish and prevent the worst abuses. I. I. Kharchenko, then Chairman of the All-Union Committee on Physical Culture and Sports Affairs, roundly condemned the practice: 'In the race for records and best results, several departments use absolutely impermissible means. Buying-up and enticing have somehow become the basic job of sports "entrepreneurs". An athlete only has to give a moderate performance and he becomes an object of buying and selling. Selling goes on all over: in Gor'ky, Voronezh, Rostov and Taganrog.'[16]

Reports in the press confirmed Kharchenko's strictures: 'Sports

[15] Ibid., 5 January 1939.
[16] Ibid., 27 June 1936.

businessmen have appeared from somewhere during the turbulent growth of Soviet sport. In order to enhance their club's prestige, they have replaced hard work in increasing the proficiency and training of first-rate athletes with primitive and quite underhand methods. Why train when you can 'bu ' the finished product? Why create when you can entice? So we have sports societies which have hardly existed for more than a few weeks before they suddenly come up with record breakers, champions and Masters of Sport. This system has spread far and wide. Things have got to such a pitch that you have to pay even the rank-and-file players, the "mini-masters", to remain in the ranks.'[17]

The disputes and abuses attendant upon professionalism everywhere continued and, in 1939, the new Chairman of the All-Union Committee, Vasily Snegov, warned that he would 'severely prosecute all attempts to entice players from other teams'.[18]

Even more than their counterparts in industry, the sports stars began to receive large sums of money, priorities in respect to flats and scarce commodities for establishing records and winning championships. A former Soviet sports official who defected during the war has written that the sportswoman Nina Dumbadze received a special bonus for setting an All-Union record and a 25,000 ruble bonus for breaking the European women's discus record. 'My friends and the former USSR record breakers of the early 1930s, M. Shamanova, G. and S. Znamensky, Dyachkov and Malin lived well on bonuses and rewards from sport alone. Masha Shamanova once received a radiogram as a bonus – then a priceless commodity.'[19]

Seen in its wider context, this was part of a general process of élite-creation in society at a time when the cult of Stalin's personality was at its height. All these practices were largely started in the mid-1930s (and most continue to the present day, although, officially, money prizes were discontinued in the late 1940s before the USSR joined the International Olympic Committee). It would be hard to imagine a system for developing talent in Soviet conditions that would not harbour the danger of abuse.

[17] Ibid., 11 January 1937.
[18] Ibid., 10 October 1939.
[19] F. Legostaev, *Fizicheskoye vospitanie i sport v SSSR* (Munich, 1951), p. 25.

The biggest problem has remained that of keeping a 'reasonable' balance between mass participation and the development of a professional élite.

Facilities for sport and physical culture

One of the circumstances giving rise to the problems mentioned above was that of allocation of the limited available sports facilities among all those who wanted to practice the sports. Although the economic results of the industrialisation programme enabled absolutely more government funds to be allotted to physical culture, the paucity of inherited amenities and the neglect and destruction of the war years meant that it would be a long time before facilities would be adequate to meet even part of the needs of sports enthusiasts. As with other countries that made a late start in industrial development (in contrast to Britain, in which each of the many sports in which she was a pioneer have developed separately, independently and far from simultaneously with the others), the predominant feature of sports facilities became the multi-sport centre.[20]

This was the era of the designing of giant stadiums in the form of vast amphitheatres – e.g. the Kirov Stadium in Leningrad, with seating for 150,000 spectators, the Bagirov Stadium in Baku for 80,000 spectators and the projected Stalin Izmailovsky Stadium in Moscow for 250,000 spectators (which was never built). It is not surprising, however, that the sports with the greatest following tended to be those which required little and unsophisticated equipment. Chess, for example, is available to all ages and sexes, and independent of the weather. All the same, an effort was made to match the increasing demand with some sort of adequate supply. Between 1931 and 1940, the provision of sports facilities roughly quadrupled.

[20] The Russian word *stadion* (stadium) usually denotes a multi-sport centre or complex (e.g. the Lenin 'Stadium' in Luzhniki, Moscow, has facilities for swimming, tennis, basketball, *gorodki*, ice hockey, etc.).

Sports activities

Events and tournaments

The 1930s were the period *par excellence* for competition at all levels – *spartakiads* (from individual farms to All-Union festivals), league and cup competitions, and All-Union championships for a variety of sports. Medals, certificates, banners and special prizes were awarded to factories with the largest number of enrolled sportsmen, to individuals, towns, villages, teams and so on.

Spartakiads and mass events. Sports contests took a number of forms; one of the most important, and one that was to become the basis of all future competitions, was the intra- and inter-workplace *spartakiad*. The biggest such sports festivals were the Urals–Kuzbas *Spartakiad* of 1932, held in Sverdlovsk and dedicated to the commissioning of the first stage of the Urals–Kuzbas Combine, the Trade Union Summer *Spartakiad* of 1932, held in Leningrad, and the *Spartakiad* of Students in Heavy Industry Colleges, held in Moscow in 1934.

The now traditional May Day sports display in the Red Square was first held in 1931; in that year, it involved some 40,000 participants, in the next year – 70,000, and in the next – 105,000; concurrently, in Leningrad, some 96,000 athletes of all ages marched through the city in 1933. Sports parades, marathons and displays in the streets and squares of large cities were becoming increasingly common as a means of advertising sport, encouraging emulation and civic pride. As just one example, in 1936, a green fibre carpet was rolled across part of the Red Square, and a soccer match played between two Moscow *Spartak* teams. On 16 July 1939, the government decreed that 18 July was to be 'Physical Culturist's Day'. After that year, the Day was marked annually on the second Saturday in August (when, traditionally, such big occasions as the Football Cup Final or opening of the *Spartakiad* of the Peoples of the USSR take place).

In athletics, inter-city tournaments became common, as did mass district or town cross country runs in which whole families were urged to take part. Some 1,500 people, for instance, took part in the Voroshilov Cross Country Run in Moscow in 1930 and 3,000 in a similar run at Krasnoye Selo near Leningrad.

Marathons took place through the streets of Moscow – e.g. the annual *bul'varka* (a run round the inner-ring road, then known as the *Bul'varnoye kol'tso* – now the *Sadovoye kol'tso*) became a popular festive event for spectators and runners alike. Newspapers began to sponsor events that have since become traditional – e.g. the evening *Vechernyaya Moskva* sponsored an annual marathon and ice hockey tourney, the Moscow *Moskovskaya pravda* – a road cycle race, and *Pravda* – an international marathon race.

Gymnastics. Gymnastics came into its own in the middle of the decade: by 1940, it was fourth among sports in registered number of participants for both sexes.[21] It received official encouragement at the First All-Union Conference on Gymnastics in 1933, which resolved to make gymnastics the basis both of the whole sports movement and of physical education in primary, secondary and higher schools. The working man and woman were constantly urged to acquire the dignity, grace, deportment and bodily grandeur worthy of the free citizen of the first workers' state. Gymnastics was to be used, too, as a cultural medium to draw athletes into the orbit of a culture which was a novelty to the vast majority of them; thus, gymnastics was often linked with the ballet and other forms of cultural expression. The aesthetic value of human movements engendered in gymnastics was, it was urged, synonymous with that which emanates from art at its best; a new and dynamic cultural force was presented as emerging through the symbolic media of gymnastics, calisthenics, the dance, mass formation displays (as in the *spartakiads*) and other sporting activities. It was argued that both sport and art were means of modifying and enriching man's experiences, and that gymnastics enabled a person to discover and develop in himself cultural resources that had lain dormant.

[21] How far popularity of a sport, like gymnastics or chess, was autonomous is uncertain. What is certain is that the extent of the practice of a sport was greatly determined by the Party, which effectively controlled all the mass media, the organisation of sport and provision of facilities. That is not to say that non-approved but genuinely popular sports and pastimes were outlawed; horse racing, cards and dominoes, for example, were tolerated (and, in the case of horse racing, even encouraged) by a government willing at least temporarily to bow to popular demand for the sake of not prejudicing the attainment of pressing short-term economic goals.

Volleyball, soccer, rugby and skiing. The most popular team sport of the decade was *volleyball*, a game that required few facilities (virtually all courts were outdoor) and which both men and women could play. Soccer continued to be the most popular spectator sport in summer.[22] The number of teams increased rapidly. In 1931, for example, as many as 124 soccer clubs with over 400 teams and 5,000–6,000 players registered for the Leningrad championships – almost as many teams and players as in the whole of the Russian Empire in 1914. By 1939, as many as 2,000 teams entered for the cup competition (established three years before). The next year, a record total of 2,150 teams entered the qualifying cup rounds.

Attempts were made to popularise other organised team sports, sometimes capitalising on similar national folk games, but not always with much success. Rugby, for instance, was introduced into several secondary schools and colleges in 1926, and again in 1932. It was not until 1934, however, that two teams were assembled in Moscow for exhibition matches. In October 1935, the first inter-city rugby tournament took place between Moscow and Minsk (which the former won 6–0). Two years later, an unofficial All-Union championship was played with the two best Moscow teams competing against a team from Minsk and one from Gor'ky. However, facilities were rather primitive and the game did not attain sufficient popular support at the time to warrant the authorities continuing their efforts to implant it in the Soviet Union. It was not until the late 1950s that Soviet teams once more began to be formed.

In winter, skiing was the obvious favourite. Some 800 skiers competed for the trade union championships in 1938, and, to celebrate the twenty-third anniversary of the Red Army, 120,000 competitors took part in a cross-country ski run in the winter of 1940–1941.

[22] Women also took up soccer (and ice hockey); there were enough women's teams to form a women's league in 1940. This did not, however, survive the war. Grass hockey was another sport that women played, the first All-Union women's championships being won by the *Komsomol* team in 1935. (*Sport v SSSR*, 1970, No. 8, p. 31.)

Sports and military preparedness

The association between several sports and the armed forces was patently obvious during the 1930s, especially in the immediate pre-war years. In October 1929, the Revolutionary Military Council of the USSR issued an order that obliged every serviceman to make sport an important part of his training. 'The skill of a sniper, machine-gunner, scout, signaller, engineer, diver and flyer depends equally on his special technical and his physical training.' It demanded that servicemen should 'pursue a sport regularly and that the Red Army should become a mass school of physical education'.[23] Outside the army, an army reserve was unofficially forming around paramilitary sports groups, mostly under the patronage of the Central House of the Red Army (*TsDKA*) and the civil defence organisation *Osoaviakhim*. The latter had, in 1930, more than 15,000 rifle circles with over 4,000 shooting ranges at their disposal; these were important because 'the training of snipers began in these circles; they were later to distinguish themselves in battles at Khasan and Khalkhin-Gol, and in the Finnish–Soviet conflict.[24] Rifle and sniping contests were held between Moscow and Leningrad.'[25]

The *GTO* system is, as its name implies, of special relevance to the army, since it embodies a national fitness programme that includes such direct military training as tossing a hand grenade and rifle shooting. As mentioned above, the first people to obtain *GTO* 2 badges were twelve students and officers at the Frunze Military Academy – who received special mention in an order of the High Command (10 May 1934) as citizens who 'set an example to the entire personnel of the Red Army'.[26] By January 1935, 85 per cent of all servicemen were said to have passed their *GTO* 1 tests.

Some sports were completely dominated by the army which, in some cases, had a monopoly of the facilities. Parachute jumping,

[23] Chudinov, *Osnovnye postanovleniya*, p. 117.
[24] The battles around Lake Khasan in the Soviet Far East and the Khalkhin–Gol River in Mongolia were against the Japanese in 1938 and 1939; the Soviet–Finnish war lasted throughout the winter of 1939–1940.
[25] N. P. Korol'kov, *Sport i zashchita rodiny* (Moscow, 1969), p. 15.
[26] Ibid., p. 17.

gliding, mountain climbing, horse riding, fencing, shooting and skiing all had an exceptionally large proportion of servicemen-practitioners. In 1933, for example, three soldiers, led by Ivan Lukin, commander of a detachment in the Turkestan military district, scaled the highest Soviet mountain (for the first time) – Stalin Peak (formerly Garmo Peak and, latterly, Communism Peak) in the Pamirs, which is 7,495 metres (24,590 feet) high. Three years later, another army group made the first winter crossing of the Pamirs (410 kilometres – at a temperature of –45°C). Army teams won the All-Union weightlifting, skiing and ice hockey championships in 1939. In just a few years, this sports training was to have vital application in World War II – in which, it was claimed, 'sportsmen were the heart of the ski units'.[27]

Among combat sports, fencing, wrestling and boxing were popular, the first securing a high place in number of participants because it had both male and female adherents and was particularly encouraged by the armed forces. A new unarmed combat sport was introduced in 1938 by order of the All-Union Committee on Physical Culture and Sports Affairs. It was called *sambo* – an abbreviation of the Russian *samozashchita bez oruzhiya* (self-defence without weapons) and was based partly on ju-jitsu and partly on various national styles of wrestling. Unarmed combat had long been popular both in the army and *Dinamo* clubs and had been included in the *GTO* 2 programme in 1932. It was not until 1938, however, that official rules were published and All-Union *sambo* championships established.[28]

---

[27] Ibid., p. 20. Writing in 1936, the former organiser of the Red Army and current exile, Lev Trotsky, emphasised the important part various paramilitary sports had played within the army and the population as a whole: 'All sorts of athletic sports developed tumultuously in the army and around it. Among the workers, officials and students, the badge of distinction for marksmanship enjoyed great popularity. In the winter months, skis gave the regiments a hitherto unknown mobility. Startling successes were achieved in the sphere of parachute jumping, gliding and aviation. The arctic flights and flights into the stratosphere are known to everybody. These high points speak for a whole mountain chain of achievements.' L. Trotsky, *The Revolution Betrayed* (Faber and Faber, London, 1937), p. 195. Trotsky here is evidently harking back to the 'good old days' of the Soviet 'workers' state' and the organisation (the Red Army) essentially created by himself.

[28] I suspect that this 'new' sport was, in fact, a form of judo which was

Horse racing came back into official favour; the various race-courses ('hippodromes') were re-opened or returned to their original horse racing purposes, and new All-Union races were held in 1938. It had, of course, been repressed during the 1920s because it had been regarded as encouraging the vice of gambling and passive spectatorship. Now, with the accent on spectacle and pageantry, horse racing was re-admitted into the fold of tolerated, if not fervently encouraged, sports – along with state facilities for totalisator betting and programmes that gave the horses' form and betting odds. Horse racing had, too, a military usefulness, most of the stud farms being run by the army; that probably influenced the official encouragement of the sport in view of the deteriorating international situation.

Motor cycling and motor racing were held back by the lack of production of racing cars and motorcycles. The All-Union Committee had taken over motor racing and set up the USSR Motor Sports Club in 1935, which inaugurated All-Union rallies. It also ordered the manufacture in 1938–1939 of the first prototypes of Soviet sports and racing cars; previously, sports drivers had adapted saloon cars or used foreign racing cars. Nevertheless, the sports administration came in for criticism for their alleged neglect of these sports, which were regarded as important for the country's defence. Kharchenko admitted that the 30 existing motor car clubs were inefficient and had trained only 6,000 drivers in the whole of 1936. He promised that steps would be taken forthwith to remedy the situation, one of which was to make the driving test obligatory, from 1 May 1937, for all candidates for the *GTO* 2 test. Criticism continued, however, and opened the way to all manner of other accusations which may have contributed to Kharchenko's downfall in July 1937 (alternatively, it may be, of course, that the impending downfall evoked the criticisms). It was not until after the war that both sports were to develop at all widely.

Chess was, according to figures on participation by sport in 1940, the most 'popular' sport, or at least the one with most registered players. Other figures bear out the popularity of the game: in 1936, the enormous total of 700,000 people are said to

disguised in view of judo's association with a foreign militaristic philosophy.

have played at some stage in the trade union championships and, in 1940, the country had a total of 950,000 registered chess players. Soviet chess masters were good enough to compete against 'bourgeois' masters, and the Party gave permission for the leading Soviet player, Botvinnik, to compete in several foreign tournaments after 1933.

Achievements: peak prewar performances

How high Soviet standards were generally at this time is not easy to judge, since Soviet sportsmen did not compete in many 'bourgeois' international events (like the 1936 Olympic Games held in Berlin) and were not members of any international federations or committees.[29] It is the Soviet claim, however, that a number of athletes were of world class and that several Soviet records surpassed existing world records; they were not, of course, ratified by world sports bodies, since the Soviet Union was not a party to these organisations.

One source asserts that, as far back as 1934, six world marks had been improved on – in weightlifting, swimming and speed skating. In athletics, between 1938 and 1940, it was estimated that 'Soviet women athletes were overall in second place, and the men in fourth place in unofficial world rankings'.[30] Nina Dumbadze from Georgia threw the discus 49 m 54 cm – a world record; Nikolai Ozolin pole vaulted 4 m 30 cm, V. Alekseyev threw the javelin 69 m 65 cm – all then European records. In the field events, two other Soviet women achieved results very close to official world records: K. Lapteva threw 45 m 38 cm in the javelin, and T. Sevrukova – 19 m 54 cm in the shot. Altogether, by 1 January 1939, as many as 44 unofficial world records were said to have been set – over half of them (23), significantly, in

[29] It has been asserted (by Legostaev, *Fizicheskoye vospitanie*, p. 28) that Soviet participation in bourgeois sport, after being discussed, was rejected in 1939. Nevertheless, gold rubles are said to have been released for subscription to foreign sports magazines; a Soviet magazine, *Sport za rubezhom* (*Sport Abroad*) began publication in 1939 (with a circulation of only 1,000 copies). Despite it being reserved 'for special use only', it did not survive beyond the fifth issue.

[30] I. A. Tarabrin (ed.), *Pyat'desyat shagov sportivnoi Rossii* (Moscow, 1967), p. 178.

weightlifting; the remainder were in shooting (9), athletics (9), swimming (2) and in speed skating (1).[31]

There is little doubt that standards were rising quite rapidly and that the rankings system and the decision to train a group of what were effectively professionals had largely been instrumental in bringing this about. Given a different international climate, the USSR might well have tested its strength against the world's top sporting nations before the war.

It was on the base of mass participation that the outstanding achievements were said to have been obtained. By 1940, the sports movement had grown to 5,332,400 sportsmen (from 759,000 in 1929 and 4,700,000 in 1934), the bulk of whom were members of primary sports collectives.[32]

In the national republics, sport was, as we have pointed out, a means of creating and encouraging a sense of Soviet national identity and unity. Although standard organised sports, team games and gymnastics were encouraged in the non-Russian republics, there was also a concerted attempt – in line with the then general cultural and educational policy of developing ethnic cultures within a Soviet framework – to sustain and organise a number of national games. But not all. The Soviet sports movement, like all aspects of culture, was to be 'national in form and socialist in content'. It was to include 'only those types of national sport which can enrich the already existing physical culture'.[33]

Physical education

Schools

This was a period in which significant changes took place in the schools and in the provisions for the training of physical educa-

[31] F. I. Samoukov (ed.), *Istoriya fizicheskoi kul'tury* (Moscow, 1956), p. 300. The director of the Museum of the History of Physical Culture and Sport of the USSR at the Lenin Stadium, Zoya Romanova, herself a former vice-chairman of the All-Union Committee, told me that Soviet athletes had by 1940 established 49 unofficial world records.

[32] Compiled from statistics provided in *Malaya sovetskaya entsiklopediya*, Vol. VIII (3rd edition) (Moscow, 1960), p. 838, and Samoukov, *Istoriya fizicheskoi kul'tury*, p. 306.

[33] V. I. Elashvili, *Znachenie etnograficheskikh materialov po narodnomu sportu* (Moscow, 1964), pp. 7–8.

tionalists. After the decision to create a fully centralised school system in 1931, a set of new syllabuses for all subjects came into force on 1 January 1932 which was to operate in a uniform curriculum throughout the comprehensive school system. A new physical education programme was therefore issued – influenced considerably by the introduction of the *BGTO* system in that year and by two Party resolutions: the first 'On Primary and Secondary Schools' passed on 5 September 1931, and the second 'On Curricula and Timetables in the Primary and Secondary School' passed on 25 August 1932. In these resolutions, the Central Committee of the Party strongly attacked the 'complex' ('project') method of combining individual subjects in the school curriculum.

New physical education curricula. The new physical education syllabus laid down the guidelines for every physical education lesson, which was to be distinct from lessons in other school subjects proper. Like its predecessor, the new physical education syllabus stressed the health side of physical education, but added two new elements: elementary knowledge of (1) sports theory and (2) first-aid. As before, no specific sports were mentioned by name, nor was gymnastics recommended. Instead, the syllabus described the motor skills that were to be developed – walking, running, swimming, balancing, climbing, jumping, throwing, combat exercises and dancing, along with some theoretical knowledge of hygiene and sports. Children were to be trained to pass their standards for the *BGTO* test. They had to meet one standard in form 1 (at the age of seven), two in form 2, 8 in form 3 and 9 in forms 4–7. The time allotted to physical education was to be two-and-a-half hours in forms 1–4 and three hours in forms 5–10, spread over the then 10-day school 'week'.

With the encouragement of competition and organised sports in the country at large, the physical education syllabus was formalised in the second half of the 1930s in order to incorporate intra-school competition. In the new syllabus set for 1937, gymnastics was included for the first time and made the basis of the physical education lesson: exercises were prescribed, using the rings, parallel bars, horse and horizontal bars; some elements of acrobatics were also recommended. No longer was the material classified according to basic motor movements, but now according to specific formal sports: gymnastics, athletics, skiing, team games, swimming, and so on. The time devoted to physical education was, however, reduced to one hour per week for all classes, with no time allowed separately for games – as a concomitant of the growing stress on formal academic lessons.

With war clouds gathering, another syllabus was introduced in 1940 which inserted military training (drilling, hand-to-hand fighting, etc.) into the curriculum for the senior forms. Furthermore, schools were instructed that, besides giving children an all-round introduction to a wide range of sports, they were to encourage them to pursue one sport in particular, which was to be an optional choice for each school. Although this demand fitted in well with the trend in sport in the country as a whole, it was, of course, wishful thinking to imagine that a physical education instructor could attain much in the way of specialist training in just one hour a week.

Sports amenities. What most prevented the new syllabuses from being effective was the inadequacy of resources to realise the aims: the simple fact was that the vast majority of schools had neither sports facilities nor trained instructors. Only one school in 235, for example, had a gymnasium, and only one in 346 had any kind of playing field for its use.[34] More importantly, few schools had a qualified physical education instructor. Even if all the qualified physical education instructors *had* worked in schools, there would still not have been enough for every two-hundredth school to have one. In fact, nearly all worked in sports collectives and trade union sports societies. Given the dearth of equipment and instructors, the stress had had to be put on extra-curricular children's activities. On 21 April 1932, the Party had issued a decree 'On the Work of the Young Pioneer Organisation' in which it stressed the responsibility of the Pioneers for providing sporting facilities and contests. Since virtually all children of school age were members of the Young Pioneer organisation, it may be assumed that many children had an opportunity to pursue sports activity with the Pioneers. Further, a number of sports societies set up junior sections and permitted their junior members to use club equipment; it should be recalled, too, that any society member had the right to bring members of his family into the

[34] *Fizicheskaya kul'tura v shkole*, 1967, No. 10, p. 23.

society. Thus, the *Dinamo* Society created a Junior *Dinamo* section ('*Yuny Dinamovets*') and *Spartak* – a Junior *Spartak* section ('*Yuny Spartak*'). Where individual sports were organised, it was common to arrange children's teams (for soccer, volleyball, athletics, swimming and rowing) alongside the adult. In some towns, special children's clubs (called 'sports schools' – *detskie sportivnye shkoly*) were instituted for the most promising junior athletes; the children would attend the clubs after the day's schooling. By 1939, there were 300 such schools and one-and-a-half million children were said to have passed their *BGTO* test.

Physical culture institutes

The situation with regard to facilities and clubs was somewhat better in higher educational institutions. Inter-collegiate competitions helped to fire students' sports enthusiasm, and all students were exhorted to acquire their *GTO* badge.

Meanwhile, three new physical culture institutes were set up with higher educational status – in Tbilisi, Kiev and Stalingrad. Departments of physical education were opened in teacher training colleges, and special research institutes were founded in Tbilisi and Leningrad (1931), Moscow (1932) and Khar′kov (1934) – joining the already established Lesgaft Institute of Physical Culture in Leningrad, the Frunze Military Academy and the Stalin Central State Institute of Physical Culture (nowadays the Central State Order of Lenin Institute of Physical Culture) in Moscow.

Production gymnastics

One of the major areas of research engaged in by the above mentioned institutes was physical culture and production – i.e. how to utilise physical exercise rationally to improve productivity, cut down absenteeism through sickness and injury, reduce fatigue and spread hygienic habits among the millions of new workers who only recently had lived in bug-infested wooden cottages in the villages.

In the early years of Soviet power, a council[35] had been set up

[35] The Council for the Scientific Organisation of Labour (*SovNOT*) was formed in September 1923 by order of the USSR Council of People's Commissars.

to conduct research into the 'Scientific Organisation of Labour' (*'Nauchnaya organizatsiya truda'* – *NOT*) which, though not mainly concerned with recreation, did investigate the part 'active rest' and exercise might play at workplaces. The implications of physical recreation for higher productivity had been emphasised by pre-revolutionary scientists like Lesgaft and Sechyonov, whose work now received much wider publicity. Further, in 1925, the Party pronouncement on the rôle of sport in socialist society had spread the limits wide: 'Physical culture should not be confined merely to physical exercises in the form of sport, gymnastics, motor activities and so on; it should embrace both the public and personal hygiene of work and everyday life, the use of the forces of nature, and a proper régime of work and leisure.'[36]

With the start of full-scale industrialisation, attempts were made to employ physical culture and sport for directly utilitarian purposes, to link physical culture with factory work to the benefit of the latter. On 5 February 1931, the People's Commissar of Labour issued a decree calling on all organisations and enterprises throughout the country to introduce physical exercises at workplaces 'as a measure to make labour and everyday life healthier, to combat industrial disease and to raise productivity. The implementation of this measure should be planned separately for various branches of industry and for enterprises of various branches.'[37]

As a result, experiments were begun to observe closely the results of various methods of incorporating physical education into production. The All-Union Physical Culture Council created a special commission to study the effects of physical exercises on work and the Moscow and Leningrad Physical Culture Institutes were put in charge of the research; they, in turn, set up special 'Production Faculties' to specialise exclusively in this work. They carried out surveys first at 27 undertakings (in 1932) and then at 100 more (in 1932–1934) with the participation of some 70,000 employees. The experiment appears to have been a success: it was claimed that 'production gymnastics' not only improved efficiently, but reduced the incidence of industrial disease and waste. Labour productivity at the Leningrad factory *Skorokhod* was up by 6.2 per cent, at the Moscow *Krasny Treugolnik* by 2.8 per

[36] *Izvestiya Tsentral'novo Komiteta RKP (b)*, 20 July 1925.
[37] *Pravda*, 5 February 1931.

cent, at *Tryokhgornaya Manufaktura* by 2.1 per cent, at the
Anisimov Weaving Mill by 4.3 per cent, and at the Khar'kov
Tractor Plant by 6.3 per cent. In a leader, *Pravda* wrote: 'It has
been proved in practice what an enormous benefit physical culture
can be in improving productivity and in implementing cultured
methods of work in production.'[38]

Despite the apparent success, the idea was not taken up at once
(it was only after the war that physical exercises at all enterprises
were again to be officially recommended). One reason for the lack
of response was that factory managements had often proved
hostile to the recommendations of the zealous research brigades –
which they viewed as a threat to the vital task of fulfilling the
plan. When every minute counted in working towards the set
targets, time taken out for physical exercise was regarded as time
wasted. Workers, too, did not always take kindly to the idea of
an invigorating exercise session in the middle of their already
exhausting labour – particularly if it interfered with their chance
of earning a bonus. In many cases, the physical education break
was dropped as soon as the research brigade moved on.

Summary

With the embarking of the USSR on a course of rapid industrialisation, the pattern of sport for the new society began to take
shape. By the end of the 1930s, the basic organisational pattern
had already been set – with its sports societies, primary sports
collectives, sports schools, formal physical education syllabus,
GTO programmes, and uniform ranking system. The Soviet
society of the 1930s differed from that of the preceding period in
seeing the flourishing of all manner of competitive sports (soccer,
basketball, volleyball) with mass spectator appeal and the official
encouragement of leagues, stadiums, cups, championships, popularity polls, cults of sporting heroes – all the appendages of a
sub-system consciously designed to provide general recreation for
the fast-growing urban populace.

One of the most profound social consequences of industrialisation was the very rapid shift of people from country to town.[39]

[38] Ibid., 24 July 1934.
[39] It has been calculated that a shift of labour comparable to that which

Millions of people, uprooted from centuries-old traditions, were pitched into new and strange environments and found themselves building vast ironworks and blast furnaces in previously un-inhabited wastes like Magnitogorsk, oil refineries and pipelines in the Caucasus or railways across the deserts of Turkestan, working on the new collective farms – or in labour camps in Siberia. This social upheaval was bound to have a reflection in the nature of and requirements for sporting activity. Besides pouring into factories, the newcomers to industry joined factory clubs and looked to them for the recreation they had previously enjoyed in an open-air rural setting. Since urban living conditions were spartan and deteriorating,[40] sports served many townsmen as an escape from the drudgery of their domestic and work environ-ments.

The integrating functions of sport for a new urban community took on an altogether new dimension after 1928. The authorities based most sports clubs directly on the workplace and gave full rein to 'professional' teams representing factories or trade unions with which the workers could identify themselves. The state also provided sports amphitheatres in the fast-growing towns which, by their titanic scale, their architectural forcefulness and national décor, furthered a sense of grandeur, excitement and mass unity that, coupled with the spectacle presented, could evoke feelings among participants and spectators of civic pride and patriotism. At the same time, not unlike the Olympic Games of ancient Greece, the circuses of ancient Rome, the bullfighting and other festivals in the giant bowl-like stadiums of Spain and Latin America (or even the exotically-named and styled picture theatres

took place in the USSR in the twelve years between 1928 and 1940 had taken from thirty to fifty years in the countries of Western Europe and North America that had industrialised earlier. See C. E. Black, 'Soviet Society: A Comparative View', in A. Kassof (ed.), *Prospects for Soviet Society* (Praeger, New York, 1968), p. 32. The transformation of the population is reflected in the rapid annual rate of increase in the popula-tion of cities of over 50,000. Moscow, for example, increased in popula-tion from just over one million in 1920 to over two million in 1926, nearly three million in 1931 and over four million in 1939, *Moskva: arkhitekturny putevoditel'* (Moscow, 1960), p. 6.

[40] In 1926, the average housing space per person had only been 8.2 and, by 1940 it was down to about 6.4 square metres. *Narodnoye khozyaistvo SSSR v 1970g.*, 'Statistika' (Moscow, 1971), pp. 7, 546.

of Britain), these helped distract the masses from the hard and exacting life beyond the stadiums. The many sports parades and pageants which constituted a background to the sporting competitions of the 1930s were intended, too, to create and reinforce this group feeling and demonstrate to people (abroad as well as at home) how happy and carefree life was under socialism in the USSR – 'under the sun of the Stalin Constitution', as it was said after 1936. It is significant that physical culture rallies often accompanied major political events or festivals (May Day, Constitution Day and the Anniversary of the October Revolution). In this way, sport became a means of linking members of the public with politics, the Party and, of course, Stalin (his portrait, in hundreds of copies, deputising for his person – since he preferred to cultivate the image of himself as a remote godhead).

At a time when, it seemed, everything was devoted to industrialisation, sport had the utilitarian function of furthering, directly and indirectly, the success of the economic plan, of helping to raise labour productivity by encouraging in the new, recently peasant, labour force the cultivation of such characteristics as cleanliness, sobriety, punctuality, resourcefulness, discipline, collectivism, efficiency and patriotism. Physical exercise and sport, therefore, received attention mostly because of their interdependence with work. Specialised work in the factory or on the construction site was a far cry from that on the land or in handicraft production. Whatever the effectiveness of using sport and physical exercise to develop desired moral and physical qualities may actually be, there can be no doubt that the Soviet authorities believed in it and encouraged it with precisely these aims in mind: hence the *GTO*-based national fitness campaign and the attempts to introduce daily physical exercises or 'production-exercises' directly into the workplace – and into the home, by means of daily radio physical education broadcasts (begun in 1929).

Sport became, in effect, professionalised. Athletes were enjoined to treat their performance as part of their plan-fulfilment. Excellence in sport became the equivalent of the achievements of the shock-worker in industry and a reinforcing example of endeavour to the rank-and-file. This had two purposes. At home, the proficient athlete was to inspire emulation from the mass of workers and engender local pride among spectators. Its international significance sprang partly from the implications of Stalin's doctrine of the possibility of building socialism in one country – a doctrine that revived in a new form the whole cult of Russian messianism: backward Russian would lead the world; Moscow – the third Rome. Skilled athletes possibly capable of world-class performance were encouraged and given every inducement to perfect their skills – even though they still had few opportunities to compete against 'bourgeois' sportsmen.

A relatively close link was re-established between sport and the military. It stemmed partly from the leaders' conviction of the need for a state surrounded by unfriendly powers with a different social and political system to be strong militarily and constantly on the alert. This conviction became widespread in the 'besieged fortress' atmosphere of the 1930s, encouraged in part by the rise of fascism in Europe and by the deliberate playing up of the danger from without (and from the 'enemy agents' within) to justify the hardships and sacrifice which the intensive industrialisation campaign entailed. Sport openly became a means of providing pre-military training and achieving a relatively high standard of national fitness for defence. Several sports with potential military applications – e.g. skiing, shooting, gliding and mountain climbing – came to be dominated by servicemen. The two largest and most successful sports clubs in the country were those run by the army and the security forces, the Central House of the Red Army (*TsDKA*) and *Dinamo*. And, after 1931, the 'Ready for Labour and Defence' sports system was expressly intended to train people, through sport, for work and military preparedness.

A comparison between the USSR and Nazi Germany in the 1930s, between the Stalin and Hitler dictatorships in their manipulation of sport for military purposes is tempting (for both régimes displayed certain similar attitudes towards sport) and to some extent instructive: the flag-brandishing sporting parades and displays with distinctly military overtones, the use of sports events for explicit political purposes (the delivery of political speeches), central direction and control of sport, national fitness campaigns closely allied to military and patriotic aims and the dream of a disciplined athletic youth movement. But there are dangers in the comparison: the Soviet use of sport for military purposes was explicitly (as in the title of the 'Ready for Labour and Defence' system) and actually *defence* of the motherland, while the German was explicitly *aggressive* and linked to territorial aggrandisement through military conquest.[41] The main Soviet emphasis in sport was on the training of better workers (rather than better soldiers); the priority was labour first, defence second in the *GTO* system. The Soviet leaders were dealing with a still predominantly rural population and were concerned with transforming a relatively raw labour force in the throes of a gigantic industrialisation campaign.

[41] Adolf Hitler wrote, 'Give the German nation six million bodies with flawless athletic training, all glowing with fanatical love of their country and inculcated with the highest offensive spirit, and in less than two years if necessary a national state will have created an army.' A. Hitler, *Mein Kampf* (London, 1969), p. 497.

6

World War II, 1941–1945: the supreme test of physical training

Background

The Soviet involvement in World War II lasted from June 1941 to August 1945.[1] Hitler's armies had struck deep into the country to the very outskirts of Moscow and Leningrad, to the Volga and the Caucasus, before they were finally driven out. They left behind them great areas of devastation in the west of the country, including most of the Ukraine and much of European Russia. Loss of life was officially estimated at over 20 millions. Material damage was extensive – 17,000 towns, 70,000 villages, 31,000 factories, 84,000 schools and 40,000 miles of railway track. In reporting six years after the war, at the 19th Party Congress, Malenkov was to state that 'the war retarded our industrial development for eight or nine years, that is, approximately two five-year plans'.[2]

The war was a critical test of the principles that lay behind the 'Ready for Labour and Defence' sports system and, to some extent, of the utilitarian functions which sport had been assigned during the 1930s. The war brought home to many people that sport and physical fitness did actually perform a social function that far exceeded in significance the subjective satisfaction they had gained from it at the time. The cross country running, skiing, hurdling, shooting, combat sports and grenade throwing all now proved highly relevant both to soldiers at the battlefront and to partisans behind enemy lines. It is, of course, impossible to measure the contribution made by the mass sports movement to

[1] For a detailed treatment of this period, see A. Werth, *Russia at War, 1941–1945* (Pan, 1964).
[2] G. Malenkov, *Report to the Nineteenth Party Congress* (*FLPH*, Moscow, 1952), p. 52.

preparing Soviet people for their war effort. There is no doubt, however, that it was useful to have reserves of people who were physically fit, who could endure long months of fatigue, thirst and hunger, and who had been trained in the sort of discipline and moral qualities valuable in war. As Marshal Konev, Commander of the Second Ukrainian Front, wrote in a letter to the editorial board of *Fizkul'tura i sport* in the first months of the war:

Only physically fit people can stand the strain of heavy fighting, can march long distances under perpetual bombardment and quite often have to start fighting at the end of a long march. We owe it primarily to the sports organisations that Soviet people were trained and had imparted to them such qualities as courage, persistence, will power, endurance and patriotism. The soldier needs such qualities in the war we are fighting. The same qualities will be very much needed in peacetime, too.[3]

The war reinforced a patriotism that was to inspire the performance of Soviet athletes abroad for many years to come and which, indeed, to a large extent, had its real origins in the 'Great Patriotic War' – as the Soviet leaders significantly called their part of World War II. This particularly Soviet brand of patriotism was later to be rather awkwardly but poignantly recalled in this account by the twice Olympic sculling champion Yuri Tyukalov:

I am reminded [by J. V. Stalin] of the legend of Anteus who became invincible once he touched the soil of his motherland. . . I recall the 1952 Olympics and the sculling race. Everyone thought that the Australian, Wood, was bound to win the single sculls. Yet I beat him. My 'swallow' flew towards the finishing line as if on wings, and Wood could do nothing about it. And yet, in theory, he should have won.

Back in February 1942, Wood was living in Australia, and I was living under the Leningrad blockade. Wood probably had eggs and bacon for breakfast washed down with orange juice; my mother and I received 125 grammes of bread a day. In February 1942, Wood was relaxing in the sun. At any rate, he didn't have bombs falling all around him or shells smashing his house to smithereens. When he woke up every morning, he didn't have the worry of whether he would live to see the evening. He had it 'O.K.'. In that same

[3] *Fizkul'tura i sport*, 1941, No. 12, p. 2.

February, in our room, my uncle's corpse lay on the table, and those of my dead aunt and cousin on the bed. We didn't have the strength to take them out and bury them. Our windows had been blown out by a blast and the flat was freezing cold. I don't know how we managed to survive. . . But my father somehow smuggled some mutton to my mother and me. It saved us.

I mean no offence to Wood. He is a fine sportsman. I make the comparison with one aim in mind: to show that succulent steaks and a comfortable life are not the only recipe for victory. Patriotism is also needed. For me, a Soviet sportsman and citizen of Leningrad, it was incomparably higher than for Wood. And that is the reason I won.[4]

The story is *simpliste*, but it does contain a clue to the sort of patriotic motivation behind Soviet participation in sport both at home and abroad to which the war undoubtedly contributed.

The reformation of Vsevobuch

The entire sports movement was put on a war footing from June 1941. *Vsevobuch* was resurrected and attached to the People's Commissariat of Defence; all the sports committees, societies, collectives, government sports departments and physical culture institutes were subordinated to it. Sports programmes and physical education in schools were switched over to the acquisition of military skills. Students and lecturers (316 of them) of the Lesgaft Institute, for example, formed 13 partisan detachments which were active behind the lines in German-occupied territory – for which the Institute was awarded, in 1944, the Order of the Red Banner. When a special services independent motorised task-force (*Otdel'naya motostrelkovaya brigada osobovo naznacheniya – OMSBON*) was set up in June 1941, the Stalin Central State Institute of Physical Culture in Moscow was approached for its lecturers and students to form the core of its brigade of skiers, drivers, marksmen and flyers. The Institute was evacuated to Sverdlovsk in the Urals and there trained skiers, drivers, swimmers, grenade throwers and specialists in armed and unarmed combat.

In September 1941, the All-Union Committee on Physical Culture and Sports Affairs decreed that 'the implementation of

[4] N. P. Korol'kov, *Sport i zashchita rodiny* (Moscow, 1969), pp. 21–22.

the Law on universal military training for all citizens capable of handling a weapon requires all physical culture organisations to make a really big effort to step up physical training'.[5] As a result, over 13,000 skiing instructors were given 'crash' training courses during one winter, 1941–1942, in Siberia, the Urals and other areas. In Kazakhstan, more than 31,000 became instructors in hand-to-hand fighting and paramilitary sports.

Contests during hostilities

In order to boost morale, sports contests continued despite the desperate situation. As a retort to those who thought the Soviet Union was on its knees, Feodosy Vanin is said to have set a new (unofficial) world record for the marathon (20 km) on 23 September 1942. In the same year, some five-and-a-half million people are said to have taken part in ski races and cross country runs organised jointly by the *Komsomol* and the trade unions; the number increased to over seven million in 1944; altogether, some 30 million people are said to have taken part in such races during the war. The All-Union athletics championships that had begun in 1936, though interrupted in 1941 and 1942, were resumed in the town of Gor'ky in 1943. As an example of a morale-boosting sports event, on 6 May 1942, a soccer match took place in Leningrad between *Dinamo* and a Leningrad Garrison team; a commentary on the match was broadcast throughout the Soviet Union and all along the battlefront. 'Despite the bombardment and shell explosions around the stadium, the match continued to the end in the presence of a large number of spectators.'[6] Two further matches took place, on 31 May and 7 June, between *Dinamo* and a Nevsky Factory team. A *'Blitz-Turnir'* was held on 11 October between Leningrad Garrison 'A' and 'B' teams and a student team (the Garrison 'A' team, despite drawing in the Final, won the tourney by winning an 11 x 100 metre relay race, held prior to the match). In 1943, Moscow held Soviet speed

[5] I. D. Chudinov (ed.), *Osnovnye postanovleniya, prikazy i instruktsii po voprosam fizicheskoi kul'tury i sporta, 1917–1957* (Moscow, 1959), p. 175.
[6] *Fizkul'tura i sport*, 1970, No. 5, p. 16. A former English sailor, Len Wincott, then living in Leningrad, who witnessed the match told me that about ten thousand spectators were present.

skating championships in February, Sverdlovsk – skiing championships, with 140 participants in March, Chelyabinsk – fencing,
combat sport and shooting championships in September, Gor'ky
– wrestling championships in November (after a 3-year lapse)
and boxing championships in December.

The *GTO* system underwent a change of orientation so as to
encourage purely military training; in 1942, by order of the
All-Union Committee, it was to include 'a knowledge of topo-
graphy, first-aid, rifle handling, running and jumping in full
dress, river crossing, bayonet drill and hand grenade tossing from
a prone position'.[7]

In education, the People's Commissariat of Education of the
Russian Federation issued an order in July 1941, introducing
'military-physical education in senior classes' (3, 4 and 5 hours a
week for forms 8, 9 and 10 respectively) and on 24 October 1942,
the USSR Council of People's Commissars passed a resolution
'On the Introduction of Military-Physical Training for Pupils at
Incomplete Secondary and Secondary Schools and Tekhnikums'.
And in July 1943, one of the Soviet Union's most important
sports societies was formed, The 'Labour Reserves' All-Union
Voluntary Sports Society, to represent pupils and staff in the
trade, railway and factory schools and colleges which had been
established in 1940. Its wartime function was 'to provide tempered
fighters for the war'.[8] Right at the end of the war, partly as a
mark of recognition of the contribution of physical fitness through
sport to the military victory, three new physical culture institutes
were established: the Armenian State Institute of Physical Culture
in Yerevan, the Kazakh State Institute of Physical Culture in
Alma Ata, and the Lithuanian State Institute of Physical Culture
in Kaunas.

On the debit side, the war caused immense material and
human damage to Soviet sport, which no doubt set it back many
years. Many of the country's leading sportsmen were killed – such
popular heroes as the marathon champion Babarykin, the sprinter
Puzhny, the record holder in the walk, Shkodin, and Kaplinsky,
who had established a new Soviet record in speed skating just one
year before his death in 1942. The famous woman ski champion

[7] F. I. Samoukov, *Istoriya fizicheskoi kul'tury* (Moscow, 1964), p. 313.
[8] V. A. Ivonin (ed.), *Sputnik fizkul'turnovo rabotnika* (Moscow, 1972), p. 15.

Lyubov' Kulakova was executed by the Nazis after operating as a partisan for five months behind the lines. Athletes were, of course, by virtue of their assumed superior stamina, strength, skill and moral qualities, often assigned dangerous missions such as partisan work, and were therefore particularly exposed.

The decline in sports facilities

The setback in sports facilities was the harder, bearing in mind that they were, prior to the war, only beginning to approach an adequate level.

TABLE 3   *Sports facilities during the war (numbers)*

Amenity	1940	1945
Sports centres	7,858	6,401
Gymnasiums	6,684	4,694
Soccer pitches	9,172	3,741
Volleyball courts	25,137	23,725
Basketball courts	5,439	2,744
Tennis courts	1,270	272

Sources: Fizicheskaya kul'tura v shkole, 1967, No. 10, p. 36; N. A. Makartsev, *Stranitsy istorii sovetskovo sporta* (Moscow, 1967), p. 114.

The figures do not tell the whole story of destruction, since rebuilding was started in some places in 1943 as soon as Nazi-occupied territory was liberated, and no indication of the sophistication of facilities is provided in the statistics. It is reasonable to assume that, being mostly open-air playing grounds, they were on the whole rather primitive. The least complex, volleyball courts – necessitating only a rough clearing and a net – appeared not to suffer as much as the rather more sophisticated soccer pitches, basketball and tennis courts.

Summary

The war years cannot simply be seen as a wasted interlude that retarded the sports movement. They had certain consequences, some intangible, but nonetheless quite far-reaching, whose effect was to be evident for many years ahead.

The war convinced the authorities that they had been absolutely right to 'functionalise' sport and make countrywide physical fitness a prime target through, primarily, (1) the *GTO* and *BGTO* programmes and (2) a production-based organisational structure.

It reinforced belief in a military bias in physical training and sport. It was, after all, 'the most hardy, courageous and resourceful people who had received their physical tempering in the circles run by *Osoaviakhim*, the gliding schools and boxing rings who made the greatest contribution to victory'.[9] (After the war, the rôle of army and military organisations like *Dinamo* and *DOSAAF* was to be increased and these organisations made the organisational pillars of the whole sports movement. A national physical fitness programme was to be the principal goal, and sports with explicit military utility were to become compulsory in all educational establishments and sports societies.)

The emotional effect of the war on Soviet people was capitalised on by the holding of sports festivals named after eminent athletes who had died in the war. Even though virtually everyone had lost a close relative (many children had, of course, lost their fathers), a *national* grief could be evoked at the loss of a popular sporting hero. The names and memories of these were now to be invoked both for keeping the memory of the war alive in people's minds and for drawing people to sport: 'Sports contests for prizes dedicated to the memory of outstanding athletes and heroes of the Great Patriotic War are of special significance. They are very important educationally both for the sportsmen and for the spectators.'[10]

Finally, victory in the war gave the Soviet people a sense of pride in their achievements, a feeling that the period of pre-war industrialisation and sacrifice had been justified. Now they could take on the world in another – peaceful – form of combat, in sport, and test their potential. But the war had been won at a

---

[9] Korol'kov, *Sport i zashchita rodiny*, p. 23.
[10] G. D. Kharabuga, *Sovetskaya sistema fizicheskovo vospitaniya* (Leningrad, 1970), p. 13.

price; many people felt – and they were told this by their leaders – that they had borne the brunt of German might and had made untold sacrifices to free the world from the blight of fascism. The resultant feelings of patriotism and urge to avenge the honour of those that had fallen were to be an evident part of the motivation for victory in foreign competition after the war.

7

Restoration and consolidation, 1945—1958: aiming for world supremacy in sport

Although the war had brought German invasion and extensive damage to the Soviet Union, it also brought Soviet power and influence into the heart of Europe – a source of seemingly interminable friction with the Western powers. In these conditions of international conflict and economic devastation, the Soviet people had to turn to the task of reconstruction, which, once again, had to be accomplished largely from the country's own resources. Peace, in fact, brought no relenting in either economic tempos or political pressures.

Within the new boundaries of the USSR, the urban share of the population increased from 31.6 per cent in 1940 to 38.4 per cent in 1950 and to 46.9 per cent in 1958 – a tremendous demographic shift, despite the war. By 1958, five years after the death of Stalin and two years after Khrushchov's speech to the 20th Congress, the Soviet Union was on the verge of becoming a more leisure- and consumer-orientated society, and was not far off having a predominantly urban population for the first time in its history. Already at the end of 1958, there were 151 cities with a population of over 50,000 (an increase of 52 since 1939). All this, inevitably, was to have its effect on social policies and social life,[1] not least of all on sport.

The control of sport

With the conclusion of the war and the setting of a new national target – to catch up and overtake the most advanced industrial

---

[1] For an economic overview of this period, see M. Dobb, *Soviet Economic Development since 1917* (Routledge, 1966), Chap. 13.

powers (and that included catching up and overtaking in sport) – the pre-war pyramidal structure of sports administration had to be re-established and refashioned to suit the new circumstances. As in other spheres, the incentive to produce top results was to be 'material interestedness', the awarding of cash prizes and priorities in the allocation of flats and scarce commodities for setting records and winning championships. This the government officially encouraged (or at least tried to control via a 'white market') by a decree issued in October 1945 establishing a cash-bonus system; the decree read in part:

> To stimulate greater sports proficiency, the Council of People's Commissars of the USSR has permitted the All-Union Committee on Physical Culture and Sports Affairs to award monetary prizes for outstanding sports results. An award ranging from 15,000 to 25,000 rubles will be given for setting an All-Union record that betters the world record, and from 5,000 to 15,000 rubles will be given for setting an All-Union record; 1,000 to 3,000 (in the form of valuable gifts) for setting an All-Union junior record. Those who come first, second or third in USSR championships will be awarded prizes to the value of from 2,000 to 5,000 rubles.[2]

All athletes also received salaries and bonuses according to their sports ranking, thus further encouraging the formation of an élite of sports stars. The above-mentioned decree also announced the setting up 'of 80 sports schools for young people. These schools are to train top-class athletes without interference with their everyday jobs.'[3] It soon became clear that, officially, a blind eye was to be turned to the non-observance of this last aspect of the decree (of athletes not letting their sports training and participation interfere with their normal jobs) and the body of professional sportsmen quickly grew to quite large proportions.

Joining international federations, 'shamateurism' and the target of world supremacy

It became evident that, if the USSR were to compete internationally, it would have to join existing international federations and comply with their regulations. Since most of these bodies had

---

[2] *Pravda*, 22 October 1945, p. 1.
[3] Ibid., 22 October 1945.

been established for amateur sportsmen at the end of the 19th century and their definitions and rules reflected in sport the social distinctions then current in society, they laid down quite stringent rules about remuneration of competitors in each amateur sport and the maximum amount of time they were to devote to that pursuit. Despite the Soviet distaste for the kind of social privilege reflected in bourgeois 'amateur' status, Soviet sportsmen had to play the game according to these rules if they were going to play at all against the world's best athletes. The appearance, at least, then, had to be given that they complied with the definition of an 'amateur'. In July 1947, the USSR Council of Ministers issued a special resolution 'On Remuneration of the Sporting Attainments of Soviet Sportsmen' in which it reversed its earlier prescription of monetary rewards and now declared that the only awards to be made for All-Union and world records were to be gold and silver medals and silver and bronze badges.[4]

Having solved the problem of remuneration to the apparent satisfaction of international federations, there remained the problem of classifying athletes according to some kind of occupation so as to retain their amateur status. Henceforth it was asserted that *there were no professional entertainers* in Soviet sport in the sense that there were strong social and official sanctions which prevented sport from interfering with an athlete's all-round development and his success in a non-sporting profession. There had always been, it was pointed out, an elaborate apparatus for facilitating the physical and talent development of every sports enthusiast (for example, all competitors, if qualifying, got expenses and leave).

It transpired that normally, in fact, proficient sportsmen would be following one of three occupations: student, serviceman or physical education instructor, under the sponsorship of a trade union or other (such as *Dinamo* or army) sports society. A master sportsman (i.e. one who more or less devotes all his time to training for and playing a sport during his active career as a sportsman) is paid by his sports society – according to his ranking, results and several other factors – so that he can devote much time to sport (unencumbered by a job of work outside sport, but not free from

---

[4] I. D. Chudinov (ed.), *Osnovnye postanovleniya, prikazy i instruktsii po voprosam fizicheskoi kul'tury i sporta, 1917–1957* (Moscow, 1959), p. 189.

academic studies) and be coached under the auspices of and using the facilities of the society. In the case of the country's two best-endowed sports societies, *Dinamo* and the Central Army Sports Club, the sportsman would normally hold a commission but not be expected to undergo normal military service.

The system which was reinforced after the war was obviously open to abuse. In November 1950, the All-Union Committee had passed a resolution 'On Rules Regulating the Transfer of Sportsmen from One Society to Another'.[5] It had stressed that sports activity should be based on the production principle and that, therefore, the basis on which an athlete belonged to one or another sports group must be his regular place of work, study or service in the armed forces. This did not go to the root of the problem, however, since units and enterprises were retaining people on their payrolls at the request of societies because of their sports ability. Given the circumstances of the 'world supremacy' policy and the prestige that top-flight sportsmen could bring to the sports societies, towns, national groups and factories, it was perhaps inevitable that the official directives should fall on deaf ears (it may even have been so intended).

Another problem resulting from the amateur–professional distinction has been the creation of a double moral standard in sport – one for 'stars' and one for the rest – as a result of the granting of material benefits[6] and high status to outstanding individual players. Certain of the latter have abused (and today continue to abuse) their position and violated the Soviet code of morality, as a consequence of which they have been censured officially and sometimes even barred from competition.

These problems were aggravated by the official decision to aim for world titles in all the major sports in the Olympic programme. In order to try to contain the worst of these abuses and balance up the movement by giving priority encouragement to mass participation, certain modifications were made to the organisation and structure of sport.

[5] Ibid., p. 183.
[6] Players of Moscow *Spartak*, for example, are generally known to receive bonus payments for winning matches from such organisations as the Moscow City Soviet, whose employees are members of the *Spartak* trade union sports society. The biggest bonuses are said to be received by soccer players in the *Dinamo* and army teams (personal communication).

If the Soviet Union were to achieve its aim of pre-eminence in world sport, intensive, as distinct from extensive, application to sports would have to be encouraged – i.e. participants would have to concentrate on a few sports or even a single sport rather than become all-round athletes (which the pre-war system had favoured). In 1946, therefore, the *GTO* programme was simplified: the number of *BGTO* norms was cut to seven (from 16), *GTO* Stage 1 – to 9 (from 15), and Stage 2 – to 9 (from 22). This made the programme more accessible and gave a boost to the number of badge holders, who increased from 470,000 to 1,433,000 (*BGTO*) and from 936,000 to 2,624,000 (*GTO*) between 1945 and 1948.[7]

The stage was now set to qualify for international contests and to take on the best in the world. In December 1948, the Party Central Committee set the targets in a resolution 'On the Work of the All-Union Committee on Physical Culture and Sports Affairs in Implementing the Directives of the Party and Government on the Development of the Mass Sports Movement in the Country and in Improving the Skill of Soviet Athletes'. Once again, the Party made it clear that improved proficiency could and should be based on mass participation; it called on all interested parties – sports committees, the *Komsomol*, trade unions and Party organisations everywhere – 'to spread physical culture and sport to every corner of the land, and to raise the level of skill, *so that Soviet sportsmen might win world supremacy in the major sports in the immediate future*'.[8] (My emphasis.)

The 'world supremacy' target was something new to the sports movement and flatly contradicted the condemnation of 'record-mania' that the Party had made in its 1929 resolution. But it reflected the social trends in the country and the popular mood after the war, and was not greatly dissimilar from the contemporary aims – though these were not always so explicitly stated – of other great sporting nations, particularly since the Cold War was increasingly dividing the world into two opposing camps, vying for influence over the rest of humanity.

The Party resolution outlined a specific programme for attaining the targets it had set; it entailed reinforcing the organisation

[7] N. A. Makartsev, *Stranitsy istorii sovetskovo sporta* (Moscow, 1967), p. 32.
[8] *Kul'tura i zhizn'*, 11 January 1949, p. 3.

of sports collectives; ensuring the all-round expansion of all sports but with particular attention given to sports that featured prominently in the Olympic Games – athletics, cycling, gymnastics, skiing, speed skating and swimming; improving the sports amenities available to collectives and societies; coordinating the activities of all voluntary sports societies and trade union committees at all levels; bringing Master's and ranking standards into line with All-Union and international records; heightening the responsibility of coaches and instructors for the performances of their charges (by awarding them bonuses for high attainments by their athletes); and extensively utilising the press, radio and cinema for popularising sport among the public.

Purges of sportsmen

Apparently to bring greater discipline to the All-Union Committee and more drive to the reorganisation campaign, a new chairman was appointed to succeed Nikolai Romanov, who had acceded to the post in 1945. Significantly, given the leading rôle of *Dinamo*, the purge of sportsmen that now began and the entry of Soviet sportsmen into the world arena, the new chairman, who assumed office in May 1948 was Colonel Appolonov, an officer in the security forces who had previously commanded the frontier guards. He remained as chairman for five years (until Stalin's death in 1953) when he was replaced by his vice-chairman, the previous incumbent, Romanov.

Two features of the immediate post-war 'national chauvinism' were: (1) a purge of famous sportsmen who had had contacts with foreigners prior to the war; and (2) an attempt to 'Russify' sports terminology. Purges were not new to the sports movement; indeed, practically the whole sports administration had vanished in the purges of the latter part of the 1930s. But attacks on Soviet players for 'counter-revolutionary activities' were novel. The four footballing Starostyn brothers, Nikolai, Alexander, Andrei and Pyotr, for example, who were household names before the war, were arrested immediately afterwards and all received between eight and ten years in labour camps because, it is alleged, 'they had all been abroad and told friends about foreign life'.[9] Their

[9] A. Ekart, *Vanished Without Trace* (Max Parish, London), 1954, p. 188.

time spent abroad had, in fact, been with Soviet soccer teams playing against foreign opposition. The second brother, Alexander, is reported to have told a fellow inmate of his at the labour camp in Kotlas on the Northern Dvina that the *NKVD* (security police) had been 'most interested in his sweaters, suits and hats bought abroad'.[10] Nearly thirty years later, when he published his autobiography, Andrei Starostyn was still only able to make a veiled reference to the 'missing' decade: 'People's destinies were varied and difficult in the war years. Life took its toll. But when I returned to Moscow in 1954 *after several years beyond the Arctic Circle*, the capital was already constructing a new life.'[11] (My emphasis.)

These arrests paralleled those of people tainted with foreign associations in other spheres; they included a number of Jews (accused of 'cosmopolitanism'), foreign residents living in the USSR,[12] Soviet ex-prisoners-of-war and Soviet officers who had, in their course of wartime duty, come into contact with their allied colleagues. The purges of well-known sportsmen served warning on Soviet athletes about to compete on a wide scale with foreigners that they needed to be careful about nurturing personal contacts abroad or spreading tales at home about the foreign way of life. Victory in sport abroad was to be regarded as propaganda in favour of the Soviet system both for foreign and domestic consumption. As a former medical adviser to the pre-war All-Union Physical Culture Council, Dr Matveyev is reported as saying (while in a labour-camp):

Sport in the Soviet Union has two objectives: propaganda for abroad, and the physical training of the Red Army and the *NKVD*. . . . Professionals have privileges only as long as they win, especially abroad, like race horses. The victories abroad make excellent domestic propaganda. People have little to be proud of otherwise. . . The average Russian thinks 'If *Dinamo* can beat a French team, obviously the French have even less bread and meat than we do.' This is exactly what the Soviets wish people to think, as a sort of justification for their hunger and a consolation for the evils of the system.[13]

[10] Ibid., p. 188.

[11] An. Starostyn, *Povest' o futbole* (Moscow, 1973), p. 168.

[12] The ex-sailor, Len Wincott, mentioned earlier, was arrested and sentenced to 11 years in an Arctic labour camp for having 'defamed Stalin' in a conversation during the war.

[13] Ekart, *Vanished Without a Trace*, p. 207.

Russification of sporting terms

For sports terminology – much of which was largely English – new, Russian terms were recommended, 'Russian being a language rich enough to express the appropriate concepts'.[14]

This occurred in the context of a general atmosphere of Great Russian chauvinism then prevailing. Thus, as regards soccer terminology, approximate Russian equivalents were invented, such as, '*futbol*' was to become '*nozhnoi myach*', '*offsaid*' – '*vne igry*', '*gol'kiper*' – '*vratar'*', '*korner*' – '*uglovoi*', '*pass*' – '*podacha*', '*forvard*' – '*napadayushchii*', '*butsy*' – '*botinki*', '*shorty*' – '*trusiki*' and, ironically enough, '*penal'ti*' – '*shtrafnoi*' (actually from the German '*Straf*'). It is interesting to note that, at a Soviet soccer match today, one can hear a mixture of all these terms (often used by the same person), although '*nozhnoi myach*' never caught on (unlike '*ruchnoi myach*' which competes equally for modern usage with '*gandbol*').

Restructuring the sports administration

Both the *Komsomol* and the trade unions had, of course, to respond to Party calls for action. At its Eleventh Congress, in 1949, the *Komsomol* called on its members to organise sports groups and bring more young people into the movement. The All-Union Central Council of Trade Unions reacted (at its Tenth Congress in 1949) by creating sports committees as branches of the All-Union Council at Republican, territorial and regional levels.

After Stalin's death, a general consolidation of ministries took place which swallowed up the All-Union Committee on Physical Culture and Sports Affairs. On 15 March 1953, its functions were taken over by the Ministry of Health, in the shape of a Main Board of Physical Culture and Sport. The new centralised structure soon proved unwieldy, however, and the crisis concentrating authority came to a natural end. So the old Committee re-appeared on 11 February 1954, with enhanced powers, as did its committees at all levels. Thus it was to continue until its dissolution in 1959.

[14] *Sovetsky sport*, 20 July 1948, p. 2.

To conform with the decentralisation of the economic administration and its reorganisation along territorial lines, initiated by Khrushchov in 1957, the sports administrative structure was similarly reorganised – a far more radical change than had occurred for many years. According to the plan which went into effect in July 1957, 27 central industrial ministries were abolished in favour of 105 Regional Economic Councils (*SNKh*) which were put in charge of the large economic regions into which the USSR was divided.

With the industrial ministries disbanded, there was no longer any administrative reason for having sports societies organised along industrial lines. It was therefore decided to adopt a new pattern of trade union sports societies organised on a territorial basis. At the end of 1957, the All-Union Central Council of Trade Unions resolved to dissolve its 99 sports societies and unite them into a single society for all workers and employees in industry and construction for each of the fifteen republics, regardless of union affiliation – i.e. on a territorial basis. Within each republic, the Republican Council of Trade Unions had to choose the name of its society: in the Russian Republic, it was *Trud*; in the Ukraine, it was *Avangard*; in Latvia – *Daugava*; in Georgia – *Gantiadi*; and so on. Appendix VI gives a full list of the 26 voluntary sports societies (and their relative contribution in number of collectives, Masters, First-Rank athletes and registered members) – 34 of which are run by the trade unions, including 15 urban Republican, 15 rural Republican and 4 All-Union (*Spartak, Burevestnik, Vodnik* and *Lokomotiv*); the two non-trade union societies are *Dinamo* and *Trudovye rezervy* (Labour Reserves). The only sports organisations that do not come within this category of voluntary sports society are the army sports clubs, *DOSAAF*, the Hunters' Society (*Obshchestvo okhotnikov*) and the Ministry of Education Children's Sports Schools (*Detskie sportivnye shkoly*).

At the time of the reorganisation in 1957, two All-Union trade union sports societies, because of the nature of their membership and work and to match surviving ministerial structures, were left intact: *Lokomotiv* for all railway workers, and *Vodnik* for river and canal transport employees. Further, an All-Union students' sports society was set up in 1957 – *Burevestnik* (unrelated to the industrial sports society of the same name which was swallowed up in the reorganisation). Three years later, *Spartak* came under trade union authority and became a fourth All-Union sports society – representing people employed in communications, road transport, health, the civil service, trade, food, culture, building, education and local industry. Prior to 1960, it had represented Producers' Cooperatives, which were at this time absorbed into the state system.[15]

To coordinate the activity of all the trade union sports societies, an All-Union Council of Trade-Union Voluntary Sports Societies was formed; the new administrative structure is shown in Appendix III. With only slight modifications, it has remained in this form up to the present day.

Although the new organisation of trade union sports societies created substantial problems, it did bring a more rational deployment of existing physical amenities, finance and coaches and the encouragement of wider participation. Previously, members of the smaller unions had suffered from a lack of amenities and opportunities for competition; now a union member had gratuitous use of any of the facilities in his area, previously available only to members of one sports collective. Nevertheless, by far the best-endowed and most successful sports organisations remained those outside union control – *Dinamo* and the army clubs.

Improving sports qualifications

New honours

After the war, the government for the first time introduced honorary awards for coaches and instructors. On 26 June 1945, it passed a resolution 'On Instituting the Badge "For Outstanding Service to Physical Culture" (*Otlichnik fizicheskoi kul'tury*)', intended for people who promoted sport and assisted with the training of outstanding athletes; this award was supplemented in

---

[15] Despite the changes over the years, *Spartak* is still popularly referred to as '*lavochniki*' (the 'shopkeepers'), *Dinamo* players and teams as '*gorodoviki*' ('policeman' – pre-revolutionary ones), and army players as '*konyushnye*' ('stable-men'). As a translator in Moscow, I was eligible to join *Spartak* – and did so, on payment of 30 kopecks per annum, which gave access to the club's facilities and team membership; I subsequently became a member of the Moscow *Spartak* badminton team.

March 1956 by the institution of the higher title 'Merited Trainer of the USSR'. This was now the highest institutionalised status to which a Soviet coach could aspire: he could gain the title by training Masters of Sport, champions and record holders at All-Union, European and world levels. This was a further encouragement to concentrate on top-class athletes and, at the same time, recognition of the efforts of the country's best coaches in producing a pleiade of world-class athletes.

The reorganisation of the GTO and BGTO programmes and tests

As before the war, sports activity in most schools and colleges, the armed forces and primary collectives was directed to preparing people to take the *GTO* and *BGTO* programme and tests. With the onset of the 1950s, millions of people were gaining their badges every year. In 1957, for example, 2,567,700 people were said to have met the standards for *GTO* Stage 1, 445,000 for Stage 2 and 1,498,000 for *BGTO*.[16]

Nonetheless, since the end of the war, there had been increasing criticism of the *GTO* programme and the way it operated. It had been revised in 1946 and the number of sports in a test reduced; although the smaller number of obligatory tests made the *GTO* more accessible, the tests were now criticised for being of uneven quality in the individual optional sports and for taking no account of age. It was apparent, too, that the programme was not producing as many active sportsmen as had been hoped and that those produced were not of a high enough level of skill. Again the norms were modified (in 1955) and, this time, the optional sports were eliminated and uniform compulsory standards were once more established for all candidates: 10 for *BGTO*, 12 for *GTO* Stage 1 and 11 for Stage 2. Once again, however, the results did not come up to expectations. The schools were particularly critical that, although they were called upon to prepare their pupils for the *BGTO* and *GTO* tests, the latter did not coincide with the physical training syllabus laid down by the Ministry of Education, nor was there enough time to combine the two.

16 Samoukov, *Istoriya fizicheskoi kul'tury*, p. 332.

One distinct advantage of the programme inaugurated in 1955, however, was that it did take some account of age differentials: the *BGTO* was specified for schoolchildren aged 14–15, the *GTO* Stage 1 for young men and women of 16–18, and Stage 2 for the over-18s.

The response of young people and the levels of skill attained, however, did not accord with the targets set by the All-Union Sports Committee. Many sports collectives were once more accused of ignoring the mass of members, of allowing the ranked athletes to monopolise available physical facilities and instructors, and of concentrating on a narrow group of sportsmen. It was not that they showed a decrease in *GTO* badge holders, but they often, it was said, *bent the rules* to get their quota of *GTO* passes (a perennial problem in all plan-fulfilment campaigns); in many cases, it was apparent that those awarded their badges had not actually fulfilled their sports norms. All this led to a fall in the popularity of the *GTO* programme among young people and provoked further changes. A new (third) *GTO* programme was drawn up during 1958 and came into operation on 1 January 1959.

The reorganisation of the rankings system

With the entry of the Soviet Union into international 'bourgeois' sport soon after the war, it was found necessary to revise the sports classification system regularly so as to adjust to rapidly improving world standards. Qualification standards for each of the four rankings and for the Master of Sport title were all raised in 1947 and again in 1949 (in response to the December 1948 Party appeal for greater excellence and world sporting supremacy). The new targets affected all sports in the rankings system. Henceforth, the All-Union Committee on Physical Culture and Sport ruled, the standards would be revised every four years in accordance with prevailing world standards.

In 1957, rankings existed for a total of 47 sports – a big increase over previous years and an indication that there were now Soviet candidates of reasonable standard in the bulk of the world's organised sports. In some sports – athletics, swimming, cycling and rowing – standards were raised appreciably. Despite regularly revised standards, the numbers of ranked athletes increased rapidly: 1,273,000 to 6,154,000 between 1945–1948 and 1957–1960.[17]

The percentage of ranked sportsmen among all sports participants was steadily rising. While ranked athletes, in 1940, constituted only 1.8 per cent of all sportsmen, in 1948, they made up 5.8 per cent of the total and in 1958, as much as 13.9 per cent.

If account is taken of the heightened proficiency norms, the overall improvement in skills is even more significant. Thus, if we select from amongst the results achieved in 1948, 1952, 1956 and 1957 those in which the norms for a Master of Sport rating had not been changed in the immediate future (1961–1964), it would appear that Master of Sport standard was achieved by one athlete in 1948; by 27 athletes in 1952; by 51 athletes in 1956; and by 377 athletes in 1957.

One reason for the evident rise in skill may, of course, be that these particular norms were too low. Yet other comparisons provide evidence of considerable improvement in skill – not least of all, the performance by Soviet athletes in the Olympic Games and other international sporting events.

Sports and sports events

The biggest domestic sporting event of the 1950s was the First *Spartakiad* of the Peoples of the USSR (*Spartakiada narodov SSSR*) whose final was held in Moscow between 6 and 16 August 1956. The decision to hold the games had been made in January the year before by the USSR Council of Ministers (which awarded the main prizes). It instructed every sports collective in the country, every district, regional, town, village and Republican sports organisation to prepare for the event, hold qualifying contests, construct the requisite amenities and make the forthcoming games the biggest and most widely publicised sports festival in the country's history. It was to be, too, the forerunner of regular sports festivals to be held every four years in the year preceding the Olympic Games; it was also a much publicised demonstration

[17] Makartsev, *Stranitsy istorii sovetskovo sporta*, p. 35; V. V. Stolbov and I. G. Chudinov, *Istoriya fizicheskoi kul'tury* (Moscow, 1970), p. 191.

of the mass (and especially the multi-national) nature and the proficiency of the Soviet sports movement.

It is claimed that as many as 23 million people took part in the competitions leading up to the First *Spartakiad* finals. On the way, some 1,500 sportsmen won their Master of Sport title, 26,000 – the first ranking, 150,000 – the second, and more than 700,000 – the third. Moreover, 415 All-Union records were set – of which 142 surpassed world records. As a means of popularising sport and organising tests of skill, the games certainly did their job.

The finals were held in the newly opened Lenin Stadium in Luzhniki, on the banks of the Moscow River at the foot of Lenin Hills, with seating in the main stadium for 104,000 spectators. The importance of the occasion was marked by the presence of all prominent Party leaders and a number of eminent foreign guests, including the presidents of many international federations and the then president of the Olympic Committee, Avery Brundage.

Over a period of ten days, a total of 9,244 participants representing the 15 republics and the cities of Leningrad and Moscow competed in 20 sports (the Olympic programme except for field hockey). In the team score chart, Moscow came first, followed by the Russian team and Leningrad. This underlined the supremacy of Russians and of the country's traditional sporting centres – the places of maximum concentration of urban population.

As an event, the *Spartakiad* was certainly unsurpassed in the history of Soviet sport. It was intended to be precisely that: an event of political and social significance in the lives of Soviet people. It was not merely a taking stock of Soviet sports achievements and a launching pad for the coming Olympic Games, it was also meant to be a culturally unifying force; the authorities relied on the popularity of sport to bring representatives and ordinary people from all sections of Soviet society together in a festive, patriotic mood on a great occasion organised by Party and State. It was to bind together in friendly contest the forty nationalities represented in the finals, on a larger scale than ever before, as the ancient and modern Olympic Games had been intended to do, and to encourage more extensive involvement in sport throughout the country.

The former IOC President, Avery Brundage, has described the scene at a similar massive sports event, not dissimilar to the First *Spartakiad*. His description, here quoted at length, helps one to understand the importance given at these events to their functions as a nationally unifying force, as artistic spectacles, and as ritualised political campaigns.

The Sports Parade I was invited to see was fantastic. It wasn't a parade at all. It was a huge demonstration of physical culture and gymnastics. I have seen many such things in various parts of the world, but never anything that would even approach this one, either in magnitude or in beauty. The participants were brought from all over the Soviet Union. There were Uzbeks and Tadzhiks and Cossacks and Armenians and Georgians and Kirgiz. They came from Karelia, Moldavia, Aberbaidzhan and other remote places. . . Each delegation included from 400 to 3,000 boys and girls. They told me there were altogether 34,000 participants. First, they paraded around the stadium; then, the field was turned over to the delegations one at a time and they gave mass demonstrations. . . One delegation brought collapsible gymnastic apparatus and erected 70 to 80 horizontal bars on which, in a trice, were 70 to 80 gymnasts doing giant swings together to classical music. Another erected a framework 30 to 40 feet high, and participants draped themselves on it with different coloured costumes like a huge living bouquet of beautiful flowers. It went on for five hours like clockwork. How they organised this event with such mechanical precision, with delegations coming from the Ural Mountains, the deserts of Central Asia, the Arctic Provinces, and the remote interior of Siberia, I do not know. It was amazing. Worked into the displays by the various groups were slogans, very cleverly designed to bind the young people to the régime, which were spelled out on the field by the performers: *ready for labour and defence; glory to the Fatherland; hail Lenin and Stalin; three million bales of cotton for the nation; success to the Communist Party; peace–peace–peace.*[18]

Despite the great increase in the range of sports practised and the attention devoted to international sport in the period 1945–1958, one glimpse of the Party's view of sport in its scale of priorities may be gained by noting the fact that it provided no greatly increased financial backing: although budgetary expendi-

[18] From a speech to the Economic Club of Detroit on 7 February 1955; quoted in H. W. Morton, *Soviet Sport* (Collier Books, New York, 1963), pp. 61–62.

ture on physical culture rose absolutely between 1946 and 1958 from 20 million to 50 million rubles, its share in total budgetary expenditure actually fell – from 0.07 per cent to 0.06 per cent in the same period. It remained at this level until the end of the 1950s.[19]

Physical education

The immediate need, on the conclusion of hostilities, was to adjust the school physical education syllabus to peace time conditions and to utilise it as far as possible, given continuing food shortages, to fortify the health of children deprived and debilitated during the war.

New sports curricula

In the new syllabus scheduled for 1947, therefore, the stated aim was to improve children's health. Back came the classification by motor skills rather than by sport and the virtual elimination of team games. Nonetheless, this somewhat conflicted with the requirement of schools to adapt their physical education lessons to the *BGTO* programme and to gain as many passes as possible. All physical education instructors received detailed instructions on how to conduct each lesson, their attention being drawn to the biological and psychological requirements of children, particularly the physically weak. Yet the amount of time allotted in school hours was small: 33 hours a year for forms 1–2 and 8–10, and 66 hours for forms 3–7.[20]

The Party decision of 1948 to campaign for improved skill in all sports and the earlier decision to compete on a wide scale in international sport were bound to affect school sport and physical education. A radically new syllabus was drawn up for 1954 which again changed the orientation from basic motor skills (running, climbing, throwing, and so on) to competitive sports, and instructed schools to 'teach the basic skills in gymnastics, sports and team games'.[21] For the first time since the 1937–1941 physical

[19] *Narodnoye khozyaistvo SSSR v 1958* (Moscow, 1959), pp. 900, 903–904.
[20] *Fizicheskaya kul'tura v shkole*, 1967, No. 9, p. 7.
[21] Ibid., p. 7.

education syllabus, physical education in schools was to be centred around gymnastics, organised sports and team games. The instructions included material on specific sports and games. The new physical education syllabus, in conjunction with all other school sport activities, was based on the *GTO* programme, and it was intended that each pupil completing the seventh form (at the age of 14 or 15) would gain his *BGTO* badge, and each pupil completing the tenth form (at the age of 17) would gain his *GTO* Stage 1 badge.

At colleges and universities, the compulsory physical education in the first two years of the students' courses (instituted in 1929) was, from 1947 to 1948, made subject to an examination which, if failed, might hold the student back a year. In 1956, the physical education course was made more flexible and students could choose a sport in which to specialise.

Sport in schools and colleges

The school physical education syllabus was, clearly, a highly ambitious programme – possibly unrealistically so – but the targets had been set and the schools played a vital part in developing young talent. Between 1949 and 1958, some 42 per cent of the country's registered sportsmen were schoolchildren and, by 1958, nearly half of all *GTO* and all *BGTO* badge holders were in school. Over a quarter of all ranked sportsmen, including 23 per cent of the third-ranked and 14 per cent of the second-ranked sportsmen were school pupils.[22]

Many of the achievements were not due to the efforts of school physical education instructors, but to the extra-curricular children's sports organisations, to sports clubs in the Young Pioneer Palaces and Houses, Pioneer camps and sports societies. By a special government decree in 1952, all sports organisations in the country were obliged to allow schoolchildren free use of their amenities during the daytime. This was to compensate for the lack of sports facilities in the schools (virtually all schools still had no gymnasium or sports ground) and, since many schools still

---

[22] Makartsev, *Stranitsy istorii sovetskovo sporta*, p. 80; *Kul'turnoye stroitel'stvo* (Moscow, 1956), pp. 76–77, 80–81; *Narodnoye obrazovanie, nauka i kul'tura* (Moscow, 1971), pp. 44–45, 121.

worked on a shift system, to provide a socially beneficial – or, at least, harmless – occupation for children in out-of-school time. Nevertheless, subsequent complaints in the press made it clear that many sports organisations were refusing to permit children access to their facilities, primarily out of fear that the children might damage their scarce resources.

Expansion of children's sports schools

In a number of sports, contemporary world standards can only be achieved by intensive training at an early age. Swimmers, for example, as a rule reach their peak in their 'teens, and sprinters and gymnasts – in their late 'teens and early twenties. In these and several other sports for which amenities were few and for which intensive training is necessary at an early age (like tennis) there was the problem of identifying and 'creaming-off' as expeditiously as possible the potential talent early and developing it intensively, using such facilities as were available. For these purposes, it was decided to expand widely the network of children's sports schools (*detskie sportivnye shkoly*). These are select sports clubs which promising children can attend after the normal daily school lessons are over. The first such schools had been set up in 1934 in Moscow and Tbilisi under the auspices of the Ministry of Education. Their growth had been quite slow, since finance and physical amenities were not made available on a large scale; the Ministry of Education had more urgent priorities in its expenditure. By 1940, the number of such schools had, then, risen to 262; these were mostly concentrated in the central, more industrially developed areas of the country. Turkmenia and Kazakhstan, for instance, had no more than one school each.

After the war, particularly after the government's call for excellence in 1948, they received somewhat greater financial support and – although their organisation remained largely in the hands and at the whim of Republican educational bodies – the trade union sports societies were also ordered to establish junior sports schools in many of their bigger collectives – or at least to establish junior sections. By 1958, the number of such schools had expanded to over a thousand and their membership had increased six-fold compared with the pre-war figure; their average size rose from 179 pupils in 1940 to 229 in 1948 and 260 in 1958. They had varying numbers of sports groups: in some areas, they concentrated on a particular sport (e.g. swimming – where a good swimming pool or the sea was to hand). The sports most commonly pursued in the schools were gymnastics and athletics, followed by basketball, volleyball, skiing, swimming, fencing, soccer and speed skating.

After 1954, the time devoted to physical education in schools was increased to 66 hours per year for all forms. Altogether, this meant two physical education lessons per week of 45 minutes each, plus a daily 15–20 minute period of setting-up exercises before classes, six days a week.[23] As an American physical educationalist noted: 'If the times for morning exercises and physical education lessons are considered, this equals 200 minutes, which is more than the time allotted in most American schools.'[24]

Spartakiads for children and students

Nationwide competitions and tournaments were initiated for schoolchildren in 1954, when the first children's *spartakiad* was held in Leningrad; for the next six years, such an event was held annually. Students had had their All-Union *spartakiad* from as early as 1951. The student voluntary sports society, *Burevestnik* (set up in 1957) soon became one of the most powerful societies in the country. This was hardly surprising, since a large number of more or less full-time athletes were combining their training and competition with study or research at physical training institutes.

Graduations in physical culture

Training of physical education instructors, athletes, coaches and sports officials continued as before and, although the number of qualified instructors greatly increased in the decade and a half following the war, it by no means satisfied the demand in schools

---

[23] *Fizicheskaya kul'tura v shkole*, 1967, No. 9, p. 9.
[24] A. Esslinger, 'Health, Physical Education and Recreational Programmes in the USSR', in *Journal of Health, Physical Education, Recreation*, September 1958, p. 28.

and elsewhere. By 1958, courses of four or five years' training were available at 16 physical culture institutes, in physical culture faculties at 42 colleges of education (*pedagogicheskie instituty*) and universities and at technical colleges (*tekhnikums*) and schools for coaches. Further, many more qualified instructors were trained by correspondence courses and evening classes; special 6-month courses were also arranged through the trade unions. The growth in numbers and their distribution among the various establishments is shown in Table 4.

TABLE 4 *Graduations from higher and secondary physical-culture establishments: selected years, 1946–1958*

Type of educational establishment from which graduating	1947	1950	1956	1958
Graduations from all establishments (number)	1,780	4,576	8,108	6,887
of total from:				
1. Physical culture institutes (number)	539	1,185	1,625	1,949
(percentage of total)	30.4	25.7	20.4	28.3
2. Physical culture faculties of higher educational establishments (number)	–	106	1,225	1,821
(percentage of total)	–	2.1	15.1	26.4
3. Correspondence courses and evening classes (number)	–	119	621	1,208
(percentage of total)	–	2.4	7.6	17.5
of total 3, from:				
a. physical culture institutes (number)	–	119	608	836
b. Other secondary educational establishments (number)	–	–	13	372
4. Physical culture technical colleges (number)	1,096	2,943	4,352	1,571
(percentage of total)	61.5	64.1	53.6	22.8
5. Schools for coaches (number)	145	223	285	438
(percentage of total)	8.2	5.7	3.3	5.0

Source: N. A. Makartsev, *Stranitsy istorii sovetskovo sporta* (Moscow, 1967), p. 93.
Note: It should be noted that government control in the USSR implies a standardisation of curriculum, teaching, staff and facilities for teachers of physical education (as for other specialities) which is quite unlike the situation in Anglo-Saxon countries.

The table shows that, after 1956, the number of part-timers with only a secondary special education qualification (line 4) actually started to decline, while the number with higher education was continuing to increase. This was in line with the requirement of 1957 that instructors engaged in coaching schoolchildren and working in junior sections of the sports societies should have higher educational qualifications.

Summary

As in the pre-war years, after the war, the big industrial effort and its concomitant rigid centralisation were accompanied by intellectual and cultural constraints and massive repression. These were the years of the Iron Curtain and the Cold War, when xenophobia characterised many pronouncements, when something very like Great-Russian chauvinism was practised (if not overtly preached as such). These aberrations emanated from several sources: the fear of attack from the Western powers, the Western monopoly of atomic weapons, the weakened state of the Soviet Union following the war and the personal power and attitudes of Stalin. The tension gradually subsided, however, after his death in March 1953 as the most pressing shortages were overcome and as Soviet authority and prestige in the world (to which sporting success abroad made some modest contribution) grew.

During the war, Stalin and the Soviet leadership had played down class conflict and proletarian internationalism (the mass of the German working class self-evidently backing Hitler) and had played up, in the interests of national unity, the old glories of the Russian heroic past and the virtues of the Russian people. The leaders seem to have objectively encouraged Great-Russian chauvinist sentiments among the public by their denigration of and attempts at eliminating things 'tainted' by foreign influence – by measures such as (in relation to sport) the 'purification' of terminology. Sport was a means of continuing the war peacefully – now against the remaining enemy, the bourgeois-democratic states of the world, utilising the sentiments aroused during the recent 'hot' war against the bourgeois–fascist states – aggressiveness, intense patriotism, partisan attachment to 'one's own side' (Stalin, Party, USSR, *Dinamo* FC, etc.).

For those Soviet citizens whose military service had taken them outside their country during the war and who had seen for themselves that life had not everywhere been as black as it had been painted by Soviet propaganda, sports success abroad was intended to be a morale booster to assuage doubts about the superiority of the Soviet system, to provide a justification for all the efforts and sacrifice made to attain a strong state and higher standard of living. At home, the pomp of sports festivals like the 1956 *Spartakiad* and the competitive excitement of the burgeoning sports contests helped to obscure memories of foreign life and divert or diminish any yearning for a more liberal, relaxed and consumer-orientated society to be introduced into the post-war USSR. The faith in national success and belief in national superiority so created were thus conducive to strengthening group identification and constituted a compensation for frustrated aspirations in other areas. At the same time, particularly in the period up to Stalin's death in 1953, by strict control of the sports movement through functionaries of the security forces and by the latter's timely warnings that players, too, were subject to the insistence on active political conformity and to coercion, any dangerous aspirations to cultivate friendships with foreign sportsmen, to communicate information about foreign societies, gathered during a sports trip, to Soviet citizens, or to treat international sports contests as apolitical games were effectively extinguished.

8

The later post-war years:
urban life and leisure

Since the late 1950s, there has been a fairly steady increase in public and personal prosperity, a marked growth in the range and quantity of consumer goods available, a reduction in working time (with the introduction of the five-day week in 1967 for the bulk of the urban population) and a continuing shift in population balance in favour of the towns (the urban population first exceeded the rural in 1961); moreover, the Five-Year Plan for 1971–1975 for the first time projected a greater rise in the production of consumer goods than of producer goods. All these factors are having a qualitative effect on the pattern of recreation – which, in turn, is having social and political consequences for society as a whole.

Increasing prosperity

Since the end of World War II, the urban way of life in the USSR has altered remarkably. Figures published in the USSR indicate that national income, consumption and real incomes *per capita* more than doubled between 1959 and 1975.[1]

Part of the increased personal income is undoubtedly being spent on recreation, on the pursuit of a growing variety of sports, particularly outdoor ones, and on personal sporting durables such as skis, skates, tennis and badminton rackets, fishing tackle, tents and, to a lesser extent, on motorcycles, canoes, dinghies, yachts and cars. This would clearly seem to be a long-term trend.

[1] Thus, using 1958 as base year (100), total national income in comparable prices rose to 254 in 1972, of which the amount going to consumption increased to 244; real *per capita* incomes rose to 205 in 1974. See *Narodnoye khozyaistvo SSSR v 1960*, p. 160, *1972*, pp. 531, 533 and *1974*, p. 535.

Higher national income has also resulted in more substantial government allocations to leisure and sporting facilities, and the development of a number of sports, particularly outdoor, that presuppose a certain level of industrial development and economic surplus – for example, motor racing and rallying, yachting, other types of boating, karting, various winter sports (tobogganing, bobsleighing, slaloming, ski jumping), water skiing, aqualung diving, mountain climbing, fishing, shooting and the complex of activities that come under the rubric of 'tourism' in the USSR. All these sports showed appreciable growth in the 1960s; some, in fact, have only begun seriously in the last few years. Karting began in 1960 in Tallinn; water skiing began in 1959 and its first national championships were held only in 1965; motor car racing and rallying only seriously began in the mid-1960s – yet, in 1971, Soviet cars competed in 60 Soviet and 20 foreign rallies; it was only in 1969 that the first luge toboggan runs were constructed near Leningrad and Riga – yet, by 1970, Soviet industry had not produced any toboggans (except for children) and followers of the sport had had to make their own.[2] Some sports which had been played spasmodically earlier in the Soviet Union received a new lease of life in the 1960s when industry was able to produce equipment for them – as, for example, in the cases of rugby, archery and field hockey.[3]

State capital investment for the construction of sports facilities grew considerably during the 1960s: while the government spent an average of 16 million rubles per annum between 1953 and 1964 on new sports facilities and installations, it spent as much as 40 million rubles for the purposes in 1965 alone.[4] Furthermore, after the August 1966 government resolutions on sport, a big spending programme was drawn up, so that, in the following

[2] *Sport v SSSR*, 1970, No. 2, p. 80.
[3] A Rugby Federation was formed in 1967 and the first All-Union championships were held in 1968; archery appeared in Moscow in 1967 and a federation was formed in 1968 (it is noteworthy that archery was included in the Olympic Games in 1972 for the first time for fifty years); the first field hockey championships were held in 1969; a golf course near Moscow was being laid out in 1975 and a Soviet delegation visited Britain to examine squash facilities. Even a pigeon fanciers' federation was set up in 1975.
[4] *Fizkul'tura i sport*, 1966, No. 7, p. 43.

year, some republics increased their expenditure on sport by as much as 6–7 times. In the Russian Republic, the 1967 expenditure on sport was over twice the amount spent in all the preceding post-war years put together.[5] As a result of this campaign, between 1966 and 1970, the country gained 319 new sports centres, 185 indoor swimming pools, 31 indoor athletics stadiums and 16 artificial ice rinks.[6]

Increasing free time

The relationship of work and leisure altered radically in the decade up to 1970. In 1956, the standard (six-day) week in Soviet industry was of 46 hours; by 1961, it had declined to 41 hours – still in a six-day week – i.e. most workers had five 7-hour days and one 6-hour day each week. In 1970, the average working week in industry was 40.7 hours and, in state employment in general, 39.4 hours in a five-day week.[7] Moreover, the number of public holidays and days off for industrial manual workers increased by 36.1 days between 1960 and 1972.

Another factor of importance for sport is the *distribution* of leisure. The number of hours in the working day has diminished, leaving more free time and energy available for leisure pursuits in the evenings. More significant has been the increase in the number of whole days on which no work is done. Altogether, Soviet industrial manual workers had 95.4 days off during 1972, including annual paid holidays of fifteen days for most workers (from 1 January 1968).[8]

An idea of time use by workers in eight different Soviet towns may be obtained from the next table (Table 5).

The breakthrough that signals the greatest revolution in sports participation, just as in other advanced industrial countries, and in the pattern of recreation was the introduction of the long weekend. In March 1967, the Central Committee of the Communist Party adopted a resolution 'On the Transfer of Industrial and Office Workers to a Five-Day Working Week with Two

---

[5] *Ekonomicheskaya gazeta*, 1968, No. 19 (23 May), p. 18.
[6] *Sovetsky sport*, 13 July 1971, p. 2.
[7] V. I. Azar, *Otdykh trudyashchikhsya SSSR* (Moscow, 1972), p. 6.
[8] *Teoriya i praktika fizicheskoi kul'tury*, 1971, No. 3, p. 4.

TABLE 5   *Time use by urban manual and office workers in some Soviet cities: 1963 and 1968 (hours and minutes per week)*

Time use category	Ivanovo (1963) hrs.–min.	per cent	Gor'ky (1963) hrs.–min.	per cent	Rostov (1963) hrs.–min.	per cent	Sverdlovsk (1963) hrs.–min.	per cent	Dnepropetrovsk, Zaporozh'ye, Odessa and Kostroma (1968) hrs.–min.	per cent
Total time	168–00	100	168–00	100	168–00	100	168–00	100	168–00	100
including:										
actual working time[a]	41–00	24.4	39–30	23.5	37–50	22.5	39–50	23.7	39–50	23.7
non-working time related to the job[b]	8–50	5.3	10–50	6.4	10–10	6.1	10–10	6.1	11–10	6.2
household duties[c]	22–00	13.1	22–30	13.4	22–40	13.5	23–30	14.0	24–30	14.4
eating, sleeping and personal care	68–50	41.0	66–00	39.3	67–50	40.4	66–30	39.6	63–40	37.5
free time[d]	27–20	16.3	29–10	17.4	29–30	17.6	28–00	16.7	30–30	18.2

a   Total time for which the worker is paid.
b   Chiefly travel to and from work.
c   Shopping, cooking, cleaning, sewing, care of children.
d   Major components are studying, reading, watching TV, visiting the cinema, theatre and sports spectacles, visiting friends, and sports activities.

Source: L. A. Gordon and E. V. Klopov, *Chelovek posle raboty: sotsial'nye problemy byta i vnerabochevo vremeni* (Moscow, 1972), p. 28.

Note: Although it would be wise not to read too much into the changes between 1963 and 1968 – in view of the different nature of the towns (e.g. Ivanovo has a high proportion of women in the labour force) and the unknown quality of the statistical techniques used – the table does reveal a fairly consistent pattern of time use for all eight cities and an increase in free time of at least one hour per week) between 1963 and 1968. It would appear that workers had about 30 hours a week at their disposal as free time. It is *how much* of that which they devote to sport which is examined below.

Consecutive Free Days'. For the first time in Soviet history, the bulk of industrial workers had their weekends free. Holidays with pay and long weekends enable men and women to pursue sports which cannot be enjoyed in an evening or even in a half-day's holiday. They can then pursue games which were previously beyond their physical and emotional resources. It is this pattern of leisure that has made possible in Western Europe and America the great proliferation of sports and pastimes which take place away from the city streets and office blocks. A similar trend seems to be taking place in the USSR. The chairman of the All-Union Council of Trade Union Sports Societies, G. I. Yeliseyev, has said that 'whereas recreational activities used to take place in urban sports centres, many have now been transferred to out-of-town sports amenities, recreation camps and parks'.[9] As a consequence, the unions have had to 'refit and adapt various buildings, old passenger railway compartments and river steamers, landing craft, barges, etc. and construct rudimentary recreational areas'.[10] As an example of the impact of the long weekend, Yeliseyev quotes figures for sports participation at several factories. At the *Zaporozhstal'* Works, which operated a five-day week as early as in 1966, every employee is said to have spent on average 3 hours 27 minutes on sport and physical culture each week during 1967 while, at similar factories working a six-day week, the average was only 2 hours 14 minutes. With general conversion to the five-day week, sports participation usually increased – in some areas, very greatly. For example, in the Perm' *Oblast'*, the number of sports participants is said virtually to have trebled.

The boom in camping, fishing and hunting and, to a lesser extent, in mountaineering, potholing, water skiing, motoring and boating, is partly accounted for by longer holidays with pay and partly by the developing cult of the weekend. The Soviet Union is, in fact, rapidly developing a 'weekend' pattern of behaviour, not greatly dissimilar from that followed in most advanced Western countries – if, as yet, with far less use of motor cars.

Nothing is more indicative of the changing recreational pattern than the rapidly mounting popularity of 'tourism'.[11] In 1955, it

[9] *Teoriya i praktika fizicheskoi kul'tury*, 1968, No. 2, p. 45.
[10] Ibid., p. 47.
[11] 'Tourism' is a loosely defined term, as the following description indicates

was 14th among all sporting pursuits in numbers of participants, in 1960 – 11th, in 1965 – 4th, and in 1970 – 2nd after athletics (see Table 6). Immediately after the war, there were only 15 recognised tourist routes in the USSR; by 1968, there were over 900 and, in 1970, more than 1,000. In 1970, some 50 million people (i.e. over one-fifth of the population) took part in camping or excursions around the country.[12] In 1972, the number had increased to 74 million (nearly one-third of the population).[13] Several factories have their own recreation 'tourist' camps. The big *VEF* engineering works in Riga, for example, has its own camp between the rivers Gauya and Vausozer, which 6,000 of its employees and their family members visited during 1967. Most of the cost is borne by the factory, the employees contributing 1 ruble a day for their three meals, use of sports equipment, and accommodation. During 1970, 50 tourist passes were available for issue for every 1,000 workers (as compared to 11 per 1,000 in 1965).[14] As a step to encourage tourism – and also to control it and the way people spend their free time – the Party, government,

only too clearly: 'Tourism includes more or less lengthy journeys with the aim of active rest and better health, tempering the organism, acquiring new knowledge and experience, and performing, on the way, socially useful work. . . An important part of tourist activity is moving about on foot, skis, bicycle or boat and overcoming natural obstacles, often in extremely difficult climatic conditions and even in dangerous situations, e.g. mountaineering or rock climbing. . . Many tourist journeys involve self-service, such as arranging a camp, campfire, food and washing. . . Tourism comprises rambling (*progulki*), excursions and tourist journeys (*pokhody*). Sporting tourism, however, also includes mountaineering and orienteering. . . The Uniform All-Union Sports Classification details the complexity of routes, the number of journeys and the length of the journeys, and the difficulty of natural obstacles that the tourist has to negotiate in order to attain a ranking.' G. D. Kharabuga, *Teoriya i metodika fizicheskoi kul'tury* (Moscow, 1969), pp. 69–71.

[12] P. A. Rakhmanov (ed.), *Turistskie marshruty, 1970* (Moscow, 1970), p. 151.

[13] *Sport v SSSR*, 1973, No. 6, p. 21.

[14] Rakhmanov, *Posobie organizatoru turizma*, p. 156. Both as a student and as a Soviet employee, I was able to take advantage of these facilities; in the former case, the recreational centre was a delightful camp in the pine woods on the edge of a forest lake about 20 miles from Moscow; food, accommodation and use of sports equipment cost no more than one ruble a day.

Komsomol and the All-Union Central Council of Trade Unions jointly issued a decree in 1969 'On Measures for the Further Development of Tourism and Excursions within the Country'. The decree noted that 'tourism and excursions, besides being forms of recreation, are becoming important means of raising the cultural level and of ideological-political education'.[15] The rôle that the decree ascribed to tourism was distinctly a functional one: 'to improve health, inculcate patriotism, develop greater knowledge of one's country and popularise the revolutionary, military and labour attainments of our people'.[16]

TABLE 6 *Sixteen sports by order of number of participants: selected years 1940–1970*

Sport	1940	1945	1955	1960	1965	1970
1. Athletics	3	3	1	1	1	1
2. Tourism	14[a]	18[a]	14	11	4	2
3. Volleyball	5	6	2	3	2	3
4. Skiing	2	1	3	2	3	4
5. Pistol shooting	6	7	5	6	5	5
6. Soccer	7	9	7	8	7	6
7. Basketball	11	12	9	7	8	7
8. Chess	1	2	4	4	6	8
9. Draughts	–	4	6	5	9	9
10. Fishing	–	–	–	–	–	10
11. Table tennis	–	–	12	10	10	11
12. Shooting (game)	–	–	–	–	–	12
13. Swimming	8	8	11	13	11	13
14. Cycling	9	10	10	12	12	14
15. Gymnastics[b]	4	5	8	9	13	15
16. Speed skating	10	11	13	14	14	16

[a] In 1940, the missing numbers (12 and 13) represent sports not here listed (ice hockey and fencing respectively); in 1945, the missing numbers (13 and 14) represent wrestling and ice hockey.

[b] Gymnastics (*sportivnaya gimnastika*) does not include here modern rhythmic gymnastics (*khudozhestvennaya gimnastika*), or body-building (*atleticheskaya gimnastika*) or keep fit exercises at work (*proizvodstyennaya gimnastika*).

Sources: Stranitsy istorii sovetskovo sporta (Moscow, 1967), pp. 54, 72, 93; N. A. Makartsev and P. A. Sobolev, *Govoryat tsifry i fakty* (Moscow, 1968), p. 87; N. A. Makartsev and P. A. Sobolev, *Govoryat tsifry i fakty* (Moscow, 1969), p. 62.

[15] *Materialy XVI s"yezda VLKSM* (Moscow, 1970), p. 194.
[16] Ibid., p. 195.

Fishing and shooting have also both greatly increased their following and relative position of popularity (see Table 6). In 1961, a total of 1,856,800 engaged in fishing and shooting; in 1968, the following of these was 5,324,300, and they had moved up to 10th and 12th places respectively from 17th and 23rd in 1961. During 1968, a total of 3,181,700 people are said to have engaged in fishing and 2,142,600 in shooting.[17]

Other outdoor sports have increased their following and their position of popularity in the list of participant sports (whereas indoor pursuits like chess, draughts, gymnastics and table tennis have declined relatively). It would seem that the increase in leisure is resulting in a change in the pattern of Soviet sport towards non-urban outdoor recreation.

It has been argued by some that the increase in leisure and prosperity in the Soviet Union has paralleled the consolidation of a Soviet élite. It is true that, although some facilities may be had free of charge or hired at very low cost through a club at one's workplace or place of residence and although trade unions do grant special subsidised passes for visits to well-equipped out-of-town recreational sites, it is the richer and more influential members of the community who are increasingly able to afford such pleasures (and even acquire their own facilities – e.g. a motor car, a motorcycle, a boat or camping equipment). There are indications that the social stratification of Soviet society finds expression in recreation. Members of élite groups at present noticeably tend (as seen below) to be concentrated in the three largest cities, Moscow, Leningrad and Kiev, even though the trend appears to be away from such concentration. Furthermore, to the extent that functional 'importance' is reflected in greater remuneration, a high income gives some groups access to certain opportunities not available to the masses: country houses (*dachas*), cars, boats, larger apartments and travel – even abroad.[18] It is, in

17 A. Dobrov, *God sportivny* (Moscow, 1969), p. 143.

18 In my travels in the Soviet Union, I have noted an extravagantly-equipped billiard-room at the home of a high Party official in a southern republic, a spacious table-tennis room in the apartment of a high-ranking army officer in Moscow, a private swimming pool at the *dacha* of a Soviet journalist just outside Moscow, a car and a river-yacht belonging to a professor at a Moscow Institute and lavish gambling on horses at the Moscow Hippodrome racecourse by army officers – all in

fact, admitted that 'certain free time activities require considerable expenditure on special equipment and clothing, payment for transport and services. Of course, our widespread use of public forms of leisure organisation and the extensive use of workplace and trade union funds substantially equalise the opportunities of different income groups. Nonetheless, there still remains a certain differentiation in opportunities.'[19] The same authors found that, with the change-over from the six- to the five-day week, the lowest paid workers tended to spend even less time 'on reading, visiting the cinema or stadiums, pursuing a sport, self-improvement and out-of-town recreation' – the reason being that they spent part of the weekend earning extra cash by doing work at home (dressmaking, furniture and handicrafts making), doing odd jobs, etc.[20] Not everyone, therefore, is in a position to take full advantage yet of the extra free time and leisure facilities available.

It is also true, however, that, for members of the élite, time for recreation may be a problem, since they are more involved with their occupation and greater demands are made upon them. This is, in particular, the case for urban intellectuals. Furthermore, there are several distinctions to be made between the social differentiation in sport that exists in the Soviet Union and that in some Western societies. First, because Soviet sport in general has not been commercialised, no particular sport can be exploited without control, or turned virtually into the preserve of particular income and social status groups, as has happened with such sports as polo, yachting, show jumping and fencing in England, and golf in the USA. Second, Soviet leisure patterns probably reflect income differentials to a much lesser extent than in most Western industrial societies; the greater social mobility and the existence of wider educational and sporting opportunities have kept open the channels to sports. Certainly, there are sports which are preferred by certain groups more than others – e.g. rural Russians enjoy *gorodki* and *lapta* more than their urban counterparts; the Estonians have access to water, hence have a tradition of yachting

striking contrast to the modest living space and material facilities available to the bulk of the population.
[19] L. A. Gordon and N. M. Rimashevskaya, *Pyatidnevnaya rabochaya nedelya i svobodnoye vremya trudyashchikhsya* (Moscow, 1972), p. 65.
[20] Ibid., p. 64.

and have the grass for lawn tennis, while the Kirgiz and the Bashkirs have the horses and conditions for equestrian sports. All the same, sport seems to have spread far and wide among all sections of the population, and chess, soccer, skating, skiing, fishing, gymnastics and volleyball appear to be popular with old and young, worker and intellectual, townsman and countryman. It is, moreover, the declared aim of the Party and government – and their desire for greater social control through mass sport – to involve the entire population in sport. In a recent (1972) statement, Sergei Pavlov, Chairman of the Committee on Physical Culture and Sport, said: 'We make no secret of the fact that mass participation in sport is of obvious advantage both to every citizen and to society as a whole. Sport is a vital tonic, is uplifting and increases one's capacity for work, and that, in turn, has a beneficial effect on the results of that work.'[21]

Increasing urbanisation

Over half the Soviet population now lives in a relatively modern, urban, industrial society, a human condition which, in itself, regardless of the character of the polity, promotes and predisposes people to certain kinds of recreational activities.

The rate of population shift from the rural localities to the cities reflects the general course of industrialisation. Since Russia was an agrarian country before the 1917 revolutions, the level of its urbanisation was very low: only 11 per cent of the population lived in the towns in 1870 and only 18 per cent in 1913 and 1926. By 1976, the number of town dwellers was over 150 million persons – i.e. more than 60 per cent of a population exceeding a quarter of a billion.

Furthermore, the USSR by the end of 1975 had eleven cities with a population exceeding one million,[22] and 35 cities with a population of over half a million with an aggregate total population of 42.8 million. The biggest city, Moscow, had an estimated

---

21 S. Pavlov, 'Glavnaya nasha zadacha', in N. A. Nemeshayev (ed.), *Glavny rekord-zdorov'ye* (Moscow, 1972), p. 9.
22 Moscow (7.5 million), Leningrad (4.2 million), Kiev (1.9 million), Tashkent (1.6 million), Baku (1.4 million), Khar'kov (1.3 million), Gor'ky (1.3 million), Novosibirsk (1.2 million), Kuibyshev (1.1 million), Sverdlovsk (1.1 million), and Minsk (1.1 million).

population in January 1976 of 7,528,000. By comparison, it had had a population of 1.854 m. in 1917, 2.080 m. in 1926, 4.542 m. in 1939 and 6.044 m. in 1959. Greater Moscow now occupies about 875 square kilometres and stretches 35 kilometres from west to east and 40 kilometres from north to south.[23]

At the same time as people have migrated into the towns, the government has followed a policy of high density building in multi-storey blocks of flats. Town planning tends to allow for sizeable courtyard facilities for each block of flats and now for a certain minimum of sports amenities for urban residents (a norm of one sports centre, one gymnasium and one indoor swimming pool for every 50,000 people in 1970.[24] Further, in accordance with a Party Central Committee resolution of 1966, *Gosstroi* of the USSR approved a list of sports amenities whose provision was 'compulsory for all neighbourhood units (*mikroraiony*) and groups of blocks of flats (*gruppy zhilykh domov*), in the building or reconstruction of residential districts (*zhilye raiony*), small towns and factory settlements (*promyshlennye posyolki*)' (*Gosstroi* Order No. 65, issued on 28 April 1967). (A *zhiloi raion* is defined as an area of up to 250 hectares (1 hectare = 10,000 square metres) with a population of 30,000–50,000; these are divided into *mikroraiony* which have an area of 50 hectares and a population of up to 20,000 and which, in turn, are divided into *gruppy zhilykh domov* which each have a population of 2,000–3,000.) The optimum allocation of sports facilities was redefined in 1968 by the Central Research Institute of Model and Experimental Design of Entertainment, Sports and Administrative Buildings and Installations of the State Committee for Civil Construction and Architecture attached to *Gosstroi* of the USSR. The desired norm is for sports facilities for daily use to be situated within 5–7 minutes walk of home – i.e. within a radius of 250–700 metres. For regular use, the facilities should be within 15–20 minutes by foot or transport – i.e. within a radius of 2.5–7.5 kilometres. Amenities for daily use are to include an area of 1,200 square metres with equipment for gymnastics, athletics, basketball, volleyball and table tennis; in winter, the same area is to be used for ice skating, figure skating,

[23] Em. Dvinsky, *Moskva:kratky putevoditel'* (Moscow, 1971), p. 7.
[24] H. E. Shmidt and A. S. Poleyev, *Sportivnye sooruzheniya v SSSR* (Moscow, 1970), p. 71.

ice hockey and providing a ski track. Amenities for regular (but not necessarily daily) use by adults, individually or in sports sections, should include a sports ground with facilities for soccer, volleyball, basketball, tennis, badminton and *gorodki*, gymnasiums for gymnastics and games, indoor and outdoor swimming pools, shooting ranges and service facilities (cafeteria, changing rooms, etc.). A third type of sports complex covers organised games and training and should include a soccer ground surrounded by athletics and speed skating tracks, skating rinks, an indoor athletics stadium, indoor swimming bath and artificial ice rink. A fourth category is facilities designed for sportsmen with a first ranking, masters of a particular sport and sportsmen who pursue certain other sports (wrestling, boxing and weightlifting). This last amenity should be within a distance of 30 minutes' travel; it is also recommended that a children's sports school should be formed using these facilities. Beyond this 30-minute travel limit are to be big stadiums, 'palaces of sport', artificial ice rinks and indoor swimming baths for public use.[25]

Nonetheless, the problem of providing adequate outdoor amenities for games and sports is becoming ever greater in the most densely settled urban areas. In Moscow, for example, it was reported in 1971 that its districts were grossly under-provided with sports amenities: Krasnaya Presnya, where 213,000 people resided, should have had 68 hectares of sports facilities according to prescribed standards, but, in fact, had only ten hectares – one-seventh of the prescribed standard; Krasnogvardeisky district, with 160,000 residents, had only 4.5 hectares of facilities instead of 51 hectares; Gagarin district, with 250,000 residents, had only 2 hectares instead of 80 hectares. Despite an order by the Executive Committee of the Moscow City Soviet to prevent any new district being commissioned without the requisite sports amenities, the city as a whole had only a quarter of the sports amenities it should have had (and only one-ninth of the prescribed facilities in the new (constructed since 1960) districts). In the period 1966–1971, some 2,250 sports grounds should have been built, but only 250 (11 per cent) were actually constructed.[26]

[25] Ibid., pp. 20–24.
[26] *Sovetsky sport*, 8 January 1971, p. 2. The problem would seem to be common to other towns: a lack of coordination in financing and building

As the Moscow example would indicate, while the already established multi-sport centre fills the need of some, it is becoming increasingly difficult to accommodate the casual as well as the serious participant in sport. There simply are not enough sports facilities and parks in the towns to go round.

The changing leisure pattern

The present pattern of sport is not easy to delineate; it is even more difficult to estimate how far the pattern satisfies people's needs and aspirations. Facilities and opportunities, and their limitations, determine to a great degree not only what Soviet citizens actually do with their leisure, but also their aspirations. In developed Western countries, for example, the motor car has had a considerable impact on the way families spend their leisure time. Since the output of passenger cars was 344,000 in 1970 and only 3 million over the 15 years 1955–1970, it would obviously be idle for the average Soviet family to crave yet for a Sunday motor car ride in the country. However, it is estimated that, by 1980–1985, the USSR will have some 15–20 million passenger cars – i.e. approximately one for every 4–5 families.[27] How great an impact the car will have on Soviet leisure patterns is already being forecast by some Soviet sociologists; thus 'like the television set, the appearance of the family motor car will stimulate the emergence and development of a whole number of activities, will lead to a change in habits and traditions and, ultimately, will transform the psychology of millions of people. When the car becomes part of everyday life, it is no longer simply a "means of transport"; it becomes a means of transforming everyday life, a weapon in the domestic revolution.'[28]

sports amenities (they are mostly financed from non-centralised sources – trade unions, ministerial departments, factories, offices and farms) and a low priority accorded to them by the city Soviet: 'The Soviets as a rule act as passive onlookers instead of following a concerted policy in building sports facilities corresponding to the needs of town-planning.' Shmidt, Poleyev, *Sportivnye sooruzheniya v SSSR*, p. 29.

[27] L. A. Gordon and E. V. Klopov, *Chelovek posle raboty* (Moscow, 1972), p. 273.

[28] Ibid., pp. 275–276.

Rising personal prosperity, an increasing amount of free time, particularly the long weekend, and the pressures of an urban-industrial environment have certain implications for sport. For example, people tend to form smaller (often family) groups for recreation and holidays (going on family rather than individual subsidised-ticket (*putyovka*) trips). There appears to be an increasing desire to 'get away from it all' rather than to 'get together'. On the whole, the government has, in the past, endeavoured to see to it that the facilities available to the population at large predispose them toward some form of public, collective recreation – mainly through the sports club, workplace, trade union, public park or play centre behind a block of flats.

In a survey in Lithuania, undertaken in 1966, to discover where sports participants practised their sport, it was found that 55.6 per cent of the men and 48.4 per cent of the women mainly used the facilities provided at their places of work. Of the school-children studied, 70 per cent said they practised their sport mainly using facilities at school.[29] But this pattern is largely due to the location of sports amenities at places of work or study: 'the overwhelming majority of urban clubs and most sports groups are today associated with workplaces and are orientated primarily on serving their needs'.[30] Now that most workers have a long weekend away from work, these production-based facilities no longer suit them because the clubs are 'ill-adapted to family forms of free time activity or to the active leisure activities of a small group linked by personal – and – friendly rather than formal relations'.[31] There is clearly a trend away from 'public and mass' leisure activities towards 'individual, domestic, family and passive'[32] leisure – especially watching television. 'Televiewing' has become the single most important time-consuming leisure activity: 'the amount of time spent on watching television in an urban worker's family exceeds the combined time spent on read-

[29] V. Stakioniene and S. Dulinskas, 'Nekotorye rezul'taty razvitiya fizicheskoi kul'tury v bytu shkol'nikov i trudyashchikhsya Litovskoi SSR', in N. Solov'ov, J. Lazauskas, Z. Yankova (eds.), *Problemy byta, braka i sem'i* (Vilnius, 1970), p. 217.

[30] L. A. Gordon and N. M. Rimashevskaya, *Pyatidnevnaya rabochaya nedelya i svobodnoye vremya trudyashchikhsya* (Moscow, 1972), p. 115.

[31] Ibid., p. 115.

[32] Ibid., pp. 38–39.

ing and visiting places of public entertainment, and comprises a third of all time spent on culture outside work'.[33]

It is an oft-stated belief that the social controls within the working collective are more effective than those embodied in formal institutions, and that conformity to social norms can therefore more readily be exacted through the collective. Collectivised sporting activities are seen as discouraging excessive individualism, introspection leading to doubt, and the development of tastes for privacy that might interfere with loyalties towards the collective. Sport has a further function in regard to young people. To the extent that, in every society, the young – particularly adolescents – are more concerned with sport than adults, the authorities are interested in using and guiding their leisure time (through sport) – especially in view of the rebellious, deviant and anomic tendencies sometimes observable among some Soviet youth. The above mentioned Lithuanian survey maintained that 'sociological studies reveal the rôle of sport and regular physical education in the fight against juvenile delinquency. According to the headmaster of secondary school No. 7 in Kaunas, for the last five years none of the members of the school or town teams has been brought before the juvenile commission of the Town Executive Committee or sent to a reform school. Schoolchildren who regularly pursue a sport much more rarely have bad marks for behaviour. Only 0.6 per cent of the members of the sports group have low marks for discipline. The picture is the same in most other schools in the republic.'[34] Apparently, some potential delinquents have a penchant for combat which, so it is said – and organisers of boys' clubs in Britain would probably agree – can be

---

[33] Klopov, Gordon, pp. 160–161. In the surveys whose results are presented in the two above mentioned books (based on five industrial centres: Dnepropetrovsk, Kostroma, Odessa, Zaporozh'ye and Taganrog), it was found that 75 per cent of the men and 64 per cent of the women had watched TV at some time during the three-day survey; two-thirds of all workers in the survey had TV sets; furthermore, men watched TV on average 8–9 hours a week, women – 3–4 hours (Gordon, Klopov, pp. 159–160); in Taganrog, adults spent a weekly average of 6–7 hours watching TV (Gordon, Rimashevskaya, p. 76). In the space of nearly 15 years, 1960–1973, the USSR has moved from a national average of 22 to 195 TV sets per 1,000 population, from 8 per cent to 67 per cent of family ownership. *SSSR v tsifrakh v 1973 godu* (Moscow, 1974), p. 192.
[34] Stakioniene et al., pp. 217–218.

used to draw them into sport and away from crime: 'Physical culture has great importance in combating hooliganism, drunkenness and other vices. On the initiative of the *Komsomol*, physical culture work has recently been carried out with young people who have violated public order. Experience has shown that these young people display great interest in soccer, wrestling, boxing and acrobatics. It is no secret that they often take up sport initially, especially boxing and wrestling, to fortify themselves and be a menace to others. But many subsequently become real sportsmen and some take an active part in maintaining public order.'[35] It is noteworthy that, when the Central Committee of the Communist Party launched a special campaign against drunkenness and alcoholism in June 1972, it gave special mention in its resolution ('On Measures for Intensifying the Fight against Drunkenness and Alcoholism') to the need for providing more and better sports facilities: 'We must increase the number of out-of-town recreational centres, using, in particular, the premises of Pioneer camps when the children are not occupying them; we must build in these recreational areas more ski centres, ice rinks, pavilions and boating lakes, hire points for sports and tourist equipment; we must increase the number of sports grounds, tennis courts, ice rinks, etc. on collective and state farms, in urban residential districts and in workers' settlements.'[36] Sport, as much subsequent press and official comment has shown, was to be a principal diversion from vodka drinking, especially on weekends and holidays. It was felt that youth, in particular, needs the challenge and adventure of sport, that competitiveness – or conflict – in sport provides an outlet for young people. Using sport as an antidote to deviance among young people is illustrated by two sports sections in Moscow, set up exclusively for juvenile delinquents – the Olimpya ice hockey club and the *Burevestnik* special combat young people's sports school. The latter has 240 children enrolled in its boxing and wrestling groups (one of whom won a gold medal in wrestling at the 1973 European Championships).

Another aim of the authorities has been to see that sporting activities and free time generally are used in a rational way, that

[35] G. D. Kharabuga, *Sovetskaya sistema fizicheskovo vospitaniya* (Leningrad, 1970), p. 13.
[36] *Sovetsky sport*, 17 July 1972, p. 1.

sport should be socially functional. The prevailing functionalised conception of sport stresses not so much the needs of the individual as those of society. As Party Secretary Leonid Brezhnev has made clear: 'In socialist society, time free from work is a measure of public wealth. But free time can only be considered genuine public wealth when it is used in the interests of the all-round development of the individual, of his capabilities, and, thereby, for an even greater increase in the material and spiritual potential of our society.'[37] Time well spent on sporting activities is held to be important because of the contribution it makes to production and the smooth functioning of society in general. It should enrich the individual so that he may enrich society. Only under socialism, it is argued, is this possible: 'Various systems of exercises for strengthening the body and mind have existed through the ages, but they have all been based on the narrow interests of exploiting classes, aimed at limited groups of people and have not envisaged the harmonious development of every person. Our country was the first to elaborate a system of physical education and sport embracing the whole of a person's life, from early childhood to old age, a system noble in its aims – to improve people's health, physique and labour performance.'[38]

Nonetheless, a number of games exist that clearly are at odds with notions of rationality – horse racing (as a spectator sport for gamblers), dominoes, lotto (bingo) and many card games. That they are tolerated is an indication that the authorities are willing to compromise with the strong personal desires of sections of the public on such matters – perhaps in order to gain compliance or at least the absence of active resistance in other, more important spheres. They are the equivalent in sport of such semi-tolerated or tolerated but non-approved actions as vodka drinking, tipping and religious observance. The position of dominoes is particularly illustrative of the ambivalent status of such games. Some say dominoes is a serious game, interesting, useful, intellectual. It has "won its spurs" among such games as chess and draughts. . .'[39] Others maintain that 'the domino cult deals a blow at real mass

[37] *Komsomol'skaya pravda*, 21 March 1972, p. 3.
[38] N. N. Bugrov (ed.), *Fizkul'tura i podgotovka molodyozhi k trudu* (Moscow, 1963), p. 3.
[39] *Sovetsky sport*, 12 May 1971, p. 2.

physical culture work. . . It is not necessary to encourage an increase in the ranks of domino bangers; it is a notoriously irrational game.'[40] Academician Strumilin, on the other hand, was more tolerant: 'No one will object to a game of cards or dominoes [in Communist society]. Nor will anyone interfere with a person who wastes his leisure or kills time, as they say. Such a person, however, might meet with the censure of his friends.'[41]

Some sociologists believe that such seemingly wasteful and irrational games as cards and dominoes are in fact an important part of urban life, and that official sanctions will not stop people playing them: 'before campaigning against such non-sporting games, people ought to realise that neither the cinema, books, nor even television, can "defeat" dominoes, because they all fulfil different leisure functions. Neither propaganda, nor ridicule, nor administrative sanctions will have any effect.'[42] The authors do not specify these functions, but one may assume them to include compensations for the lack of outlet for such motivations as love of chance successes and speculation, and a response to the needs of the 'less cultured'. One may further assume that Soviet society, like all cultures, has and plays a large number of games of different kinds, not all of which confirm or reinforce established values – rather, which contradict and flout them, thus representing compensations or safety valves for its citizens. As the French sociologist, Roger Caillois, has written in regard to national lotteries: they may 'go against the professional idea. Nevertheless, they play a significant, perhaps indispensable, rôle in that they offer an aleatory counterpart for the recompense that – in principle – work and merit alone can provide.'[43]

A number of sports or games have been attacked for their allegedly exhibitionist nature or for the fact that they lend themselves to commercial exploitation (even within the Soviet Union), thereby detracting from the *sporting* element – as it is understood in the Soviet sports system. Such games include women's soccer and unarmed combat (*sambo*), and male body-building. By a reso-

[40] Ibid., p. 2.
[41] S. G. Strumilin, *Your Questions on Communism* (Moscow, 1964), p. 13.
[42] Gordon and Klopov, *Chelovek posle raboty*, p. 145.
[43] R. Caillois, *Man, Play and Games* (Thames and Hudson, London, 1962), p. 89.

lution adopted by the USSR Sports Committee in January 1973 ('On Certain Facts Concerning the Incorrect Development of Some Physical Exercises and Sports'), sports organisations were instructed to disband sections practising women's soccer, body-building, hatha-yoga, karate and bridge.

An activity with an undoubtedly large following among men is body-building, which has been difficult to keep within state-desired limits. The state has been concerned that 'athletic gymnastics' should not step over the border into 'culturism'. With an eye to the 'excesses' that exist in the West, the authorities fear it will become an excuse for exhibitionism and narcissism: 'egotistic love and dandified culture of the body and one-sided, unhealthy development of the organism are alien to the Soviet system of physical culture'.[44] The sport has not been banned, but all the various '*Gerkules*', '*Atlant*', '*Atlet*' and '*Anteus*' studios up and down the country, from L'vov in the Ukraine to Tyumen' in Siberia, from Tallinn in Estonia to Alma Ata in Kazakhstan, have been officially warned (1970 and 1973) to keep their activities 'strictly in accordance with scientific, medical, and hygienic recommendations, thus precluding all manner of contests and exhibitions that include posing and the judging of the body'.[45]

Another reason for attacking certain activities is that they are said to be associated with a philosophy that is alien to that of Soviet society. This applies to such oriental pursuits as hatha-yoga and karate. Yoga had become quite popular, particularly among intellectuals, in the early 1970s and had received some official encouragement – including two films shown on television. During 1973, however, it was roundly condemned as being potentially injurious to health, but particularly for two ideological reasons: first, 'yoga does not involve team-work; it encourages individualism and advocates that "yogis" should lead a closed ascetic life outside of society and even of the family'; second, it is 'based on idealist philosophy and mysticism'.[46] The latter accusation was also levelled at karate.

Card games have regularly been condemned throughout Soviet history as empty, time-wasting activities often associated with

---

[44] *Sovetsky sport*, 25 January 1973, p. 3.
[45] *Teoriya i praktika fizicheskoi kul'tury*, 1973, No. 10, p. 63.
[46] *Sovetsky sport*, 25 January 1973, p. 3.

gambling and luck (rather than skill), so it was no surprise to see bridge condemned in 1973 as a 'perversion' of sporting activities. It was revealed that bridge schools had existed in places as far apart as Leningrad, Vilnius, Tallinn, Kiev, Tbilisi, L'vov, Riga and Moscow; Estonia and Lithuania had even had their own bridge federations and, for several years, had held inter-city and Republican bridge tournaments. The official reasons for condemning bridge were not given, but one may surmise that the game was regarded as a potential menace to productivity, as an 'irrational' use of free time and as a game partly based on chance.

All the above mentioned 'sporting activities' had gained a hold, the January 1973 resolution stated, 'due to the connivance, acquiescence and unprincipled position of certain sports administrators. Instead of determined and daily work in introducing the new *GTO* complex or using sport as an effective and necessary means for organising the free time of the workers and for training top-class sportsmen, they became involved in charlatanism and roguery, helping to implant and popularise all manner of "fashionable" exercises designed to excite people and to encourage a spirit of profit that is detrimental to the health of participants and also, to some extent, to Soviet society.'[47]

The emphasis on the special interdependence of work and games stems from the paramount importance attributed to work and from the claim that, in socialist society, it has acquired a uniquely satisfactory character owing to the absence of exploitation and alienation. Yet, as with other media of recreation and leisure – e.g. television and the cinema – the official descriptions must be understood as arising largely from a desire to *educate* the population in the broad sense of the word and to prevent the wasteful dissipation of energy and time.

At the same time, with more money, more free time and a wider range of recreation to choose from, Soviet people are increasingly able to select the recreational activity that most accords with their personal desire and aspiration. With improved facilities and opportunities, participation in sport is becoming less ruled by the official utilitarian-instrumental approach – despite official attempts to regulate the use of increasing leisure – and more

[47] *Teoriya i praktika fizicheskoi kul'tury, 1973*, No. 10, pp. 63–64.

governed by the idea that a game, a sport or outdoor activity of any kind is desirable in itself, for its own sake.

Improving health

The link between sport and better health has been noted throughout this work, particularly the Party's desire to use sport for inculcating habits of hygiene and health in a culturally backward population and for improving physical fitness. It is, in fact, inscribed in the Fundamental Law of the USSR on Public Health (Article 49) that 'State bodies, trade unions, the *Komsomol*, sports societies, factories and offices *must* promote physical education and fitness programmes, sport and tourism, they *must* set up and constantly improve sports groups and tourist clubs and arrange production gymnastics'.[48] There have been many factors behind the all-round improvement in Soviet vital statistics (and, too, the advances in sport), but the interaction between sport and health can certainly be said to have been mutually beneficial. The improvements in vital statistics and health generally in the Soviet Union have been particularly marked since the end of the last war; these have certain implications for sport that will be discussed after a description of the changes themselves.

In 1913, in the Russian Empire, both the birth rate and the death rate were extremely high: births were 45.5 per 1,000 inhabitants, deaths were 29.1 (infantile mortality was as high as 269 per 1,000) – within the present territory of the USSR. The natural yearly population increase was, therefore, 16.4 per 1,000. What is particularly interesting is that, in 1940, on the eve of the German invasion of the USSR and 23 years after the revolution, the situation was not very greatly different from that of 1913: by 1940, births had dropped to 31.2; deaths to 18.0 and the natural net increase to 13.3; infantile mortality had fallen from 269 to 182: an unquestionable progress, but by no means sensational. The decisive turn has come since the war (see Table 7).

It is noteworthy that the Soviet statistics for the 1960s are quite close to those for the advanced countries of Europe. Thus, taking

[48] Pavlov, 'Glavnaya nasha zadacha', p. 7. See Art. 82 of RSFSR Law of 29 July 1971 on Health Protection, published by 'Izvestiya' (Moscow, 1971), pp. 33–34.

TABLE 7   *Birth and death rates: selected years, 1958–1973*

Year	Births	Deaths	Natural increase	Infantile mortality[a]
1958	25.3	7.2	18.1	41.0
1959	25.0	7.6	17.4	41.0
1960	24.9	7.1	17.8	35.3
1965	18.4	7.3	11.1	27.2
1966	18.2	7.3	10.9	26.1
1967	17.3	7.6	9.7	26.0
1968	17.2	7.7	9.5	26.4
1969	17.0	8.1	8.9	25.8
1970	17.4	8.2	9.2	24.7
1971	17.8	8.2	9.6	22.9
1972	17.8	8.5	9.3	24.7
1973	17.6	8.6	9.0	26.0

[a] Deaths up to age 1 per 1,000 live births.
Sources: *Narodnoye khozyaistvo SSSR, 1922–1972 gg.* (Moscow, 1972), p. 40; *SSSR v tsifrakh v 1973 godu* (Moscow, 1974), p. 18.

the years 1960, 1965 and 1970, the figures for the USSR, France and England are indicated in Table 8.

The Soviet trends are very interesting: the death rate has remained almost stationary at around 7–8 per 1,000, the birth rate has been sharply declining and the rate of natural increase has halved. Infantile mortality has dropped from 35 to around 25. If, compared with those for 1913, the figures for 1940 are not spectacular (the infantile mortality rate in 1940 was still only one-third less than in 1913), those for 1970 represent a considerable improvement.

The lower birth rate and smaller family mean more leisure time available for parents; they are no longer so tied to the home and can travel and afford equipment, such as skis and camping equipment (some – even a car) and the time to use them. The lower death rate and high life expectancy (in 1975, it was 66 for men and 74 for women) mean that more middle-aged and older people can go in for sport. It is a particular feature of Soviet sport and physical education that so many older people are preoccupied with keeping fit. The *Bodrost' i zdorov'ye* ('Fitness and Health') groups for older people that have mushroomed since about 1956 are just one example of this. Some 5,000 people over 35 (women)

TABLE 8 *Vital statistics 1960, 1965 and 1970: USSR, France and United Kingdom*

	Birth rate	Death rate	Natural increase	Infantile mortality
			Indicator	
1960				
USSR	24.9	7.1	17.8	35.3
France	17.9	11.4	6.5	27.4
UK	17.5	11.5	6.0	22.5
1965				
USSR	18.4	7.3	11.1	27.2
France	17.8	11.2	6.6	21.9
UK	18.3	11.5	6.8	19.6
1970				
USSR	17.4	8.2	9.2	24.7
France	16.7	10.7	6.0	18.2
UK	16.2	11.7	4.5	18.4

Sources: *Narodnoye khozyaistvo SSSR v 1972 g.* (Moscow, 1973), pp. 123–125; *SSSR v tsifrakh v 1973 godu* (Moscow, 1974), pp. 18, 59; *UN Statistical Yearbook* (1970), pp. 371–377; *UN Demographic Yearbook* (1968), pp. 371, 373; *Social Trends, 1974* (HMSO, 1974) pp. 208–209.

and over 40 (men) are said to belong to such groups attached to the Lenin Stadium in Moscow: they pay five rubles a month and may attend three times a week for two-hour sessions.[49] Since 1966, tests and norms have existed on a parallel with the *GTO* system for the *Bodrost' i zdorov'ye* badge.

The reduction in infantile mortality and general improvement in children's health are results of many factors – not least of all state care for the health and fitness of children. Some measure of

[49] During my second stay in Moscow (October 1970–March 1971), I joined just such a *Bodrost' i zdorov'ye* group at the Lenin Stadium, attending two mornings a week; there were said to be up to 5,000 registered members attending keep fit classes in the stadium every week, although the Tuesday and Thursday morning classes averaged about 25–30 people (with an average age of about 50). Most had been recommended by their doctors to attend, although it was remarkable that, while being keen on exercise, hardly anyone observed a diet; indeed, immediately after the sessions, we would retire to the canteen where the women (most rather buxom) in particular would consume several buns with their glasses of cocoa.

the improvement in the physical development of children may be seen from a Lithuanian study covering the period 1958–1966 which shows that children in some age groups were, in 1966, taller by 3–4 cm and heavier by 2–3 kg than in 1958. They could jump higher and farther, run faster and were generally stronger. Nonetheless, the study sounded a warning note familiar to health authorities in other developed urban communities: 'there is a tendency towards excess weight which makes for passivity, inhibits movement and is detrimental to character formation and aesthetic views'.[50]

There have, of course, been many factors (living standards, hygiene levels, medical provisions, etc.) behind the overall improvement in vital statistics and the Soviet advances in international sport, but the effect of the practice of sport on health has certainly had a part to play in improving people's health and the quality and achievement in sport. About that, Soviet political leaders have no doubt, as Brezhnev has more than once stated: 'We want to see our young people healthy, tempered, physically tough as well as widely educated and cultured. . . We must continue to raise the international class of our sport, but the main thing is the health of the millions in the sports movement, the development of physical culture embracing all young people, the tempering of their will power, the physical preparation of young people for work and defence.'[51]

This chapter has gone into some detail to describe the main processes which have influenced the Soviet sports movement in the years since the beginning of the 1960s and the resultant tensions they have brought between official and personal desires in recreation, because they are central to an understanding of Soviet sport today. These processes lie behind many of the changes in structure and aims which the next chapter examines.

[50] *Sport v SSSR*, 1970, No. 6, p. 6.
[51] *Teoriya i praktika fizicheskoi kul'tury*, 1971, No. 5, p. 55. The quotation comes from a speech Brezhnev made at the opening of the plenary meeting of the *Komsomol* Central Committee in 1969.

9
Contemporary organisation of Soviet sport and physical education

Background

At the Twenty-First Congress of the Communist Party in 1959, the then First Secretary of the Party, N. S. Khrushchov, declared that the Soviet Union was entering the period of full-scale construction of communism, that it was in the final stages of socialism – the transitional period between capitalism and communism – and could begin seriously to build the foundations of complete communist society. One feature of this development, in fulfilment of Marx's and Engels' forecast many years earlier, was to be the 'withering away of the state' – i.e. the transfer of duties, previously undertaken by paid state functionaries, to voluntary unpaid popular bodies. One of the first indications of the new policy, consequent on Khrushchov's dictum, was seen in the form of a new administrative structure for sport.[1]

Union of Sports Societies and Organisations established

In a government resolution of 9 January 1959 'On the Administration of Physical Culture and Sport in the Country', it was proclaimed that, 'at the present stage of communist construction, when the rôle of mass workers' organisations – especially of the unions and the *Komsomol* – is acquiring growing importance in handling state affairs, there is no longer a need to concentrate the administration of physical culture and sport in the hands of

---

[1] Other innovations of the time, as part of the 'withering away of the state', were, in non-sporting spheres, the comradely courts and the *druzhiny* (unpaid volunteers who help to keep public order and control traffic).

government agencies; there exists every opportunity for the sports movement to be completely based on broad democratic principles and for its administration to be undertaken by an elected popular organisation'.[2]

Further elucidation of this reorganisation was provided in the Party Programme adopted at the Twenty-Second Party Congress in October 1961: 'What we have to do is to reduce the state salaried apparatus, to get more and more people to acquire the habits of administration and to ensure that the work in this apparatus gradually stops being a special profession.'[3]

As a consequence, the All-Union Committee on Physical Culture and Sport Affairs was dissolved, along with all its local committees. In its place 'had been found a more expedient form of organisation of sport in which the dominant rôle would be played by the popular organisations that participate in the sports movement. A Union of Sports Societies and Organisations of the USSR is to be set up, which would be a public – not a state – agency.'[4]

In theory, at any rate, the new public organisations were to be much more democratic than their predecessors; they would be based on direct popular administration and encourage popular initiative and self-government. In practice, the 'withering away' of the sports administrative apparatus appears to have been somewhat premature and no fundamental changes occurred, apart from a degree of reduction in central control and the replacement of some coercion by greater incentives and public discussion. Romanov continued until 1962 as the person chiefly responsible for sports administration and was then replaced by Yury Mashin, a relatively young Party worker who appeared to have no previous experience in this field. Romanov became Secretary of the All-Union Central Council of Trade Unions.

On 19 February 1959, draft statutes for the new Union were presented for public discussion. The 46 articles defined the proposed organisational structure, which somewhat resembled that of other Soviet administrative bodies – i.e. in following the prin-

[2] *Fizkul'tura, sport i turizm* (Moscow, 1963), p. 5.
[3] *Materialy XXII s"yezda KPSS* (Moscow, 1961), p. 399.
[4] N. S. Khrushchov, *O kontrol'nykh tsifrakh razvitiya narodnovo khozyaistva SSSR na 1959–65 gg.* (Moscow, 1959), p. 120.

ciple of 'democratic centralism', whereby the lower-level organs formally elect delegates to those on the next higher level, ranging upwards from the sports collectives and clubs through city, *raion* (district), *oblast'* (regional), *krai* (territorial) and Republican levels to an 'executive' Central Council and a 'legislative' All-Union Congress. This Congress, like Party, *Komsomol* and trade union congresses, was to be a 'supreme organ' and was to meet once every four years. Between meetings, the Central Council, convening twice a year, was to implement the directives of Congresses. Day-to-day administration was to be carried on by a Presidium of the Council. The organisational structure of the All-Union Football Federation in the Soviet sports movement as a whole is described in Figure 3.

The 1961 Party Congress formulated a new (third) Party Programme intended to be relevant to the new period of 'construction of the material and technological base of full-scale communist society'; it also endorsed the reorganisation of sports administration which had taken place. As before, sport was to be a means of raising productivity: recreation, properly organised, and physical exercises during the working day were seen as helping to restore energy and as powerful factors making for higher labour productivity. Furthermore, sport was to help combat the physical and mental inertness and lethargy that, it was averred, had been attendant upon higher standards of living in other societies. Now that sport was to be self-administered, the new organisational structure was intended to inject new vitality into the sports movement at all levels, not least in the factory.

A new dimension was given to sport: a character training appropriate to the construction and nature of communist society. The Congress emphasised a previously neglected aspect of the functions of Soviet sport for the immediate future: the 'all-round development of the personality'. This notion implied that there was more to sport than mere recreation; no person could consider himself properly developed if he neglected the physical side of his education. In the new period of a final transition to communism, there was to be every opportunity 'for educating a new person who would harmoniously combine spiritual wealth, moral purity and a perfect physique'. The official desire was to make sport as common a part of everyday life as eating or teeth cleaning. As

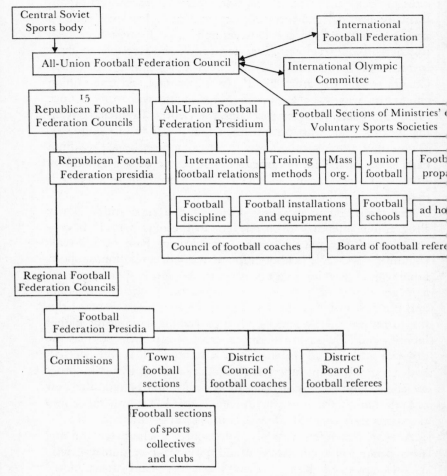

Fig. 3. Structure of the All-Union Football Federation

the new Party Programme put it: 'People will increasingly devote their leisure to public pursuits, cultural intercourse, intellectual and physical development, scientific, technical and artistic creative endeavour. Physical culture and sport will become part and parcel of everyday life.'[5]

[5] *Materialy XXII s"yezda KPSS*, p. 412.

The official insistence at this time on the proximity of the full-scale communist social order therefore had important implications for the new interest in sport. 'Rationally utilised' recreation was said to go to meet the need for the ever-higher level of productivity and efficiency associated with complete communism and to contribute to the full development of the New Soviet Man. Thus, the prerequisites of Communist society included both changed values, or complete development of the New Soviet Man, and an economy of abundance to provide for his material and cultural needs. It must be added that the strong utopian elements in the Party Programme and Soviet ideology, particularly during the Khrushchov era (Khrushchov had, for instance, predicted the creation of the 'material basis' of communism by 1980[6]), have since been toned down and some have been dropped altogether (such as the predicted early arrival of communism); their use in appealing to an expectant audience virtually dictated that some account be given of what, besides material abundance and freedom from fatiguing toil, would comprise the 'good life' of the future.

The reorganisation of sport was to give added impetus to the campaign to draw more people into sport. This was not a new policy. But it was now presented as a feasible reality for the mass of the population: 'The Party considers it of fundamental importance to ensure the education, from a very early age, of a physically strong younger generation which harmoniously combines physical and spiritual forces. This necessitates the extensive encouragement of all forms of mass sport and physical culture, including in the schools, and the involvement in the sports movement of increasingly wider sections of the population, especially young people.'[7]

There was, therefore, an intention to make sport part of everyday life. Partly to this end, the first conference of the new Union set its sights on a total of 50 million regular and active sportsmen by the end of 1965. At the same time, sporting proficiency was not neglected: by the end of 1965, there were to be 17 million ranked athletes, including 400,000 in the first ranking and 30,000

[6] *Pravda*, 6 March 1962, p. 2.
[7] *Materialy XXII s"yezda KPSS*, p. 393.

Masters of Sport.[8] These targets, which were virtually double the figures for 1959, were, it was claimed, achieved. Subsequently, the target was to be 60 million regular participants by 1970 and, then, the less ambitious figure of 60–65 by 1980[9] – perhaps indicating that the earlier targets had been fulfilled on paper only. In fact, the figures and targets were revised downwards in 1969–1970 in view of the blatant falsifying of figures that was widespread. A more precise definition of a *fizkul'turnik*[10] or sports participant was given, a new and revised *GTO* programme was introduced (with warnings to all that it was to be treated seriously and that no one was to be awarded a badge without meeting all the requisite standards – and more realistic targets were set). Thus, in 1972, it was claimed that 45 million people regularly pursued a sport[11] – almost the same number claimed for 1965.

All-Union Federations for individual sports

Another new organisational step taken in 1959 was the setting up of All-Union Federations for individual sports; by 1970, there were 56 of these. In tune with the new appeal for voluntary work and local initiative, the Federations were to be backed up in the localities by individual sports sections attached to the *krai* (territorial), *oblast'* (regional), city and *raion* (district) councils and run by local sports enthusiasts rather than by full-time functionaries. In this way, more than three million 'volunteers' were drawn into the sports administration. Throughout the sports movement, the trend was towards the encouragement of public support on a voluntary unpaid basis, whether as referees, coaches, instructors or as sports administrators. It is regarded as the duty of many athletes and coaches, particularly Masters of Sport, to make their

[8] *Fizkul'tura i sport*, 1960, No. 3, p. 3.
[9] *Sovetsky sport*, 29 June 1971, p. 1.
[10] A '*fizkul'turnik*' was now defined as 'a member of a physical culture collective who engages in physical exercise or sport in a section, group or team under the supervision of a full-time or part-time coach *not less than twice a week* (including participation in sports-competitions) over a period of six months' (my italics – JR). (I. Pereverzin, *Prognozirovanie i planirovanie fizicheskoi kul'tury*, Moscow, 1972, p. 6.)
[11] *Narodnoye khozyaistvo SSSR v 1972 g.* (Moscow, 1973), p. 693.

voluntary and unpaid contribution to society by giving coaching lessons, instructing in schools and clubs. This trend away from direct state forms of administration to 'popular' forms of self-government was said to signify the beginnings of a new, communist relationship of people to matters of state importance.

1966 Resolutions on sport

Despite the reorganisation, whose effects do not appear to have been very great, the level of participation and performance in sport did not come up to expectations – even though the paper targets for numbers of 'sportsmen' were claimed to be fulfilled. How *real* the changes were is hard to assess, but the Party leadership remained unhappy about the persistent imbalance in participation.

Defects in participation

The provinces and rural areas, as well as the casual athletes in the cities, were still being largely ignored in the desire to concentrate efforts and facilities on potential stars. Facilities and qualified staff were still extremely limited in the schools and colleges. At least two-thirds of all teachers taking physical education lessons in schools in 1965 were unqualified.[12] Of the 663 colleges and universities, only 45 (less than 7 per cent) were considered to have 'adequate' sports facilities.[13] Not enough attention was being paid to the lower and upper reaches of the population – all those outside the 19–35 age range. Yet the nature of contemporary industry and the increasing leisure time made it essential greatly to extend the facilities available for recreation, particularly for older workers. In the countryside and generally in certain less industrially advanced republics, the lack of both physical facilities and qualified personnel was hampering sports development. Consequently, the gap between town and village, metropolis and outlying areas was increasing rather than diminishing. Another under-represented group was women. On 1 January 1966, of the

[12] V. Mikhailov, *Sovetskaya fizicheskaya kul'tura i sport na novom etape* (Moscow, 1967), p. 12.
[13] Ibid., p. 18.

46 million sports participants, fewer than 16 million (i.e. 34 per cent) were women. Whereas 20 per cent of the total population regularly engaged in sport, only 13 per cent of the female population did so. Moreover, of the 4,678 Master of Sport titles awarded during 1965, only 1,052 went to women – i.e. less than a quarter. This was despite the fact that, as a result of the war, there were far more women (54 per cent) than men (46 per cent) in the 1966 population.

With the dismissal of Khrushchov in October 1964, the policy of the gradual extension of the transfer of state functions to activists and the handing over of local full-time agencies to voluntary unpaid and untrained bodies was largely discontinued. Although the structure of the sports administration was in the main permitted to stand until 1968, the encouragement of voluntary unpaid bodies was tacitly dropped.

It would seem that one result of the encouragement of greater 'popular initiative' and self-administration was a shift from mass to individual recreation. (This was also due, no doubt, to the higher personal incomes obtaining at this time.) Clubs concentrated on the business of winning cups and medals, and the masses, released from the pressures for public sport participation, either took up more individual pursuits (tourism, boating, fishing – see the popularity chart above, p. 189), or 'dropped out' altogether. As the future chairman of the supreme sports authority, Sergei Pavlov, was later to put it: 'By the mid-1960s . . . many undertakings had forgotten that the main index of success of the primary sports group was not innumerable certificates and cups, but the wide regular involvement in sport of all who can play volleyball and table tennis, ski and skate. In many sports organisations, sport, competition and training were used not for educational work, propaganda was low; there were not enough sports centres and facilities. Many young people had a poor idea of the rôle of sport and regular participation in raising productivity, fortifying health and broadening their range of interests and recreation.'[14]

What worried the authorities was, perhaps, not so much the lack of mass participation as the fact that the general decline in

[14] S. P. Pavlov, 'Novaya stupen'', in V. A. Ivonin (ed.), *Velenie vremeni* (Moscow, 1969), p. 11.

administrative and other pressures had led to a measure of individual independence or separation from institutional and public organisations. The use of sport as an agent of social control through the *Komsomol* and trade unions had weakened, and this important link had to be reforged. Party concern with the free time of individuals has always been more consistent with a centrally directed model of social organisation. The effort to regulate recreation, and not merely to provide facilities for its use plus a modicum of guidance, is part of the desire to control a large segment of the life of the citizen and use it for his or her moral education (*vospitanie*).

To remedy this situation, the Party and government sent out directives to 'Party central committees and Republican Councils of Ministers, Party committees and Executive Committees of Soviets of Working People's Deputies, the All-Union Central Council of Trade Unions, the *Komsomol* Central Committee and to all sports organisations'.[15] The subsequent resolution (of 11 August 1966) 'On Measures to Promote Physical Culture and Sport' obliged them 'to improve administration of the sports movement as an important part of educative work among the population, to set out clear-cut measures for developing physical culture so that it might become a more active means by which society would influence the formation of Soviet people's moral and spiritual outlook, would encourage their all-round harmonious development and highly productive labour, would help them stay healthy and creatively active until old age, and would prepare them for defending their Homeland'.[16]

Not since the 1925 Party resolution had the utilitarian and social functions of Soviet sport been spelled out so forcibly; for several years to come, hardly any official article on sport would go into print without due acknowledgement of the 'August Resolutions' of 1966, as they became known. The resolutions were strong meat and put sport on the agenda, for the first time, of many Party Committee meetings: 'Between 1966 and 1968, the Communist Parties of Latvia, Armenia and Tadzhikistan *for the first time ever* examined problems of sport at meetings of Republican Party organisations. In 1969, the Uzbek and Georgian

[15] *Pravda*, 11 August 1966, p. 1.
[16] *Pravda*, 25 August 1966, p. 2.

Supreme Soviets ratified legislation on measures to improve mass sport.'[17] (My emphasis.)

The highlight of the resolutions was the desire to make sport universal: 'The Soviet physical culture movement must be universal (*obshchenarodny*) and be founded on a scientifically based system of physical education which consistently embraces all groups in the population from a very early age.'[18]

Establishment of an All-Union Committee on Physical Culture and Sport

Two years later, on 17 October 1968, the sports movement was once again taken under direct government control with the creation of an All-Union Committee on Physical Culture and Sport attached to the Council of Ministers of the USSR. The now defunct Union, being a 'social' organisation, was said to have had insufficient power to implement the 1966 resolutions. The new Committee's resolutions and instructions on sport were to be binding on all ministries, departments and public organisations. Similar government committees were set up in all Union Republics. The new Chairman taking over from Yuri Mashin was Sergei Pavlov, who had been Secretary of the Central Committee of the *Komsomol* from 1959 to 1968.[19] Apparently as a result of the Committee's proposals, three important steps were taken. First, real efforts were made to provide the countryside with more facilities and qualified instructors, and farm chairmen were instructed to facilitate the achievement of this goal: the amended Collective Farm Regulations ratified at the 3rd All-Union Congress of Collective Farmers in 1969, for example, included the following passage: 'the collective farm shall take steps to improve the cultural and everyday living conditions of collective farmers, shall display daily care for their health *and the physical education of members of the collective farm and their families . . . shall build and equip . . . sports installations, and promote physical culture and sport*'.[20]

17 Pavlov, 'Novaya stupen'', p. 12.
18 *Pravda*, 25 August 1966, p. 2.
19 See Appendix I for a list of sports leaders, brief biographies and a note on their selection.
20 *Sovetsky sport*, 5 November 1969, p. 3.

Second, in late 1969, the Supreme Soviet of the USSR passed a law 'On the Ratification of the Fundamentals of Legislation of the USSR and Union Republics on Health.' Article 49 of the Law lays down detailed obligations and rights in regard to the organisation of physical culture, sport and tourism.

Third, the government itself carried out a drive to increase and improve sports facilities; in May 1969, it passed a resolution 'On Increasing the Production, Assortment and Quality of Sports and Tourist Equipment'. How effective the campaign was is still too early to say, but the pages that follow give some ideas of the quantitative and qualitative changes that have taken place in Soviet sport since the 1966 resolutions.

Revision of the classification systems

'Ready For Labour and Defence': revisions

To cover a wider segment of the population, the *GTO* programme was in 1966 to embrace all age groups from 14 to 60 and to consist of five stages for men and four for women: (1) a category for boys and girls of 14–15 (*BGTO*); (2) one for juniors aged 16–17; (3) a new category for (male) pre-conscripts called 'Ready for Defence of the Homeland' (*Gotov k zashchite rodiny – GZR*); (4) one for the age group 19–39 for men and 18–34 for women; and (5) a 'Fitness and Health' category (*Bodrost' i zdorov'ye – BZ*) for males over 40 and females over 35.

In the armed forces, the *GTO* programme was replaced from 1966 by one with a greater military bias: the Military-Sports Programme; a corresponding badge 'Soldier–Sportsman' (*Voin–Sportsmen – VS*) was awarded at three levels. Parallely, special sports rankings were instituted for servicemen and they no longer followed the general classification system.

Each stage of the new *GTO* system necessitated a certain minimum performance in gymnastics, running, jumping, throwing, swimming, shooting (except in the *BGTO* programme) and skiing (the 'Fitness and Health' group had its own less vigorous programme). A points system was used to estimate performance. Each event had a minimum pass mark and, the better the performance, the more points earned. To gain a badge, every event had to be performed and it was not enough to achieve a bare minimum qualifying mark in each event; a certain number of points above the overall minimum had to be reached. On this basis, a competitor was awarded either a 'pass' or an 'excellent' mark. One year was allowed for the 'pass' qualification and two years for the 'excellent'.

As an example of qualifying marks in the *GTO* standards chart (for 1964), men in the 19–39 age group had to climb 4 m up a rope or pole, run 100 m in 14 seconds and 1,500 m in 5 minutes 30 seconds, long jump 4.3 m, hurl a 700 gm grenade (unfused) 35 m, swim 100 m in 2 minutes 20 seconds, ski 10 km in one hour five minutes and score a certain number of points firing a small-bore rifle at 50 m. In addition, they had to perform eight morning exercises satisfactorily, and answer questions on first-aid, sport and hygiene.[21]

GTO planning quotas were set for every region, club, society and collective, and tests were held throughout the year under the supervision of *ad hoc* commissions – primarily to prevent collectives falsifying results to fulfil or overfulfil their set targets. The main concern of most sports collectives is, in fact, to see that their members obtain their *GTO* badges. There is competition among the various collectives and all other levels, including Republics, to attain the highest number of badges or proportion of badges in relation to total work force or population. Seventy million people had qualified for badges by 1961 in the thirty years since their inception in 1931. In the next nine years, 1962–1970, another 86 million qualified – an average of some 10 million a year[22] – i.e. nearly five per cent of the population.

A revised All-Union Physical Culture 'Ready for Labour and Defence of the USSR' programme came into effect from 1 March 1972;[23] the new requirements and qualifying standards had been drawn up jointly by the All-Union Committee on Physical Culture and Sport, the All-Union Central Council of Trade Unions and the Central Committee of the *Komsomol*. The official reasons for the overhaul of the system just six years after the last

---

[21] N. A. Makartsev, *Organizatsiya raboty fizkul'turnova kollektiva* (Moscow, 1964), pp. 84–85.

[22] *Sovetsky sport*, 27 February 1972, p. 2.

[23] *Sovetsky sport*, 25 February 1972, pp. 2–3 gives full details of the new Statute.

change were given by Sergei Pavlov, the All-Union Committee's Chairman:

We have to admit that the opportunities offered by the *GTO* system have, on the whole, been poorly used for improving the vocational and applied military training of young people. At many establishments they no longer concern themselves with workers' physical education. The means of physical culture and sport have been used in an extremely limited way in organising workers' labour and leisure scientifically, in improving workers' health and preventing industrial diseases, in combating bad habits, in tightening up labour and social discipline, and in improving educative work with young people.[24]

Yet another campaign was therefore launched, in a great blare of publicity, to keep sports officials and factory managers on their toes and to attract more people to regular exercise. The changes entailed the following: lowering the age limit to cover the range 10–60 instead of 14–60, dispensing with the *BGTO*, introducing names for each of the five stages, establishing an All-Union *GTO* Council to coordinate activities and supervise the qualifying for and awarding of *GTO* badges, increasing the military content, and going over to qualifying standards through competition rather than a points system (which, it was alleged, had been open to abuse). Inasmuch as it is through the *GTO* that most Soviet people are involved in organised sport and as it is regarded as the *foundation* of the Soviet system of physical education and sport, a description of the new stages, requirements and qualifying standards is given below with an example for Stage 4 (the remainder may be found in Appendix IV). There were now, as before, five stages, but for different age groups:

(1) a category for girls and boys of 10–13, called *Smelye i lovkie* ('Bold and Skilful');
(2) one for 14–15 year olds, called *Sportivnaya smena* ('Sporting Reserve');
(3) one for 16–18 year olds, called *Sila i muzhestvo* ('Strength and Courage');
(4) one for men, 19–39, and women, 19–34, called *Fizicheskoye sovershenstvo* ('Physical Perfection'); and
(5) a *Bodrost' i zdorov'ye* ('Fitness and Health') category, as before, for men 40–60 and women 35–55; older people could compete only with their doctors' permission.

[24] *Sovetsky sport*, 27 February 1972, p. 2.

The first four stages all awarded either a Gold or Silver Badge, the fourth (basic) stage having an additional mark – a Gold Badge with Distinction. The fifth stage had only a Gold Badge.

The motives for the modification of the *GTO* may be assessed as follows:

(1) to attract children to sport at an early age: this was desired first because it was felt that the earlier they became engaged in physical fitness and sport, the more likelihood there was of them taking part in regular sporting activity later; second, because there were now more facilities for children to pursue a sport and keep fit – and children are maturing earlier to use them (the minimum age limit had been at 14 since the *BGTO* was introduced in 1934); and, third, because, to achieve success in many international sports, it was increasingly necessary to spot talent and nurture it at an early age.[25]

(2) to use the *GTO* more for direct military training than it had been used in the past; a civil defence test and gas mask training were now found at each stage, and rifle firing at three stages (instead of one as before). The element of military preparation was especially evident for the 16–18 age group. Efforts were now to be made to extend this form of military training to the public at large and also to see that the army got suitably trained conscripts: 'Our clubs and sports-federations will make every effort to see that most young people of conscription age obtain a good training and enter the armed services with their *GTO*.'[26]

(3) to draw more people into the fitness campaign with a view to cutting down absenteeism from work through illness, making workers physically and mentally more alert (through sport) to cope with the changing techniques of industry – and thus raising productivity. It might also be seen as another attempt to rationalise the use of the increasing free time that people had, or at least to see that it was spent in relatively healthy and officially approved ways, as Pavlov indicated in his speech quoted above.

[25] Moreover, the average age of international champions in some sports is declining – e.g. in the 1972 Olympic Games, the winners of most gold medals among women were the 17 year old Soviet gymnast, Olga Korbut (3 gold medals) and the 16 year old Australian swimmer, Shane Gould (3 gold medals).

[26] *Sovetsky sport*, 4 March 1972, p. 3 (interview given by General A. I. Pokryshkin, Chairman of the Central Committee of *DOSAAF*).

(4) to keep organised sport and the fitness campaign in the limelight – and officials on their toes. It is noteworthy that such revisions and campaigns had occurred at frequent intervals: 1939, 1941, 1947, 1955, 1959, 1966 and 1972 – every five years on the average. (This sort of regular campaign is, of course, a feature of other spheres of Soviet life too.) There had undoubtedly been concern, however, that the *GTO* badge was 'becoming tarnished',[27] that people no longer took it seriously and that officials simply falsified *GTO* statistics and handed badges out to people who had not qualified for them: 'Exaggerated *GTO* lists, badges awarded to those who have not met all the standards . . . formalism and, simply, going through the motions (*paradnost'*)',[28] were some of the sins of which organisations were accused. To try to prevent this sort of thing happening in future, a special All-Union *GTO* Council was set up, headed by the cosmonaut, A. A. Leonov, and involving representatives of the All-Union Central Council of Trade Unions, the Central Committees of the *Komsomol* and *DOSAAF*, and of a number of government ministries and departments. The Council was to be responsible for qualifying competitions[29] (no longer could organisations hold unsupervised *GTO* qualifying contests or award points to candidates, since the points system had also been dispensed with). In other words, it was admitted that too many people had been 'cooking the books' so as to meet desirable targets and that the *GTO* was beginning to lose its meaning. It was hoped the new measures would put 'the golden and silver shine' back on the badges. In the meantime, the press spotlighted continuing malpractices: Samarkand Region (*oblast'*), for example, had handed out over 63,000 *GTO* badges in 1972, yet two-thirds of the recipients had not met the qualifying standards:[30] there had been widespread '*ochkovtiratestvo*'

[27] This was the title of an article on the new *GTO* in *Sovetsky sport*, 27 February 1972, p. 2.

[28] Ibid., p. 2.

[29] It is interesting that when I attended a soccer match at the Kirov Stadium in Leningrad in July 1972, the match was preceded by a *GTO* athletics qualifying contest in which several hundred young people took part. The giant slogans round the stadium urged people to obtain their *GTO* badge. Again on a special sports visit in late 1975, such *GTO* contests were much in evidence – at the Lenin Stadium, Moscow University and factory clubs.

[30] *Sovetsky sport*, 8 May 1973, p. 2.

TABLE 9   The All-Union physical culture system 'Ready for Labour and Defence of the USSR' (GTO), 1972

Stage 4–'Fizicheskoye sovershenstvo' ('Physical Perfection') (for men 19–39 and women 19–34)

Academic requirements (to be examined)

1. To have a knowledge of the subject 'Physical Culture and Sport in the USSR'.
2. To know and carry out the rules for personal and public hygiene.
3. To know the basic rules of civil defence and to wear a gas mask for 1 hour.
4. To be able to explain the importance of and to perform a set of morning exercises.

Physical exercises: qualifying standards

Type of exercise	Men 19–28 Silver Badge	Men 19–28 Gold Badge	Men 29–39 Silver Badge	Men 29–39 Gold Badge	Women 19–28 Silver Badge	Women 19–28 Gold Badge	Women 29–34 Silver Badge	Women 29–34 Gold Badge
1. Run 100 m (sec)	14.0	13.0	15.0	14.0	16.0	15.2	17.0	16.0
2. Run 500 m (min sec)	–	–	–	–	2.00	1.45	2.10	2.00
or 1,000 m (min sec)	3.20	3.10	3.45	3.30	4.30	4.10	5.00	4.30
or 3,000 m (min sec)	11.00	10.30	11.30	11.00	–	–	–	–
3. High jump (cm)	130	145	125	130	110	120	105	110
or long jump (cm)	460	500	400	460	350	380	320	350
4. Hurl a hand grenade of								
500 gm (m)	–	–	–	–	23	27	20	23
700 gm (m)	40	47	35	40	–	–	–	–
or putt the shot of								
4 kg (m cm)	–	–	–	–	6.50	7.50	6.20	6.50
7.257 kg (m cm)	7.50	9.00	6.50	7.50	–	–	–	–
5. Ski 3 km (min)	–	–	–	–	19	17	21	19
or 5 km (min)	25	24	30	26	35	33	38	35
or 10 km (min)	54	50	–	–	–	–	–	–
In snow-free regions:								
Run cross country 3 km (min)	–	–	–	–	19	17	21	19
6 km (min)	36	33	38	36	–	–	–	–
or cycle cross country								
10 km (min)	–	–	–	–	28	25	30	27
20 km (min)	46	–	48	–	–	–	–	–

Type of exercise	Men 19–28 Silver Badge	Men 19–28 Gold Badge	Men 29–39 Silver Badge	Men 29–39 Gold Badge	Women 19–28 Silver Badge	Women 19–28 Gold Badge	Women 29–34 Silver Badge	Women 29–34 Gold Badge
6. Swim 100 m (min sec)	2.05	1.50	2.15	2.05	2.20	2.00	2.30	2.20
7. Pull-ups: one's own weight up to 70 kg	9	13	6	9	–	–	–	–
one's own weight of 70 kg and over or lift weights above one's head (as a percentage of own weight)	7	11	4	7	–	–	–	–
own weight up to 70 kg	55	75	50	55	–	–	–	–
own weight of 70 kg and over or press-ups	65	85	60	65	12	14	8	10
or raising and lowering the trunk in a lying position, hands behind head, and feet held	–	–	12	14	40	50	30	40
8. Fire a small-bore rifle at 25 m (points)	37	43	35	37	37	43	35	37
or at 50 m (points)	34	40	34	40	–	–	–	–
Fire a heavy weapon at 100 m (points)	70	75	60	65	–	–	–	–
9. Tourist hike with test of tourist knowledge	1 hike of 25 km or 2 hikes of 15 km	1 hike of 30 km or 2 hikes of 20 km	1 hike of 20 km or 2 hikes of 12 km	1 hike of 25 km or 2 hikes of 15 km	the same as for men			
10. Obtain a sports ranking at any sport	–	II	–	–	–	II	–	–

Note: for the Gold Badge, one must attain not less than 7 qualifying standards at Gold Badge level plus 2 at Silver Badge level (except item 10). To obtain a Gold Badge with Distinction one must complete all the requirements and qualifying standards for the Gold Badge and obtain one first sports ranking or two second rankings.

('blinding with science') in Kirgizia (it provoked an order of the USSR Sports Committee 'On Serious Deficiencies in the *GTO* Work in Sports Groups in Kirgizia'); and 'businessmen' had been selling badges of the *GTO* and of Awards: a Merited Master of Sport badge had sold for 35 rubles, a Master of Sport for 20 rubles and a *GTO* badge for 10 rubles.[31] Nonetheless, there seems little doubt that a great many people did and do qualify for their badges fairly and are caught up in the fitness campaign.[32]

The following description of the new rankings system gives some idea of the qualifying obligations for each standard and age group.

The sports ranking system: revisions

While emphasising the primacy of mass participation, the 1966 resolutions by no means played down the importance of sporting proficiency. In the previous year, 1965, two new sports rankings had been introduced: (1) Master of Sport of the USSR, International Class; and (2) Candidate Master of Sport. At the same time, all rankings requirements for new candidates were revised to bring them into line with current world achievements and records.

The principal aims of the rankings system are stated in the book of rankings that is periodically published whenever the system is revised, giving qualifying standards for all recognised sports. In the edition – *Uniform All-Union Sports Classification, 1969–1972* – these aims were stated to be: (1) to establish uniform principles for the award of sports rankings and titles in order to promote the mass development of sport, the all-round training of Soviet athletes, the improvement of their health and their skill; (2) to help promote better educational work with athletes, aimed at improving their health, all-round physical development, mental and physical abilities, and their education in the spirit of the principles of the Moral Code of the Builder of Communism and of sporting ethics; (3) to help train young athletes capable of

---

[31] *Sovetsky sport*, 14 February 1973, p. 2.
[32] During 1974, nearly 18 million people obtained a *GTO* badge. *Sport v SSSR*, 1975, No. 10, p. 8.

winning Soviet and international tournaments and of establishing records.[33]

The range of sports to be included in the classification was very broad and covered both the type of sport that had a fairly extensive popular following and sports for which there existed official backing with a view to successful participation internationally. The following fifty sports were listed with appropriate standards for the period 1969–1972:

Acrobatics	Modern pentathlon
Archery	Motor racing
Athletics	Mountaineering
Badminton	Pistol shooting
Bandy[34]	Rhythmic gymnastics
Basketball	Rifle shooting
Boxing	Rowing
Canoeing	Rugby
Chess	Skiing (racing, biathlon)
Cycling (road and cross country racing)	Ski jumping
	Skiing (slalom, Nordic skiing)
Cycling (track)	Soccer
Diving	Speed skating
Draughts	Sub-Aqua sport
Equestrian sport	Swimming
Fencing	Table tennis
Field hockey	Tennis
Figure skating	Tobogganing
Firemen's sports[35]	Trampoline
Fishing	Volleyball
Gorodki	Water polo
Gymnastics	Water skiing
Handball	Weightlifting
Ice boating	Wrestling (free-style, Graeco-
Ice hockey	Roman and *sambo*)
Judo	Yachting

[33] *Yedinaya vsesoyuznaya sportivnaya klassifikatsiya, 1969–1972* (Moscow, 1969), p. 4; the new rankings were ratified in a resolution of the Committee on Physical Culture and Sport of 26 February 1969. The 'Moral Code of the Builder of Communism', referred to in the aims, was included in the new Programme of the Communist Party of the Soviet Union, launched at the Twenty-Second Congress of the Party in 1961.
[34] Bandy or Russian hockey is played with a ball instead of a puck, usually on ice.
[35] Firemen's sports (*pozharno-prikladnoi sport*) were launched in 1937,

By arrangement with the Committee on Physical Culture and Sport, certain other organisations are permitted to set norms for other sports within their special range of interest. These are as follows: (a) Republican Sports Committees – for a variety of folk games; (b) the Central Council for Tourism and Excursions – for orienteering, potholing and 'tourism'; (c) the Sports Committee of the Ministry of Defence – for sports with a military bias that are performed by athletes in uniform or carrying equipment: cross country driving, decathlon, athletics, skiing, parachuting, swimming, shooting, weightlifting, forced marching and certain initiative tests; (d) the Central Committee of *DOSAAF* – model aeroplane flying, automobile sport, model-car racing, helicopter sport, motor boating, combined sea sports, motorball, motor-cycling, parachuting, gliding, sub-aqua sport, radio sport, aeroplane sport, and model-boat racing.

For all the above sports – however esoteric they may sound – entire sets of qualifying standards, rankings and titles are laid down in the Uniform All-Union Classification system.[36]

At the top of the ranking system are two sports titles: *Master of Sport of the USSR, International Class*, and *Master of Sport of the USSR*. Then come the following sports rankings: *Candidate Master of Sport, First-Rank Sportsman, Second-Rank Sportsman, Third-Rank Sportsman, First-Rank Junior Sportsman, Second-Rank Junior Sportsman*, and *Third-Rank Junior Sportsman*.

In chess and draughts, the title *Grandmaster of the USSR* is the equivalent of *Master of Sport of the USSR, International Class* for other sports. Chess also has a fourth ranking. The only other exception to the above rankings is in folk games in which, instead of the above titles, the title *Master of* (the appropriate folk sport) *of the Republic* is awarded, since these sports do not feature in international competition.

when contests were held at all levels; three sports rankings and Master of Sport were introduced in 1959. The sports programme consists of events and exercises for training firemen for fire-fighting, performed in full uniform and equipment.

[36] Altogether there are said to be 75 sports pursued in the USSR today (*Sport v SSSR*, 1976, No. 6, p. 8).

The two titles are honorary titles for life. The only higher award to which an outstanding athlete may aspire is *Merited Master of Sport of the USSR*, but this is a state honorific decoration outside the classification system.

The *Master of Sport of the USSR, International Class* is awarded for international success either in sports in the Olympic programme, World or European championships, or (in certain sports) in other important international championships. The title of *Master of Sport* is awarded for international success or for exceptional results in a particular sport. In order to earn either title, an athlete must first meet all the ranking standards for the specific sport.

Sports rankings 1–4 are awarded on the basis of results achieved in official competition and are valid for two years only, after which time they either lapse or have to be renewed – or, of course, the athlete may try for a higher ranking. To obtain a second or third ranking, he must also have satisfied the requirements of the *GTO* programme for his particular age category. Junior rankings are awarded to athletes between 15 and 18 years of age, who have also met the qualifying standards of the appropriate *GTO* programme for their age.

The physical token of having gained one of the rankings is a badge and a certificate awarded by the All-Union Committee on Physical Culture and Sport. Ranked sportsmen receive a badge from the primary sports collective or club to which they belong. Councils of sports collectives, school head-teachers and college principals have the right to present the badges.

Titled or ranked athletes have the right to take part in official competitions and to receive preference in admission to sports schools and physical education colleges and faculties (after passing the entrance examinations). Along with these rights, however, go certain prescribed duties: (a) to conduct oneself in accordance with the Moral Code of the Builder of Communism and the code of sporting ethics; (b) constantly to improve one's political and cultural standards, physical accomplishments and sporting skill; (c) to be a member of a sports collective and actively take part in contests on behalf of one's collective; (d) to observe a sporting régime and good health standards, to fortify one's health and constantly to be under medical supervision; (e) to take an active and regular part in the Soviet sports movement and to pass on to others one's experience and expertise.[37]

Any violation of these obligations may result in deprivation of the ranking or title – a not infrequent occurrence.

The qualifying standards for each category are high and are regularly revised to keep pace with changing world standards. In some sports, the athlete competes against the clock. In athletics, for example, the 1969–1972 standards for the men's 100 m and the high jump were as shown in Table 10. (For comparison, 1970 world record figures were: 100 m – 9.9 seconds; high jump – 2.28 metres.)

TABLE 10 *Ranking standards in two athletics events: 1969–1972*

		Requirement for award of:								
		Title			Ranking					
Event	Unit of measure	Master of Sport International Class	Master of Sport of USSR	Candidate Master of Sport	1st	2nd	3rd	1st Jr	2nd Jr	3rd Jr
100 m	Seconds (max.)	10.0	10.3	10.5	11.0	11.5	12.3	12.6	13.0	13.5
High jump	Metres (min.)	2.20	2.08	2.02	1.90	1.75	1.55	1.50	1.35	1.25

Source: Yedinaya vsesoyuznaya sportivnaya klassifikatsiya, 1969–72 (Moscow, 1969), pp. 107–109.

In other sports, the rankings may depend on the number of victories in contests with athletes of equivalent or higher ranking. In tennis, for example, the top title was awarded to a player who reached the quarter-finals of the singles or doubles at Wimbledon, or who won or was runner-up in the European zone matches of the Davis Cup, or who took first or second place in singles or doubles at a major world tournament, or who won two matches in the course of two years in singles against players seeded in the

[37] *Yedinaya vsesoyuznaya sportivnaya klassifikatsiya*, 1969–1972, pp. 14–15.

world top ten, or three victories over opponents seeded in the European top ten players.

In team games, victories in regular league and cup games and in international matches count. For example, each member of the Soviet ice hockey team was awarded the first-ever *Master of Sport, International Class* title after the retention, in 1965, of the world championships. Again, for example, for the third basketball ranking, a player had to be present in a team that had won no fewer than seven matches during a year over teams of any qualification, as long as the player had made at least 14 appearances for the team.

The two systems, the *GTO* and the rankings, are intended to operate together so that (a) general public interest in sport is sustained from school onwards, and (b) as little potential talent as possible is lost. In a country as vast as the Soviet Union, they are a means of establishing uniformity and a yardstick for measuring progress in the proficient and deficient areas of the Soviet sports movement. Combined, they form an instrument that, despite the paucity of sports equipment and amenities, has enabled the Soviet Union to sift out its most promising performers and nurture them to world-class attainments and international competition in a relatively short time. The pyramidal structure may be seen in Figure 4.

Massovost' and masterstvo

In theory, at least, this instrument can from *massovost'* hatch *masterstvo*. The long-lived Soviet President, Mikhail Kalinin, once said: 'In our country, physical culture means sport for the whole people; in our country, millions participate in the physical culture movement. And it is obvious that talented athletes will sooner be found among those millions than among thousands, and that it is easier to find talented athletes among thousands than among hundreds.'[38] That the Party and government so frequently stress *massovost'* is not mere lip-service to ideology, but a sincere attempt to put pressure on societies, clubs and coaches to pay more attention to the ordinary public. Since the war, when the

[38] M. I. Kalinin, *O voprosakh sotsialisticheskoi kul'tury* (Moscow, 1938), p. 132.

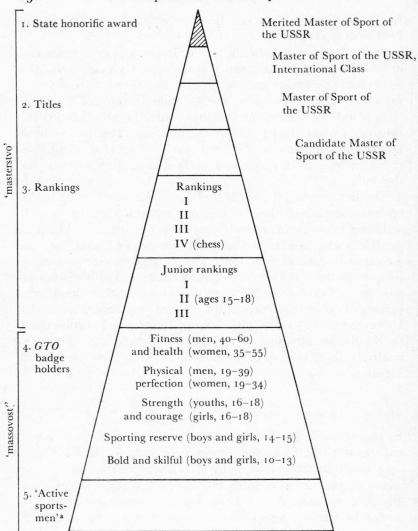

Fig. 4. The USSR sports pyramid, 1976

[a] Active sportsmen are now officially defined as members of sports groups who engage in physical exercise or sport under the supervision of an instructor not less than twice a week over a minimum period of six months. In 1975, the number was put as 51 million people – i.e. nearly one-third of the population between 10 and 60 (see *Sport v SSSR*, 1975, No. 10, p. 8). By contrast to this 'global' figure, many micro-sociological surveys indicate one-tenth of the population as a more realistic figure.

accent has been on producing champions who would help to establish and maintain Soviet supremacy in world sport, the twin aims have sometimes tended to interfere with rather than to supplement one another. With the increasing complexity of the sports movement 'it is clear that an increase in mass participation does not automatically today guarantee an increase in proficiency. The connection between them presupposes a high degree of organisation by sports societies and clubs, the presence of qualified instructors, rational sports training and so on.'[39] The trend is towards an administrative separation and funding of sport with the serious sportsman who shows talent being channelled at an early age into a privileged environment of qualified trainers, good facilities and intensive training, and the casual sportsman independently following his inclination in a more or less unsupervised way. This separation was indicated quite clearly by the head of the department of Forecasting and Planning of Physical Culture Development at the All-Union Physical Culture Research Institute: 'A tendency is already evident in the sports movement today towards a differentiation of big-time sport from mass physical culture. This process will be even more marked in the future. Sport will develop principally through specialised sports organisations like the children's and youth sports schools, schools of higher sports skill, sports boarding schools, etc. . . . Mass participation will develop largely through independent forms of physical culture.'[40] If, however, this bias is too blatant, it can evoke unfavourable comment, as occurred in relation to the Georgian sports authorities in 1973, who were accused of being 'only interested in a specially selected band of athletes in sports schools, specialised sports boarding schools, local and Republican teams – from which swift and high results are expected. They are not interested in mass sport.'[41]

A number of studies present quite a different picture of mass sports participation to that given in the statistics produced by various sports organisations and released by the Central Statistical Board.

The Secretary of the *Komsomol*, S. Arutyunyan, speaking in

[39] *Fizkul'tura i sport*, 1970, No. 8, p. 3.
[40] Pereverzin, *Prognozirovanie i planirovanie*, p. 26.
[41] *Sovetsky sport*, 12 January 1973, p. 2.

1972 at the Seventh Plenary Meeting of the *Komsomol* Central
Committee, revealed the findings of a survey carried out by the
Komsomol, that 'only 1 in 10 young workers and farmers
engaged in sport regularly'.[42] A number of recent sociological
surveys have also given data at variance with earlier published
figures. Thus, 'according to Taganrog city organisations, the city
had 30,000 sportsmen in 1966 and even 40,000 in 1970 – i.e.
some 27 per cent of the entire employed population. But these
figures (and, incidentally, it would seem, those for the country as
a whole) include every single person who, just once during the
year, took part in some sports activity; moreover, the same people
were double-counted if they participated in more than one contest.'[43] This survey showed that 'regular sports activity – and that
determines the real level of physical culture – is undertaken by
only five per cent of the manual workers and eight per cent of the
office workers. Evidently, the main body of the 40,000 sports
participants in the city comprise people who engage in sport only
now and again. *Eighty per cent of the manual workers and 70 per
cent of the employees revealed that they have absolutely nothing
to do with physical culture and sport* (my emphasis). Even among
young people, not more than 10 per cent take a regular and active
part in sport.'[44] The table below confirms this picture. It also
reveals other trends affecting sport: first, almost three times more
men engage in sport than women, both regularly and occasionally
– though the sex discrepancy is not so great in regard to out-of-
town recreation – indicating, perhaps, that this tends to be undertaken by families rather than individuals. Second, the changeover
from the 6- to 5-day week has not appreciably affected sports
participation – though it has boosted out-of-town recreation for
men and women. At the same time, it has evidently given greater
scope to family cultural activities, like theatre and cinema going,
while resulting in far less time being spent on such workplace
organised and non-family events as attending lectures; similarly,
going to soccer matches (usually only a male pastime) has not
seen any significant increase.

[42] *Teoriya i praktika fizicheskoi kul'tury*, 1972, No. 4, p. 5.
[43] L. A. Gordon and N. M. Rimashevskaya, *Pyatidnevnaya rabochaya
nedelya i svobodnoye vremya trudyashchikhsya* (Moscow, 1972), p. 61.
[44] Ibid., p. 62.

TABLE 11 *Use of free time among industrial manual workers in Taganrog: 1968 (percentage)*[a]

Free time activity	Of all persons surveyed			Of men surveyed			Of women surveyed		
	Working new 5-day week	Working old 6-day week	Per cent 'difference'	Working new 5-day week	Working old 6-day week	Per cent 'difference'	Working new 5-day week	Working old 6-day week	Per cent 'difference'
Reading newspapers regularly	79	75	+4	89	81	+8	72	69	+3
Reading books[b]	53	52	+1	56	55	+1	51	49	+2
Going to the cinema[b]	64	59	+5	70	60	+10	59	57	+2
of whom: four or more times per month	27	19	+8	33	20	+13	22	17	+5
Going to the theatre[c]	54	44	+10	51	46	+5	57	42	+15
Studying independently:									
regularly	3	1	+2	4	–	+4	2	1	+1
occasionally	5	2	+3	6	1	+5	4	4	0
Attending sports spectacles[b]	16	14	+2	30	28	+2	5	–	+5
Taking part in sport:									
regularly	5	4	+1	7	5	+2	2	2	0
occasionally	15	14	+1	22	21	+1	9	9	0
Enjoying out-of-town recreation[b]	51	45	+6	54	49	+5	47	38	+9
of whom: four or more times per month[b]	13	13	0	15	16	–1	11	7	+4

[a] The survey was undertaken in the fairly 'typical' industrial centre of Taganrog shortly after the transfer of most of the workers to a 5-day working week. Some 600 manual workers on a 5-day week, and 250 on a 6-day week completed questionnaires.
[b] During the month prior to the survey.
[c] During the previous year.
Source: L. A. Gordon and N. M. Rimashevskaya, *Pyatidnevaya rabochaya nedelya i svobodnoye vremya trudyashchikhsya* (Moscow, 1972), p. 48.

For those who do make sport a career, sport can be an attractive, relatively non-political sphere of activity. It can also be materially worthwhile. As the cancer-stricken young girl in Solzhenitsyn's *Cancer Ward* says: 'Anyone can be a sportsman. You've only got to train a lot. And it pays! You travel for nothing. You get thirty rubles a day for food, *and* free hotels, and bonuses on top! And think of the places you see!'[45] Poor Asya could boast she had been to Leningrad and Voronezh, but others can travel to Los Angeles, Montreal and London. In a comparatively 'closed' society like the Soviet Union, foreign travel can be a particularly attractive inducement among other attractions that can include relatively high monetary rewards, a car and a large flat in the big city for successful sportsmen. Sport can, therefore, be a remunerative and attractive career for successful athletes.[46] Moreover, since coaches and club administrators can also share in this affluence and bask in the reflected glory, there is an understandable inclination to ignore the non-proficient athlete – the one who is not likely to win medals and earn perquisites for the club – and concentrate on the proficient. However, so as not to appear biased towards the latter, not to receive official cautions (not to fail to meet sports participation norms), clubs may be tempted to put forward even grossly inflated registration and participation figures to the Central Statistical Board. Hence the over-high figures given for mass participation in sport.

Contemporary problems

The pressures on clubs and players to be successful have built up in recent years. Training schedules have been intensified, previously weak teams beyond the capital – especially in non-Russian areas – have risen to prominence and problems typical of 'professional' sports (particularly soccer and ice hockey) in the West – e.g. unruly crowd behaviour, rough play and the 'procuring' of

45 A. Solzhenitsyn, *Cancer Ward* (Penguin, London, 1971), p. 142.
46 I do not mean to imply that money values are the sole or even main ingredient in that complex phenomenon, motivation, in Soviet sport. Least of all is it fear of being punished for failure (otherwise some would defect – and not one sportsman, to my knowledge, has ever done so). There is another facet of motivation – a mixture of discipline, patience, dedication and patriotism that should not be underestimated.

players – have grown more acute. The apparent increase in violent behaviour, especially on the part of spectators, may also be attributed to the decline in official coercion and strong social discipline that were such prominent features of the 'Stalin era' and tended to discourage overt anti-social activities. Official concern about the seamier side of Soviet big-time sport stems from a number of factors. There have always been abuses of official regulations and prescriptions for the organisation and functioning of Soviet sport – as this study has revealed in previous chapters. After all, competition, conflict and the outbreak of violence are not the preserve of Western societies; they are features of social life in the Soviet Union, too, and the field of sports is no exception. Fights among players, illegal yet widely acknowledged privileged treatment of players and riotous behaviour on the part of spectators have accompanied Soviet sport at least since the organisation of club competitions in 1924. Official strictures against such practices have come at regular intervals but little would appear to have been done to enforce the rules. In recent years, however, there have been marked attempts to see that the rules and the 'norms of Soviet living' are abided by, particularly in the most popular of all Soviet spectator sports – soccer. Examples of malpractices have received wide publicity in the press, as the illustrations that follow show; they are described at some length because, first, they reveal the type of behaviour that exists behind the idealised picture that the Soviet press is more prone to project; second, they appear to parallel some of the problems facing sport in the West today and, third, they contain certain elements that are new to the Soviet sports movement.

Scandals in soccer

The extremes to which the undercover-bonus system[47] in soccer can lead were revealed in an article in *Komsomol'skaya pravda* in 1971. It came to light when two members of the Odessa

---

[47] As an example of the financial arrangements for top soccer players (though these are never published), a player in the top national league (in 1976) received a basic salary from his sports society (for one of whose teams he plays) of about 180 rubles a month. By comparison, the average monthly earnings of an industrial worker were 135 rubles in 1976. If the

Chernomorets soccer team were involved in a car crash – one fatally. Both were drunk and accompanied by their girl friends; the soccer player who survived, Victor Lysenko, had evidently knocked down a pedestrian a year before and had had his licence suspended for a year – but the local militia chief had 'reviewed' the case and let him off. Lysenko is said to have been a habitual debauchee and frequently to have gone on drinking bouts with four of his team mates, after which they would roar around the town in their private cars. The Assistant Manager of the Odessa Steamship Line explained, 'Of course, Lysenko should have been punished. . . But we have to consider the interests of the team. . . Thousands of people, the whole town, support it. And what don't these soccer players have? We invite them here from other towns and give them all they need.' The Steamship Line had paid for a million ruble training camp out of town, with three football pitches, steam baths, a luxury hostel and garages for the players' cars. It was now adding an indoor stadium, swimming pool and giant aquarium. As an incentive to players, the Line had paid out 2,000–3,000 rubles each to five *Chernomorets* players over a few months. The Ilychevsky Port Authority had paid out 50,000 rubles as 'financial stimulus' to the team over a brief span of time. The team's benefactors not only came from the docks, but the Odessa *Stroigidravlik* Factory had been paying 100 rubles every month to a *Chernomorets* player and double that amount to the chief trainer.

The club itself had provided well-furnished flats, cars and 'pocket money' as inducements to attract the best soccer players to the club; sometimes players would arrive, accept the flat and the car and then move to another club (*Shakhtyor* was cited)

player had a Master of Sport ranking or had represented his country, he would receive another 30 or 40 rubles respectively, paid to him by the All-Union Committee on Physical Culture and Sport. Additionally, he would probably get unofficial payments from various organisations associated with his sports society as bonuses for team success and for playing extra matches outside the normal league programme. Players of Moscow *Spartak*, for example, receive bonus payments for winning matches from such organisations as the Moscow City Soviet, whose employees are members of the Spartak trade union sports society. A player's 'utility' value may also secure him certain other perquisites, such as a spacious apartment and a foreign car.

where they would get another flat and car, while retaining the old ones.

Several state organisations had apparently turned a blind eye to the misdemeanors. The city militia chief, Major Marushchenko, disclaimed all knowledge of Lysenko's motoring offences; the Chief Auditor of the Odessa Regional Auditing Board of the Ukrainian Ministry of Finance reported that the documents showing evidence of illegal payments to players had been taken from him; the *Chernomorets* team's *Komsomol* secretary denied all knowledge of the restaurant 'debauchery' and drunkenness and claimed that the political and educational work in the team was 'on a high ideological level'.

While the one Odessa 'professional' soccer team and its players had everything they needed in the way of facilities and material benefits, the public had extremely limited facilities for sport: junior soccer practically did not exist in any organised form, and *Chernomorets* had completely neglected all the mass sport sections that came under the club's tutelage. The town did not have a single swimming pool, because no Odessa organisation was prepared to contribute funds towards building one. The article's author concluded by asking the pertinent questions: 'So, why does Odessa need a soccer team of masters? In order to propagandise sport among thousands of people – or to maintain dubious sporting prestige?'[48]

Similar 'scandals' have been exposed in regard to the Azerbaidzhan football team *Neftchi*, whose players had been involved in drunken brawls in public and misbehaviour on the field. During a match against the Rostov army team in 1971, the *Neftchi* goalkeeper, Kramarenko, 'after letting in a second goal, attacked the referee with his fists, punched him twice, knocking him to the ground. . . After the match the referee required urgent medical attention.' In the same match, another *Neftchi* player, Mirzoyan, 'spat in a linesman's face', the captain, Banishevsky (who had previously been banned from football for life by the USSR Football Federation for his part in a drunken brawl at Baku airport – but who had subsequently been reinstated by the Azerbaidzhan Sports Committee and made captain of *Neftchi*) ordered his players to leave the field in protest at the referee's decisions, and

[48] *Komsomol'skaya pravda*, 20 July 1971.

another player, Kuliev, 'demonstratively kicked the ball high onto the terraces after a decision had been given against him'. The response of the Azerbaidzhan Sports Committee to all this was to hand out a 'token' punishment of a three-match ban on Kramarenko and an admonition to the other members of the team. The USSR Soccer Federation took a much more serious view and proposed to the Board of the USSR Sports Committee that *Neftchi* be suspended from the league until the end of the season (three games, in effect), that Kramarenko be banned from soccer for three years 'for an offence of hooliganism unprecedented in our major league', that Kuliev be banned for a year, that Banishevsky be relieved of the captaincy, and that the team be reformed.[49] Although these proposals were ratified, the *Neftchi* team in the following season (1972) contained roughly the same players excluding Kramarenko but including Kuliev, Mirzoyan and Banishevsky.[50]

As the *Chernomorets* and *Neftchi* investigations revealed, soccer clubs are 'supported' by wealthy patrons, referred to as 'Mycaenases' who grant players financial inducements for winning. There also exists a band of 'soccer merchants' who work independently or for a club, scouting for talent and enticing players from other clubs. The newspaper *Sovetsky sport* has reported on the shady dealings of these 'merchants' who 'buy up talented youngsters with big money offers',[51] or who 'pester players while they are training or even in their private lives'.[52] Both the *Komsomol* and trade union leaders have spoken out against these and other malpractices. The *Komsomol* secretary, S. Arutyunyan, has said that 'buying up players, enticing them to other clubs, infringements of financial regulations, non-observance of training régimes and an atmosphere of all-forgiving toleration can be found in some teams'.[53] He warned, too, that many players were spoilt (he cited several by name) and that trainers spent their time and money pandering to the whims of the masters and did nothing at all for the younger players.

[49] *Sovetsky sport*, 22, 26 and 30 October 1971.
[50] See *Sovetsky sport*, 21 September 1972, p. 3.
[51] *Sovetsky sport*, 5 December 1971, p. 3.
[52] *Sovetsky sport*, 15 July 1972, p. 3.
[53] *Sovetsky sport*, 2 April 1972, p. 1.

The Presidium of the All-Union Council of Sports Societies put out a statement in 1972 condemning sports societies and administrators who turned a blind eye on these nefarious activities because they wanted to see their club or society win at all cost: 'Some leading sports administrators want to have their team succeed at any cost and therefore ignore serious breaches of discipline and immoral acts on the part of players.[54] Soccer clubs such as *Neftchi*, *Kairat* (Alma Ata, Kazakhstan) and *Karpaty* (L′vov, Ukraine) were cited as persistent offenders. 'Labour hirers journey from town to town offering blandishments to players. . . It is intolerable that many councils of voluntary sports societies do not pay proper attention to the development of soccer, even connive with trainers and team managers in their unprincipled attempts to get players developed by other clubs, seducing them by financial offers paid for out of state and public funds.'[55] After meting out a long gaol sentence to the ex-manager of the *Torpedo* Football Team in Togliatti for misappropriating club funds, a warning was issued to 'the administrators of sports work at big new construction sites. It is no secret that crooks, including sports businessmen, go there in search of a "long ruble".'[56] Rather than seek success, some club organisers are evidently willing to 'throw' a match if the price is right – although no evidence has been published on this in regard to major clubs. In 1972, however, a case was reported in the press of teams in the Dnepropetrovsky Regional *Kolos* league (including the *Progress* kolkhoz team) being ordered to lose by their managers. The results

---

[54] *Sovetsky sport*, 6 July 1972, p. 3.

[55] Ibid., p. 3.

[56] *Sovetsky sport*, 14 December 1972, p. 2. To curb this practice, the transfer regulations were tightened up on 5 October 1972, when the USSR Sports Committee issued new 'Regulations for Player Transfers in Master Football Teams from one Physical Culture Organisation to Another'. Accordingly, transfers henceforth were to be: (1) only permitted from lower divisions upward ('to prevent lovers of an easy life in soccer moving from team to team, avoiding training by going to lower divisions'); (2) only permitted for First and Second Division clubs which could take on three new players each year (Third and other Division teams have to consist entirely of local players); (3) only permitted to the extent of three players per club annually; and (4) considered by the Sports Committee only from 5 to 30 November. *Sovetsky sport*, 12 January 1973, p. 2.

were 'prearranged by interested parties'. Surprisingly, official reaction was extremely light: all the 'fixed' results were annulled and the guilty parties – including a referee, trainers and a league official – were merely reprimanded.[57]

Rough play and unruly crowds

The 'dirty' play of soccer players and the unruly behaviour of spectators have been further causes of lively comment and official action in recent years. The first-ever conference concerned with the problem of rough play was held in April 1972 with the participation of sports, trade union and *Komsomol* officials in addition to players and trainers from all leading clubs. New measures were forthcoming, including the ruling that a player was to miss a match automatically after being sent off or 'booked' twice; 4 'bookings' – or 1 sending-off plus 2 'bookings' – were to result in the player being banned from soccer until the end of the season. There were reported to be two players banned until the end of the season during 1972.[58]

There have been a number of incidents reported about unruly crowd behaviour at soccer matches which tend to suggest that Soviet soccer spectators are no less prone to misbehaviour than their counterparts in England[59] – although they have not reached the stage of whirling rattles, shaking flags, singing abusive songs, throwing stones, bottles, darts and beer cans at opposing players or fans – actions which, needless to say, would be very much discouraged by the Soviet authorities. Soviet soccer grounds (where spectators *sit* and soldiers ring the pitch between specta-

[57] *Sovetsky sport*, 13 December 1972, p. 2.
[58] *Sovetsky sport*, 25 July 1972, p. 3. On the whole, Soviet soccer would appear to be less 'violent' than in 'the West'; in the Soviet Union, 20 players were sent off in first-class matches in 1970, 11 sent off and 163 'booked' in 1971, and 7 sent off and 77 'booked' during over 300 first-class and reserve matches in the six divisions in 1972. On the other hand, a record total of 105 soccer players were sent off during English League matches in 1972–1973 season.
[59] *Sovetsky sport*, 25 November 1971, p. 3; 25 July 1972, p. 3. During the 1972–1973 English Football League season, a total of 276 fans were arrested at the Sheffield United ground and 250 at Manchester United Football Club. No Soviet statistics on arrests are available, but it is my observation from watching many Soviet and English matches that Soviet soccer fans are generally much better behaved.

tors and players, thus presenting less opportunity for hooliganism') have, nonetheless, come, over the years, to enjoy a reputation as locations for drunken festivities; for some Soviet fans, getting drunk is part of the natural ritual of attending a match. During a campaign against drunkenness, launched in 1972, a special drive was made at all soccer grounds to prevent the sale of liquor and to see that no bottles were brought into the ground. Nonetheless, drunkenness and violence continue: a soccer fan was sentenced to death for fatally stabbing a youth during a match in Kiev in 1973.[60] After a match in the Ukraine, 'a hooligan hit a Lipetsk player over the head with a hard object wrapped in paper'.[61] But it is not only players and 'fans' who lose control of themselves. Club trainers and managers are accused of encouraging infringement of soccer's written and unwritten code of conduct. Some even show the way: 'the senior trainer of *Avtomobilist*, I. Livshits, ran onto the pitch during the match, harangued the referee and, despite the requests of officials and his own players, for a long time refused to leave the field. Unfortunately, some Zhitomir players followed his example and acted like hooligans. . . The referee had to abandon the match.'[62]

The increasing official concern with these and other irregularities in Soviet soccer may be attributed to the following factors.

First, the rough play, crowd hooliganism and malpractices are officially considered to be against Soviet morality. The 'victory at all costs' mentality is said to be contrary to Soviet ethics and presents a bad example to young people and a bad image to world opinion: 'victory at all costs is spoiling our sport; it perverts supporters, not educates them.'[63] It is recalled that the old English residents' club in St Petersburg, *Victoria*, had as its motto 'Lose With Honour'[64] and that the English soccer player, Stanley Matthews, had not had one booking in his long career;[65] these were the models to follow.

[60] *Sovetsky sport*, 23 September 1973, p. 2.
[61] Ibid., p. 2.
[62] *Sovetsky sport*, 3 October 1972, p. 3
[63] *Sovetsky sport*, 13 May 1971, p. 3.
[64] *Sport v SSSR*, 1970, No. 6, p. 12. This motto was referred to after it was reported that the *Pakhtakor* (Tashkent, Uzbekistan) soccer club captain did not thank a linesman at the end of a game.
[65] *Sovetsky sport*, 29 December 1971, p. 3.

Second, the rough play and resultant injuries and official bans, the 'spoiling' of so many leading soccer players, have reduced the chances of Soviet teams winning against foreign clubs. Misconduct in international matches is also bad for the Soviet 'image' abroad. Thus, the Georgian Sports Committee warned at the start of the 1974 season that 'soccer players who dressed untidily, had long hair and wore charms would not be permitted to play in international matches in future'.[66]

Third, the increasing preoccupation – even obsession – on the part of spectators with their favourite clubs and, on the part of sports clubs, with achieving success in their soccer playing activities have exacerbated the perennial problem of clubs tending to direct all their attention and resources towards 'professional' sport – at the expense of the mass of casual players.

Falling attendances and changing tastes

In recent years, a number of articles in the Soviet sporting press have complained of falling attendances at soccer matches. Until recently, the soccer season traditionally began in Moscow on 2 May, with clubs playing an average of two matches a week until October; soccer, then, has been a summer sport. The season is now in two parts, however, to enable Soviet teams to be 'in form' when competing in the major European championships. In the 1972 season, the three best-supported clubs in Division 1 (16 teams) were Leningrad *Zenit* (average 'gate' 41,200), Kiev *Dinamo* (average 'gate' 39,000) and Voroshilovgrad *Zarya* (average 'gate' 34,600); at the other end of the scale were Baku *Neftchi* and Alma Ata *Kairat* (average 'gates' 15,600) and Moscow *Lokomotiv* (average 'gate' 11,400). It is interesting that while *Zenit* and Kiev *Dinamo*[67] attracted attendances of over 50,000 seven times, the 74 League matches played in Moscow drew a total of 1,245,850 spectators (an average of 16,836 per match) – a figure well below the national average for a First Division match. As if to highlight the comparatively low attrac-

---

[66] *Sovetsky sport*, 8 February 1974, p. 2.

[67] From 1975, this consistently successful club was chosen to represent the USSR in all international matches. This ceased in mid-1976.

tive power of Moscow clubs, *Lokomotiv* recorded the Division 1's lowest-ever attendance figure – 200.[68]

Among the reasons voiced for the falling attendances were: (1) the unattractive style of much modern play (few goals, 'defensive' soccer, increasing violence); (2) the lack of international success of Soviet teams; (3) the counter-attraction of other forms of entertainment – notably the television; and (4) the surfeit of matches.

Some observers explain this change by the evolving pattern of leisure in modern urban-industrial societies. With rising living standards, less time worked, the 'long weekend', a family car, television, and a wide range of 'newer', more individual or 'small-group' sports (boating, hiking, horse riding, badminton, tennis – and, soon, squash and golf), people are turning to more individualistic or small-group leisure activities centred on the home, the family or a group of friends, rather than pursuing public, mass activities centred on workplace or public entertainment. To give one example, people still watch soccer, but they do so by TV in their home rather than in a stadium: 'In essence, time is used here on the same spectacles, but in a passive – i.e. a family and domestic (and not a public and mass) – form.'[69]

The increasing demand for sports televiewing has been matched by an increase in the hours given over to sports on TV – roughly 1 hour 25 minutes every day in 1970 (from 55 minutes in 1966).[70] The authors of the Taganrog survey make the point that 'most town clubs and sports groups are ill-adapted for family recreation'; they suggest that boating 'firms', riding schools and out-of-town recreation centres should be built – all open to the general public.[71] These changes in leisure patterns are clearly affecting attendances at the more traditional sports like soccer – a trend that applies equally to Western industrial societies.

[68] This information was culled from *Sovetsky sport* during the 1972 season by Ted Woodgate, to whom I would like to record my gratitude.

[69] Gordon and Rimashevskaya, *Pyatidnevnaya rabochaya nedelya*, p. 39.

[70] V. A. Ivonin, *Sputnik fizkul'turnovo rabotnika* (Moscow, 1972). In 1973, there was one TV set for two families out of three in the USSR. It is also noteworthy that sports events, including soccer and ice hockey matches, are normally transmitted 'live' and in full on television.

[71] Gordon and Rimashevskaya, *Pyatidnevnaya rabochaya nedelya*, p. 76.

Clubs and competition

Sports clubs

In 1960, the All-Union Central Council of Trade Union Voluntary Sports Societies created the honorary title of *Sports Clubs* for conferment on the best-equipped and most successful sports collectives at factories and other urban workplaces. The calendar of competitions was becoming overcrowded, with a multiplicity of collectives of varying ability taking part. With the best collectives made into sports clubs, therefore, a separate channel for superior competition could be devised, running parallel to that of the sports societies (there were 29 with over 25 million members in 1972) of which the collectives were members. Furthermore, employees of factories with their own club would be more likely to identify themselves with such a club of their own – having its own emblem, name, uniform and newspaper – than with the much bigger and more impersonal sports society. The right of clubs to take part in All-Union and international tournaments might encourage factory managements to meet the qualifying standards for club status by boosting the sports budget and encouraging more workers to take part in sport or even to gain a ranking.

According to the regulations for awarding the title of Club, a sports collective must have at least 40 per cent of the labour force of its workplace pursuing a sport regularly, it must engage in no less than 12 sports and these must include athletics, gymnastics, swimming, cycling, weightlifting, and certain winter sports (where climatic conditions permit); it must have a permanent group of referees responsible for all its competitions and at least one part-time coach for every 12–15 athletes who compete in one of its teams; it must do its best to see that a certain proportion of its members become Masters of Sport and must every year gain rankings for 5–6 per cent of its employees; it must run a children's and youth sports school; no less than 80 per cent of its employees must take part in daily physical exercises at their workplace; it must have at its disposal good sports facilities and a training camp, and finally, it must act as patron of one or more rural sports collectives.[72]

[72] N. A. Makartsev, *Organizatsiya raboty fizkul'turnovo kollektiva* (Moscow, 1964), pp. 134–136.

Running a club is the joint responsibility of the factory trade union committee and the council of the parent sports society with assistance from the *Komsomol*. On an executive level, the club's affairs are run by a collegiate board consisting of the senior and assistant trainers (*starshy i mladshy trenery*), manager (*nachal'nik*), team captain (*kapitan*) and *Komsomol* organiser (*Komsorg*). The most important person here is usually the *starshy trener*, and he it is who is held responsible for the club's success or failure; in some clubs, one dominant personality as *starshy trener* can dictate the club's policy – as long as it and he are successful.[73]

By the end of 1961, more than 50 workplace collectives had become Sports Clubs; by 1965, there were 360 and, by 1972, 540 (of which 282 were at factories, 236 at specialised secondary schools and 22 at collective and state farms). Clubs' rights include participation in All-Union championships and international friendly matches. A club also has the right 'to provide full-time training for up to 12 days prior to a Republican, All-Union or international contest'.[74] Here is official sanctioning of more or less full-time sportsmen, for if an important (Republican or All-Union) match takes place weekly, then players are able to train continually throughout the season without breaking the 12-day rule (before *each* match). A number of Clubs concentrate on a single sport; for example, the Riga *TTT* (*Tramvainotrolleibusny trest*) women's basketball team had, by 1970, been All-Union champions eight years in succession; the Moscow Aviation Institute Club is noted for rugby (of the 20 league teams in 1970, as many as 15 were student Sports Clubs); the Alma Ata *Stroitel'* ('Construction-Worker') Club is the most successful team in the country in women's volleyball, and so on.

[73] If the club fails to do well, the senior trainer's fate is usually that of a soccer team manager in the West – he gets the sack. Thus, at the end of the 1972–1973 soccer season, the senior trainers of *Torpedo* Moscow, *Lokomotiv* Moscow and *Dinamo* Kiev were all peremptorily dismissed. Although the USSR Sports Committee condemned the 'gross violation of sporting ethics' by the Moscow and Ukrainian Sports Committees, nothing was done to reinstate the trainers. See *Sovetsky sport*, 28 October 1973, p. 3. In 1976 the two trainers of the Soviet national team were replaced for lack of success.

[74] Ivonin, *Velenie vremeni*, p. 57.

As an example of Club administration and functions, the *Pervoural'sk* Pipe Plant Club receives 400,000 rubles annually from trade union and factory funds; plant facilities in 1970 included an indoor stadium (cost – over a million rubles), two soccer pitches-cum-ice rinks, three gymnasiums, an indoor swimming pool, a ski centre, a slalom course and a mountain hostel. Forty full-time trainers administered 34 sports sections in which 10,000 employees (one-third of the total labour force) were registered.[75] As another illustration, the staff of the Ukrainian Academy of Sciences in Kiev have their own Sports Club, *Nauka*, which, in 1966, ran sports groups in 49 research institutes in the city and involved half the total staff. The Club had 29 Masters of Sport and had at its disposal an aquatic centre, two recreation camps and several sports grounds.[76]

In 1965, the right to form Sports Clubs was extended to secondary schools and rural sports collectives. A school may call its sports section a club if over 75 per cent of its pupils over the age of ten take a regular part in sport, physical education and tourism, if no less than 50 per cent of its 15–18 year olds annually gain a junior ranking, if at least 90 per cent of its school-leavers have *GTO* badges, and if it has fully qualified instructors, a permanent pool of referees and adequate amenities.[77]

The Club innovation has undoubtedly encouraged workplaces and educational establishments to draw more participants into sport, but it has also had the, at times contradictory, effect of encouraging the largest workplaces to concentrate their resources on producing masters and full-time teams.

The structure of sporting competitions

An extensive network of competition is seen as the most effective 'means of involving many millions of people in sports, of consistently improving the attainments of Soviet athletes and of taking stock of the quality of the work being done in the various sports organisations'.[78]

[75] *Sport v SSSR*, 1970, No. 1, pp. 4–9.
[76] N. Lyubomirov and P. Sobolyov, *Na pyati kontinentakh* (Moscow, 1967), p. 14.
[77] *Fizkul'tura i sport*, 1968, No. 1, p. 43.
[78] Makartsev, *Organizatsiya raboty*, p. 191.

Two distinguishing features of the Soviet programme or 'calendar' of tournaments are: (1) consistent planning – from the lowest level of the sports collective up to All-Union championships – and (2) the extensive opportunities available for collectives, teams and individual sportsmen to take part at some stage in All-Union tournaments. Indeed, everything possible is done to use the attraction of competition to sustain interest and draw people into both regular training and sport.

Annual and long-term plans are drawn up by the Committee on Physical Culture and Sport and these provide the guidelines for the principal sports and the coordination of the activities of all sports organisations in the country. When the calendar is drawn up, the Committee takes into consideration coming international contests – World and European Championships, the Olympic Games, USSR v USA Athletics Match, and so on – so that athletes for a particular event may be brought to the peak of their training at the right moments for the major international event through domestic competition. International competition always has priority. Figure 5 illustrates the three-channel pattern of planned competition in use in the 1970s.

The first column is for competitions on the basis of place of work or study – e.g. a schoolchild may work up from his local school competition through town, regional and republican tournaments eventually to the annual schoolchildren's *spartakiad*.

The second column shows the organisation of tournaments on a residential or territorial, as opposed to workplace, basis. Here an athlete may represent his local residential sports collective, or his town, or Republic right up to the All-Union championships and become a champion of each in turn. In the third channel of competition, the competitor is organised by voluntary sports society (*VSS*), irrespective of his place of residence or his workplace.

This structure of competition exists both for multi-sport tournaments and for individual sport championships. The competitions also provide a useful medium whereby a number of sportsmen are able to receive or improve their rankings.

FIGURE 5 *Scheme for conducting sports competitions*

Level	Branch (*vedomstvenny*) competitions	Territorial competitions	*VSS*, club and sports collective competitions
1. All-Union	All-Union contests and *spartakiads* (e.g. Railwaymen v Builders)	All-Union championships and *spartakiads* (e.g. Moscow v Leningrad)	All-Union tournaments (e.g. *Uralmash* v *ZIL*)
2. Republican	Republican tournaments	Republican championships	Republican tournaments
3. Territory, region and autonomous republic	Territorial and regional tournaments	Championships of territories, regions and autonomous republics	Territorial and regional tournaments
4. City	City tournaments	City championships	City tournaments
5. District	District tournaments	District championships	District tournaments
6. City-district	–	Tournaments in residential districts	–
7. Primary	Tournaments in primary organisations (schools, military units, colleges and universities)	Tournaments within sports collectives	Tournaments within sports collectives

Source: I. I. Nikiforov and V. S. Pol'shansky (eds.), *Organizatsiya fizicheskoi kul'tury* (Moscow, 1965), p. 194.

N.B. An inter-school nationwide tournament 'Starts of Hope' (*Starty nadyozhd*) was introduced in late 1975.

Spartakiads

The greatest multi-sport competition is the *Spartakiad* of the Peoples of the USSR, largely patterned on the official programme of sports of the Olympic Games. In recent years, the word '*spartakiad*' has taken on a broader meaning and now *spartakiads* are held for trade unions, collective farms, schools, Pioneer camps and even backyard teams. But the big event still is the *Spartakiad* of the Peoples of the USSR – held in two seasons, summer and winter, now every four years, normally in the year preceding the Olympic Games. These games have become so massive, with so many participants in the qualifying tournaments, that the Fifth *Spartakiad*, in 1971, was held in four parts: the first two being mass tournaments in individual sports, taking place in the various sports collectives and including district and city championships. The third stage comprised competitions for regions, territories, Autonomous Republics, the 15 Union Republics, Moscow and Leningrad. The fourth and final stage was the Finals which took place from 4–31 July 1971 simultaneously in Moscow, Riga, Ufa, Voronezh, Kiev and L'vov.

How important this sports festival is for popularising sport may be judged from the numbers of people said to have taken part. Some 23 million took part in the First Summer *Spartakiad* in 1956, with over 9,000 competing in the finals in 21 sports. Some 40 million took part in the Second *Spartakiad* in 1959, with nearly 8,500 athletes representing 43 nationalities competing in the finals. As many as 66 million people are said to have participated at some stage of the Third Summer *Spartakiad* during 1963 – more than a quarter of the Soviet population at that time, and three million more than the first two *Spartakiads* put together. The Fourth Summer *Spartakiad* was held in 1966 and 1967, dedicated to the fiftieth anniversary of the Soviet Union. Figures for participation vary from a reported 57.5 million to 80 million;[79] over 11,000 people contested 26 sports in the finals held in Moscow during August 1967. Simultaneously, the All-Union Schoolchildren's Spartakiad was held with 20 million schoolchildren participating and 5,222 contesting the finals.

The Fifth Summer *Spartakiad* was held during 1970 and 1971, the finals taking place in July 1971. Figures for participation were lower (but probably more realistic) than at the two previous *Spartakiads*: 44 million. As a spur to proficiency, it is noteworthy that 4,000 became Masters of Sport for the first time and 186 All-

---

[79] The second figure was quoted in N. A. Makartsev and P. A. Sobolyov, *Govoryat tsifry i fakty* (Moscow, 1968), pp. 80–81; the first (revised) figure was given three years later in *Sport v SSSR*, 1971, No. 1, p. 3.

Union records were set during the preliminaries; in the Finals, 237 Republican records, 31 All-Union, 19 European and 18 world records were broken.

How reliable these and former data on the *Spartakiads* are is hard to say, but if the highest figure for participants, 80 million in the Fourth *Spartakiad*, is correct, it means that well over half the population between the ages of 15 and 60 participated. Bearing in mind that rural and female sports participation is not very high, the claim that over half of all eligible men, women and young people took part seems dubious in the extreme.

A survey into the 4,294 finalists of the Fifth *Spartakiad* revealed that 76.2 per cent were men (23.8 per cent women); 4.7 per cent were Party members, 61.1 per cent *Komsomol* members and 34.2 per cent unaffiliated; in social composition, only 7.3 per cent were manual workers, 45 per cent white collar workers, 23.7 per cent students, 4.5 per cent schoolchildren, 18.8 per cent servicemen and the tiny figure of 0.8 per cent collective farmers; 30 per cent had a higher education, 65.2 per cent secondary and 4.65 per cent only primary.[80]

The Sixth *Spartakiad* was held in 1974 and 1975 and dedicated to the thirtieth anniversary of the ending of the war. Over 80 million contestants are claimed in 25 sports,[81] the Finals taking place for the first time in all 15 Republican capitals and 12 other major cities. But the *Spartakiads* are not simply a means of drawing people into sport and preparing athletes for international success. The Chairman of the Committee on Physical Culture and Sport, Sergei Pavlov, highlighted another aspect of the festival in his speech at the opening ceremony of the 1971 finals: 'The *Spartakiad* is a true festival of fraternal friendship of the peoples of our multi-national country. In that sense, it acquires special significance as we approach the fiftieth anniversary of the formation of the USSR. The *Spartakiad* reflects a major component of our Leninist nationality policy – the convergence of cultural levels of all our peoples.'[82] As the number of points attained by

[80] I. I. Pereverzin, 'Rol' sredstv massovoi informatsii v upravlenii razvitiem fizicheskoi kul'tury i sporta', in Yu. V. Borisov et al., *Problemy upravleniya fizkul'turnym dvizheniem* (Moscow, 1973), p. 29.

[81] *Sport v SSSR*, 1975, No. 10, p. 9.

[82] *Sovetsky sport*, 9 July 1971, p. 1.

the 15 Union Republics and teams from Moscow and Leningrad would indicate, the *Spartakiads* have tended to be dominated by the European centres like Moscow and Leningrad, the Ukraine and Belorussia; nonetheless, there is a noticeable shift in sports success over the last decade in the direction of a levelling-up of sports performance for all republics.

Another distinct function of the *Spartakiads* is to demonstrate patriotic feelings through festive parades and mass displays. A conscious attempt is made to simulate the sports ceremonies and rituals of the Ancient Greek Games that were held quadrennially at the foot of Mount Olympus between 776 BC and AD 395. Torch bearers run single-kilometre laps, starting in Moscow from the tomb of the unknown warrior in the Alexandrov Gardens alongside the Kremlin Wall, through the streets to the Lenin Stadium in the south-west of the city. As the official programme explicitly states, 'Following the Olympic tradition, born in ancient Hellas, sports contests should be embellished by creative contests and the winners should receive medals, prizes and diplomas.'[83]

Attempts are made in the *Spartakiad* to present sport as something ennobling, a cultural force that enriches man's experiences. Emphasis is put on the pageantry, the mass gymnastics and formation displays as art forms. The aesthetic element in sports parades and the *Spartakiads* – and in sport in general – is deliberately highlighted. In 1971, for example, the finals of the *Spartakiad* were accompanied by a giant cultural festival that linked sport with the arts. Throughout July, Moscow staged three special exhibitions: first, the 'Third All-Union Exhibition of Physical Culture and Sport in the Arts' held in the Central Exhibition Hall (the *Manezh*) displayed over a thousand paintings, sculptures, graphics and various applied art exhibits (cups, vases, plaques); second, a 'Sport and Philately' exhibition contained more than 250 display stands of stamps on sporting themes; and, third, an exhibition entitled 'Books and Sport in the USSR' had on show over a thousand books and other publications, including 400 from other socialist countries, on sport. At the same time, Moscow was host to a festival of sports films and other artistic events which included a display of sports photographs and of sports goods.

One other aspect of the *Spartakiads* is of note here, since it is

[83] *Teoriya i praktika fizicheskoi kul'tury*, 1970, No. 5, p. 4.

relevant to other features of Soviet sport and competitions in general – that is, the ritualistic paraphernalia of parades, mass displays, flag and banner waving, and the fanfares preceding events. It is noteworthy that the Soviet Union has always resisted attempts to downgrade or abolish ritual in the Olympic Games. In an editorial comment on an interview with the late Avery Brundage, criticising his attempts to 'cosmopolitanise' the Olympics by banning the raising of flags and the playing of anthems for winners, *Sovetsky sport* wrote, 'One can only hope that certain people, including, incidentally, certain circles in West Germany [the 1972 Olympic Games were held in Munich] will fail in their attempts to revise the Olympic ritual which vividly illustrates the Olympic oath obliging an athlete to fight on behalf of his country's honour.'[84] The 16th *Komsomol* Congress emphasised the importance of ritual at even the lowest levels of the Soviet sports movement: 'We must constantly promote the best traditions of sports groups and see that each of them has its own emblem, pennant, badge, uniform, ceremonial and festive ritual for accepting new members and farewell ceremonies for graduates and veterans.'[85] And elsewhere: 'The observance of rituals that accompany competitions is just as important as graciousness, respect, fair play and respect for opponents.'[86]

Nearly all Soviet stadiums are flag-bedecked, garlanded with banners and pictures, and decorated in the imagined style of their ancient Greek counterparts. Spectators sit for the performance, which is often preluded by musical fanfares and marches; the contestants then emerge together and engage in an elaborate opening ceremony before play commences. In the case of a soccer match, the sides may first emerge for a 'warm up' and then leave the field in order to reappear in the orderly and ceremonious fashion that decorum demands.

The vivid mass sports displays that accompany major Soviet festivals like May Day and 7 November perform the same ritualistic function. The timetable of events immediately after the military parade through Moscow's Red Square on 1 May 1971 ran as follows:

[84] *Sovetsky sport*, 22 July 1971, p. 3.
[85] *Materialy XVI s"yezda VLKSM* (Moscow, 1970), p. 198.
[86] *Sport v SSSR*, 1970, No. 6, p. 13.

10.20 – 800 Labour Reserves gymnasts give a display;

10.25 – members of the *Trud* Society give a mass display of exercises;

10.27 – a mass military gymnastics display by young members of the *DOSAAF*, Young Sailor and Cosmonaut societies;

10.32 – 100 athletes march through Red Square carrying the banners of all the voluntary sports societies, culminating in the flag and emblem of the Olympic Games;

10.33 – motorcycles bear through the Square the flag and emblem of the Fifth *Spartakiad* of the Peoples of the USSR, followed by a procession of the country's champions;

10.37 – 800 young athletes give a gymnastics display;

10.45 – 5,000 athletes of the Labour Reserves Society parade through the Square.[87]

Certainly, the concepts of empathy and catharsis[88] that Aristotle identified in the rituals of the Greek theatre are just as relevant to Soviet sports arenas and parades. For newly urbanised people who spend much of their time in a colourless industrial setting, the cathartic experience of the sports ritual may be a welcome diversion both from the workplace and the cramped residential environment. At the same time, the authorities value the integrative and patriotic significance of sports pageant and ritualistic competition, especially in such grand festivals as the *Spartakiad* of the Peoples of the USSR.

Finance

The financing of the Soviet sports movement is effected by various means – from state budget allocations to state lotteries. Although it is recognised as an important ingredient in the Soviet way of life, sport comes relatively low on the list of priorities.

All state-run organisations connected with sport receive money from the state budget to spend on sport and physical education.

---

[87] *Sovetsky sport*, 2 May 1971, p. 1.

[88] See Aristotle, *Politics*, Book VIII (Heron Books, London, 1970), p. 232. In his discourse on musical education, he writes, 'We find that such [emotional] persons are affected by religious melodies: when they hear those which fill the soul with religious excitement they are brought back to normal as if they had received medical treatment and catharsis. Men who are subject to pity or fear, and indeed all emotional people, experience the same kind of effects; and so, indeed, do we all in proportion as we are susceptible of feeling.' Ibid., p. 1.

This government expenditure is intended to cover the expenses that the physical culture and sports committees bear in maintaining their councils, in arranging international sports contacts and conducting training sessions, competitions and mass sports activity in the country. To cover the costs of training instructors, the physical culture and sports committees are granted funds for financing the work of physical education institutes, and for the construction of sports installations and establishments under the auspices of the Committee on Physical Culture and Sport. Besides finance from the Budget, the Committee obtains capital from the profits of *Glavsportprom*, the *Sovetsky sport* Publishers, various commercial enterprises and other sources.

The principal sources of finance are:

The state budget

These resources are allocated to the committees on physical culture and sport and to various ministries and departments for financing work connected with sport. In 1968, some 8,100 million rubles in the state budget were allocated to health and physical culture; this increased to 8,400 million rubles the next year,[89] and to 9,300 million in 1971.[90] Between 1960 and 1970, state budgetary allocations to physical culture actually decreased both absolutely (from 52 million to 47 million rubles) and relatively (from 0.07 to 0.03 per cent). It is an interesting note on the parsimonious government attitude to sport that the relative share of physical culture in state budgetary expenditure in 1970 was exactly the same (0.03 per cent) as it was in 1924 (when the government had far more pressing priorities for expenditure). In the same period (1960–1970), the share of government budgetary expenditure going to all social and cultural purposes increased: from 17.2 to 36 per cent, including from 11.7 per cent to 12 per cent for Education, from 4.5 per cent to 6 per cent for Health, and from 0.9 per cent to 8 per cent for Labour Protection and Social Security. Only physical culture alone of social expenditures did not improve its relative share in the budget. At the same time,

[89] *O gosudarstvennom byudzhete SSSR na 1969 god* (Moscow, 1970), p. 19.
[90] *Sport v SSSR*, 1972, No. 9, p. 3.

the government has tried to find other means of financing sport – such, for example, as recourse to state 'sport' lotteries.

State social insurence

All organisations, both state and public, which employ hired labour contribute to the state social insurance fund in the proportion of 4 to 9 per cent of their wage funds, depending on the branch of industry. The All-Union Central Council of Trade Unions, by permission of the government, is entitled to distribute the social insurance fund as it sees fit, subject to legal requirements. Part of this money goes on the payment of benefits and allowances for sickness, industrial injury and for health treatment in sanatoria and holiday camps. Part also is allotted to sport and recreation – e.g. the construction of student recreation centres, partial financing of sports schools, development of tourism, mountaineering and other outdoor recreation. It is reported that over half (56 per cent) of the sports amenities that were being constructed during 1969 were being financed out of the funds of enterprises and government departments, 20 per cent from local Soviets, 18 per cent from trade unions and 6 per cent from the voluntary sports societies.[91]

Trade union and cooperative allocations

The trade unions and cooperatives (collective farms, fishery collectives, consumer cooperatives) assign sums of money to their sports sections. The trade union budget is made up of membership dues[92] and income from various undertakings. Part of this money is earmarked for the trade union voluntary sports societies. *Ekonomicheskaya gazeta* reported in 1967 that trade unions spent 10–13 per cent of their funds on sport;[93] that means that approximately 307 million and 367 million rubles were assigned

---

[91] G. V. Yasny, 'Arkhitektory – sportu', in V. A. Ivonin (ed.), *Velenie vremeni* (Moscow, 1969), p. 288.

[92] At my place of employment, in Moscow, dues amounted to 3 per cent of each person's pay.

[93] *Ekonomicheskaya gazeta*, 1967, No. 34, p. 5.

from the trade union budget in 1969 and 1970 respectively;[94] 403 million rubles were allotted to sport in 1971.[95]

All enterprises of industry, transport, communications, agriculture, construction, service industries, retail and wholesale trade and public catering allocate 0.15 per cent of their wages fund to their local trade union committees for entertainment and recreation. The factory works committee includes this money in its annual estimate and determines what proportion of the total will be spent on recreation.

If an enterprise does well and makes an excess profit for over-fulfilling its plan, it may dispose of the accumulated funds as the management and trade union committee think fit: part will be ploughed back into production and part will go to recreation and other cultural requirements (including – and probably with high priority – sport).

Collective farms, fisheries and cooperatives help to finance the work of the rural sports societies by means of an annual contribution. The exact amount is specified in the regulations of each rural sports society. The rural sports societies *Urozhai* in the Russian Republic, *Urozhai* in Belorussia, *Varpa* in Latvia and *Kairat* in Kazakhstan, besides membership dues, farm contributions and other income, receive money from the trade unions, insofar as they are known as trade union cooperatives. The Russian *Urozhai*, for example, received three million rubles from the trade union budget in 1966 and eight million in 1970; in the same years, it received 2.8 million and 6.5 million rubles respectively from membership dues and farm contributions.

Commercial income

Sports committees, societies and clubs receive income from renting out and using sports facilities, making, lending and selling equipment. The Ukrainian Committee on Physical Culture and Sport, for example, has at its disposal in Kiev, the Ukrainian capital, the Kiev Central Stadium, Kiev Palace of Sport, the Palace of Physical Culture and a rowing and aquatic centre. All these amenities may be let out to various organisations and the money

[94] *Sport v SSSR*, 1971, No. 3, p. 15.
[95] *Sovetsky sport*, 19 March 1972, p. 2.

the latter pay for the hiring goes into the committee's coffers. A local sports collective is in the same position: it can let out its amenities and equipment, make a profit from using them itself (from spectators' entrance fees), lease out equipment, boats and other property. All the income it gets is tax-free. By a law passed in March 1957, sports amenities are free of contributions to the state budget in the form of deductions from profits or tax on the profits made from utilising sports amenities. Moreover, by a decree of the Presidium of the USSR Supreme Soviet in April 1962, all sports centres, stadiums and other sports amenities became exempt from entertainments tax. This enabled the Central Council of the Union of Sports Societies and Organisations in 1966 to finance the whole of its sports activities out of the money it received from utilising sports amenities, conducting contests, profits from industrial firms, publishing houses and market.

Income from sports tournaments and displays

Sports organisations conduct a number of sports contests, displays, social gatherings and other ventures for which admission fees are charged. The money raised is entirely at the disposal of the organisation that controls the premises and runs the function. The only exception is profit from selling tickets for the major league soccer matches (in the two premier leagues) where there is a special arrangement whereby the proceeds are distributed among a number of bodies, including the clubs that take part.

Membership dues and entrance fees received by VSSs and membership dues of corporate members of the rural VSSs

Each voluntary sports society establishes its own entrance fees and membership dues (which are very small). *Spartak* and other trade union sports societies, for example, have no admission fees to the society but stipulate that each member of the society pay a yearly subscription of 30 kopecks (1 ruble = 100 kopecks). The Labour Reserves Sports Society and *Dinamo* require new members to pay 20 kopecks admission fee and a contribution of 40 kopecks per annum. For members at school and college, the entrance fee and the annual contribution are both 10 kopecks.

The contributions of corporate members of the rural sports society *Kolgospnik* (in the Ukraine) vary according to the financial position of the rural establishment. For instance, a collective farm that is a member of *Kolgospnik* pays an annual membership due of 0.1 per cent of its cash profits, but not more than 600 rubles a year. Individual members of *Kolgospnik* pay a yearly fee of 30 kopecks. In all cases the contributions of members of sports collectives, clubs and societies are altogether nominal and do not prohibit anyone from joining the organisations and having the right to use its facilities – even expensive ones as in equestrian sport, parachuting and mountaineering.

Lotteries

One means by which the government can raise money for sport is by running special lotteries. This began as a means of helping to finance the Soviet Olympic team to go to the Olympic Games in Tokyo in 1964 and again to Mexico in 1968. In 1970, the government announced that, henceforth, it intended to run monthly 'sport lotos' in order to obtain money to spend mainly on more sports amenities.

In the second 'Olympic lottery' held in 1968, a total of 50 million tickets were issued at 1 ruble each (approx. 1 ruble = $1.00; £.55). Prizes to the value of 30 million rubles were presented to 3,415,000 winners. The prizes included 50 *Volga* cars, 500 *Moskvich* cars, 1,250 *Zaporozhets* cars, 1,500 motorcycles, 300 tickets for international sports events in Eastern Europe (or their monetary equivalent), 6,150 double tickets for an 18-day trip on the Black Sea, a 20-day trip on the Volga, a 22-day tour of Central Asia and Lake Baikal and a 20-day coach tour of Transcaucasia, and a large variety of sports goods – e.g. imported *Neptune* canoes, inflatable dinghies, sleeping bags, transistor radios, skis and skates plus money prizes ranging from 3 to 25 rubles.

Part of the proceeds of the 1964 lottery went to building a new Palace of Sport in Leningrad, a lift for the *El'brus'* ski jump, new wings for the Moscow Central State Institute of Physical Culture, the reconstruction of the Kiev Central Stadium, new sports goods factories, and for training the Soviet Olympic team. Of the

8 million rubles obtained for sport from lotteries in the 18 months from 1970 to mid-1971, part went to building a 'tartan' running track in the Lenin Stadium (Moscow), a bobsleigh run at Bratsk in Siberia, a winter sports' resort and sports' school in the Khibin Mountains, a sports centre at Kalinin and an artificial ski run in Kavgolov.

The idea of sports lotos is not new. Some Eastern European countries had been running them long before 1970 to raise money for building sports amenities. In the Soviet Union, the tickets for the monthly sports loto cost 30 kopecks each; the draw takes place three times a month. On each ticket there are six numbers; when the draw is made, if the holder of a ticket has on his ticket three or more of the six numbers drawn, he stands to win up to 5,000 rubles.

In the 14th draw, on 25 May 1971, the first prize (six numbers correct) was 5,000 rubles to the single winner, the second prize – 4,438 rubles (for five correct numbers), the third prize – 115 rubles (for four correct numbers), the fourth prize – 8 rubles (for three correct numbers). Over three million tickets were sold in eight cities during the first lottery draw. Half of the receipts from each draw is given back in prizes; the other half is spent on improving sport.

No reference is made in Soviet publications to any ethical principles possibly being involved in the holding of lotteries, despite the fact that it is a principle of socialist development in the Soviet Union that rewards should be 'according to the quality and quantity of work done'. The criterion of justice is work performed, by which the society is said both partially to satisfy the principles of equity and to stimulate the accelerated production of goods and services – by making attractive to the individual the most rational and efficient utilisation of abilities and skills possible.

Shortfall

The fact that sport is largely state-controlled certainly does not mean that it possesses a Fortunatus Purse, as both the small budgetary allocations and the recourse to state lotteries shows. Sports officials have to compete with other interests for priority in their demands for more money. Some republican ministries and organisations are more sympathetic than others to the needs of sport, particularly for improved facilities. For example, while in 1967 Georgia with a population of 4.6 million had 97 sports centres, 708 gymnasiums, 48 swimming pools and spent 1.8 million rubles on sport, another Transcaucasian republic, Azerbaidzhan (admittedly poorer than Georgia) with approximately the same population (4.8 million), had only 35 sports centres, 512 gymnasiums, 20 swimming pools and spent only 1.2 million rubles on sport. At the Fourth All-Union *Spartakiad* of the Peoples of the USSR, held that same year, Georgia came 5th and Azerbaidzhan 11th.

The large scale on which capital sums were allocated after the 1966 resolutions and strong criticisms of the country's inadequate facilities may be judged from the fact that as much as 100 million rubles was earmarked in 1967 for construction of sports amenities over the next five years by the Central Council of the Union of Sports Societies and Organisations, the All-Union Central Council of Trade Unions and the Labour Reserves. Altogether, taking into account all sources of finance, the planned sum of capital investment in sport (1967–1971) was 300 million rubles.

Facilities

The major purpose of the 1966 resolutions on sport was to announce a concerted effort on all sides radically to improve the quality and quantity of amenities for sport and recreation in the country. It was all very well aiming for an ever-greater number of sportsmen and for increasing leisure time but, without the recreational facilities with which to enjoy sport and games, increased participation could only result in frustration and overcrowding. Apart from the need to build the more traditional amenities – e.g. stadiums, gymnasiums, swimming pools, skating rinks – there grew, throughout the 1960s, a demand for a greater variety of recreational facilities and for special amenities and equipment for the newer sports (e.g. for ski runs, slalom, bobsleigh and toboggan courses; for equipment for racing cars and tracks; for sophisticated equipment for aquatic sports – water skiing, boating, skin diving and fishing; for ice rinks for figure skating, hockey and speed skating). Furthermore, with the transition to a five-day week and a rising standard of living, more families were eager to pursue outdoor sports and games at the weekend and to go camping, touring, hiking and even rock climbing, potholing, and mountaineering. With the rise in world standards and the increasing utilisation of technically sophisticated equipment and modern training methods throughout the world, the Soviet sports authorities had the problem of matching the best facilities that other advanced industrial nations were currently producing. Hence, particularly in the late 1960s, there was a big effort to produce more indoor athletics stadiums, swimming pools, tartan tracks (or something similar, like bituminous surfaces), fibre glass poles and mountain training camps and to create training centres (for soccer, boating and athletics) that could be used all the year round.

This has entailed an extensive campaign to build enough facilities to meet the growing demand. Although overall allocations to sport in the latter part of the 1960s greatly exceeded the sums spent in all preceding periods, there was still much criticism of the poor quality, the inadequacy and the bad planning of sports facilities.

It has to be remembered that, like the country's industrialisation in general, facilities for sport were only recently *at an extremely low and primitive level* – and that many of those that did exist in the 1930s had been destroyed in the war. Some indication of the improvement of sports facilities over the years is seen in the fact that in just one decade (1960–1970), the number of stadiums, soccer pitches, gymnasiums and tennis courts roughly trebled; indoor swimming pools, ski jumps and indoor athletics stadiums grew from virtually nothing to over a thousand, nearly 100 and 50 respectively. In 1967 alone, a further 195 swimming pools (including 60 indoor), 13 indoor athletics stadiums, 52 artificial ice rinks (including 10 indoor), 332 stadiums (with seating for a minimum of 1,500 spectators) and 3,493 gymnasiums were opened to the public. This 'great leap forward' in construction of facilities was matched by the production of equipment and the construction of tourist camps. In 1964, Soviet tourist camps could accommodate a little over 1,500,000 people; by 1970, they had room for 8,200,000 people, and, by 1971, for 12.6 million.

Production of sports amenities and sportswear

Even this pace of construction was considered insufficient by the government; in May 1969, the USSR Council of Ministers issued a resolution 'On Increasing the Current Assortment and Quality of Sports and Tourist Equipment', setting out new targets. The resolution also voiced a note of alarm at the 'mad rush' to put up slapdash facilities without regard for safety standards, quality and assortment. In fact, a number of newly opened installations were closed down after a government inspection commission from *Glavsportprom* (set up in 1966 to supervise the production and quality of sports goods and to set production targets) had announced that they did not meet the requisite standards. In 1972, it rejected almost a quarter of all standard items it inspected.

The inadequate supply and quality of sportswear and equipment, and of facilities in general, despite the big attempts in recent years to equate supply with demand, continue to give more concern to the sports authorities than any other single feature of the sports movement.

Sports centres

In regard to the construction of facilities, much depends, as always, on local initiative, particularly that of the *Komsomol*, and the ability and inclination of factories, farms and city councils to allocate money for sports purposes. As a result, some factories, schools, towns and republics are much better equipped than others.

Three cities have central stadiums that can (and often do) seat over 100,000 spectators – Moscow, Leningrad and Kiev. The Moscow Lenin Stadium in Luzhniki, built in 1956, stands at the foot of the Lenin Hills on the north bank of the Moscow River in the South-West of the city. The whole sports complex covers an area of 180 hectares and includes as many as 140 separate sports installations where 26 sports can be pursued simultaneously, watched by a maximum of 160,000 spectators. Besides its Central Lenin Stadium with seating for 104,000 spectators, the Luzhniki sports centre has a 'Palace of Sport' which can accommodate 13,000 spectators and an outdoor swimming pool for 12,000 spectators. The many sports pursued in the sports centre range from shooting, field hockey and archery to show jumping, tennis and *gorodki*. It is estimated that 10,000 people between 18 and 70 pursue a sport in the Luzhniki sports centre *every day*.[96]

In addition to the *Luzhniki* sports centre, Moscow had, on 1 January 1971, 70 stadiums, 228 football pitches, 964 gymnasiums, 21 swimming pools, 1,500 volleyball courts, 830 basketball courts, 240 tennis courts, 23 swimming pools, 27 rowing bases, seven artificial ice rinks, two cycle tracks and one horse race track. It is claimed that more than two million of the capital's seven million population regularly pursue a sport. The Moscow City Soviet ruled in 1967 that, henceforth, any sports facility, irrespective of the organisation to which it belonged, could be used free of charge by anyone residing in the district in which it was situated. It has, not surprisingly, been extremely difficult to get sports organisations to advertise the free availability of facilities and to comply with the order.

The Baku *Neftyanik* ('Oilman') Stadium is much older, dating back to 1926, when it was a dirt soccer pitch, on the shore of the Caspian Sea, surrounded by several rows of wooden benches for spectators. The whole sports centre covers an area of nine hectares and the central stadium has accommodation for 10,000 spectators; in addition, it has a three-storey pavilion with three halls and stands for 7,000 spectators, a junior stadium, a sports hall for other sports, a training area, a swimming pool, several pitches and courts, a hotel for visiting athletes, a clinic and a research-laboratory. Other towns, however, present a different picture. Dnepropetrovsk, for example, was reported in 1973 as having only one tennis court for its one million inhabitants.[97] And empirical studies that rely less on official statistics and more on sociological on-the-spot investigations tell quite a different story. The Taganrog survey of 1969, mentioned above, made the point that 'the situation in the city is hardly different from the average for the country as a whole ... the town has only 10 soccer pitches, 117 sports grounds, 36 gymnasiums (1 hall per 6,000 people over 15 years of age), most of which belong to schools and colleges; in

[96] V. I. Zholdak, *Stranitsy moskovskovo sporta* (Moscow, 1969), p. 7. The stadium is, of course, the central arena for the 1980 Olympic Games.
[97] *Sovetsky sport*, 19 January 1973, p. 2.

effect, only 6 gymnasiums are generally open to the public'.[98] The Taganrog figures revealed in the survey and official data on sports amenities for the USSR as a whole are compared in Table 12.

TABLE 12　*Reported sporting amenities in Taganrog and the USSR as a whole compared: 1969*[a]

Amenity	Taganrog survey results	USSR		
		TsSU data[b]	Taganrog provision extrapolated	Estimated inflation of *TsSU* data (times)
Soccer pitches:				
(number)	10	89,100	9,549	9.3
(per 1,000 pop.)	0.04	0.37	0.04	9.3
(per 1,000 males aged 10+)	0.11	1.01	0.11	9.3
Courts for basketball, volleyball and tennis:				
(number)	117	383,000	111,728	3.4
(per 1,000 pop.)	0.46	1.59	0.46	3.4
Gymnasiums:				
(number)	36	42,200	34,378	1.2
(per 1,000 pop.)	0.14	0.17	0.14	1.2

[a] End of year.
[b] Rounded.
Sources: Gordon and Rimashevskaya, *op. cit.*, pp. 113–114; *Narodnoye khozyaistvo SSSR v. 1970 g.* (Moscow, 1971), p. 14.

If, as the authors maintain, Taganrog is fairly typical of Soviet towns in its provision of sports facilities, then, once again, a substantial discrepancy between official sports statistics and information obtained from empirical studies is revealed. Other reports in the press and my own investigations within the USSR tend to confirm the latter type of data.

A number of large factories have ample sports facilities. It is a

[98] Gordon and Rimashevskaya, *Pyatidnevnaya rabochaya nedelya*, p. 114.

feature of Soviet sport in general that workplaces are expected to regard the health and recreation of their employees as an essential part of the responsibility both of management and the trade union. Much sport, in fact, is practised using factory facilities, and, as we have seen, a large number of factories have earned the title of Club for their sportsmen and the right to take part in major leagues and competitions. One such factory Club, at the *Uralmashzavod* (the Urals Heavy Engineering Works in Sverdlovsk), has four soccer pitches, a stadium, four basketball and five volleyball courts, two handball courts, three *gorodki* squares, two ice hockey rinks, two gymnasiums (20 m x 40 m), a wrestling and boxing hall, a weightlifting hall, an indoor swimming bath, a camping site, three holiday recreational centres and fishing and hunting lodges. The factory itself pays for the equipment and its maintenance: between 1960 and 1966, it spent nearly 600,000 rubles on acquiring and constructing new facilities. In skiing alone, 1,200 of the factory's employees and their families pursue the sport regularly; the factory sports club has over 1,000 pairs each of skis and boots for hire and has a 3-km floodlit ski track. The factory regularly engages in inter- and intra-factory contests; in 1967, some 3,500 employees took part in the skiing, skating, swimming, rowing, volleyball and athletics contests.[99]

Such well-equipped factories are, of course, in the minority. But it is clearly in the interest of the sports authorities and of many factory managers to develop facilities at workplaces, not only as a means of providing recreation for their employees and encouraging integration – i.e. by evoking feelings of togetherness around the factory and pride in the factory's achievements – but also as an important means of raising productivity. This latter aim takes on new significance as leisure time increases and new methods have to be found of increasing production largely by means of greater productivity. In a study carried out at *Uralmashzavod* in 1967 into the number of days lost through illness, it was found that, among active sportsmen, only 300 days per 100 workers every year were lost through illness; among non-sportsmen, on the other hand, 950 days were lost per 100 men during the year. It was further estimated that sportsmen had 50–55 rubles less in sickness benefits in a year than other workers;

[99] *Teoriya i praktika fizicheskoi kul'tury*, 1968, No. 10, pp. 66–67.

from this, the factory management concluded that it would gain by spending more money on sports equipment and facilities.[100] In another study, the All-Union Research Institute for Physical Education found that, taking the average monthly norm-fulfilment as 100, the average for *sportsmen* at the Moscow GPZ–1 Factory was 103.4, at the Kazan' *Spartak* Footwear Trust – 104.3, at Kazan' Lenin Linen Mills – 105.8, at the Taganrog *Krasny Kotel'nik* ('Red Boilerman') – 106.3, and at *Uralmashzavod* – 109.8.[101]

Attention to sport at workplaces is not, therefore, devoid of utilitarian interest. Moreover, factory managers are undoubtedly under trade union and popular pressure to provide recreational facilities. The provision of such facilities would probably loom quite high in the priorities of ambitious managers courting popularity.

Sports personnel

Breakdown of personnel

People working in the sports movement may be engaged full-time or part-time (referees, instructors and voluntary workers, who give up some of their spare time to sport). Of the full-time sports personnel, there are those directly employed in physical education and sport (coaches, physical education instructors at schools and workplaces and sports specialists) and those responsible for sports administration and the construction of sports amenities.

Over half the personnel (58.2 per cent) were teachers in full-time education in 1970; this figure was actually larger (67.8 per cent) if one includes those teachers, coaches and administrators working in sports schools, which operate mainly in the evenings (with the exception of the sports boarding-schools). The seemingly high figure of 13.7 per cent for production gymnastics specialists (*metodisty po gimnastike v rezhime truda*) gives an idea of the number of people employed by workplaces principally to organise physical exercises during the working day. It is also interesting that the number of coaches was only about two-thirds

[100] *Ekonomicheskaya gazeta*, 1968, No. 19, p. 13.
[101] Ibid., p. 13.

that of the number of people employed in the administration of sport.[102] Below we examine two of the full-time categories, physical education instructors and coaches, and a part-time group, that of referees.

Physical education instructors

As the survey of shortcomings in the sports movement, made public in the 1966 resolutions, demonstrated, one of the most intractable of all problems was the position of the school physical education instructor, particularly in rural schools. School sports staff, the report stated, were often treated as second-rate members of the teaching profession and their subject not infrequently came last in the school list of priorities and was trespassed upon by more 'important' subjects. One reason for this was that marks in physical education were not considered as important as those in other subjects, so that children could never be kept down at the end of the year if they received 'unsatisfactory' (2 out of 5 or less) marks for physical education in the end-of-year examinations. Physical education, furthermore, was not included in the school-leaving certificate. After 1966, the situation changed: physical education was added to other school subjects in the certificate and, during 1970, the end-of-year physical education marks were put on a par with others in deciding whether a child would proceed to a higher class or not. Physical education lessons were also increased in several republics to three or four from two periods a week. This did much to raise the prestige of the subject and of the school physical education instructors.

Nonetheless, the deficiencies in the supply of trained physical education instructors to the schools will take far longer to erase. The 1966 report stated that 'in two-fifths of the country's schools, primarily in the countryside, physical education is entrusted to people who do not have a special physical-education and pedagogical training'.[103] In the first three years of school (age 7–9), 'games lessons are conducted irregularly and by unqualified teachers'. In fact, a senior-form pupil may be given the job of

[102] I. I. Pereverzin, *Prognozirovanie i planirovanie fizicheskoi kul'tury* (Moscow, 1972), p. 29.
[103] Mikhailov, *Sovetskaya sistermna*, p. 12.

taking the games lesson in the primary classes.[104] In 1973, two schools in Leningrad (Nos. 194 and 203) were reported as having conducted no physical education lessons for the past year because of lack of an instructor.[105] M. I. Kondakov, Deputy-Minister of Education of the USSR, estimated in 1968 that 'it would take 10–15 years, at the present rate of growth in training physical education teachers, before the lack of trained instructors could be eradicated'. He further revealed that 43 per cent of rural physical education teachers were unqualified.[106]

In 1970, some 60 per cent of all secondary school physical education instructors were trained; 36 per cent had a higher education diploma, and 24 per cent had had a secondary special physical education training. The percentage of unqualified instructors had fallen from 49 in 1958 to 40 in 1969. In 1972, it was reported that this percentage had now fallen to 32.[107] Despite the marked improvement in the supply of qualified instructors, the problem of inducing trained physical education graduates to return to teach in schools, particularly in the countryside and outlying republics, remains. Despite the 'posting' system, whereby graduates are normally assigned to a specific job for a minimum of two years, the demands and pressures for qualified instructors appear to be great enough (or the students are astute enough to take advantage of their great utility) to prevent an adequate number getting sent to the countryside. Between 1950 and 1965, for instance, only half of the physical education graduates returned to schools as physical education instructors; the others went largely into the sports societies and into college teaching and training. Several central institutes of physical culture every year fail to meet their quota of specialists to be sent to Central Asia.[108]

Because of the reluctance of sports personnel to go to teach in the countryside and outlying republics where sporting facilities (among other things) are not so sophisticated, the government and sports organisations have taken a number of measures since 1966

104 V. Starikov, *Shkol'nikam o sporte* (Moscow, 1968), p. 51.
105 *Sovetsky sport*, 19 January 1973, p. 2.
106 M. I. Kondakov, 'Osnova osnov', in V. A. Ivonin (ed.), *Velenie vremeni* (Moscow, 1969), p. 15; *Fizkul'tura i sport*, 1968, No. 5, p. 7.
107 *Sovetsky sport*, 25 July 1973, p. 1.
108 *Teoriya i praktika fizicheskoi kul'tury*, 1973, No. 3, p. 2

to try to right the situation. Crash-courses (of from three to nine months) were instituted specially for rural physical education instructors and a large number of trained sports instructors were drafted into the villages immediately after the 1966 resolutions so that whereas, for example, on 1 January 1966, only 822 sports specialists (*metodisty*) were operating in the rural areas, by 1 January 1967, the number had risen to 9,162, while the number of full-time instructors in rural sports societies had doubled. By 1973, seven institutes of physical culture had special preparatory departments for collective and state farmers. The Armenian Minister of Education explained the situation as follows: 'I am not revealing a major secret if I say that a section of our graduates are not very keen on working in the countryside. Therefore, we have acted thus: when we receive applications [to colleges and departments of physical education] from the villages, we give them priority entrance on condition that, on graduation, they return to work in their own village.'[109] This is a measure that has been adopted elsewhere, along with the setting up of special sports centres in the countryside. This seems to show government concern that material facilities and sports personnel be distributed in as balanced a way as possible as between urban and rural areas. The resons for this concern are discussed below (see, in particular, the section on rural sport).

Coaches

The position of the professional coach is likely to be materially better than that of the physical education instructor, though the former's tenure may well be more precarious and his salary may well depend on the performance of his charges. Many leading coaches are, naturally, former athletes themselves. The former gymnast, Larissa Latynina, for example, became senior trainer of the Soviet women's gymnastics team, and Gavriil Korobkov, for long the senior trainer of the Soviet athletics team, is a former Soviet decathlon champion. The majority of professional coaches have had special training, either in higher education or on special courses, some at schools for coaches.

In 1967, as many as 65 per cent of all professional coaches

109 *Fizkul'tura i sport*, 1968, No. 3, p. 2.

were academically qualified: 42 per cent had higher education diplomas and 24 per cent had secondary-special diplomas. This is a considerable number and indicates the importance the authorities attach to the qualifications of coaches; thus, over two-fifths of all professional coaches had passed through a five-year higher educational course by 1967.[110]

Throughout the 1960s, there was a big drive to increase the number of trained coaches in the country, many of whom would be able to work with leading athletes and at the best sports schools and sports clubs. This was particularly necessary to meet the growing demand for specialists in a range of 'newer' sports in which the USSR had little international or even domestic experience.

In 1966, in no Olympic sport was the ratio of coaches to Candidate Masters of Sport and 1st-Rank athletes greater than 15:1, in most, it was lower than 7:1 and, in some sports (gymnastics, show jumping, speed skating, athletics, swimming, diving, modern pentathlon and figure skating), it was 3:1 or even less. It is noteworthy that, in those sports in which the USSR was making a big effort to excel internationally – gymnastics, show jumping, speed skating, athletics, swimming, diving and figure skating – the athletes were well served by coaches.

For the country's top coaches, the rewards can be high. In 1956, the title of 'Merited Trainer of the USSR' was instituted – to be awarded to coaches responsible for 'training Masters of Sport, champions and record breakers at Soviet, European, world and Olympic levels, and also for popularising new training and instruction methods'.[111] A little later, another honorary title was introduced: 'Merited Trainer of the Republic', to be awarded by Republican Councils of the Union of Sports Societies (now Committees on Physical Culture and Sport) for outstanding successes with Republican sportsmen. At the same time, the basis of remuneration was altered so as to be based on the coach's education, length of service, any honorary title, the success rates of his charges and the organisation and geographical location in which he is working. In 1967, the Central Council of the Union of Sports Societies and Organisations of the USSR introduced gold

---

[110] Makartsev and Sobolev, *Govoryat tsifry i fakty*, p. 93.
[111] Makartsev, *Stranitsy istorii sovetskovo sporta*, p. 99.

medals and bonuses for coaches who had trained athletes winning international honours. The first beneficiaries were the two coaches of the Soviet ice hockey team, Arkady Chernyshev and Anatol' Tarasov – the Soviet ice hockey team having won the world and Olympic titles frequently since 1954. The penalty for failure, on the other hand, as elsewhere in the world, is normally the sack – as successive trainers of the USSR soccer team have discovered.

Professional coaches are engaged on a full-time basis and receive a more or less fixed salary; it is a statutory rule that 'the normal working time of coaching instructors, production gymnastics "methodists", and instructors in physical culture, tourism and mountaineering cannot exceed 41 hours per week'.[112] As two examples, first a senior coach at a children's and youth sports school with a full ten-year education and a dozen years' coaching experience would receive 115 rubles a month; second, a senior coach with a higher sports qualification, with the title of Merited Trainer of the USSR and ten years' coaching experience, who is engaged at a ten-day training camp (preparing his charges for competition) would receive a monthly salary of 170 rubles (120 basic + 20 for his title + 30 rubles extra for work at the training camp).[113] Since many coaches surpass the set norm of hours, they receive additional increments: thus, a senior coach with higher education, ten years' coaching experience and a Merited Trainer title would receive 210 rubles a month if he worked 150 hours instead of the set 100 hours.[114]

Coaches may be employed on a part-time basis and paid according to the amount of time they spend with their charges. The part-timers make up nearly two-thirds of the total professional coaching personnel (63 per cent or 26,799 in 1967). Over half had attended special coaching schools or colleges. In 1974, just over 75 per cent were fully qualified.

Apart from these professional coaches, there are many coaches working on a voluntary, unpaid basis at factories, farms, offices and sports societies. They may be concerned with coaching in a particular sport, instruction in general sports and games, or

112 V. N. Uvarov, *Trudovye prava rabotnikov fizkul'tury i sporta* (Moscow, 1974), p. 37.
113 Ibid., p. 75.
114 Ibid., p. 77.

responsible for physical exercises at places of work and study. No payment is officially given for this type of work, but a great variety of token badges, certificates and banners may be won, up to the lapel badge 'Voluntary Instructor' (for all part-time coaches who have worked two years or more in a sports collective and who have a good record) and the top award, 'Outstanding Worker in Physical Culture' (*Otlichnik fizicheskoi kul'tury*). Part-time instructors are encouraged to obtain some coaching qualifications, and are given time off from work with pay to attend 20-day intensive courses. Further, all graduates of children's and young people's sports schools (*CYPSSs*) are automatically qualified for the job of part-time sports instructors.[115]

In 1970, there were nearly four million such part-time coaches and instructors, which meant an average of one part-time instructor to every 19 sports participants in the country as a whole.[116] The target set by the second conference of the Union of Sports Societies and Organisations in 1966 was one part-time instructor for every 10–15 sports participants. It is interesting that the best provided-for sports participants are those in sports that have the closest association with military training, viz. the combat sports, fencing, shooting and weightlifting. It is likely that many of the part-time instructors in these sports are servicemen or ex-servicemen working in the army societies or *Dinamo*.

Referees and sports organisers

Since the present supply of trained sports personnel cannot keep pace with the rapidly growing sports movement at all levels, a great deal of responsibility is laid on the people who undertake such work on a voluntary, unpaid and part-time basis. The public-spiritedness involved in this form of work is just the kind of popular participation that the Party and government wish to encourage as a sign of a developing 'communist' outlook of Soviet citizens. A vast amount of administrative and other sports work is carried out on this voluntary basis. Thus, for example, there existed in 1972 over three million (3,243,000) referees – all part-

[115] I. I. Nikiforov and V. S. Pol'shansky, *Organizatsiya fizicheskoi kul'tury* (Moscow, 1965), p. 174.
[116] Makartsev, *Stranitsy istorii sovetskovo sporta*, p. 103.

timers.[117] They, too, are said to be given time off from their work-place for attending training courses and for taking charge of tournaments. Referees are, as in most occupations, given a formalised structure by being placed by degree of experience and qualification into various categories: All-Union, Republican, First, Second and Third Categories, with the remainder simply bearing the title 'Referee' (by individual sport). Every sports collective is intended to have its own groups of referees (*sudeiskie gruppy*) responsible for conducting tournaments and arranging the training of new referees or judges. The title All-Union Referee is now awarded by the All-Union Committee on Physical Culture and Sport; over a quarter of all referees had this title in 1970. Those with 25 years' experience are awarded the 'Honorary Jubilee' Badge, and referees with international experience are given an 'International' title.

Another two million voluntary part-time workers are engaged in the activities of the councils of sports collectives, as physical culture organisers (*fizorgy*) and members of various councils and audit commissions of the Committee on Physical Culture and Sport.

Professional training

One of the requirements for active athletes is that, at the same time as they train and engage in competition at home and abroad, they should improve their theoretical knowledge by studying. In fact, a large proportion of leading Soviet athletes, mostly Masters, are provided with the relative security of a studentship or post-graduate scholarship at one of the country's institutes of physical culture. A number of top-flight sportsmen spend as many as 10 or 15 years at these educational establishments – as long, in fact, as they remain active and successful in their sport. This is, of course, a system of 'sports scholarships' not uncommon in the USA. Unlike the American system of mostly spurious scholarships for sports stars, however, it would seem that, for many Soviet Masters, academic work is an integral and important part of their training and is taken seriously.[118] It is felt that this is one way of preparing

[117] *Sport v SSSR*, 1972, No. 9, p. 174.
[118] In early 1971, I accompanied a Soviet friend (who was then an inter-national soccer player) to the Central State Institute of Physical Culture

a sportsman for a future career once his short-lived active participation is over. Among Soviet boxers, for example – a sporting profession by repute not generally noted in the West for the high intelligence of its practitioners – former USSR champion, Konstantin Gradopol, is now a university professor, former Olympic champion, Gennady Shatkov, is rector of Leningrad University, one former Olympic champion, Boris Lagutin, is now a practising lawyer and another, Valery Popenchenko (holder of the Barker Trophy as best boxer at the 1964 Olympic Games), was awarded in 1968 a PhD (*kandidat tekhnicheskikh nauk*) for his research.[119]

Types of education establishment providing physical education

The secondary and higher education establishments teach a large number of students who become instructors, coaches and officials in schools, colleges, sports societies, clubs, factories and farms. The range of physical education teaching and research establishments is shown in Table 13 (figures for 1 January 1972).[120]

Authority over the *Institutes of Physical Culture* is shared by the All-Union and Republican Committees on Physical Culture and Sport, on the one hand, and Republican educational ministries, on the other. Students are normally accepted for one of two degree courses: *Education* or *Sport*.[121]

in Moscow – his *alma mater*. During the tour of the institute, it became quite evident that he had actually studied there for five years. He also said that nobody is permitted to play in league soccer without completing ten years of schooling. Moreover, of the 27 soccer players attached to the permanent staff of Moscow *Spartak*, 24 were studying or had studied in a higher educational establishment. On our way out of the institute, we met a group of soccer players (from three other Moscow clubs) who were just arriving for evening classes. The impression that serious study is an essential part of an active sportsman's life was confirmed during my visits in 1975 to the Lesgaft Institute in Leningrad and the new Moscow Central State Institute.

[119] *Sport v SSSR*, 1968, No. 7, p. 23. This was confirmed by my own meetings with two of the boxers named, Popenchenko and Lagutin.

[120] *Sovetsky sport*, 15 August 1972, p. 1; *Sport v SSSR*, 1972, No. 9, p. 2.

[121] Appendix V gives a detailed syllabus in operation in 1975 at the State Central Physical Culture Institute in Moscow.

TABLE 13 *Physical education establishments: 1972*

Type of educational establishment	Number
1. Institutes of physical culture (*instituty fizkul'tury*)	20
2. Physical education faculties at higher education establishments (*fakul'tety fizicheskovo vospitaniya*)	78
3. Secondary special physical culture education establishments (*tekhnikumy fizkul'tury*)	25
4. Secondary special colleges of education specialising in physical education (*pedagogicheskie uchilishcha fizkul'turnovo profilya*)	33
5. Schools for coaches attached to physical culture institutes or secondary special education establishments (*shkoly trenerov pri institutakh, tekhnikumakh fizicheskoi kul'tury*)	18
6. Physical culture research institutes (*nauchno-issledovatel'skie instituty fizkul'tury*)	4

Education degree course

On graduation after a 4-year course, students become 'teachers of physical culture and sport' with the right to work in schools and colleges, sports societies or urban and rural sports collectives. The curriculum includes four disciplines which all students must take, plus a special course of seminars and an optional course:

A. *Compulsory subjects*
  (1) *'Social Sciences'*, comprising History of the Communist Party of the Soviet Union, Philosophy, Political Economy, Scientific Communism and Scientific Atheism;
  (2) *Education*, comprising Psychology and Sports Psychology, Educational Theory and History of Education, History of Physical Culture, Organisation of Physical Education, Theory and Methodology of Physical Education and a Foreign Language;
  (3) *Medicine and Biology*, comprising Anatomy and Bio-mechanics, Biochemistry and Organic and Inorganic Chemistry, Physiology, Medical Supervision and Therapeutic Physical Training, Hygiene of Physical Culture, Hygiene and Sports Amenities;
  (4) *Sport*, comprising Athletics and Teaching Methods, Gymnastics and Teaching Methods, Team and Outdoor Games and Teaching Methods, Skiing and Teaching Methods, Swimming and Teaching Methods, Speed Skating and Teaching Methods, Weightlifting, Boxing, Wrestling and Teaching Methods (for men students only), and Tourism.

This course covers the theory, methodology and technique of teaching these sports;

B. *Special seminar and optional course*

    (1) Students may choose from a variety of seminar courses, all of which are designed to enhance knowledge of research methods used in sport; the courses include Statistics, Cybernetics and Electronics;

    (2) In the second year, a student may take options either in the History of Physical Culture or in Educational Theory; a third-year student may take either Theory and Methodology of Physical Culture or Physiology; and a fourth-year student must choose as a speciality either a particular sport, or production gymnastics or therapeutic physical training.

During his or her course, the student is also obliged to spend 30 weeks in practice, both educational practice at a school and organisational practice in a factory or farm sports collective.

In addition, there are a number of general non-examinable courses (such as Aesthetics, Soviet Literature and a variety of other sports) which the student may choose to attend voluntarily. Moreover, all students must retake their 4th Stage *GTO* test, obtain a Second Sports Ranking in their chosen sport, obtain at least a Third Sports Ranking in two (optional) sports and the title of Referee Third Category in two sports.

Undergraduates who have passed all their term tests and sessional examinations, fulfilled all their practical norms and completed the four-year course are admitted to State Finals in the following three subjects: Scientific Communism, Physiology, Theory and Methodology of Physical Education.

This course for the Educational Faculty is more or less uniform for all institutes of physical culture with the exception of the country's two major institutes – the State Central Order of Lenin Institute of Physical Culture (*GTsOLIFK*) in Moscow, and the Lesgaft Institute of Physical Culture in Leningrad. The former accepts only first-rank sportsmen-students and has a more intensive course; students also receive higher grants than elsewhere. In September 1967, by order of the Union of Sports Societies and Organisations 'On Changing the Degree Courses and Structure of *GTsOLIFK*', the Education degree course was abolished and work was concentrated on the Sports degree course. In view of the fact that 95 per cent of the graduates from the now defunct

Education degree course had gone into coaching, the motivation for change was said to be to use the Institute almost wholly as a training school for active sportsmen – a kind of élite establishment for potential international contestants. This was enhanced by a decision to turn the Sports degree course, from the 1968–1969 academic year, into degree courses for individual sports, team games, winter and technical sports. Nonetheless, the newly formed Committee on Physical Culture and Sport invited suggestions from the Institute for a new Education degree course to be set up in June 1969; it was to train, first, teachers of physical education and sport for higher and secondary special educational establishments and, second, teachers, organisers and administrators for sports work in committees, departments, societies and sports clubs.[122]

Sports degree course

For this degree course, which unofficially carries a higher status, the student specialises in a particular sport and receives the qualification of 'Instructor-Coach' with the right to work in any sports organisation, from a local collective or sports club to a city, regional, republican or sports society representative team.

His course is basically the same as that for the Education degree course. The 'Social Sciences' remain the same; the only difference in the Education subjects being the inclusion of Coaching; in the Medicine and Biology section, the student studies Biomechanics and the Sports Technology as a separate subject, and Medical Supervision and Therapeutic Physical Training replace Sports Medicine. The sports section is dominated by the particular sport the student has chosen as his speciality but, in addition, he has to study athletics, gymnastics, team games, swimming, skiing and weightlifting and their teaching methods.

The length of educational practice is the same, teaching practice being spent in a secondary school, sports school, sports club or sports society, and organisational practice in a sports collective.

The special seminar course is identical to that for the Education degree course, but the optional coursework is monopolised by the student's chosen sport. Where facilities allow, a student may

[122] *Teoriya i praktika fizicheskoi kul'tury*, 1970, No. 6, p. 5.

conduct research work in his sport instead of completing some of the normal coursework.

Stage 4 of the *GTO* programme has to be retaken and, in addition, the student must gain a First Ranking in his chosen sport, at least a Third Ranking in two other sports and a referee's certificate in the chosen sport. The Finals consist of: Scientific Communism; Physiology; Special subject. If a student has written an adequate dissertation (*diplomnaya rabota*) on his chosen sport, he is excused examination in his special subject.

Most institutes of physical culture have correspondence and evening courses. Identical degrees may be obtained by this method, but the length of study is extended to six years.

The two oldest and most famous institutes are the two already mentioned in Moscow and Leningrad; the other eighteen were, in 1972, spread among the Republics with the exception of Estonia, Tadzhikistan and Turkmenia.

The *physical education faculties at higher educational establishments* come under the jurisdiction of the USSR Ministry of Higher and Specialised Secondary Education and the corresponding Republican ministries. Graduates normally become physical education instructors in secondary schools. The courses last five years and closely follow the curricula of the institutes of physical culture. Additional subjects in the course are Calisthenics and Outdoor Games but boxing, weightlifting and a specialised sport are excluded. Teaching practice is normally spent partly in a secondary school, partly (in the third year) in a Pioneer camp (three weeks) and partly in charge of a tourist excursion (a fortnight). Final examinations are in: Scientific Communism; Physiology; Theory and Methodology of Physical Education. Post-graduate work may be conducted for a period not exceeding three years for full-time students, and four years for external students.

The *physical culture tekhnikums* come under the auspices of both the Committees on Physical Culture and Sport and the various Republican education ministries. They train physical education instructors for schools and coaches in individual sports for urban and rural sports collectives. Most of the entrants are accepted at the age of 15 or 16 straight from general secondary school and undergo a course of between four and five years;

evening and correspondence course students do an extra year. The course is generally broader and less intensive than that in higher education, but final examinations consist of similar subjects – with the exception of 'Social Science' subjects. The reason for that exclusion may be that graduates are not expected to take up a job requiring such a degree of political awareness and responsibility as graduates from institutes, some of whom are likely to travel abroad. Finals, then, consist of: Physiology; Theory and Practice of Physical Education; Chosen Sport.

Students must do teaching practice in schools, sports collectives and at Pioneer camps and meet the following standards in the sports programme and rankings: *GTO* Stage 4, the equivalent or near-equivalent of the Second Sports Ranking, a Third Ranking in one sport featured in the curriculum, and Third-Class Referee Category.

The *secondary special colleges of education specialising in physical education* fulfil more or less the same function as the *tekhnikums* in training physical education instructors for secondary schools. The study course is shorter (usually three years) than that in the *tekhnikums*, and the teaching less intensive. Their immediate authority is the Republican ministry of education and the Republican Committee on Physical Culture and Sport. Normally, entrants are taken at the age of 15, having completed eight years of general education.

Their number dwindled from 64 in 1955 to only 5 in 1960, with the campaign to get more pupils to stay on at school until 17 and to ensure that all potential physical education instructors should take a higher course at a *tekhnikum* or higher educational establishment. In recent years these colleges have again increased in number (to 33 in 1970) – mainly through the drive to overcome the shortage of physical education schoolteachers in rural areas. Thus, one-year courses were begun for rural physical education instructors in 1969, with special six-month courses available, too, for people wishing to do sports work in the countryside.

Schools for coaches are normally attached either to an institute of physical culture or to a *tekhnikum*. Although they do take students at the age of 15 or 16 from secondary school, they are chiefly concerned with evening and correspondence courses for experienced sportsmen who wish to gain a coaching certificate during their sports career. Courses last approximately four years for internal students plus a year extra for external students. All entrants for the full-time courses must take an entrance examination in Russian Language, Chemistry and Physics, hold not less than a Second Sports Ranking in one sport and have at least eight years of schooling.

The course, which is neither as long nor as academic as those for coaches at the institutes of physical culture, consists of the following disciplines:

(1) *General subjects*, comprising History of the USSR, Social Studies, Economic Geography, Literature, Mathematics, Physics, Chemistry and a foreign language;

(2) *Educational subjects*, comprising Theory of Education, Psychology, Theory and Methodology of Physical Education, History and Organisation of Physical Culture;

(3) *Medical and Biological subjects*, comprising Anatomy, Physiology and Biochemistry, Hygiene, Medical Supervision, Sports Injuries and Massage;

(4) *Sports subjects*, comprising specialisation in one main sport and in a subsidiary sport (chosen from Gymnastics, Athletics, Team-games, Skiing and Swimming).

In addition to the above subjects, a further 105 hours have to be devoted to auxiliary material in Russian Language, Refereeing, Photography and proficiency in the chosen speciality.

Since part of the entrance requirements is for students to hold a high sports ranking, no additional demands are made during the course as regards sports-practice and rankings. Finals consist of: Physiology; Social Studies; Chosen Sport.

In the system of training personnel, the tendency has been to increase the number graduating from the higher education courses at the expense of those from the secondary specialised education courses. After 1956, the number of specialists attending secondary special college courses (*tekhnikums*) diminished, while the students at higher education establishments (internal and external) increased. This is part of the desired trend to raise the qualifications of physical education instructors, coaches and sports officials.

Research

Research into physical education and sport is an integral part of the Soviet sports movement. It is conducted at a large number of higher education establishments (including all the institutes of physical culture and the physical-education faculties), at medical colleges, polytechnics, at the Academy of Medical Sciences of the USSR (most important of all, at one of the latter's institutes, the Research Institute of Physiology and Physical Education) and at four separate physical culture research institutes. A documentation centre for books, periodicals and films concerned exclusively with sport and physical education is situated in Minsk, capital of Belorussia.

As may be gathered from the description above of the various educational courses, a scientific and technological study of sport and its related sciences is regarded as vital to a real understanding of the significance of sport in everyday life and work, and as the basis for improved performance. In the early 1970s, research was also being pursued into the sociology of sport – an area hitherto largely unexplored in the Soviet Union and still circumscribed by rather narrow ideological boundaries. Thus, the first Soviet book dealing with the social rôle and functions of sport[123] came out in 1972 – but in a very small printing of only 500 copies.

The extensive research into the technical aspects of sport testifies to the careful preparation that goes into sports performance and the seriousness with which the authorities take success in international competitions. Moreover, it provides an insight into the official concern with what, it is believed, are the main functions of sport: to help improve productivity, maintain a physically fit nation ready for military action, to advertise the communist system through international sporting success and to contribute to a 'fuller life' for all citizens. Indicative of the utilitarian functions assigned to sport are the quotations from Lenin inscribed on boards in tall letters inside the foyer of the Central State Institute of Physical Culture in Moscow. Three inscriptions, stressing both patriotism and productivity, perhaps sum up official thinking about the ideas that should underlie physical education training:

[123] P. S. Stepovoi, *Sport i obshchestvo* (Tartu, 1972).

A nation will never be conquered if the bulk of workers and peasants recognise, sense and see that they are safeguarding their Soviet power – the working people's power.

Labour productivity is, in the last resort, decisive for the victory of the new social system.

Our socialist republic of Soviets will stand firm like a torch of international socialism and as an example to all the working masses.

As in other research spheres, money bonuses and gold medals are awarded for outstanding research: in 1973, the USSR Sports Committee made seven such awards for three types of research: (1) for theoretical and sociological problems of physical culture and sport; (2) for research into training and teaching; and (3) for medical-biological work into physical education and coaching.[124]

Publications

Inasmuch as the mass media are seen largely as a means of education and political socialisation, rather than mainly entertainment or even sources of information, their rôle in Soviet society is particularly important to the Party: 'The Congress [24th] attaches great importance to improvement of the press, radio and television. Party organisations must be able skilfully to use the mass media as propaganda, to ensure their effective use and improve the political maturity and skill of journalists and propagandists.'[125] The sporting press is no exception. Sport is, after all, not a recreational pursuit that people can take or leave as they see fit; it is officially regarded as a valuable, indeed necessary, component of everyday life – and the mass media are required to propagandise sport and the benefits that are supposed to accrue from participation in it. M. Shishigin, deputy chairman of the USSR Sports-Writers Federation, has stated: 'It is the task of Soviet sports-writers to reveal the purpose and functions of physical culture, its rôle as an active means of shaping people physically and culturally.'[126] Moreover, sport – and the sporting press – by virtue of its popular nature, is regarded as a convenient vehicle for carrying overt political messages: 'Sporting contests for prizes

[124] *Sovetsky sport*, 28 July 1973, p. 1.
[125] *24th Congress of the CPSU*, APN (Moscow, 1971), p. 7.
[126] *Sport v SSSR*, 1970, No. 7, p. 20.

commemorating outstanding athletes and war heroes are particularly important as propaganda both for the participants and for the spectators. . . . Similarly, cross country runs and events in honour of Party and *Komsomol* congresses and other political occasions have great political significance.'[127]

Periodicals and books

Sports periodicals, like other specialised journals, frequently carry important general political speches in leading articles or editorials, (e.g. *Teoriya i praktika fizicheskoi kul'tury*, 1971, No. 6, had a leading article, seven pages long, in bold type, devoted to the 24th Party Congress with no mention at all of physical culture or sport). During 1972 *Sovetsky sport* devoted its front page to a variety of non-sporting causes, ranging from the full text of a Party resolution on preparations for marking the 50th anniversary of the USSR (22 February) to the campaign to gather the harvest (1 October); on 22 December, *the whole issue* was devoted to Brezhnev's speech on the occasion of the 50th anniversary of the USSR. It is also usual for leading politicians to attend big sporting events, possibly to demonstrate their identity of interests with the populace, but also to receive the acclaim of sports fans and, sometimes, to make speeches, as Khrushchov often did, and as Kosygin did at the opening of the 1971 and 1975 Finals in Moscow of the *Spartakiad* of the Peoples of the USSR.

In 1975, there were 46 sports periodicals with a circulation of eight million. Of the total, 14 were published in Moscow by central agencies, such as the USSR Committee on Physical Culture and Sport, the Central All-Union Council of Trade Unions, USSR Ministry of Education and the USSR Ministry of Agriculture. The rest were published in various republics and in Moscow and Leningrad specifically for the local population.

Partly due to the serious tone of the rest of the press, sports periodicals are extremely popular and always in great demand; unless a person has a subscription to such newspapers as *Sovetsky sport* or *Futbol-khokkei*, he is unlikely to obtain a copy (from a newspaper kiosk). It is not unknown for news-sellers to sell less

[127] G. D. Kharabuga, *Sovetskaya sistema fizicheskovo vospitaniya* (Leningrad, 1970), p. 13.

popular newspapers as a 'package deal' with a sports paper.[128] Until about 1966 (the year of the important Party resolution on physical culture and sport), the supply of sports papers was kept down far below the demand – perhaps for fear of people reading exclusively the less political sports media. In the last decade, however, the Party leadership has made a concession to popular demand (no doubt also with a view to increasing participation in sport) by allowing such papers to boost circulation, sometimes considerably: the circulation of the 14 central sports periodicals more than trebled between 1962 and 1973; subscriptions to the two most popular sports papers, *Sovetsky sport* and *Futbol-khokkei*, even quadrupled. It is true that the circulation of most periodicals has risen substantially since 1962, but it by no means matches that of sports papers.[129]

Most of the Republican and local sports periodicals are run jointly by the corresponding sports committee and *DOSAAF*. It is noteworthy that the single most popular sport in terms of the number of periodicals devoted to it and of circulation is chess (four) – an indication probably not so much of the popularity of the game as of the official promotion of it as a cerebral pursuit befitting a socialist society. Such evidently more popular sports as soccer, athletics and ice hockey have only one journal each specifically dealing with their sport among both central and local periodicals, while volleyball, basketball and skiing have none. Another sport officially supported (for its aesthetic qualities) is gymnastics, for which a special 50-odd page journal was first published twice yearly in 1973. As well as the magazines mentioned above, most of the major sports (including fishing and hunting, tennis, sub-aqua sport, cycling, speed skating, rowing, swimming, skiing, boxing, wrestling and weightlifting) similarly have periodicals that come out only once or twice a year.

Comparatively, the sports periodicals do rather well. Thus, in

[128] On more than one occasion in Moscow, I have asked for *Sovetsky sport* at a newspaper kiosk, and either had it offered at over 6 times its normal price (at 15 kopeks) or on condition another newspaper was bought with it. This would appear to be not unusual, as Soviet colleagues have confirmed.

[129] See M. V. Shishigin, 'Sportivnaya pechat' – aktivnoye sredstvo propagandy fizicheskoi kul'tury i sporta', *Teoriya i praktika fizicheskoi kul'tury*, 1973, No. 5, p. 10.

1972, *Sovetsky sport* was seventh in circulation of all Soviet news-papers, standing above the teachers' and servicemen's professional newspapers (*Uchitel'skaya gazeta* and *Krasnaya zvezda* respectively).

The major sports periodicals are as follows:

(1) *Sovetsky sport* (*Soviet Sport*), published since 1924 and currently the organ of the Committee on Physical Culture and Sport attached to the USSR and RSFSR Councils of Ministers. It is a popular four-page newspaper (price 2 kopecks) that comes out daily except Mondays, containing information on the performance of teams and sportsmen at home and abroad, political news and any resolutions on sport, criticisms, readers' letters and the results of sudden 'spot checks' ('raids') on sports organisations in any part of the country.[130] On 1 January 1975, it was published in 33 Soviet cities and, in 1973, had a daily circulation of 3,600,000. It has a Sunday supplement (sold separately) called *Futbol* (*khokkei* in winter) with a circulation of over a million.

(2) *Fizkul'tura i sport* (*Physical Culture and Sport*) is a popular well-illustrated monthly sports magazine, founded in 1922, and today one of the organs of the Committee on Physical Culture and Sport (see above). It costs 30 kopecks, contains an average of 40–50 pages and was published in a monthly printing of 425,000 in 1973.

(3) *Teoriya i praktika fizicheskoi kul'tury* (*The Theory and Practice of Physical Culture*) is a theoretical and technical monthly journal published by the Committee on Physical Culture and Sport. It costs 40 kopecks, had a monthly circulation of 18,500 copies in 1973 and averages 80 pages. As its name implies, it is a serious journal averaging 30 articles an issue, and contains much interesting material and research data of value to coaches, sportsmen, physical education instructors and sociologists. Normally, the journal consists of the following sections:

1. General introductory articles – often political or historical;
2. Training, techniques and tactics;
3. Physiology and sports medicine;
4. Sport and young people;

[130] In 1972, it published as many as 193 articles or letters critical of organisations and personnel involved in sport. Many of these were obviously taken up and improvements made.

5. Sport in everyday life – articles of mainly sociological interest;
6. Physical education among students;
7. 'Consultation' – detailed and often authoritative technical surveys in the form of replies to readers' questions;
8. Sport abroad;
9. Reviews.

(4) *Sport v SSSR (Sport in the USSR)* is a monthly illustrated popular and informative magazine, begun in 1963 and mainly printed for foreign consumption as a supplement to the general magazine *Sovetsky soyuz (Soviet Union)*. It comes out in Russian, English, French, German, Spanish and Hungarian, averages 30 pages and costs 30 kopecks.

(5) *Fizicheskaya kul'tura v shkole (Physical Culture in the School)* is a monthly illustrated journal published by the USSR Ministry of Education since 1930 and intended primarily for physical education teachers. In view of the fact that about one third of such teachers are unqualified, its rôle is particularly important. It costs 30 kopecks, averages 50 pages and had a circulation of 117,000 copies in 1973.

(6) *Sportivnye igry (Sporting Games)* deals with such games as soccer, hockey, handball, water polo, tennis and badminton. It costs 30 kopecks and had a circulation of 170,000 copies in 1973. Apart from *Sport za rubezhom*, this is the only journal to have undergone a fall in circulation after 1972.

In addition to these multi-sport journals, there are several periodicals for individual sports and recreational activities, such as the chess weekly '*64*' and the two monthlies – *Shakmaty v SSSR (Chess in the USSR)* and *Shakhmatnyi byulleten' (Chess Bulletin)*, the latter two for different levels of chess ability; *Lyogkaya atletika (Athletics)*, *Futbol-khokkei (Soccer – Ice Hockey)* and *Turist (The Tourist)*.

Of course, all national, republican, regional and local daily and weekly papers also carry some sports news (rarely more than half a page).

In a survey of the reading habits of the 4,294 finalists of the Fifth *Spartakiad*, it was discovered that 70 per cent of the men and 68 per cent of the women were regular readers of *Sovetsky sport*, 22 per cent of the men and 32 per cent of the women – of *Fizkul'tura i sport*, 22 per cent of the men and 11 per cent of the women – of *Futbol-Khokkei*, and only 13 per cent of the men and 8 per cent of the women – of *Teoriya i praktika fizicheskoi kul'tury*. *Shakhmaty v SSSR* and *Chess '64'* attracted only 1.9 per cent and 1.3 per cent of the men respectively, and none of the women (though, it should be pointed out, chess did not feature in the *Spartakiad* programme).[131] Virtually all the finalists were regular readers of fiction, and some 80 per cent – of sports literature.

The sports administration has its own publishing house in Moscow, *Fizkul'tura i Sport* – reputedly the biggest in the world – which, in 1972, accounted for half the total production of sports literature: 141 publications – books, manuals, albums and brochures – with a total print of nearly nine million copies. Even so, this is estimated to be far below the demand: '*Fizkul'tura i Sport* Publishers meet the orders of book trading organisations for sports literature only by 40–50 per cent and, in some areas, only by 15–20 per cent.'[132]

Though sports periodicals occupied a relatively important place among all Soviet periodicals, the same cannot be said for books on sport. In 1975, the share of sports literature was only 0.9 per cent of the total number of titles published and of the total print and 0.6 per cent of the actual volume of printed matter produced. This was 'ridiculously small by comparison with other types of literature and does not correspond to the popular nature of sport'.[133] While willing to provide funds to meet popular demands on the sporting press, therefore, the Soviet authorities would appear to be far more parsimonious in regard to manuals, biographies, histories and suchlike.

---

[131] I. I. Pereverzin, 'Rol' sredstv massovoi informatsii v upravlenii razvitiem fizicheskoi kul'tury i sporta', in *Problemy upravleniya fizkul'turnym dvizheniem* (Moscow, 1973), p. 30.

[132] Shishigin, *Sport. Informatsiya*, p. 14.

[133] Shishigin, *Propaganda fizicheskoi kul'tury*, p. 66.

10

Social aspects of sport:
the military, peasants, nationalities,
women and schoolchildren

Since, as we have already seen, Soviet sport is encouraged and shaped by specific utilitarian and ideological designs, it will be instructive to examine the relationship between the official goals of the State and those of particular groups within the community. This will help us to understand the rationale of certain official functions attached to sporting activities.

Sport and the military

Sport and the military are connected in varying degrees during the development of all societies. For example, in the evolution of Western societies, ideological weapons such as militarised sports and their accompanying ethics have been closely associated with nationalism, militarism and imperialism. Sports fields and gymnasiums have traditionally been regarded as training grounds for building the kind of men needed to police an empire – whether in pre-war India or in post-war Vietnam. This in turn requires a civilian army both physically fit and well-socialised into conforming to a militarised view of life.

The link between sport and the military would appear to be particularly close in modernising societies which progress from a way of life which has recently been largely traditionalist in a comparatively brief historical span. In the development of the communist states, the rôle of the military in sport has been particularly heightened by centralised control over sport. All such countries have a national fitness programme with a bias towards military training, largely modelled on the Soviet *GTO* system. Moreover, they all have a strong military presence in the sports movement through army and security forces' clubs, provide military sinecures for more or less full-time sportsmen and, at times, have established direct military supervision over sport. The sporting ties between army and security forces' clubs within the socialist bloc are particularly illustrative of the utilitarian purposes to which sport is put and the formative influence of Soviet policies in sport on virtually all other communist states. (These international links are examined below in Chapter 11.)

'Militarised' sport did not spring fully armed from the head of Marx or Lenin; it was already well advanced in the Russian Empire: the tsarist régime valued sport as a factor promoting military training. This view was reinforced, as was shown above, during the early years of Soviet power when the young state was fighting for its very life. It was in these early years that the two organisations that today dominate the Soviet sports movement came into existence: the sports club of the army and *Dinamo*.

Sports Club of the Army

Figure 6 shows the organisations that have been concerned directly with ensuring the military fitness of the population since 1918. Thus, *Vsevobuch* was reorganised in 1923 into a sports organisation for the armed forces, eventually to become the Central Sports Club of the Army. *Vsevobuch* also provided the nucleus for the organisation of other military (or 'civil defence') societies during the 1920s that had some connection with recreation. In 1923, the Society of Friends of the Air Force was set up, to be followed by the Voluntary Society of Friends of Chemical Defence and the Chemical Industry. In 1925, the two amalgamated to form the Society of Friends of the Aviation and Chemical Defence. Subsequently, in 1927, all societies for the military training of civilians were combined in a single organisation, the Society for Aid to Defence and the Aviation and Chemical Industry. Today, it is known as *DOSAAF*, the Voluntary Society for Aid to the Army, Air Force and Navy. In its recreational activities, the Society concentrates on running various military sports circles such as rifle and gliding clubs. How close its involvement in sport is today may be judged by the very high proportion (70 per cent) of its members' subscriptions that it channels into sport. The resolution passed at the Seventh Plenary

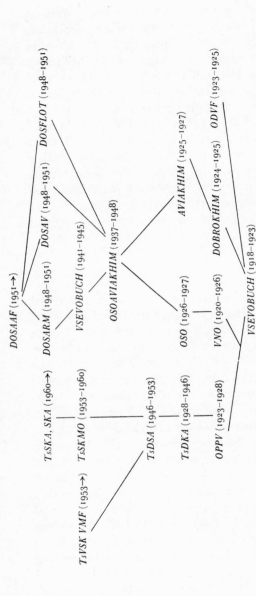

Fig. 6. Organisations concerned directly with ensuring the military fitness of the population, 1918–1976.

AVIAKHIM	Obshchestvo druzei aviakhimicheskoi oborony (Society of Friends of the Aviation and Chemical Defence).
DOBROKHIM	Dobrovol'noye obshchestvo druzei khimicheskoi oborony i khimicheskoi promyshlennosti (Voluntary Society of Friends of Chemical Defence and the Chemical industry).
DOSAAF	Dobrovol'noye obshchestvo sodeistviya Armii, Aviatsii i Flotu (Voluntary Society for Aid to the Army, Air Force and Navy).
DOSARM	Dobrovol'noye obshchestvo sodeistviya Armii (Voluntary Society for Aid to the Army).
DOSAV	Dobrovol'noye obshchestvo sodeistviya Aviatsii (Voluntary Society for Aid to the Air Force).
DOSFLOT	Dobrovol'noye obshchestvo sodeistviya Flotu (Voluntary Society for Aid to the Navy).
OVDF	Obshchestvo druzei Vozdushnovo flota (Society of Friends of the Air Force).
OPPV	Opytno-pokazatel'naya ploshchadka Vsevobucha (Vsevobuch Experimental and Display Centre).
OSO	Obshchestvo sodeistviya oborone SSR (Society for Aid to Defence of the USSR).
OSOAVIAKHIM	Obshchestvo sodeistviya oborone i aviatsionno-khimichesko promyshlennosti (Society for Aid to Defence and the Aviation and Chemical Industry).
SKA	Sportivnye kluby Armii (Army Sports Clubs).
TsDKA	Tsentral'ny Dom Krasnoi Armii (Central House of the Red Army).
TsDSA	Tsentral'ny Dom Sovetskoi Armii (Central House of the Soviet Army).
TsSKA	Tsentral'ny sportivny klub Armii (Central Army Sports Club).
TsSKMO	Tsentral'ny sportivny klub Ministerstva oborony (Central Sports Club of the Ministry of Defence).
TsVSK VMF	Tsentral'ny vodnosportivny klub Voenno-Morskovo Flota (Central Navy Aquatic Sports Club).
VNO	Voyenno-nauchnoye obshchestvo (Military-Research Society).
VSEVOBUCH	Vseobshcheye Voyennoye Obuchenie (Universal Military Training).

Session of the *DOSAAF* Central Committee on 25 May 1971 aptly sums up its aims: 'Widely to propagandise among the public, especially young people, military knowledge and the heroic traditions of the Soviet people; to improve the quality of training of young people for service in the Armed Forces, and further to promote military-technical sports.'[1]

Nowadays, the Central Sports Club of the Army (*TsSKA*) is the largest of the sports organisations run by the armed services which have a sports club (*sportivny klub armii – SKA*) in every military district. There is also a separately organised Central Aquatic Sports Club for the Navy (*TsVSK VMF*), set up in 1953, with its home in Moscow and branches at naval bases round the country; this club specialises, as its name implies, in sports associated with water: underwater swimming, water polo, rowing and sculling, motor boat sport and yachting. These clubs of the armed forces provide facilities both for servicemen and for the general public. Because a sportsman is a member of an army sports club (or of *Dinamo*), it does not follow automatically that he is a serviceman. For example, many ice hockey players and soccer players, most full-time gymnasts, figure skaters, cyclists, show jumpers, boxers, weightlifters, water polo players, rowers, scullers and yachtsmen are members either of the army clubs or of *Dinamo* because of the large and expensive amenities needed to practice these sports. They include the gymnasts Olga Korbut (army) and Ludmilla Turishcheva (*Dinamo*), the tennis players Olga Morozova (army) and Alexander Metreveli (*Dinamo*), and the figure skaters Rodnina and Zaitsev (army). Nevertheless, in a recent book on the history of *TsSKA*,[2] several well-known male sportsmen were pictured in uniform: they included the weightlifters Vlasov (Air Force Captain, p. 81) and Zhabotinsky (Lieutenant in the Motorised Infantry, p. 95), the soccer players Shesternyov (Senior Lieutenant in the Motorised Infantry, p. 137) and Fedotov (Captain in the Motorised Infantry, p. 135), the ice hockey players Firsov (Captain in the Motorised Infantry, p. 132) and Loktev (Major in the Motorised Infantry, p. 87) and the ex-ice hockey senior coach Tarasov[3] (wearing the uniform of a

---

[1] *Sovetsky sport*, 26 May 1971, p. 2.
[2] V. M. Gavrilin et al. (eds.), *S emblemoi TsSKA* (Moscow, 1973).
[3] His long-serving assistant coach, A. I. Chernyshev, is, however, a member

Lieutenant-Colonel in the Motorised Infantry Brigade, p. 120). For many full-time sportsmen and coaches, therefore, the armed services seem to provide a sinecure to enable them to have access to the best facilities and sound financial backing. It also enables them to retain their 'amateur' status in international sport. However, my impression is that army backing to an athlete does carry certain reciprocal obligations in respect of study, research, discipline and coaching.

It is also worthy of mention that physical culture plays a big part in army training; thus 'in 1969 and 1970 virtually all conscripts obtained their GZR (Ready for the Defence of the Homeland) badge'.[4] It is certainly true that 'physical culture and sport have become an integral part of military training' and that 'sport and the army are indivisible'.[5]

Dinamo

A paramilitary sports organisation, quite unrelated to the army clubs, is the All-Union Physical Culture and Sports Society *Dinamo*, set up in 1923 for the staff of the internal security agency and border guards. *Dinamo* has always held a rather unique position within the sports movement in that it has never come under trade union supervision (unlike 34 of the 36 sports societies) and has been the largest and richest of the sports societies. Its measure of independence has reflected that of its parent body – the security organs.

At first subordinate to the Party, the security organs (known under different names at different periods: *Cheka*; *GPU*; *OGPU*; *NKVD*; *MVD*; *MGB*; *KGB*) grew in importance when Stalin began to use them against his opponents within the Party, until at the time of the Great Purge in the latter part of the 1930s, they assumed the highest position in the apparatus of power, above the Party leadership itself and subordinate only to Stalin personally. During Beria's command of the security organs, their vast apparatus consolidated its position as the most powerful, privi-

of *Dinamo* (though no rank is given for him). See *Bol'shaya Sovetskaya entsiklopediya* (Moscow, 1972), Vol. VIII, p. 277.

[4] *Teoriya i praktika fizicheskoi kul'tury*, 1972, No. 4, p. 6.

[5] *Sovetsky sport*, 23 February 1972, p. 1.

leged and non-accountable section of society; in such a situation, it was not surprising that immediately after Stalin's death in 1953, Beria should have tried to seize supreme power in the state, and his failure was followed by a drastic curtailment of the powers of the security organs and their subordination once again to top Party control.

Although virtually no mention of the fact is now made in Soviet publications,[6] *Dinamo* is still today 'under the control of the USSR Ministry of Internal Affairs (*MVD*) and the Committee on State Security (*KGB*) attached to the USSR Council of Ministers'.[7] Membership of the Society is open 'to people serving in organs, units, offices and factories of the *MVD* and *KGB*; officers of the *KGB* and *MVD* who are in the reserves or in retirement, and members of their families; and other Soviet citizens'.[8] This definition of membership indicates the dual rôle of *Dinamo*: to provide facilities 'for the compulsory physical training of members of the *MVD* and *KGB*' and for 'the physical culture and health of the general public'.[9] The provision of sports facilities for the general public has the utilitarian aim of encouraging the cultivation of certain activities of a direct and indirect paramilitary nature and for developing mass physical fitness and military preparedness: 'The main aims of the *Dinamo* Society are to make physical culture and sport an integral part of the lives of all employees and servicemen of the *MVD* and *KGB* and of their families, to promote mass sport and, above all, to encourage military and service sports in accordance with the physical training manual of the USSR Armed Forces, to train proficient sportsmen and to prepare members of the Society for labour and the defence of their country.'[10]

[6] For example, neither the above mentioned reference to *Dinamo* in the Big Soviet Encyclopedia, nor a recent book on *Dinamo*, V. Vinokurov and O. Kucherenko, *Dinamo Moskva* (Moscow, 1973), nor any book or periodical I have read (except *Bunchuk*) mention *Dinamo*'s association with the security forces. It is also an association of which the Soviet public is not generally aware.

[7] M. F. Bunchuk, *Organizatsiya fizicheskoi kul'tury* (Moscow, 1972), p. 81. My attention was drawn to this unique source by Jack Badrock to whom I would like to record my thanks.

[8] Ibid., p. 82.

[9] Ibid., p. 82.

[10] Ibid., pp. 81–82.

With their considerable resources and tentacular organisation, it is hardly surprising that the Soviet security forces should also have an appreciable influence upon the sporting institutions of young people within the USSR and of several states within the socialist bloc: the largest single junior sports club in the USSR is *Yuny dinamovets* ('Young Dinamo') and the security forces' sports club (often called *Dinamo* – e.g. in Bulgaria, East Germany, Albania and Yugoslavia, on the Soviet model) is the largest sports organisation in most communist states.

Key position of army and Dinamo sports clubs

It will be gathered that, since the army and *Dinamo* sports organisations can call on the substantial material resources of their parent organisations, they are far more privileged than any other sports club or society and, consequently, command more facilities, consistently train more Masters of Sport and win more prizes both in domestic and in international competition. For example, of the 16 soccer teams in the top division of the Soviet League in 1974, four were *Dinamo* and two were army teams; in that year and the previous year, *Dinamo* teams won the league. From 1975 to 1976, *Dinamo* Kiev represented the USSR national side in international matches. In ice hockey, the Central Army Sports Club had, in 1975, won the first division title 17 times since the league was started in 1954; and 13 of the 19 players in the Soviet ice hockey squad at the 1972 Winter Olympics were army players. At the 1972 Summer Olympics, *Dinamo* members made up one-third of the Soviet Olympic team and collected twice as many medals as the nearest other Soviet sports society. Finally, in both the 1971 and the 1975 *Spartakiad* of the Peoples of the USSR, *Dinamo* and the armed forces amassed over half the total points scored – far more than their nearest rivals.

Some reasons for the close relationship

In the USSR, as in all the communist states, the army and the security forces provide many of the funds and facilities which enable people to take up and pursue a sport; they thereby help to ensure that as many people as possible are physically fit, mentally alert and possess the qualities (patriotism, will power, stamina and ingenuity) that are of particular value for military preparedness. The reasons for this close relationship between sport and the military in the Soviet Union must be sought in the following:

(a) the leadership's fear (given a 'capitalist encirclement' and shared land frontiers with twelve foreign states) of war and its conviction of the need to keep the population primed to meet it;

(b) the all-pervasive presence throughout society of the military and the security forces, necessitated by the imposition from above, should enthusiasm from below flag, of 'socialist construction' on a tired public (a state of affairs not so odd-seeming in Russian society, since this military presence had also, if for different reasons, been the norm before the revolution, in sport as elsewhere);

(c) its forming part of a policy of keeping the public in a state of controlled tension, ready to tolerate the discipline and sacrifices necessitated by rapid industrialisation, to conform to the standards set by the leaders and to acquiesce in their policies;

(d) the fact that, in a vast country with problems of communication, lukewarm (at best) popular attitudes towards physical exercise and few sports facilities for most of the Soviet period, military organisation of sport was actually an efficient method of deploying scarce resources in the most economical way and using methods of direction which were, perhaps, more effective coming from paramilitary than from civilian organisations.

In such circumstances and with such ambitious goals, the development of sport could hardly have been left entirely to civil institutions. The 'militarisation' of sport, moreover, becomes understandable in a country that has, in a short span of time, lived through such shattering events as three revolutions, a civil war, rapid industrialisation on its own resources, forced collectivisation, purges, mass terror and two world wars, in the second of which the loss of Soviet lives was more colossal than in any other country at any period of history.

Sport and the peasants

Attaining the goal of universal sports participation has always been hampered in the villages by the problems of generating

enthusiasm for and organising rural sport – and the rural population, up to 1961, constituted the majority of the population.

In societies other than the USSR, where an organised sports
movement has come into being, sports have predominantly been
cultivated to meet the needs of a growing urban populace. It was
thought, and this was to a large degree borne out in practice, that
peasant farmers, by the very nature of their lives and work –
undifferentiated and lonely – would not take part in many
organised sports – which seem generally to have reflected the
demands and requirements of newly urban communities. A study
of Anatolian peasants indicated 'that these highly tradition-
bound people cannot grasp the abstractness of modern sports.
They lack the enterprise, in their fatalistic village cultures, to see
why people want to knock themselves out for sportsmanship's
remote ideals; they cannot link such rituals, even by remote
analogy, with their own.'[11] In England, the organised sports
movement had grown up around the industrial cities in step with
the industrial revolution. Rural sport was largely a movement
distinct and apart from that pursued in the developing urban
areas; it was largely centred on the sporting squire or gentleman
whose interest was 'casual and sportsmanlike'. Where peasants
had time for sports, they mainly enjoyed traditional folk games
and competed in tests of strength, often only performed seriously
at annual fairs or village festivals.

The problems of recreation in the countryside are, of course,
not peculiarly Soviet, but universal characteristics of economic
under-development or backwardness. On the whole, the existing
Soviet rural and, to some extent, even the urban, sport situation
is the product of an uneven modernisation which has undermined
traditional forms of peasant recreation, yet not enough so as to
provide the substitutes found in the major cities.

In other industrialising countries, village sport was left mainly
to go its own way and was neglected by both government and
commercial sports organisations. In the USSR, however, the
declared aim of mass – and, after 1966, *universal* – participation
could not start to be achieved if the peasant farmers were ignored,
since they made up about half the population. Furthermore, rural

[11] J. Pitt Rivers, 'Honour and Social Status', in J. G. Peristiany (ed.),
Honour and Shame (Yale Univ. Press, New Haven, 1965), p. 127.

sport was said to be a means of assisting the gradual erosion of fundamental differences between town and country: 'all-round development in socialist society is not the exclusive privilege of the townsman'.[12] Sport was to help inculcate desired urban values (team and community spirit, rationality, discipline) and draw the farmer into the mainstream of 'socialist culture'. Nor was it lost on government and Party officials that sport could serve as a bond between the collectivised farmers and the industrial workers; it could provide a link between the village and wider units – region, republic and country – and help link the mass with the state. The peasant farmer might be encouraged to take an interest in the performance of his village or *kolkhoz* team, his fellow farmer-sportsmen – and thence to support the performance of his Republican team and ultimately the All-Union Soviet team against outsiders.

Nonetheless, there were immense obstacles to be overcome if rural interest was to be kindled to any great extent. First, there was the rural disdain for unnecessary physical exertion and the traditional peasant hostility to changes brought from outside in familiar cultural forms of expression and leisure habits. Second, the very nature of agricultural labour and Russian climatic conditions set close limits to the feasible pattern of rural sport and hindered the introduction of new forms of recreation. The great majority of Russian peasant farmers live under quite severe winter conditions which stretch from October to April.

In the Moscow *Oblast'* (region), for example, mean noon temperatures range from +4°C in October to −10.3°C in January (the coldest month) and +4°C again in April. On an average, the *Oblast'* (including the capital, Moscow) has over 150 days of below-zero temperature every year, the lowest absolute temperature ever recorded being −47°C and the highest +38°C; the mean annual temperature is 3.8°C. (See Table 14.)

These rather severe winter conditions militate against the playing in winter of the more easily organised sports like soccer, basketball, athletics and cycling. On the other hand, during the summer months, the farmers are normally at the height of their farm work.

[12] *Sovetsky sport*, 18 August 1972, p. 1.

TABLE 14 *Mean noon temperatures for Moscow oblast' during the year* (°C)

Month	Temperature	Month	Temperature
October	+4.0°	April	+4.0°
November	−3.8°	May	+12.1°
December	−7.7°	June	+17.0°
January	−10.3°	July	+19.3°
February	−9.7°	August	+17.4°
March	−5.6°	September	+10.7°

Source: Em. Dvinsky, *Moskva: kratky putevoditel'* (Moscow, 1971), pp. 10–11.

Third, the poverty and backwardness of the Soviet countryside, with its lack of gas, mains water and drainage, electricity and – especially – good roads have limited the possibilities of constructing relatively sophisticated sports amenities and of organising regular programmes of competition with other teams and areas.

Fourth, after 1929 and collectivisation, there was (in addition to exhaustion and a poor diet) widespread peasant hostility to urban 'communistic' things – and that included organised team games.[13]

Fifth, there has always been an organisational problem in the countryside in regard to sport. Who would be the *sportorg*? In urban areas, the trade unions had mostly done the job, assisted by government and Party organisations, in no small measure helped by the *Komsomol*. But primary Party organisations in the countryside were preoccupied with the vital problems of getting the farms to supply food and work more efficiently; furthermore, village Soviets were weak and understaffed. It was originally decided in the 1930s to make the *Komsomol* basically responsible for the condition and organisation of sport in the countryside. In April 1935, the *Komsomol* Central Committee passed a resolution

[13] It must be noted, however, that the widely remarked Soviet preference for group activities probably derives as much from the surviving traditions of village life as from the official liking for collectivised recreation. The British writer Wright Miller has remarked on this: 'The old communal ways are still the most powerful element in Soviet manners and morals. They show themselves vigorously, for example, in that most spontaneous and recent Soviet development, the sense of sportsmanship.' Wright Miller, *Russians As People* (London, 1963), p. 148. The influences in sport, are, therefore, to some extent retroactive – from town to country and from country to town

to launch a campaign to send members (15,000 was the planned number) to rural areas and supervise the formation of village sports circles.

In addition, the more prosperous urban sports organisations and factories were made 'patrons' of particular village sports circles – i.e. they were obliged to give political, cultural and material assistance to the village organisation. In this way, since many farms could not afford to build sports facilities, they were supposed to be helped by their richer urban 'patrons'. Thirty-five years later, however, a deputy-minister of agriculture of the Russian Federation was still complaining that 'there is much talk about patronage by town sports organisations over rural sports groups, but little, if anything, is done in practice. It should be made obligatory.'[14]

Nonetheless, a start had been made. It was a long haul until industrialisation made a larger amount of technical and other sports amenities available for the countryside. In the Ukraine, on the eve of Soviet involvement in World War II, only 117,000 rural sportsmen were registered in the republic's 3,800 rural sports collectives – an estimated one-eighth of the total number of athletes in the Ukraine in 1941. In other words, 43 out of every 10,000 people were registered sportsmen in the countryside in comparison with 676 per 10,000 in the towns – i.e. 16 times more in the towns.[15] It was not yet, of course, a question of developing proficiency; the prime aim was simply to excite interest in sport and, consequently, in better physical fitness, military training and health and hygiene standards. Not surprisingly, it was not until 1947 that a rural sportsman gained a Master of Sport award, though 884 Masters had been registered between 1937 and 1940.

It was a Party resolution of 27 December 1948 that marked a new concern for rural sport. The sports administration was severely rebuked for neglecting sport in the rural areas. The Party Central Committee recognised the need 'to give every assistance to the countryside in promoting mass sport, to send athletes, instructors and coaches to give displays in collective and state

14 *Teoriya i praktika fizicheskoi kul'tury*, 1971, No. 6, p. 55.
15 Estimated from statistics provided in F. I. Samoukov (ed.), *Istoriya fizicheskoi kul'tury* (Moscow, 1964), pp. 303, 339; *Malaya sovetskaya entsiklopediya*, Vol. VIII (Moscow, 1960), p. 838.

farms and Machine and Tractor Stations, to assist in organising competitions, to transmit to the rural sports collectives the best experience in the work of the sports societies'.[16]

Given the more solid industrial base of 1948 and this Party appeal, a sustained effort was now made to get things moving. One means of attracting farmers to sport was 'socialist-emulation sports contests' among farms and regions; a second was a new programme of rural sports festivals. In the autumn of 1948, a successful sports collective had been formed at the *Budyonny* Collective Farm in the Vinnitsa region of the Ukraine. Soon it was said to have had a big membership and its own rules and had come to embrace several other farms in the area; the farm collective grew into the first sports society, with a membership of 172,000 farmers. It was given the name *Kolkhoznaya niva* ('Collective Farm Cultivated Field') and held up as an example for other farms to copy. In the summer of 1949, mass rural sports festivals were held in the Ukraine with as many as 1,146,000 farmers taking part, six times more than had taken part in sports festivals the year before.[17] The Ukrainian example was held up for other areas to emulate and this led, between 1949 and 1952, to the formation of two big rural sports societies: *Urozhai* ('Harvest') and *Kolkhoznik* ('Collective Farmer'), the former an All-Union society embracing all farm personnel (on collective and state farms and at Machine and Tractor Stations) and the latter a society solely for collective farmers. This was followed by the formation of other collective farm societies for different parts of the country. The extent of the effort in recruiting may be judged by the fact that while, in 1948, only 37,000 rural sports groups existed, with a membership of 930,000, by 1955, there were 58,000 such groups, claiming 2,760,000 members,[18] and by 1973, some 65,000 groups, with twelve million members engaging in 42 sports.[19]

Administrative responsibility for individual farm sports groups had rested with the councils of rural voluntary sports societies

---

[16] Samoukov, *Istoriya fizicheskoi kul'tury*, p. 196.

[17] Y. N. Teper, 'Razvitie fizkul'turnovo dvizheniya v Ukrainskoi SSR', in *Ocherki po istorii fizicheskoi kul'tury* (Moscow, 1967), p. 59.

[18] Ibid., p. 72.

[19] *Sport v SSSR*, 1973, No. 6, p. 3.

(*VSSs*) attached to district, regional, territorial and Republican sports committees. Until 1950, the basic forms of organisation in the countryside were the sports collectives on collective farms and the trade union *Kolos*, *Luch* and *Kommunar VSSs* which had been formed in 1936 to represent state-farm, procurement and MTS workers respectively. The *VSSs* continued after the war, but the collectives were taken over by the collective farm sports societies which, in 1956, merged with other rural sports groups belonging to the *Urozhai VSS* into a single rural *VSS* for each republic; *Kolkhoznik* was disbanded. Henceforth, all collective and state farmers, the members of their families and others who worked in the countryside (e.g. teachers and doctors) would be eligible for membership of the single rural sports society existing in their republic: *Urozhai* for Russia, *Kolgospnik* for the Ukraine, *Varpa* for Latvia, and so on.

From 1955 onwards, annual rural sports festivals (*spartakiads*) were held, the first drawing over one-and-a-half million participants. How much rural sport was developing may be gauged by the fact that, in 1958, some four million took part in the annual *spartakiad*. By 1966, the claimed number had grown to eleven million and, in 1970, reached eighteen million. Remarking on the high figure of six million farmers who had taken part in the preliminaries and finals of the First Russian Federation Rural Games in 1970, a Russian Federation deputy-minister of agriculture made the practical point that, 'with greater participation in sport, there will be less of a mass exodus of young people from collective farms and fewer cases of violations of labour discipline and public order'.[20]

Although the participation and skill of rural sportsmen (and the amenities at their disposal) by no means yet reflect their proportion in the overall population, they have increased their share in overall participation in sport from 15.8 per cent in 1950 to 22 per cent in 1959, 21.6 per cent in 1965 and 21.9 per cent in 1970; in absolute figures, rural sportsmen have increased from nearly two million in 1950 to nearly four and a half million in 1959, over ten million claimed in 1966 and twelve million in 1970.

[20] *Teoriya i praktika fizicheskoi kul'tury*, 1971, No. 6, p. 52.

Not only have they increased absolutely and relatively, they have markedly improved in skill: while, in 1953, only 5.5 per cent of all ranked sportsmen were country people, their proportion was 9.9 per cent in 1959, 13.7 per cent in 1966 and 14.9 per cent in 1970. Nonetheless, Sergei Pavlov, Chairman of the All-Union Committee on Physical Culture and Sport, writing in 1969, regretted that only one rural athlete had ever represented the Soviet Union at the Olympic Games (Ardalian Ignatiev, in the 400 m at Melbourne in 1956).[21] At the Summer Olympics in 1972, however, 10 of the 507 Soviet athletes were said to be members of rural sports clubs,[22] four of whom won their events.

These results had long been recognised as inadequate and brought a special resolution at the 23rd Congress of the Communist Party of the Soviet Union in March 1965. In its resolution 'On Urgent Measures to Improve Soviet Agriculture', the Central Committee of the Party recommended that 'measures should be taken to increase the number of sports centres, stadiums and other installations, especially on collective and state farms. This must be the affair of the entire Party, all its organisations, the Soviets, trade unions, *Komsomol* and all groups in town and country.'[23] Subsequently, four years later, an administrative reorganisation took place in an endeavour to improve the rural sports situation. A Central Council of Rural Voluntary Sports Societies was set up and, in nine republics, the rural sports societies became trade union cooperatives.

A resolution passed jointly in 1973 by the Party Central Committee and the USSR Council of Ministers, 'On Measures to Improve Conditions in Rural Schools', pointed out with concern that while, on average, 50 per cent of schools in towns had gymnasiums, only 21 per cent of rural schools were so provided.[24]

Besides the lack of facilities in the countryside, another chronic deficiency was the lack of trained coaches and instructors. Some 90 per cent of the chairmen of district councils of rural *VSSs* did not possess the requisite qualifications in 1967.[25] Moreover, 43 per

---

[21] S. P. Pavlov, 'Novaya stupen'', in *Velenie vremeni* (Moscow, 1969), p. 15.
[22] *Sovetsky sport*, 18 August 1972, p. 1.
[23] *Sovetsky sport*, 26 March 1965, p. 1.
[24] *Sovetsky sport*, 28 July 1973, p. 2.
[25] *Teoriya i praktika fizicheskoi kul'tury*, 1967, No. 12, p. 3.

cent of rural physical education instructors were unqualified.[26]
The problem here is that familiar in other fields – of the dis-
inclination of college-leavers to take up a post in rural areas. To
try to overcome this problem, 'crash' training courses have been
instituted for physical education students who promise to work in
rural areas upon graduation. Another example of the serious
attempt to improve the situation is the allocation out of the
trade union budget of eight million rubles in 1970 (compared
with three million in 1966) to the rural sports society *Urozhai.*

Despite the problems and the obvious gulf that exists between
the rural and urban populations in respect of opportunities for
sport, there has been considerable progress, especially since the
end of the war, both in the provision of sports amenities in the
countryside and in the making of opportunities for using them.
The impression one gains from Soviet sporting literature of recent
years is that the authorities are seriously concerned in broadening
the base of the sports pyramid by involving more and more
peasants in sport. The reasons for this concern are various. One is,
of course, the belief in the mental and physical health-giving
properties attributed to sport; besides making people fitter and
therefore better workers, however, sport is supposed to implant
certain moral qualities that help to make the athlete a better
all-round citizen, hence the government desire to develop, institu-
tionalise and direct rural recreation. One investigator into rural
sport reports with regret that 'because of the insufficient penetra-
tion among rural workers of such games as the solution of chess
and draughts problems, crosswords and rebuses, table tennis and
billiards, particular success is enjoyed by lotto, dominoes and
cards which give nothing to the mind or heart'.[27]

Another rural study maintains that 'survey findings testify that
sport in the countryside is a powerful factor encouraging all-round
development . . .'. Sportsmen are evidently more cultured and
politically conscious than their non-athletic fellow villagers:
'Among rural sportsmen, there are more people doing social
work, engaged in political education, self-education, visiting

[26] Pavlov, 'Novaya stupen'', p. 15. The figure was put at 44.5 per cent in
1973. *Sovetsky sport*, 28 July 1973, p. 2.
[27] V. G. Baikova, A. C. Duchal and A. A. Zemtsov, *Svobodnoye vremya i
vsestoroneye razvitie lichnosti* (Moscow, 1965), p. 267.

libraries, regularly reading newspapers, books and magazines, attentively listening to the radio and watching television.'[28] Furthermore, sport helps to combat social evils like drinking and smoking, and 'irrational' use of leisure time like playing cards and dominoes: 'Among rural sportsmen, there were also fewer card players and spirits drinkers. Sportsmen spend on average 2r. 25k. per month on liquor and tobacco, non-sportsmen 8r. 85k.; on the other hand, the former spend 9r. 75k. on books and journals, the latter 6r. 30k.'[29] There is, therefore, more to the government attempts to promote rural sport than merely to provide relaxation after a hard day's work in the fields.

Despite official exhortations, several sociological studies have revealed a low interest in sport among farmers. One study reported that 53 per cent of rural young people never engaged in any form of sport and 31 per cent said no sporting events ever took place in their village; only some 12 per cent actually engaged in sport regularly.[30] On the other hand, it was noted with concern that '16 per cent of young people in the countryside play cards, lotto or dominoes in their spare time . . .'[31] and that 'visits of relatives are often accompanied by drinking bouts and empty games like cards, lotto and dominoes'.[32] In another survey of free time expenditure, this time on a state farm in Kazakhstan, it was discovered that only 6.8 per cent of the farm members took any interest in sport (2.5 per cent as spectators only); since the farm had no sports facilities, this was hardly surprising.[33] In another Central Asian republic, Uzbekistan, yet another survey found that only 5–6 per cent of the rural young people went in for sport on any regular basis; 'this was because the collective and state farms do not have sufficient sports facilities or qualified personnel'.[34] It was a pity, inasmuch as 'physical culture and sport are a

[28] *Teoriya i praktika fizicheskoi kul'tury*, 1969, No. 3, p. 44.

[29] Ibid., p. 45.

[30] I. M. Slepenkov and B. V. Knyazev, *Molodyozh sela sevodnya* (Moscow, 1972), p. 165.

[31] Ibid., p. 168.

[32] Ibid., p. 175.

[33] *Teoriya i praktika fizicheskoi kul'tury*, 1973, No. 11, p. 54.

[34] R. A. Abdumalikov and Yu. S. Sholomitsky, 'Nekotorye puti vnedreniya fizicheskoi kul'tury i sporta sredi sel'skikh truzhenikov Uzbekskoi SSR', in Yu. V. Borisov, *Planirovanie razvitiya fizicheskoi kul'tury i sporta sredi sel'skovo naseleniya* (Moscow, 1964), p. 85.

paramount means of communist education among young people in Uzbekistan'.[35] Even in the more developed republic of Latvia, a study revealed that as many as 71 per cent of the rural population did not pursue any sport and had no inclination to do so.[36]

All in all, it is clear that rural sport is not on a par with urban sport – with regard either to participation or to provision of amenities or to the level of proficiency. Nonetheless, the situation is certainly changing and by the 1970s, the Soviet farm worker appeared to prefer a pattern of sports recreation that was not greatly different from that of the town worker. He, too, now had improved opportunities for playing a sport (surveys show that this is not always the one he would prefer to play – there is an evident lack of such amenities as swimming pools, gymnasiums and boats of all kinds – though there does appear to be an adequate supply of facilities for chess, draughts, table tennis and cycling), for improving his skill and for taking part in competition.

Sport and the nationalities

The USSR contains more than 100 different nationalities, tribes and linguistic groups; 22 of the nationalities enumerated in the 1970 census had more than a million people each and accounted for 95 per cent of the population. The other 80 or more nationalities together totalled fewer than 10 million and only 28 of them numbered more than 100,000 persons each.[37] Official national policy is complex and has altered with the times. In a very general way, however, the overriding aim has been to convert all the peoples not into Russians (which was what the tsars wanted to do in many places) – who account for just over half the Soviet population – but into builders of socialism and of an industrial society and, ultimately, into willing members of a communist society. In Soviet Marxist theorising, 'national forms of human existence, while being an inevitable stage in mankind's development, are not eternal; when communism prevails world wide, it will create conditions for the gradual disappearance of national

[35] Ibid.
[36] I. F. Forands, 'Otnoshenie k fizicheskoi kul'ture sel'skovo naseleniya', in Yu. V. Borisov, *Planirovanie razvitiya fizicheskoi kul'tury i sporta sredi sel'skovo naseleniya* (Moscow, 1974), p. 85.
[37] B. Urlanis, *Statistika naseleniya* (Moscow, 1971), p. 6.

differences and for the formation of a non-national human society'.[38] In regard to the elements of national culture, including physical culture, which are prescribed officially as 'socialist in content and national in form', the current Party Programme maintains that Soviet nations 'change, advance and draw closer together, shedding all outdated traits that contradict the new conditions of life. An international culture common to all the Soviet nations is developing.'[39]

Similar problems to those existing in rural areas beset the development of sport in the more backward republics and national areas. With the advance of urbanisation and industrialisation, many of the old cultural forms, including national games, were forced into the background by forms that were more appropriate to the new urban setting and which could link each nationality with others throughout the country. This has been quite explicit government policy. Nonetheless, with national tenacity and, sometimes, official encouragement, a number of national sports and games have persisted to this day, while others have been modified into internationally accepted organised sports (e.g. wrestling, judo/*sambo* and weightlifting) and occupy an honoured place in Soviet sport. Thus, *gorodki* and *lapta* (described earlier) still thrive among the Slavs, while various equestrian and wrestling events are popular among the Central Asian and Transcaucasian peoples: *kyz-kuumui* – chasing a maiden on horseback, *oodarysh* – wrestling on horseback, *at-chabysh* – horse racing, are all popular in Kirgizia and, with slight variations, are also popular in all other Central Asian republics. I have witnessed these exciting folk games (and some more gruesome spectacles) at the traditional *Saban-tui* of Tatars in south-eastern Bashkiria – a colourful festival that must have continued with a modicum of change for many, many centuries. In Georgia, such folk sports as *djigitovka* – horsemanship, *lelo* – similar to polo, *tskhenburti* – a team game with ball and rackets, all seem to retain their popularity. Various forms of national wrestling are, of course, widespread: *alaman-baiga* in Uzbekistan, *kokh* in Armenia, *gyulesh* in Azerbaidzhan,

---

[38] R. V. Turyansky, 'Budushchnost' natsii i problema yazykovo obshcheniya', *Filosofskie i sotsiologicheskie issledovaniya*, Vyp. XII (Leningrad, 1971), p. 127.

[39] *The Road to Communism* (Moscow, 1962), p. 561.

kurash in Turkmenia, *chidaobo* in Georgia and *trÿnta* in Moldavia.

It has been the officially stated policy to bring the level of sports participation and skill in all republics up to a more or less similar level. As the evidence below would seem to indicate, there has been some progress towards this end.

Participation

In 1970, the most 'sporting' republics were Georgia, Belorussia, the Ukraine and Russia (with 190 or more participants per 1,000 people); then came a middle group comprising Turkmenia, Kazakhstan, Kirgizia, Uzbekistan and Estonia (from 160 to 180 participants per 1,000 people), followed by four other republics with between 129 and 145 participants per 1,000 people: Azerbaidzhan, Moldavia, Lithuania and Latvia. The most backward from the 'sporting' standpoint were Armenia and Tadzhikistan.[40] This is a pattern that in the main reflects the socio-economic background of the republics (the first four 'sporting' republics being among the most advanced economically and socially, and most urban, and four of the last six – with the exception of Latvia and Armenia – being among the most backward and rural). Certain other sources, however, suggest that the level of participation in sport may not be as even as this or that attitudes may not be so standard throughout the Union; some authorities clearly inflate their figures more than others to present a rosier picture of sport in their republics. An Uzbek newspaper report in 1971, for example, informed readers that, 'According to figures submitted, the Bukhara *Oblast'* in Uzbekistan had 904 weightlifters registered in 79 clubs. On investigation, it was discovered that there were no more than 100 weightlifters in only four clubs. A similar situation existed in Samarkand *Oblast'*, where the number of clubs and registered members had been inflated four-fold. . The same situation prevailed in four other *Oblast'*s of Uzbekistan.'[41] It is

[40] The number and proportion of sportsmen in Republican populations in 1970 were extrapolated from *Narodnoye khozyaistvo SSSR, 1922–1972* (Moscow, 1972), p. 9 and from *Sport v SSSR*, 1972, No. 12, pp. 7–13.
[41] *Sovetsky sport*, 29 May 1971, p. 2; the article was aptly entitled 'Paper Muscles and Inflated Figures'.

also interesting to learn, through the Soviet press, that all nationalities do not take their sport as seriously as the Russians evidently do or as official sources sometimes claim. At the 15th All-Uzbekistan *Spartakiad* that took place in May 1971, two Uzbek boxers suddenly vanished and another, a Candidate Master of Sport, refused to enter the ring when faced with superior opponents. As a result, the Candidate Master was stripped of his title and disqualified from boxing for two years; the other two were disqualified for one year – all for 'demonstrating cowardice and indifference'. Other infringements included the disappearance of the Namangan *Oblast'* handball team on the final day of the handball tournaments and the illegal appearance in the Samarkand fencing team of a girl from . . . Khar'kov.[42]

The achievements, nonetheless, are significant: in an area characterised by a feudal, bey-and-mullah-dominated way of life, that had no sports instructors prior to 1917 and whose people were 92.2 per cent illiterate at the time of the 1920 census, the Soviet republic of Uzbekistan (which was previously part of the Turkestan *khanate*) is said to have had, in 1970, over 4,000 qualified instructors, a State Institute of Physical Culture, physical culture faculties at the Tashkent, Andizhan and Bukhara colleges of education, thirty physical education departments in other institutes, and four sports boarding schools – more than any other republic.

Achievement

In sporting performance in a whole range of indices, the Central Asian republics tend to trail in varying degrees, with the Slav areas dominating once again. Thus, as the table below shows, the 4th, 5th and 6th *spartakiads* were dominated by teams from the three Slav republics, Russia, the Ukraine and Belorussia, which filled the first four places in 1967 and the first five places in 1971 and 1975; three Central Asian republics, Kirgizia, Turkmenia and Tadzhikistan, have consistently brought up the rear.

Moscow and Leningrad have traditionally been the major sporting centres in the USSR and attract potentially top athletes because they have generally had the best coaches and facilities.

[42] *Sovetsky sport*, 28 May 1971, p. 2.

TABLE 15 *Results of the 4th, 5th and 6th 'Spartakiads' of the Peoples of the USSR, 1967, 1971 and 1975, by Republic (plus Moscow and Leningrad)*

Republic	1967 Points total	Position	1971 Points total	Position	1975 Points total	Position
Moscow	379	1	2,294	2	7,293	2
Russia (team from regions, territories and autonomous republics)	361	2	2,503	1	8,713	1
Ukraine	357	3	1,956	3	7,024	3
Leningrad	301	4	970	5	5,204	4
Georgia	265	5	802	6	2,633	7
Belorussia	242	6	1,062	4	4,599	5
Kazakhstan	236	7	577	7	2,844	6
Latvia	226	8	478	8	2,400	8
Lithuania	211	9	340	10	2,162	10
Uzbekistan	204	10	256	11	2,329	9
Azerbaidzhan	191	11	250	13	1,582	13
Estonia	167	12	354	9	1,610	12
Armenia	127	13	257	12	1,422	14
Moldavia	119	14	202	14	1,909	11
Kirgizia	109	15	163	15	1,163	15
Turkmenia	87	16	30	17	609	17
Tadzhikistan	71	17	60	16	954	16

Sources: A. Dobrov, *God sportivny* (Moscow, 1968), p. 115; *Sovetsky sport*, 31 July 1971, p. 1; *Teoriya i praktika fizicheskoi kul'tury* (1975), No. 9, p. 3.

Nonetheless, there has been an obvious shift away from blanket Moscow–Leningrad domination from about the mid-1960s, as provincial centres built up their resources. Moscow and Leningrad teams both did worse at the 1971 and 1975 *spartakiads*, for example, than they had ever done previously, moving down from 1st to 2nd and 4th to 5th positions respectively. Moscow had come first in all three previous *spartakiads* (in 1956, 1959 and 1963) and Leningrad 3rd, 3rd and 4th. Another noteworthy point about the greater sports involvement of nationalities to emerge from the *spartakiads* is that, whereas 40 nationalities were represented in the first *spartakiad*, and 43 in the second, 70 were in the third and over 80 (of 121 enumerated in the 1970 census) in the fourth, fifth and sixth. This is cited as evidence of the 'growing rôle of sport in bringing together the peoples of the USSR'.[43]

Further evidence of the increasing 'spread' of sports success is that the eighty-two reigning Soviet world champions in 1970 resided in ten different Soviet cities; in soccer, league and cup winners in recent seasons have included teams from Kiev (*Dinamo*) and Voroshilovgrad (*Zarya*) in the Ukraine, Yerevan (*Ararat*) in Armenia, Tbilisi (*Dinamo* – the 1976 cup-winners) in Georgia and Baku (*Neftchi*) in Azerbaidzhan. In volleyball, the Riga (Latvia) *VEF* women's team has been Soviet champions for several seasons and, in basketball, the Alma Ata (Kazakhstan) women's team and the Tbilisi (Georgia) or Vilnius (Lithuania) men's teams have been the most successful in recent years; in tennis, the men's events were long dominated by a Georgian, Alexander Metreveli, and an Estonian, Toomas Leius; in weight-lifting, three Soviet world record holders in 1976 lived in the small mining town of Shakhty (Alexeyev, Vakhonin and Rigert); and in women's gymnastics, the top girls for several years have been Ukrainian (Turishcheva), Belorussian (Korbut and Lazakevich), Tatar (Saadi) and Korean (Kim).

In participation in sport, in intermediate performance and in individual sports, the provincial centres of the country appear to be not greatly outclassed by the metropolis and the gap appears to be narrowing. The time will probably soon come when the traditional centres for sport will have to cede first place in performance to other areas which were introduced to organised sport only relatively recently.

Sports personnel and facilities

It was noted in the previous section on sport and the peasants that rural areas suffered from lack of qualified personnel and facilities. In regard to national areas, however, this does not seem to be the case. Sports coaches are well dispersed among the republics, with the Transcaucasian and Baltic republics best off, filling the top five places in 1965 and four of the top six places in

---

[43] N. I. Ponomaryov, 'Natsional'noye i internatsional'noye v sporte', *Teoriya i praktika fizicheskoi kul'tury*, 1973, No. 5, p. 7.

1972.[44] Some republics that have shown themselves notably backward in relation to other indicators of sporting achievement – Tadzhikistan, Kirgizia and Turkmenia – here, in provision of sports personnel, appear better off than Russia, the Ukraine and Belorussia (which filled three of the bottom places in 1965 and the last three places in 1972). This may be an indication of deliberate government policy to attempt to raise the level of sport in traditionally the most backward sporting republics by providing coaches – without a correspondingly enthusiastic popular response – or it may be simply that some republics have given more realistic figures than others. Despite the statistics, it was reported in 1972 that the number of qualified sports personnel was only 50–60 per cent of the total number of full-time sports coaches and physical education specialists in Russia, Uzbekistan, Kazakhstan and Turkmenia.[45]

There would appear to be a fairly even spread of three major types of sports amenity – sports centre, gymnasium and swimming pool – over all republics, with Georgia clearly the best provided for overall and most of the Central Asian republics having made a marked relative improvement between 1966 and 1972 – from occupying four of the bottom five places in 1966 to occupying places in the top half of the table in 1972. The two worst-provided-for republics in 1972 would appear to be the Russian Federation and Azerbaidzhan.[46]

Irrespective of size of population, the proclaimed policy of developing higher educational institutions in national republics is not pursued in regard to sport. Three republics, Moldavia, Turkmenia and Estonia, had no such institute at all in 1972, while Russia had seven. Despite being the smallest (in population)

[44] The number of qualified (i.e. persons who have completed a college or university course in physical education) coaches and physical education specialists per 10,000 sportsmen was calculated for each Republic for 1965 and 1972. Data were taken from N. A. Makartsev, *Stranitsy istorii sovetskovo sporta*, p. 96, and *Sport v SSSR*, 1972, No. 12, pp. 6–13.

[45] V. A. Ivonin (ed.), *Sputnik fizkul'turnovo rabotnika* (Moscow, 1972), p. 195.

[46] The provision of sports centres, gyms and swimming pools per 100,000 town dwellers was calculated for each republic in 1966 and 1972. Full tables are given in my doctoral thesis: Riordan, J. W., *Sport in Soviet Society* (Univ. of Birmingham, 1975).

of all fifteen republics, Estonia, at least, might be expected to have had one, given its long tradition of organised sport and high level of culture. (It has two universities – at Tallinn and Tartu.) On the other hand, the other two Baltic republics each had one institute but no other further education establishment or faculty specialising in physical education and sport; by comparison, smaller republics like Tadzhikistan, Kirgizia and Armenia had 4, 3 and 2 respectively. Russia had 127! There is clearly here a disproportionate siting of such training establishments; it could give credence to the view that the central authorities discriminate against the comparatively well-developed non-Slav areas, like the Baltic republics and Moldavia, because they fear the encouragement of nationalism there. Sport is a convenient vehicle for nationalistic feelings. The disproportion may, on the other hand, be due primarily to an attempt to bring sport in comparatively backward sporting areas up to the level of the more advanced.

One conclusion to be drawn from the available statistics is that, since the end of the war, the republics that were previously regarded as being culturally and economically backward, and simultaneously lagging in sports participation, skill and facilities, have made considerable progress and, in a number of indices, caught up with the more advanced republics. The greatest headway has been made by the five Central Asian republics, especially Turkmenia and Uzbekistan. By 1972, application of the principles of proportionate representation had almost been achieved.

National problems

One final issue meriting attention here is that of national identification, through sport and the potentially 'unhealthy' nationalistic passions unleashed during sports contests. There are many examples in Soviet periodicals of the passions of players and spectators running high and, in some cases, spilling over into violence in Soviet international group sports contests. Here are just a few.

In a basketball match in 1973 against the Sverdlovsk team *Uralmash*, Georgian players 'caused much fighting, disputed decisions and finally attacked the umpire'.[47] As a result, the USSR

[47] *Sovetsky sport*, 26 April 1973, p. 4.

Basketball Federation imposed a life ban on the Georgian coach and suspended the team until the end of the season. Georgian soccer fans have also been known to let their feelings get the better of them – e.g. 'during the inter-Republican soccer tourney, a band of Georgians ran onto the pitch during the Ukraine–Georgia match and harangued the referee, thereby interrupting the game for several minutes after a Georgian "goal" had been disallowed'.[48] Incidentally, it has been my own experience, during the Moscow *Dinamo* v. Tbilisi *Dinamo* Cup Final of 1970, to witness a Georgian fan smash an empty vodka bottle and hold it threateningly in front of a Russian's face after the latter had made disparaging remarks about the Georgian team. (Rather judiciously, the Russian spent the remainder of the match cheering on the Georgians!) The Azerbaidzhan soccer team, *Neftchi* (which was constantly in trouble during the 1972 season), 'carries around a whole suite of "fans" who consider it their duty to support their favourites by fair means or foul'.[49] Finally, a Moldavian journal chides supporters of the Kishinyov soccer team, *Nistru*, who greeted the Odessa *Chernomorets* team with 'whistles and catcalls . . . And when the Odessa team scored, their goal was met in silence. Why? Why should we not treat our guests honourably; Kishinyov is renowned for its hospitality; yet, these so-called "fans" mocked and abused the Odessa fans. Even after the match, they hurled all manner of obscenities at them. This is shameful, comrades! One should support one's team in a cultured manner, and every genuine fan should root out the hooligans and hand them over to the militia.'[50]

Such incidents as these are attendant upon modern competitive sport the world over and are not necessarily the result of inflamed nationalistic passions or prejudices. However, the ebullience of players and fans of a particular national team does contain the obvious danger of nationalistic confrontations. With the increase in free time (especially the long weekend) and money for travel, fans are increasingly able to follow their team about the country and give it vocal support in its striving to win, sometimes inciting other fans and players to what the Soviet authorities regard as

[48] *Sovetsky sport*, 15 July 1972, p. 3.
[49] *Sovetsky sport*, 16 May 1973, p. 4.
[50] *Vecherny Kishinyov*, 16 May 1973, p. 4.

unsporting conduct. This is a problem that is likely to increase in future. To give just two examples from my own experience that illustrate this growing problem of commitment to the success of one's national team against another, especially Russian (the dominant nationality in the Soviet Union) teams, during 1975 at Moscow's Lenin Stadium, I encountered a large group of Kazakhs who told me they had travelled from Alma Ata (a five-hour jet plane flight to Moscow) just to see a league match between their team *Kairat* and Moscow *Torpedo*. Just a few years' previously I had been on a flight to Armenia; as the plane landed, the stewardess announced that the local team *Ararat* had beaten the Moscow team *Lokomotiv*: the scenes that then ensued were quite amazing – the passengers, who were mostly Armenian, hugged and kissed one another as though a great war victory had been proclaimed.

On the whole, the USSR has not witnessed the extreme violence occurring in some Western countries or Latin America partly because the state employs a number of controls and sanctions, deals quite severely with miscreants and does not permit its media of mass communication to be charged with the sort of ethnocentrism that awakens unrealistic expectations among the sporting public.

To sum up this section on sport and nationalities, it is evident that the State has quite deliberately fostered the development of organised sport among the various nationalities, above all as an agent of *integration* in its vast commonwealth of nationalities. As a recent study put the case: 'The value of sport is that it brings people together, encourages a community of interests and goals, helps to integrate the different nationalities, strengthen and cement their friendship, spread Russian as the *lingua franca*, make the progressive traditions of one people accessible to others and paves the way for the birth of international communist traditions among all peoples.'[51]

[51] K. T. Rzayev and E. F. Adzhanov, 'Rol' fizicheskoi kul'tury i sporta v internatsional'nom sblizhenii sotsialisticheskikh natsiy i narodnostei', *Teoriya i praktika fizicheskoi kul'tury*, 1975, No. 9, p. 9.

Sport and women

The participation of women in competitive sport can, some people believe, contribute to their improved status in society. As Professor Jan Felshin writes in a recent book on American women in sport: 'Both sport and women's status are changed by women serving in prestigious or unique rôles in sport. There is, of course, a danger of "tokenism" insofar as a single woman may be permitted to advance or to do something as a way of quieting criticism. In terms of social change, however, it seems more often that even a single woman fulfilling a heretofore "masculine" rôle becomes a substantial aspect of a changed consciousness as social conception.'[52] This notion of women in sport enhancing in some way women's liberation has already been noted in this book with reference to Lesgaft and Lenin, Isadora Duncan and Podvoisky. It has been an explicit function assigned to sport by Soviet policy makers. Moreover, in recent years, the *international* display of grace and strength, skill and courage by Soviet sportswomen in a whole range of sports has inspired many young women in other parts of the world to take up a sport they would otherwise have spurned. In her opening address to the first Canadian national conference on women and sport, Laura Sabia pointed to the example of Soviet women:

I don't know whether you are impressed, but I am, very much so, with the gymnastics that I have seen of the young Russian ladies. They were symphonies of the most beautiful music I have ever seen. Their bodies glowed with activity and serenity and with beauty untold. It was absolutely fantastic. These girls must have put untold hours and hours of frustration, too, in developing the skills that they have acquired. Now this is something else we have to instil in our young girls . . . this putting their all into it, the hours of frustration, the hours of practicing that are so important to achieve some of the beauty that we have seen. Now, how do we instil this in our young girls when we have told them that life is easy, you don't have to worry, you don't have to work, you don't have to do anything precise. We have to turn back the clock now, the discipline of the mind and the discipline of the body, it's extremely important.[53]

[52] J. Felshin, 'The Social View', in E. W. Gerber, J. Felshin, P. Berlin and W. Wyrick, *The American Woman in Sport* (Addison-Wesley, 1974), p. 219.
[53] *Report on the National Conference on Women and Sport*, 24–26 May 1974, Toronto, Canada, p. 12.

Women outside the USSR have also been able to quote the Soviet example when trying to gain admission to sports and sporting institutions that men had previously regarded as their 'preserve' and to play upon national pride in urging that their countries be given a chance to do just as well.

Significantly, the USSR has 'won' all but one summer and winter Olympics in which it has entered – and it is women who have given it the margin of victory (even though the summer Olympic Games normally have female competitions in only six sports as against 24 for men); it is Soviet women, too, that have given the USSR victory in virtually all the traditional USSR v USA athletics matches. Some Western writers see this as evidence of the extent of women's emancipation in the Soviet Union: 'There can be only one explanation for the pre-eminence of Soviet women among female athletes worldwide: it reflects a degree of equality for women that none of the non-communist countries has yet attained.'[54] It certainly is a remarkable achievement when one considers that competitive sports did not exist for women in Russia until the Revolution.

Any analysis of the part played in sport by Soviet women must take these advances into account. Yet the picture would not be complete without a closer examination of women in sport in the USSR.

Sports participation of men and women

A striking discrepancy in participation in sport – and in the use of free time generally – exists between men and women in all sections of the population. Women, while devoting almost as much time to work as men do,[55] continue to bear their tradition-ally unequal share of responsibility for the domestic work which has to be done in non-working time. Women everywhere in the Soviet Union seem to bear the large burden of household tasks in addition to full-time employment outside the home. Many time–budget studies note how little men actually help their wives in this

---

[54] W. M. Mandel, *Soviet Women* (New York, Anchor Books, 1975), p. 156.
[55] The 1959 Soviet census showed that only 18 per cent of Soviet women of working age were housewives, compared with 52 per cent of women in the USA. N. G. Yurkevich, *Sovetskaya sem'ye* (Minsk, 1970), p. 41.

respect and how attitudes of men towards domestic work have altered only slightly since the 1920s.

A random survey of 280 women workers in a Lithuanian radio components factory in 1966 showed that the women spent on average 4–5 hours on domestic work each working day, and 7–8 hours on their 'free' days. Further, 'as much as 65 per cent of the most arduous and exacting domestic work (shopping, cooking and cleaning) remains in the hands of women . . . They spend three times as much time on domestic work as men and have about half the free time that men have.'[56] More or less the same proportions of time distribution by sex were given in another time budget study whose results were published in 1972: women spent 18 hours per week on housework – three times more than men did (5–6 hours).[57] In another survey, published the same year, it was revealed that men had 1.5–2 times more free time and leisure than women (35 hours by comparison with 20 hours a week on average), although both men and women were employed for roughly the same number of weekly hours.[58] In both surveys, women were found to devote far less time to sport than men. In the first survey, weekly time spent on 'sport, physical culture and out-of-town recreation' averaged 30 minutes for unmarried girls, 5 minutes for newly married girls, 25 minutes for married women with a small family, 5 minutes for married women with more than two children, and 10 minutes for women over 40. The figures for men were 1 hour 55 minutes, 50 minutes, 1 hour 25 minutes, 1 hour 15 minutes respectively. Figures for men over 40 were not available.[59] On average, men spent five times more time on sport than women. In the second survey, women working a 5- or 6-day week spent 2 per cent of their total spare time on regular sporting activities and 9 per cent on casual sporting activities (now and again), whereas men on a 5-day week devoted 7 per cent of the total free time to regular sport, and 22 per cent to casual sport; men on a 6-day week spent 5 per cent and 21 per

[56] J. Andriuskeviciene, 'Zhensky trud i problema svobodnovo vremeni', in N. Solov'yov et al., *Problemy byta, braka i sem'i* (Vilnius, 1970), p. 79.

[57] L. A. Gordon and E. V. Klopov, *Chelovek posie raboty: sotsial'nye problemy byta i vnerabochevo vremeni* (Moscow, 1972), p. 97.

[58] L. A. Gordon and N. M. Rimashevskaya, *Pyatidnevnaya rabochaya nedelya i svobodnoye vremya trudyashchikhsya* (Moscow, 1972), p. 63.

[59] Gordon and Klopov, *Chelovek posle raboty*, pp. 34–35.

cent respectively.[60] On average, therefore, men spent at least three times more time on sport than women.

It would appear, therefore, that, after all their chores, Soviet women have little time left for sport and certainly have much less time than men have to spend on recreation. Yet it is a persistent theme in Soviet writing on women's emancipation that they should be drawn more into sporting activities. How successful the authorities have been in attracting women into sports participation in recent years may be judged from the figures below.

A comparison of women in sport in 1959 and 1969 reveals that whereas in 1969 women who regularly pursued an organised sport made up 14.1 per cent of the female population and 35.2 per cent of all sports participants in the case of men, this was 37.0 per cent of the male population and, overall, 21.8 per cent of the total population.[61] All the same, the women's participation was an appreciable improvement over that in 1959 (perhaps due to increases in labour-saving facilities and leisure time), when only 5.6 per cent of the female population went in for sport on any organised and regular basis (31.9 per cent of all sports participants). The improvement was most marked in areas of Muslim culture: Uzbekistan (from 3.6 per cent to 10.8 per cent), Kirgizia (from 4.1 per cent to 12.3 per cent), Tadzhikistan (from 1.7 per cent to 9.5 per cent), and in Azerbaidzhan (from 3.8 per cent to 11.4 per cent). Nonetheless, it is noticeable that the smallest percentages of women's participation in sport are still in these republics (plus Turkmenia and Armenia), while the best figures are for the most industrially and culturally advanced areas: in Belorussia sportswomen comprised 17.1 per cent of the female population and 4.1 per cent of all sports participants; in the Ukraine, the percentages in 1968 were 15.2 and 34.2 respectively; in Latvia 16.2 and 39.8, Lithuania 16.4 and 41.2 and in Estonia 17.7 and 40.9 respectively.

While sports participation figures do not show high levels of activity by women, women students make up a majority in

[60] Gordon and Rimashevskaya, *Pyatidnevnaya rabochaya nedelya*, p. 48.
[61] The percentage of women sports participants was calculated for the USSR as a whole and for each republic separately (both of the female population and of all sports participants). Statistics are taken from Makartsev, *Stranitsy istorii sovetskovo sporta*, p. 72; Makartsev and Sobolev, *Gavoryat tsifry i fakty*, p. 40.

physical education: in the 1971/1972 academic year, 56 per cent of the students of health, physical culture and sport in higher education, and 87 per cent in special secondary education, were women.[62]

Women's sport in former Muslim areas

That old customs die hard and prejudice against girls taking part at all in sport still exists is confirmed occasionally by Soviet writers. In a reference to Kazakhstan, a Kazakh writer mentions parents with outmoded views who keep their daughters from senior classes in school and higher education, from factories and construction sites, insisting on an early marriage; they 'forbid their daughters to dance or take part in sport; hence the problems the Republic has in training ballerinas, gymnasts and volleyball players'.[63] He refers to still-surviving instances of polygamy, the paying of a bride price and arranged marriages. Two Uzbek authors explain the low sports participation of Uzbek girls in part by the fact that 'some parents forbid their daughters to bare their arms and legs; schoolgirls are therefore unable to pursue their favourite sport. We need to propagandise the importance of sport among women and physical education establishments should train more specialists from among local girls who would themselves have a hand in training good sportswomen.'[64] In a third erstwhile Muslim area, Azerbaidzhan, research into the sporting interests of school-children revealed that 'vestiges of the past exist in the attitudes of many parents who disapprove of their children (especially girls) practising sport'.[65] This survey showed that Azerbaidzhanian sportswomen made up only 6 per cent of the Republican female population and 21 per cent of all sports participants in 1971. The share of sportswomen in Azerbaidzhanian teams competing in the national *spartakiads* has remained consistently low: 12.9 per cent

---

[62] *Narodnoye khozyaistvo SSSR, 1922–1972* (Moscow, 1972), p. 445.

[63] N. S. Sarsenbaev, *Obychai, traditsii i obshchestvennaya zhizn'* (Alma Ata, 1974), p. 157.

[64] Abdumalikov and Sholomitsky, *Nekotorye puti vnedreniya*, pp. 85–86.

[65] S. A. Alieva, 'Analiz uchastiya zhenskikh komand Azerbaidzhanskoi SSR v spartakiadakh narodov SSSR', *Teoriya i praktika fizicheskoi kul'tury*, 1973, No. 2, p. 49.

in 1956, 10.1 per cent in 1959, 10.1 per cent in 1963, 7.5 per cent in 1967 and 9.5 per cent in 1971.[66]

It may be hypothesised that women's participation in sport in a hitherto socially backward Muslim area under the strong influence of Islamic culture (where women were effectively excluded from all public life some fifty years ago) has assisted them in particular to gain some measure of emancipation. It is, after all, an enormous step forward for girls from Central Asia like Elvira Saadi and Nelli Kim to reach the top in a sport in which they wear nothing but a leotard. The Chairman of the Uzbek Supreme Soviet Commission on Youth Affairs has admitted that 'in Uzbekistan, as in other Central Asian republics, women's path to sport has been linked with a struggle against religious prejudices and for equal status in society'.[67] The bodily liberation and naked limbs (and faces), along with the self-acting, competing 'image' associated with sport, have not been accepted without a hard and bitter struggle, even bloodshed: 'I would call our first sportswomen real heroines. They accomplished real feats of valour in liberating women from the age-old yoke of religion and the feudal-bey order.'[68] Such events as the First *Spartakiad* for Rural Women of Uzbekistan in 1969 (with 300 finalists, three-quarters of whom were of Uzbek nationality) are conscious attempts to draw such women into sport as one means of furthering their social progress.

Officially approved and unapproved sports for women

The Soviet authorities take the view that biological sex differences affect women's rates of participation, levels of performance or predisposition for certain sports: thus, 'with training the functional potential of the female organism increases considerably and approximates in some indices to that of the male. Nonetheless, women's level of performance is often no more than 70–80 per cent that of men.'[69] In a recent study, it was found 'that stamina develops much more slowly in sports training among girls than

---

[66] Ibid., p. 49.
[67] *Fizkul'tura i sport*, 1970, No. 6, p. 5.
[68] Ibid., p. 5.
[69] *Teoriya i praktika fizicheskoi kul'tury*, 1973, No. 10, p. 62.

boys: girls only begin to show a marked improvement after the age of 15 and reach their peak at 18–22, whereas boys markedly improve after the age of 10 and level out after 18'.[70] The attitude would seem to be, therefore, that in sports the end in view is not success independent of physical equipment; it is rather the attainment of perfection within the limitations of each physical type.

We have mentioned above the campaign during 1973 to discourage women from engaging in sports that were alleged not only to be contraindicated and harmful to the female organism, but also to be morally degrading (in the light of the official view of femininity). Such discouraged activities included women's soccer and unarmed combat (wrestling) contests. In regard to women's soccer, it would appear that several teams had sprung up mainly in the Ukraine (in Kiev, Khar'kov, Dnepropetrovsk and the Transcarpathian *oblast'*) in the early 1970s and had played in and outside the republic. This activity was condemned for two reasons: (1) 'the main purpose was to obtain additional income from an unhealthy interest by some male spectators in women's soccer matches. Public organisations had connived at the setting up and commercial exploitation of such teams';[71] and (2) 'women's soccer is harmful to a woman's organism. . . Physical stress typical of soccer may cause harm to sexual functions, varicose veins, thrombo-phlebitis, etc.'[72] In some ways, this decision to discourage (not forbid) women's soccer seems to represent an abberation in the Soviet record and a remnant or resurgence of the 'it's unladylike' attitude among some leaders. The official condemnation of women's soccer had been preceded, interestingly enough, by some positive comment in the Soviet press on women's soccer abroad, including in Eastern Europe. It is likely that this decision will be rescinded in the future.

Like women's soccer, unarmed combat (*sambo*) was censured because it had been 'exploited by "sports-businessmen" and turned into "strength-and-beauty" contests that were degrading to Soviet womanhood'.[73] One can comprehend the official dis-

---

[70] V. G. Fedotova, 'Osobennosti vozrastnovo razvitiya vynoslivosti u zhenshchin', *Teoriya i praktika fizicheskoi kul'tury*, 1975, No. 8, p. 46.
[71] *Teoriya i praktika fizicheskoi kul'tury*, 1973, No. 10, p. 62.
[72] Ibid., p. 62.
[73] *Sovetsky sport*, 25 January 1973, p. 3.

quiet at such women's 'wrestling matches' being staged as public spectacles for male voyeuristic titilation given the ideological disapproval of hedonistic sex in general, of public sexuality, of 'kinky' deviations from straight marital intercourse and of commercial exploitation. Women's *sambo* was to be permitted henceforth only when confined to non-competitive military or semi-military clubs under the auspices of either *DOSAAF* or *Dinamo*.

Women, it was stated by the Soviet governing body for sport, are more suited to 'sports which develop speed, skill, plasticity, coordination and grace of movement – such as gymnastics, calisthenics, figure skating, swimming, athletics, fencing and certain team games. Women's health is also enhanced by such sports, included in the new *GTO* programme, as speed skating, skiing and shooting.'[74]

Some conclusions

Although Soviet women have less free time than men and show lower rates of participation and levels of performance when compared with men, they have certainly greatly improved their levels of participation and performance, particularly since the last war; they appear to be more 'sporting' than their Western counterparts and receive a great deal of official encouragement to be so. The sporting woman does seem to be a positive heroine of society – an image to whose features all women are urged to aspire.

It is interesting that the Soviet press, when reporting internal or international competitions, gives equal prominence to female and male events – a factor markedly at variance with the practice in the West. Furthermore, in a poll[75] conducted among sports writers (presumably all *men*) to select the sports personality of 1973, the top five places went to *women*, two of whom, significantly, represented 'muscular' field sports (shot putting and the discus):

1. Irina Rodnina – figure skating
2. Ludmilla Turishcheva – gymnastics

[74] Ibid., p. 3.
[75] See *Sovetsky sport*, 28 December 1973, p. 1.

3. Faina Mel'nik – shot-putting
4. Galina Shugurova – calisthenics
5. Nadezhda Chizhova – discus
6. Valery Kharlamov – ice hockey
7. Pavel Pervukhin – weightlifting
8. Levon Tediashvili – wrestling
9. Pavel Lednev – pentathlon
10. Anatoly Karpov – chess

A number of studies in the West in recent years have reported a traditional discouragement of women's engagement in more than a limited range of sporting activities. In cultural terms, sport has had an important function in the development of masculine gender identity and, hence, the socialisation of males in society. For males, to be tough, adventurous and daring, and to display general physical prowess in socially sanctioned play activities is important to the development of the male's self-esteem, social acceptability and dominance in peer groups.[76] The reverse tends to be true for females. From adolescence onwards, female involvement in sport, especially competitive sport, is treated in many ways as an aberration in terms of stereotyped notions of appropriate feminine behaviour: 'Women who meet the criteria (of the popular image in "femininity") are thought to be graceful, attractive, elegant, gentle and slim, and psychologically are seen to be emotional, dependent, uncompetitive, submissive, easily influenced and not too intelligent. Whereas athletic women are often pictured as muscular, strong, fit, agile, healthy, quick, energetic and somewhat masculine both in appearance and personality, which suggests that they are thought to possess the more "masculine" characteristics of aggressiveness, competitiveness and independence.'[77]

Such threats to femininity from sports do not seem to be so strong in the USSR (if not in Eastern Europe generally), where female athletic attainments have both reflected and reinforced processes of social change in the rôle and status of women. The reasons for official encouragement of women to engage in sport,

[76] See A. Hall and C. Jenkins, *A Paradigm for the Investigation of Female Athleticism* (Univ. of Birmingham, 1973), p. 5.
[77] A. Hall, 'A "Feminine Woman" and an "Athletic Woman" as Viewed by Female Participants and Non-Participants in Sport', *British Journal of Physical Education*, 1972, Vol. III, p. 43.

including physically exacting and 'muscular' activities, should be
sought in the state's economic needs *as well as its ideology*. First,
the work of women has been vital to economic advance – and
sport is thought to help make workers physically fit, mentally
alert and disciplined. The rôle of women in the Soviet economy
has been heightened by the shortfall of males in the population
after the human tragedy of the last war (the deaths of over 15
million Soviet men). Given the economic need for women to
engage in physically exhausting jobs (as, for example, road mend-
ing and house building), the physical and psychological characteristics required for or developed by successful participation in sport
are not incongruent with notions about the 'essential nature of
femininity' and desirable feminine demeanour as perceived in
Soviet conditions. The qualities of physical vigour and competitiveness (often referred to as 'masculinity' in the West) remain
compatible with the ways in which women are expected to present
themselves in everyday life and with the various occupational
rôles and identities which are available to them in society.
Second, women have been important to the country's defence
and military preparedness – and physical training through sport
(particularly as women are exempt from peacetime military service) is, again, thought to be the best way to prepare them for this.
Third, the authorities have used sport as a vehicle for that type
of women's emancipation officially desired in the USSR. The fact
of women displaying courage, grace, and skill in the sporting
arena, winning prestige for club, factory, farm, region, ethnic
group or republic and combining with men to compete at home
and abroad, has done much for the image of Soviet women,
particularly in the erstwhile Muslim-dominated areas where
women had been virtually excluded from public life prior to the
revolution.

Sport, schoolchildren and students

It is already clear that for sport and physical education there
exists a high degree of coordination between the education system,
local and national governments, trade unions and industry, health
and recreational institutions. Overall direction is provided by the
USSR Sports Committee whose job it is to see that the entire

system of physical education is based on the principle of uniformity and continuity of all links in the system. These links (or stages) consist in the following:

(1) the physical education of pre-school children in the home, nurseries and children's homes (from 1 to 7 years of age);
(2) the physical education of schoolchildren (7–17);
(3) the physical education of students;
(4) physical training in the armed forces;
(5) the physical education of working people in town and country carried out by voluntary sports societies at factories, offices and farms.[78]

Aims of physical education in school

The principal aims of physical education in school are said to be 'to strengthen health, temper the organism and raise the level of physical fitness and capacity for work; to acquire vitally necessary motor habits and skills, including those of an applied nature; to instil moral qualities and will power; to develop physical qualities (speed, strength, skill, stamina); and to master the technique for performing special sporting exercises (or sporting technique)'.[79]

Of course, none of these desired goals of physical education are the monopoly of Soviet schools; similar aims are propounded for Western schools. Where Soviet schools differ, however, is in the explicitness and directness of the application of their aims to practice, and in their standardisation of curricula and syllabuses. Thus, in relation to physical education, a detailed syllabus for every nursery, school and college in the country is laid down by the USSR Ministry of Education, although each Republican ministry has a certain degree of freedom in establishing the form, hours and marking of the subject: 'These syllabuses are mandatory state documents compiled for each age group; they are not open to arbitrary changes by teachers or school heads.'[80] In a highly centralised society like the Soviet Union's, it seems natural to all involved to have a single syllabus laid down from above. Each educational level is linked so that 'the syllabus for primary

[78] V. M. Kachashkin, *Metodika fizicheskovo vospitaniya* (Moscow, 1972), pp. 20–21.
[79] Ibid., p. 14.
[80] Ibid., p. 54.

classes is a continuation of that for children of pre-school age in nurseries or at home. At the same time, it is a necessary step in preparing children for physical education in the senior classes.'[81] All the same, as we shall see below, theory and practice do not always coincide.

The content of the physical education lesson

The 1960s and early 1970s saw much controversy over the place and content of physical education in the school curriculum and several modifications in the latter, as well as experiments and new government resolutions in the field.

Following the 1958 law 'On Strengthening the Connection of the School with Life and the Further Development of the Education System in the USSR', a new physical education syllabus was introduced in 1960 that differed radically from its predecessor. This (1954) syllabus had reflected the contemporary all-out campaign to shine internationally, and physical education had been geared to achieve this end: individual sports were practised intensively, potential stars were given special attention (often to the detriment of the mass of children), precise standards of achievement at each form level were established, and schools were obliged to participate in a large number of competitions (which further exacerbated the bias towards the best pupils). The 1960 syllabus (which lasted until 1967) did away with the compulsory standards for each form except for top classes, the number of intra-school contests was reduced, and the content of the syllabus was divided into two parts: Part 1 (classes 1–4, ages 7–11) was common for all schools and consisted of gymnastics, athletics, skiing and team games (72 hours a year); Part 2 (classes 5–8, ages 11–15) consisted of two sections, one which was common to all schools, the other offering an option: each school could select a sport in which it wanted to specialise (depending on climatic conditions and the teacher's inclinations). In addition, children were taken for a whole day once every two months to the local stadium for athletics contests and team games or were taken skating and skiing, according to season. These were officially known as 'Health Days' and they were supplemented by ten planned school tournaments

[81] Ibid., p. 54.

during the school year; in fact, five of the 'Health Days' coincided with tournament days, so children were to have approximately 11–12 complete sports days off from school each year.[82]

Standards of achievement in the 1960 syllabus were related to the *BGTO* norms. At the end of each school year, schoolchildren were awarded marks (out of five) for their P.E. and games performance and knowledge. In 1963, the Russian Education Ministry further enhanced the status of P.E. by including it in the school-leaving certificate. Subsequently, some other republics followed suit.

The Russian P.E. syllabus remained in this form until September 1967, when it was replaced. With the gradual transition from the 8-year school to the 10-year school (the school-leaving age was set for 17 by 1970) and the revision of the school curriculum, the attention devoted to academic subjects initially increased somewhat at the expense of P.E. and games. In many schools, the optional sports section was removed so that the new yearly P.E. calendar for schools in the Russian Republic was as follows.

TABLE 16 *Physical education and games lessons per school year: classes 1 – 10*[83]

Class	Age	Gymnastics	Athletics	Skiing	Team games[a]	Total
1	7+	28	–	12	30	70
2	8	30	–	12	28	70
3–4	9–10	36	–	12	22	70
5–6	11–12	19	19	14	18	70
7–8	13–14	20	20	14	16	70
9–10	15–17	19	19	14	18	70

[a] Mainly basketball, handball, volleyball, speed skating and swimming.

N.B.: Physical education lessons, 45-min periods, are normally held separately for boys and girls. Of the senior school curriculum of 36 hours per week, 2 periods are, on average, devoted to physical education – though this was increased to 3–4 periods in some republics from 1971.

An example of requirements prescribed by the USSR Education Ministry for all fifth formers (11 year olds) in the country is given below.

[82] T. N. Vasil'eva et al. (eds.), *Fizicheskaya kul'tura v V–VIII klassakh* (Moscow, 1967), p. 242.

[83] See *Fizicheskaya kul'tura v shkole*, 1967, No. 8, p. 22, and Z. I. Kuznetsova (ed.), *Fizicheskaya kul'tura v shkole* (Moscow, 1972).

1. To know and recount hygiene requirements at home and at school; to know the rules for avoiding injury at gymnastics, athletics, basketball and skiing;

2. To know the basic setting-up exercises and commands; to perform (in combination) the main arm, leg and trunk movements; the same with a gymnastics stick; to know exercises for developing the major muscle groups using a gymnastics bench; to know the folk dance 'School Polka'; to perform a long forward roll and short forward rolls from various starting positions, a side vault over 90–100 cm high obstacle; to climb a 3–4 m high rope three times; to perform group balancing exercises on the beam 100–105 cm high (crossing and passing in pairs and threes); to perform basic hangs and dismounts on gymnastics equipment;

3. To learn a short distance running technique; to high jump from an angled run-up and long jump from a shortened run; to clear a line of hurdles; to throw a small ball at target over one's shoulder from two paces;

4. To be able to ski competently and to brake on descents;

5. To learn the main basketball ploys (catching, passing, stopping, carrying, dodging);

6. To be able to use the already learned basic forms of movement in relays.[84]

Quite detailed instructions are given by the central ministry for the conducting of each physical education lesson with time structure broken down to: 5–10 minutes – Introduction, 25–30 minutes – Basic Part of the Lesson and 3–5 minutes – Conclusion.[85] In other words, the physical education teacher should be in no doubt about the tasks for a given lesson. Clearly, this makes for uniformity, but a certain degree of sterility of method; it is my impression that individual teachers use far more personal initiative than the manual appears to permit.

Although the subject lost status between 1967 and 1971 by being excluded from the school-leaving certificate, it subsequently regained its former position among school subjects and in the mid-1970s was marked out of five (as with all subjects) – a child might be kept down if he failed his end-of-year physical education examination – it again featured in the school-leaving certificate and had homework prescribed for it: twice a week, to last some

[84] Kuznetsova, *Fizicheskaya kul'tura y shkole*, pp. 7–8. A swimming requirement (25 m) exists for 10 year olds.

[85] Kachashkin, *Metodika fizicheskovo vospitaniya*, p. 184.

15 minutes on each occasion. Moreover, with the launching of a new *GTO* programme in 1972, the physical education syllabus in all Soviet schools was to be based upon it, so that 'all the principal exercises contained within the *GTO* qualifying norms are included in school physical education'.[86]

Other games and physical education activities

Besides the set physical education lesson, the school is responsible for a number of other sporting activities and performances of its charges. The education authorities urge that all children should engage in 15–20 minutes setting-up exercises every morning, either at home or in school. Since this is entirely at the discretion of parents and teachers, it is sometimes neglected. A survey in Siberia revealed that 39 per cent of the boys and 41 per cent of the girls in Khabarovsk, and 45 per cent of the boys and 43 per cent of the girls in Komsomol'sk-on-Amur did their morning exercises regularly.[87]

Teachers are also urged to conduct exercises throughout the school day, particularly in the breaks between lessons – whenever the opportunity arises, to insert a *fizkul'tminutka* ('physical culture minute').

In out-of-school time, many schoolchildren spend at least a fortnight of their summer holiday in a camp, often under canvas in a forest or by the sea or river. It was stated in 1971 that 'virtually one in three schoolchildren will be in a Pioneer, school, sport or tourist camp during the summer of 1971. . . They all have a single aim – to establish a sports and health regime.'[88] According to an official statistical handbook, however, about one in 4–5 children were served by Pioneer camps in 1970.[89]

[86] Ibid., p. 54.
[87] V. P. Kashirin, 'Razvitie fizicheskoi kul'tury i sporta v obshcheobrazovatel'nykh shkolakh', G. I. Kukushkin et al., *Planirovani razvitiya fizicheskoi kul'tury i sporta* (Moscow, 1974), p. 86.
[88] *Sovetsky sport*, 1 July 1971, p. 2.
[89] *Narodnoye khozyaistvo SSSR v 1970 g* (Moscow, 1971), pp. 633, 636.

Schoolchildren's interest in sport

Schools are given targets in respect to the sports standards to which it is hoped their children will aspire. Most schools have their own sports sections, and it is there that children who want to practice for their *GTO* badge may do so. The target in the mid-1970s was for no less than 65 per cent of a school's fifth to tenth formers to belong to a school sports section, for every fit 10–15 year old to gain a *GTO* badge and (for the 14–15 age group) to obtain the third junior ranking in a sport, for every fit 16–17 year old to gain the appropriate *GTO* badge and at least a second junior ranking in a sport, and for 17–20 per cent of 15–17 year olds to obtain the third adult ranking in a sport.[90]

Although official figures show that almost nine out of ten schoolchildren aged 12–17 pursue a sport regularly and that almost one in four become proficient enough to gain a sports ranking, they have to be treated with a certain amount of caution. Elsewhere, physical education teachers have written, for example, that, in 1967, only 15–20 per cent of schoolchildren between the ages of 12 and 17 pursued a sport regularly in a sports section in the country as a whole – though, in the capital, some 40 per cent did so.[91] The authority responsible for extra-mural children's sport became the *Yunost'* Voluntary Sports Society in 1968; in Moscow, however, only 20 per cent of schoolchildren were members.[92]

Children with a talent for or real interest in a sport must use their out-of-school time for practising it. They may join their local sports school. Facilities have, however, been at a premium. At the All-Union Conference on Physical Education, held in 1971, a speaker revealed that 'only 25 per cent of children pursued a sport regularly'. He blamed television, the lack of sports facilities and the refusal of sports societies to admit enough children.[93] Two years later, *Pravda* complained that only twenty per cent of schoolchildren regularly engaged in sport: 'in the localities, attention is centred on training representative teams; the mass involvement of children in sport is ignored'.[94]

[90] *Fizkul'tura i sport*, 1975, No. 9, p. 3.
[91] *Fizkul'tura i sport*, 1968, No. 8, p. 4.
[92] Ibid., p. 4.
[93] *Sovetsky sport*, 17 December 1971, p. 3.
[94] *Pravda*, 5 August 1973, p. 2.

In a Lithuanian study, it was discovered that as many as 70 per cent of senior form pupils and 60 per cent of junior form pupils did all their sport at school – largely because of the lack of opportunities and facilities outside school.[95]

It is clear, nevertheless, that schoolchildren make up a very substantial proportion of the country's sports participants. In 1974, school sports sections constituted nearly half the country's sports collectives and provided as many as 43 per cent of the sportsmen, over half the *GTO* badge holders and a sizeable proportion of the ranked athletes. That sport features prominently in many children's out-of-school activities is apparent from a survey in nine Russian cities in 1971: when asked how they spend their free time, the schoolchildren put sport in second place (in one town it took third place) after reading and in front of watching TV, listening to music, going to the pictures, the theatre and collecting. When asked what they valued most highly, the general consensus was health first, friends second.[96]

Not all physical education teachers are happy about official exhortations to higher sports proficiency. They argue that it militates in itself against developing the very principles of mass participation, collectivism and comradeship that physical education is supposed to nurture. One teacher writes that she tries to teach three principles to her physical education class of 23 girls: 'To develop an appreciation of beauty, to value friendship and to be fond of hard work. But what would the district inspector say? He would probably ask me how many girls gained a sports ranking at the end of the year. That's precisely the trouble: we gallop after rankings without stopping to think what we are doing. Scarcely is a child out of the cradle than we fix his fate as a Master of Sport. Yet how many children are thrown overboard in our race for results!'[97] This is a fairly common complaint among physical education teachers, who so often find themselves in the invidious position of striving to sustain the interest of their charges with few facilities and a hostile or indifferent headmaster,

---

[95] V. Stakioniene and S. Dulinskas, 'Nekotorye rezul'taty razvitiya fizicheskoi kul'tury v bytu shkol'nikov Litovskoi SSR', N. Solovyov et al., *Problemy byta, braka i sem'yi* (Vilnius, 1970), p. 217.

[96] *Teoriya i praktika fizicheskoi kul'tury*, 1972, No. 4, p. 35.

[97] *Fizicheskaya kul'tura v shkole*, 1967, No. 9, p. 26.

yet being judged by results measured in terms of the success of the few.

Student interest in sport

As with the schools, higher education institutes are first and fore-most academic institutions with little time and few facilities allotted to physical education and sport. If students wish to engage seriously in sport, they must do so outside of lecture hours if they have time left over from their exacting programme of studies. Unless the student is excused by doctor's certificate, he (or she) must, however, attend physical education classes for the first two years of the (normally) five-year course. If the student does not attend enough physical education classes and does not put up a satisfactory showing in the end-of-session test, he may be refused permission to continue his studies – irrespective of attendance and performance in academic subjects. Altogether, students must attend 140 hours of physical education during their first two years of study. After that, physical education and games are voluntary. The physical education department is responsible for conducting the statutory physical education lessons, but, since 1957, the sports society, *Burevestnik*, has been responsible for all sports activities in free time. It is *Burevestnik* that is responsible for seeing that the planned percentage of students engage in sport and that a certain number of ranked students is produced every year. Because the study load for students is usually very great, however, most students find little time for sport. A survey in Moscow in 1970 found that 'normally, once they have taken their physical educa-tion test, most students virtually stop all sports activities'.[98] *Burevestnik*, therefore, has found it hard to meet its target for Masters of Sport and Candidate Masters; in six republics, in fact, it was reported to be defunct in 1968.[99]

Physical education instructors also have quotas to fulfil, but they have the advantage of coercion during the undergraduate's first two years. This, however, can lead to abuses: 'In assisting students to choose a sport, teachers are in most cases guided not so much by a desire to eradicate deficiencies in their physical

[98] *Teoriya i praktika fizicheskoi kul'tury*, 1970, No. 10, p. 51.
[99] *Fizkul'tura i sport*, 1968, No. 8, p. 5.

training as by an urge to coach them as quickly as possible so that they can get a sports ranking.'[100]

One of the principal reasons for the lack of student participation in sport is simply lack of free time. In a 1967 survey of students at the Drogobych Institute of Education, it was found that 38 per cent of language students put lack of free time as their prime reason for not engaging in sport, as did 31 per cent of music students, and 54 per cent of physics and mathematics students.[101] Another major reason is the lack of adequate facilities and the small range of sports for which amenities exist. In the same survey, over half the students blamed lack of facilities for their neglect of exercise, and the overwhelming majority called for better facilities. Some indication of the academic study load (or of a distaste for physical education) is the firm rejection by 84 per cent of students in the survey of an extension of compulsory physical education and games to the third, fourth and fifth years.[102]

Certainly, the poverty of physical facilities and the shortage of qualified instructors inhibit both participation and high performance among students, but the principal factor in the low level of student participation in sport remains the big classroom study load that leaves little time or energy for active recreation. Despite official exhortations that the younger generation should be developed mentally and physically, there is evidence to suggest that many students do not accept physical fitness as a necessary part of their lives or a worthwhile competitor for the time they spend on intellectual and other pursuits.

Lack of facilities

The two deficiencies that have constantly hampered the development of sport and games among schoolchildren have been lack of physical facilities and lack of qualified instructors. The simple fact is that most schools built prior to 1960 do not have even the most rudimentary grounds suitable for games and athletics; by no means every school has proper accommodation even for indoor exercises. Although, in recent years, many schools have had

---

[100] *Teoriya i praktika fizicheskoi kul'tury*, 1970, No. 10, p. 50.
[101] *Teoriya i praktika fizicheskoi kul'tury*, 1967, No. 7, p. 60.
[102] Ibid., pp. 61–62.

special sports wings built onto the main building and there are projects for building area sports centres to be used jointly by several schools, schools are still, by English and American standards, grossly underequipped. The Soviet Deputy-Minister of Education, M. I. Kondakov, at an All-Union conference on questions of improving sport among schoolchildren held in March 1968, reported that approximately 80 per cent of all secondary schools had no sports grounds, 75 per cent had no gymnasiums, 50 per cent did not have even the sports equipment necessary for conducting compulsory physical education lessons according to the state programmes, and that some 40 per cent of physical education instructors were unqualified.[103] In primary schools, the situation was even worse: of the 85,000 primary schools, 80,000 were understaffed and underequipped for physical education and games.[104]

It was mainly this situation that gave rise to the measures proposed in the 1966 resolutions on improving sports facilities. Soon after the resolutions, the various Republican education ministries announced two-, three-, four- and five-year programmes of construction of sports facilities for schools. Nearly all the Republican ministries set up special sports departments under the ministries intended to work with the Republican councils of the Union of Sports Societies and Organisations (after 1968, of the Committee on Physical Culture and Sport). Among their jobs were supervising the carrying out of the new law that stadiums, sports grounds, gymnasiums, courts and skiing centres should be made available free of charge to schoolchildren. Clearly, not many sports organisations were enthusiastic about lending their facilities to children without remuneration, especially when they could earn money from hiring them to adult groups. They had to be given a reminder of their obligation in a resolution of 17 September 1968 – 'On the Implementation of the Resolution of the CPSU Central Committee and USSR Council of Ministers "On Measures for the Further Improvement of Physical Culture and Sport" in Relation to Children's Sport'.

In late 1967, the RSFSR Ministry of Education and the Board

---

[103] M. I. Kondakov, 'Osnova osnov', in V. A. Ivonin (ed.), *Velenie vremeni* (Moscow, 1969), p. 26.
[104] *Teoriya i praktika fizicheskoi kul'tury*, 1970, No. 8, p. 59.

of the Central Council of the Union of Sports Societies and Organisations had agreed on a set of minimum standards that all schools were to meet by 1970. The standards stipulated the minimum number and size of sports facilities that each school had to have according to the number of pupils enrolled. As an example, Table 17 shows the facilities which an 8-year school with between 320 and 960 pupils was to have by 1970.

All newly built schools were to be built to these standards and all other schools were to do their best, where space allowed, to bring facilities up to them. How well the schools responded is not yet clear, but a tremendous effort is obviously needed if all the demands are to be met in the near future. Judging by current figures, most rural schools have no chance at all of meeting the requirements, nor have many schools in metropolitan centres where space is at a premium. Some Republican ministries have, nevertheless, made considerable efforts to improve their school sports facilities, frequently with the assistance of local enterprises and even the schoolchildren themselves. The Armenian Deputy Education Minister, B. A. Bagdasaryan, gave the example of a swimming pool being built in Leninakan at a cost of only 3,000 rubles (instead of the estimated 8,500 rubles), thanks to the work done by children from local secondary school No. 18.[105]

In Moscow, as one would expect, the situation is not so bad as in the provinces. In 1970, only 70 secondary schools were without a gymnasium. Significantly, though, not one Moscow school had its own swimming bath in 1968. The first school in the capital to get a swimming pool was a new secondary school for 1,500 boys and girls on the Degunino housing estate on the outskirts of the city, which opened in 1970 with a 25 m swimming bath with ten lanes.[106] In 1968, however, the authorities had launched a campaign 'to teach all children to swim in the next 3–5 years'. The campaign was sparked by the lack of provision of swimming facilities and instruction and the number of children drowning. Since 1968, several small pools, called *lyagushatki* ('tadpole pools') have been built, some attached to kindergartens. The first prefabricated swimming pools (25 m long, 12.5 m wide and 1.2 m deep) went into production in 1973 for schools and Pioneer camps.

[105] *Fizkul'tura i sport*, 1968, No. 3, p. 2.
[106] *Fizkul'tura i sport*, 1970, No. 3, p. 7.

TABLE 17   *Standard sports provisions for an incomplete secondary school: 1970*

Facility	Number	Size
Athletics field:		
running track (circular)	I	200 × 5 m
running track (straight)	I	135 × 7.5 m
high jump pit	I	2.75 × 6 m
long jump pit	I	2.75 × 6 m
multi-purpose jumping pit	I	32 × 5 m
shot putt sector	I	16 m radius
Total area		4,900 m²
Games and athletics ground:		
discus throwing area	I	
javelin, hand grenade or ball throwing area	I	
small soccer/handball pitch	I	40 × 60 m
Total area		2,950 m²
Gymnastics area:		
combined installation of suspended equipment (rings, ropes, poles, trapezes), wall bars and long horses	I	15 × 40 m
wall bars, 12 sections	I	
boom	I	
beam	I	
parallel bars (sets)	I	
combined court for basketball and volleyball	I	18 × 30 m
combined court for volleyball, basketball, 'pioneerball'	I	20 × 24 m
table tennis area	I	162 m²
Total area		27,864 m
Sports training area		7,450–9,632 m²
of which:		
lawned area (*ploshchad' ozeleneniya*)		520–670 m²
Total area of sports zone		7,900–10,300 m²

Source: Fizicheskaya kul'tura v shkole (1967), No. 12, pp. 21–22.

Special sports courses and schools

Young people who wish to pursue a sport seriously after school hours may do so in one of several specialised sports establishments. At the base of this sports preparation pyramid is a variety of extra-curricular courses in children's and young people's sports schools (*detsko-yunosheskie sportivnye shkoly*); for example, all 16 First Division and 20 Second Division soccer clubs run their own junior schools (after normal school hours) with a full course of training for boys from the age of ten. It is also possible to attend a full-time 'sports' school from the age of seven which combines a normal school curriculum with sports training (like the 'foreign language' oriented schools). Above these schools come sports proficiency schools (*sportivnye shkoly masterstva*) and, then, higher sports proficiency schools (*shkoly vysshevo sportivnovo masterstva*); these are normally for students rather than schoolchildren. At the apex of this pyramid is the sports boarding school (*sportivnaya shkola-internat*).

During the 1960s, a number of changes were introduced into this system of sports schools and the number of schools grew considerably. By 1975, there were 4,938 children's and young people's sports schools with a total membership of 1,633,132 children (from some 1,500 schools with half a million children in 1960).[107] The range of sports each school cultivated was cut from about ten to three or four and, then, after 1966, to just one or two. At the same time, the age limits were extended either way, so that children were admitted from 7 to 18 (previously 10–16): hence the change of name in 1966 from 'children's sports schools' to 'children's and young people's sports schools'.

The aim of the schools is to use the best of the limited facilities available to give special and intensive coaching to children and young people in a particular sport so that they may become proficient, gain a ranking and graduate to an All-Union or Republican team. As the 1966 government resolution on the schools stressed, these are 'special sports institutions and are intended to train highly qualified athletes'.[108] The specialised gymnastics schools, for example, admit girls and boys from seven onwards; they are expected 'to pass from novice to master in six to seven years'.[109]

An examination of the sports pursued in the schools leaves no doubt that the chief targets for the schools' members are the

---

[107] *Zhenshchiny i deti v SSSR, 1961* (Moscow, 1962), pp. 174, 210; *Sport v SSSR*, 1976, No. 6, p. 9.
[108] Makartsev, *Stranitsky istorii*, p. 87.
[109] *Teoriya i praktika fizicheskoi kul'tury*, 1968, No. 12, p. 35.

Olympic sports. They are, in the opinion of some, 'forges preparing Olympic reserves'.[110] The head of the department for Forecasting and Planning Physical Culture Development at the All-Union Research Institute of Physical Culture has written that 'to ensure the success of Soviet sportsmen in important international competitions, especially the Olympic Games, we must consciously and purposely train athletes; this requires early specialisation, a large time expenditure, highly qualified coaches working in this sphere, better technical equipment and, correspondingly, more financial expenditure on each athlete being trained. . . In future, sport will develop principally through special sports institutions like the children's and young people's schools, the sports proficiency schools, the sports boarding schools, etc.'[111] The trend towards Olympic sports in these schools was accentuated by the move towards single sport specialisation. Of the 33 sports pursued in the schools in 1966, only six were outside the Olympic programme (acrobatics, calisthenics, chess, handball, table tennis and tennis). The most practised were athletics (155,000 members), basketball (117,000), gymnastics (106,000), volleyball (89,000), swimming (62,000) and skiing (58,000).

One advantage of these schools is that they have access to facilities, especially for technical sports, that may generally be in short supply in the country. In 1967, for example, over 80 per cent of the country's figure skaters and high divers, many of the swimmers and a third of all young gymnasts pursued their sport by grace of the sports schools. They were also well served by qualified coaches. Of the 25,000 coaches working in them in 1967, some 80 per cent were qualified, compared with just over 55 per cent of physical education instructors in secondary schools and 58 per cent of all full-time physical education instructors and coaches in the country as a whole. Of the country's 42,310 full-time instructors and coaches in 1967, therefore, over half were working in the sports schools.

It is certainly the case that the best coaches are drafted into the schools, and it is prescribed as the duty of many of the country's best athletes to do some coaching and demonstrating in a school

110 *Teoriya i praktika fizicheskoi kul'tury*, 1970, No. 8, p. 5.
111 Pereverzin, *Prognozirovanie i planirovanie fizicheskoi kul'tury* (Moscow, 1972), p. 26.

regularly. How much the coaches are paid depends on the school. Some schools pay according to the number of hours the coach puts in, others according to the number of children registered for each section – and yet others according to results, so that a coach in the Leningrad District of Moscow, say, can earn 150 rubles a month, while one in the *Pervomaisky* District can get only 100 rubles a month.[112] Sometimes abuses occur in payment to coaches: an acrobatics coach at a *CYPSS* in Chirchik, Uzbekistan, obtained an extra 2,536 rubles in one year for claiming for more hours than he had actually worked; when his time schedule was checked, it was discovered he was claiming to have put in over 24 hours of training each day. Another coach at the same school had claimed for 'dead souls' – children who had not registered for his group.[113]

The sports schools, like all school sports institutions, are not greatly endowed with their own sports amenities. The vast majority (95 per cent, in fact, in 1967) did not have their own sports centre but had to make do with facilities belonging to other organisations.[114]

In Moscow, only six of the 25 sports schools had their own sports amenities in 1968. The remainder had to hire gymnasiums, indoor running tracks, swimming pools, stadiums, and so on. In Armenia, apparently, conditions are somewhat better. The Armenian Deputy Education Minister stated in 1968 that fifteen of the republic's 44 sports schools had their own sports grounds. 'But, in the coming two or three years, all the others will also have their own sports amenities.'[115] That may be characteristic Armenian optimism. Certainly, some Armenian sports schools are not badly off: the Igor Novikov Pentathlon School has a fencing hall, indoor and outdoor shooting ranges, an outdoor 50 m heated swimming pool, a horse riding academy and a hotel with accommodation for 300 visiting athletes – no wonder the junior world pentathlon championships were held there in 1970. Also in the republic is the Grant Shaginyan Gymnastics School with two gymnasiums (one each for girls and boys), a cinema and various

---

[112] *Fizkul'tura i sport*, 1968, No. 4, p. 29.
[113] *Sovetsky sport*, 15 January 1972, p. 2.
[114] V. Mikhailov, *Sovetskaya fizicheskaya kul'tura i sport na novom etape* (Moscow, 1967), p. 15.
[115] *Fizkul'tura i sport*, 1968, No. 3, p. 2.

other special sports halls. The Yerevan Soccer School has its own stadium with accommodation for 5,000 spectators, three additional training pitches, a 26 × 18 m gymnasium and a swimming pool.

Children are considered for a sports school on the recommendation of their school physical education instructor or at the request of their parents. Attendance and coaching are free. Although most of the schools take children at 11 years of age, for some sports they may accept them earlier or later. For example, entrants to swimming sections may be accepted at 7–8, although cyclists and speed skaters can only be taken at 13–14. How often they train depends on the sport and the school, but coaching is intensive and classes are often long and frequent. In the Pervomaisky District of Moscow, for instance, the sports school had, in 1975, preparatory groups of 11–13 year olds who had to attend three times a week for two-hour sessions out of normal school hours; each group had fifteen members. Some of the top groups did even more training: the youngsters working for their Master of Sport ranking had to attend four or five times a week for two-hour sessions.

The Committee on Physical Culture and Sport laid down the conditions of work for all sports schools in a statute on the schools published in February 1970. The programme for special gymnastics schools gives some idea of how serious training is taken.

TABLE 18   *Training conditions for a gymnastics school: 1970*

Name of group	No. of groups	Age boys	Age girls	No. of pupils in the group	No. of sessions per week boys	No. of sessions per week girls	Length of each session (hours) boys	Length of each session (hours) girls
Preparatory	3	9	8	15	2	2	2	2
'Young Gymnast'	3	10	8–9	15	3	3	2	2
3rd Ranking	3	12	11	12	3	4	3	2
2nd Ranking	2	13	12	8	4	3	3	3
1st Ranking	2	15	13	6	4	4	4	3.5
Candidate Master of Sport	1	17	14	4	5	5	4	3.5
Master of Sport	1	18	15	3–4	5	5	4	3.5

Source: *Tipovoye Polozhenie o detsko-yunosheskoi sportivnoi shkole* (*DYUSSH*) (Moscow, 1970), p. 25.

Thus, a 15 year old boy or 13 year old girl attending a gymnastics school and working towards a First Ranking will be in a group of some six gymnasts, attending training sessions four times a week for 3.5–4 hours each session. That is, by any standards, a considerable load in addition to school work. On a visit to the *Spartak* gymnastics school in Leningrad in the autumn of 1975, it was instructive to watch three young girl gymnasts in training (one was the then 14 year old Olga Koval, a new member of the Soviet national squad) with as many as four specialists in attendance: coaches in gymnastics and acrobatics, a choreographer and a conservatoire-trained pianist. They trained from 10 to 2 each day ('because that is the optimum period for gymnastics training'), six days a week, and attended normal school in the afternoon – in the case of Olga Koval, this was the Leningrad Sports Boarding School. All instruction, facilities and equipment were, of course, free of charge.

The organisations responsible for financing and running these schools are mainly the Republican education ministries (via the city and district education departments in the localities), the trade union sports societies and the big sports clubs run by *Dinamo* and the armed forces. Of the 2,772 sports schools that existed in 1967, the education ministries were responsible for 1,605 with an enrolment of 567,400 members, the trade union societies for 1,044 with an enrolment of 296,600, and *Dinamo* and the armed forces for 123 with an enrolment of 74,700.[116]

A new sports society for young people, *Yunost'*, was set up in 1967 to coordinate the activities of all children's and young people's sports schools and to ensure that minimum standards were established in regard to facilities, coaches, age and other qualifications for entrance.

Sports boarding schools

The USSR opened its first sports boarding school in Tashkent in 1962 on the model of similar schools established several years earlier in East Germany. Soon afterwards, other such schools were founded – at first, one in each of the fifteen Republics, then in some provincial centres. It was not until 1970, however, that a

[116] Makartsev and Sobolev, *Govoryat tsifry i fakty*, p. 40.

special government resolution set an official seal on their creation. By that time, about 20 already existed and another 24 were planned for the immediate future.[117] The first one in Moscow was opened in 1971, followed by a second, the Znamensky school, in 1973. While some concentrate on a single sport (gymnastics, volleyball, soccer, etc.), others cultivate a whole range. (The Leningrad sports boarding school, founded in 1972, takes children in ten sports.) Significantly, only sports in the Olympic programme are taken up by the schools.

They follow other special boarding schools (e.g. for cultivating mathematical, musical and other artistic talents) in adhering to the standard Soviet curriculum for ordinary schools, but having an additional study load in sports theory and practice. Their aim is for pupils to obtain the school-leaving certificate in addition to proficiency in a particular sport. Boarders are accepted from between 7 and 12, depending on the sport, and stay on until 18 – a year longer than at normal schools.

It would seem axiomatic that such schools should possess first-class amenities. The one I visited in 1970 in Tallinn, capital of Estonia, had four sections: gymnastics, basketball, volleyball and athletics. It commanded three gyms, a 25 m indoor swimming pool, a ski centre, an athletics stadium, and courts and fields for a variety of games. In Uzbekistan, the Tashkent school takes pupils in soccer, swimming, athletics and gymnastics; the school grounds cover an area of 20 hectares, and included a 3-hall wing for gymnastics, indoor and outdoor swimming pools, and an indoor running track.[118]

Not all such schools are well-equipped. Children at the Pervomaisky school in Moscow have to travel to other parts of the city in order to use a swimming pool and indoor athletics stadium. The Leningrad sports boarding school had no facilities at all to speak of in 1975 (except a small swimming pool and residential accommodation for 270 boarders) – although plans had been approved for an indoor stadium, swimming pool, medical 'research' centre and new residential wings (at a cost of 6.5 million rubles). Down in Central Asia, in Frunze, the sports boarding school there, opened in 1968, had no sports amenities at all in

---

[117] *Moskovskaya pravda*, 26 February 1971, p. 4.
[118] *Fizkul'tura i sport*, 1968, No. 7, p. 5.

1974 and its pupils had to train on even days in a local sports club and on odd days in a physical culture institute – both at the other end of the city. This lamentable state of affairs was blamed on higher authorities: 'The school would have long had everything necessary if persons in high places, from the Ministry of Education to the Kirgiz Sports Committee, had displayed any real concern for their offspring.'[119] Similar poor conditions existed in 1973 in Rostov-on-Don, where the sports boarding school had no indoor stadium, inferior equipment, only one shot per ten shot putters and no stop watch.[120]

Boys and girls are normally invited to the schools on the basis of their performance in Republican school games. With the consent of their parents, they can enter the school if they pass a 10-day entrance examination. Allocation of periods to sport in the timetable rises with each successive year of the course. For example, 12 year olds in the gymnastic section of the Tallinn school spent 25 hours per (six-day) week[121] on standard subjects, plus eight hours on gymnastics, two on swimming and two on physical education. In the top form, at 18, they devoted 23 hours a week to sport, including 19 hours of gymnastics. Roughly the same number of hours had to be spent on academic work. At the Tashkent school, 11 year olds studied their chosen sport for 6 hours a week, 12–13 year olds for 8 hours, 14–15 year olds for 10 hours, 16–17 year olds for 12 hours, and 18 year olds for 14 hours a week. Despite these rigorous schedules, it is asserted that the pupils have a better-than-average health and academic record: the physical and mental aspects apparently supplement and reinforce one another. A gymnastics school in Dnepropetrovsk claims to attain better academic results (as well as better discipline and health) than ordinary local schools; and the head of the Leningrad school, Leonid Shapiro, insisted that his principal concern was academic work: 'general knowledge first, sport second'.

The Tallinn Sports Boarding School had a teaching staff of 50

[119] *Sovetsky sport*, 29 June 1974, p. 2.
[120] *Sovetsky sport*, 25 September 1973, p. 2.
[121] This is three hours less than in ordinary schools. See M. A. Prokof'ev et al. (eds.), *Narodnoye obrazovanie v SSSR, 1917–1967* (Moscow, 1967), p. 91.

in addition to 17 qualified coaches to instruct its 750 pupils in 1970. The syllabus included such specialist subjects as the psychology of sport, physiology, history of physical education and educational philosophy. Virtually all pupils were boarders, though some returned home at weekends; fares home for holidays and weekends were paid by the school. Annual expenditure amounted in 1970 to 650,000 rubles (i.e. 850 rubles per pupil), the bulk of which came from the Estonian Ministry of Education – the remainder from the USSR Ministry of Education. Of this sum, chief expenses comprised the provision of hostel accommodation, instruction, sports equipment and clothing (all supplied gratis to boarders) and a specially nutritious diet; at the Tashkent school, the daily food expenditure per pupil amounted to 1 ruble, 64 kopecks, virtually double that (84 kopecks) at ordinary boarding schools.[122] Most of the boarders in the Tallinn school spent at least a fortnight of their summer holidays at the school's summer camp on the sandy shore of the Gulf of Finland. The Leningrad Sports Boarding School had 570 pupils (65 per cent boys, 35 per cent girls), 27 academic staff and 63 part-time coaches in 1975. In addition to the finance it received from the Ministry of Education and the Leningrad education authority, it obtained some assistance from twenty Leningrad factories, which acted as 'patrons' of the school.

The headmaster explained during my visit in 1975 that the school was very popular: some 300 children were selected for each of the ten sports in the school out of 1,000 applicants for each sport; 150 were taken to special summer camps of which, after a further special test, 30 were accepted as pupils. There had been an inevitable rejection of children during the first four years of the school's existence, but this was now declining: from 120 out of 480 pupils leaving in the first year, 80 in the second to 40 in the third. An advertisement in *Sovetsky sport* for the new Znamensky Brothers Sports Boarding School in Moscow attracted 900 letters from 823 towns and villages all over the country during six weeks in 1973.[123] The school had winter and summer stadiums, seven Merited Coaches of the USSR and the Russian

---

122 *Fizkul'tura i sport*, 1968, No. 7, p. 6.
123 *Sovetsky sport*, 5 May 1973, p. 4 (for advertisement); *Sovetsky sport*, 2 August 1973, p. 2 (for response).

Federation and twelve Masters of Sport on its staff. Some 150 children were selected for tests, fourteen days of which were taken up with medical examinations. Several candidates were rejected on academic grounds (too many low marks), others were given acceptance conditional on improved school marks. As with other schools, a minimum sports requirement for entry to forms 6–10 was a Third Adult Ranking in a sport – a high achievement for 13–17 year olds. In the case of the Znamensky school, an exception was made for children with exceptional physical attributes: over 170 cm in height for 13 year old girls and 180 cm for 13 year old boys.

The rationale behind such schools is the conviction that precocious talent in sport, as in art, music and mathematics, has to be nurtured. It is regarded as natural and advantageous to bring together children of natural and instinctive aptitudes for sport in a 'controlled' environment of a residential school, served by the best coaches and amenities, nurtured on a special diet, constantly under the supervision of doctors and sports instructors, and stimulated by mutual interest and enthusiasm. Moreover, early specialisation, especially in such sports as athletics, swimming and gymnastics, is regarded as essential to the attainment of high standards and success in present day international competition. In the opinion of the above mentioned Leningrad headmaster, 'sports boarding schools are the only way to win world championships these days'. It is no secret that their ultimate aim is to produce Olympic winners: 'The sporting vocation has a particular significance not for mass sport, but for specialised sports schools in such sports as athletics, swimming, gymnastics, team games, figure skating, skiing and speed skating – i.e. in sports that constitute the basis of the Olympic programme. In evaluating the meaningfulness of sport in international tournaments, one must not forget that, while world and European championships have great importance, victory at the Olympic Games acquires a political resonance.'[124] The point made is that the Olympic Games bring more publicity and more national prestige. They are regarded as *the* measure of a nation's health and power. And as many as 70 per cent of the Olympic medals are concentrated in

[124] *Teoriya i praktika fizicheskoi kul'tury*, 1968, No. 5, p. 42.

only three sports: athletics, swimming and gymnastics. In the first two of these, countries like the United States, East Germany and Australia have had overall superiority. It is felt in the USSR that they attained this superiority not only by the provision of excellent facilities for young athletes and swimmers, but by careful selection and intensive coaching of these youngsters at schools and colleges.

The sports boarding schools are not without their critics. Some object that they lack depth and cannot produce a sustained flow of world-class athletes: they compare sporting prodigies to early flowering plants which make a colourful showing, as it were, in early season only to fade when 'normal' flowers are blooming. An article in *Fizkul'tura i sport* claims that no more than five soccer players made the grade from an original group of 1,500 in specialist sports schools and that the normal 'drop-out' from swimming schools was between 50 and 60 per cent. Other detractors decry the privilege implicit in the existence of the schools and the possible encouragement of an asocial life style conducive to 'starsickness'. The well-known economic 'reformer' Professor Birman, in a letter to *Sovetsky sport*, recalls Lenin's words that 'libraries should take pride in the number of readers they attract, not in the rare books they keep in their repositories'; surely, he writes, 'Lenin's words apply equally to sport?'[125] Some educationalists fear the narrowness of experience owing to the amount of time and energy needed for sport, and the possibility of academic work being overshadowed. There is also the geographical and time problem of getting from classroom to running track. The biggest stumbling block so far, however, seems to have been the opposition by some parents who are anxious about the slackening of family bonds or, eager for young Ivan or Olga to 'get on', are uncertain about the status of sport as a career. One source has admitted that 'the sports boarding schools so far do not show the slightest popularity among parents – for various reasons. First, parents do not like the word *internat* [boarding school – perhaps because of its association with institutionalised care of the deprived]. Their logic is simple: "Can't I feed my child myself?" Then the word "*sport*" puts them off; they find it embarrassing to tell their neighbours that "my Sasha is in a

125 *Sovetsky sport*, 18 October 1974, p. 1.

sports school".'[126] A similar complaint about parental opposition
has come from a volleyball coach who describes the difficulties in
recruiting for volleyball at six boarding schools: 'The word
internat frightens parents; they fear their children will be torn
from their sight and love. . . The mass media ought to explain to
parents how immensely valuable the schools are for health and
general education.'[127]

Largely because of such parental opposition, the Minsk Sports
Boarding School was on the verge of closing down in 1971, and
the situation was just as precarious in several others. The soccer
boarding school (with 100 boarders) in Voroshilovgrad, attached
to the 1972 Soviet champions *Zarya*, had trouble getting started –
but not because of parents. It met opposition from trainers of
children's and young people's sports schools who were afraid of
losing some of their charges.[128] The nature of such comments and
the apparent effectiveness of parental opposition suggest a low
status for sport as a vocation, at least in the opinions of a fairly
important section of the public.

Perhaps such teething troubles are inevitable. Despite the quite
frank criticisms voiced in the Soviet press, the schools seem to
have passed the test and the future of serious Soviet sport would
appear to lie with them. Whatever the prospects, the concept of
the sports boarding school has far-reaching implications for theory
and practice: the purists may well argue, with some justification,
that this is yet another step in the race for medals and irrational
glories that should find no place in a workers' state. The practitioners, on the other hand, may consider it to be a natural and
sensible development in a centrally planned state to concentrate
resources to maximum effect in order to win victories in today's
highly competitive and specialised world of sport.

[126] *Moskovskaya pravda*, 26 February 1971, p. 4
[127] *Sovetsky sport*, 26 October 1972, p. 2.
[128] *Sovetsky sport*, 21 October 1972, p. 3.

II

Soviet sport and Soviet foreign policy

Sport everywhere, being bound up with the values of communities, has a political aspect and is seldom (if ever) free of politics. The influence of politics on sport is particularly evident in relation to foreign policy, where sporting success is seen by many as a measure of national vitality and prestige; it can therefore serve as an unobtrusive form of propaganda. As a consequence, 'international competitive sport has become an arena for ideologies, mirroring the same tensions as are seen throughout the world on the purely political plane'.[1] UNESCO drew attention in the mid-1950s to the increasing 'politicisation' of international sport, to the extent that 'the Olympic Games are now regarded by many as merely a testing ground for two great political units'.[2]

With the division of much of the world into two camps in the 1950s with the nuclear stalemate and the intensifying 'battle for men's minds', sport became an area of great social significance. It is today employed by statesmen in East and West as a propaganda weapon in world affairs, a relatively modern method of psychological warfare. By its nature, sport is suited to the task: it excites nationalist instincts and encourages group identification; it is superficially apolitical and readily understandable; sporting activity can take place across barriers of race, class, religion and nationality; and, through modern means of communication, sporting spectacles can be transmitted throughout the world.[3]

[1] A. Nathan, 'Sport and Politics', in J. W. Loy and G. S. Kenyon (eds.), *Sport, Culture and Society* (Macmillan, 1969), p. 206.

[2] *The Place of Sport in Education*, UNESCO, Paris, 1956, p. 57.

[3] The 1973 USSR v USA athletics match in Minsk, for example, was attended by over 200 journalists, half of whom were from the West; BBC TV transmitted two half-hour programmes on the two days of the

A Soviet writer has noted that 'the deepening and widening influence of socialist sport on the condition of and trends in the world sports movement is one of the best and most comprehensible means of explaining to the masses the advantages which the socialist system has over capitalism'.[4]

It is apparent that, today, the nations of the world rank differently according to the amount of interest their governments take in the organisation and conduct of sport. On the one side are those states whose sports movement is fully integrated into the social and political system and thus becomes an important instrument of government policies. On the other are countries in which sport is largely organised by non-government bodies and tends to be free of state control – except, possibly, when it involves international competition. It is efficiency and command over resources that today count most towards success in international sport – and this is a factor that favours state-socialist systems, the Soviet Union's above all.

While sport in the West is by no means free of politics or foreign policy aims, in centrally planned, Soviet-type societies, it occupies a more central position and its functions and interrelationship with the polity (especially the military), the economy and the culture are more manifest than in Western societies. In the USSR, the dependence of sport on politics has always been explicit – and that includes the area of foreign policy. The following three points from a Soviet sports book make explicit some of the political tasks which Soviet sports organisations are today expected to discharge:

(1) to ensure top performance by Soviet athletes abroad as a means of widely publicising our attainments in building communism and in promoting physical culture and sport and to gain a prominent position internationally in the major sports;

(2) systematically to propagate the aims and tasks of the Soviet sports movement, to explain the attitudes of Soviet sports organisations to the principal problems confronting the international sports movement, vigorously to combat slander and misinformation in regard to Soviet sport, anti-communism and

tournament at peak viewing times (6.45 p.m. and 7.30 p.m.) – even though no British athletes were involved.

[4] Y. A. Talayev, 'Sport – oblast' mirnovo sorevnovaniya', *Teoriya i praktika fizicheskoi kul'tury*, 1973, No. 1, p. 8.

ideological diversions made by imperialist circles in world sport, to expose the real nature of bourgeois sport and the strategy and tactics of bourgeois sports organisations, to thwart actions directed against the sports organisations of the Soviet Union and of other socialist and young independent states;

(3) to unite progressive forces in the international sports movement, to consolidate the united front of sports organisations of the socialist states, of the young independent states and the workers' sports organisations in capitalist states for the purpose of reaching progressive decisions on issues facing the international sports movement and of using sport as a weapon in the campaign for peace and mutual understanding.[5]

These do not, in fact, exhaust the overtly stated aims assigned to Soviet sport as an instrument of Soviet foreign policy. This chapter attempts to examine these and other aspects of Soviet sport in relation specifically to Soviet foreign policy since 1917. During this period, six aims seem to have been pursued in Soviet sporting relations with the rest of the world – some more or less consistently throughout the whole period and others only in one or other phase of foreign policy. We can consider the pursuit of these state goals as functions assigned to the sports movement and attempt to assess how successfully it has coped with fulfilling them:

Continuously: (1) *promoting good-neighbourly relations both with states bordering on the USSR and with those in strategically important areas close to the USSR* (such as the Baltic, Balkans and Middle East) – a policy promoted both for reasons of strategy and, where regional contacts were encouraged with bordering states, for demonstrating the progress made by kindred peoples under socialism;

Pre-war – 1917–1928: (2) *promoting 'proletarian internationalism' and undermining 'bourgeois' and social democratic authority in order to advance world revolution*;

1929–1945: (3) *strengthening the Soviet Union as a nation-state*;

Post-war: (4) *attaining superiority as a nation-state* – a policy aimed at enhancing the status of the USSR and Soviet communism abroad;

(5) *maintaining and reinforcing the unity of the socialist bloc and the Soviet 'vanguard' position within it*;

(6) *winning support for the USSR and its policies among developing states of Africa, Asia and Latin America*.

[5] A. O. Romanov, *Mezhdunarodnoye sportivnoye dvizhenie* (Moscow, 1973), p. 185.

The history of Soviet participation in international sport, therefore, falls roughly into four periods:

A. 1917–1928;
B. 1929–1939;
C. 1939–1941;
D. 1945 onwards.

Promoting proletarian internationalism: 1917–1928

On the assumption that world revolution was not far distant and
that, until then, the world would be split irreconcilably into two
hostile camps,[6] the Soviet authorities at first ignored 'bourgeois'
sports organisations, refused to affiliate to their international
federations and boycotted their competitions, especially the
Olympic Games (of whose committee Russia had been a founder
member) which were characterised as designed 'to deflect the
workers from the class struggle while training them for new
imperialist wars'.[7] In any case, as the writer Maxim Gorky put it:
'Bourgeois sport has a single clear-cut purpose: to make men even
more stupid than they are... In bourgeois states, sport is employed
to produce cannon fodder for imperialist wars.'[8]

[6] The Declaration on the Formation of the USSR, adopted on 30 December
1922, stated clearly the fundamental preconceptions of the Soviet leaders
in international affairs: 'Since the formation of the Soviet republics, the
states of the world have been split into two camps: the camp of capitalism
and the camp of socialism. . . The USSR is to serve as a decisive new
step on the way to uniting the workers of the world into a World Socialist
Republic'. See *S"yezdy Sovyetov. Sbornik dokumentov*, Vol. III (Moscow,
1960), p. 16. The spreading of communism throughout the world was
regarded not simply as an ideological precept, but as a practical necessity
on which depended the very existence of the Soviet state. As Trotsky
explained in 1919: 'The dictatorship of the Russian working class will be
able to consolidate itself finally and to develop a genuine, all-sided
Socialist construction only from the hour when the European working
class frees us from the economic yoke and especially the military yoke of
the European bourgeoisie, and having overthrown the latter, comes to our
assistance with its organisation and its technology.' See L. Trotsky, *The
Age of Permanent Revolution* (Dell, New York, 1964), p. 130.
[7] V. P. Koz'mina, 'Mezhdunarodnoye rabocheye sportivnoye dvizhenie
posle Velikoi Okt'yabrskoi sotsialisticheskoi revolyutsii', in F. I. Samoukov
and V. V. Stolbov (eds.), *Ocherki po istorii fizicheskoi kul'tury* (Moscow,
1967), p. 165.
[8] *Pravda*, 14 August 1928, p. 3.

Initially then, excursions beyond Soviet borders were largely confined to the sport the USSR was best at (soccer – having inherited well-equipped clubs from many of the foreign, particularly British, factories in Russia) and to playing against foreign workers' teams. The first international soccer match was against the Finnish Labour Team ('*TUL*') in 1922 (won 7–1 by the old Moscow Zamoskvoretsky Sports Club). The next year, a Russian Federation side visited Berlin and Stettin to play workers' teams; these matches became an annual fixture (until relations with Germany and Poland were broken off in 1933). In 1924, a Leningrad team played Finnish, Norwegian and German workers' associations (winning 4–0, 5–3 and 7–1). The following year it played two games against Revel[9] (drawing 1–1 and winning 1–0) and eight games against Finnish teams. In 1926, a Moscow team played the French communist trade union *CFGT* team in Paris.

Nonetheless, the need to co-exist (especially with the USSR's neighbours), a desire to compete against the world's best teams and the consideration that the 'bourgeoisie' in certain backward states were playing a progressive rôle brought some limited contacts. A Soviet soccer team visited Sweden and Norway in 1923; in Sweden, it beat the national team 2–1 and drew 5–5 with a Stockholm eleven; in Norway, it won all its matches. In the following two years, the USSR twice met Turkey (winning 3–0 and 2–1). The contacts might well have been more extensive but for the refusal of certain governments to grant visas: intended soccer matches in Spain and Czechoslovakia in 1926 and 1927 had to be put off because of the refusal of their governments to grant entry visas to Soviet players. The Austrian government declined permission for the Lower Austrian Football Association to make a soccer tour of the USSR in 1926.

Limited participation in other sports began to take place in the late 1920s, even in 'bourgeois' tournaments, as long as Soviet representatives stood a reasonable chance of winning. As *Shakhmatny listok (Chess Bulletin)* wrote at the time, 'In certain circumstances, the participation of working class chess players in bourgeois tourneys would be politically advantageous, inasmuch as it would unite working people around the idea of class solidarity

[9] Present-day Tallin, capital of the Soviet republic of Estonia, Revel was then an independent Baltic state.

and of opposition, as a class, to the bourgeoisie. The Chess Section therefore deems it possible for the proletarian chess organisation to take part in international matches so as, through victories over bourgeois masters, to enhance self-respect among the proletarian masses and faith in their strength and youthful talents.'[10]

For the most part, however, as long as the USSR remained isolated and weak internationally, foreign sports relations were restricted to worker sports organisations and reflected the policy of the Communist International (*Comintern*).[11] Soviet foreign sports policy was, in fact, largely identical with and conducted through the International Association of Red Sports and Gymnastics Organisations, better known as Red Sport International (RSI). The RSI was formed at the First International Congress of Representatives of Revolutionary Workers' Sports Organisations as an affiliate of the *Comintern* in Moscow, July 1921, two years after the *Comintern*'s inception. Founder members were workers' sports organisations from eight countries – Czechoslovakia, Finland, France, Germany, Hungary, Italy, Soviet Russia and Sweden. By 1924, it had 2,214,000 members in nine sections distributed in Bulgaria, Czechoslovakia, Estonia, France, Italy, Norway, Uruguay, the USA and the USSR. Its first president was Nikolai Podvoisky, then concurrently head of *Vsevobuch*; its secretary was F. Reisner of Germany.[12]

The RSI was formed partly to counterbalance the social-democratic (Lucerne-based) Workers' Sport International (WSI – in 1929, renamed the Socialist Workers' Sport International), which had been set up in 1920 on the initiative of Belgian, French and German social democrats and was composed of workers' organisations from these three countries plus others in Britain, Czechoslovakia, Finland and Switzerland. The RSI made its concern for sport and the class struggle manifest in the second article of its Statutes: 'The Red Sport International embraces all

[10] *Shakhmatny listok*, 7 October 1925, p. 3.
[11] The Third or Communist International was set up in Moscow in March 1919, with the avowed objective of working to spread communism throughout the world. As Trotsky put it: 'If today the centre of the Third International lies in Moscow then tomorrow . . . it will shift westward: to Berlin, to Paris, to London. . .' Trotsky, *The Age of Permanent Revolution*, p. 131.
[12] *Krasny sport*, 1924, No. 14, p. 3.

workers' and peasants' sports organisations which support the proletarian class struggle. . . Physical culture, gymnastics, games and sport are a means of proletarian class struggle, not an end in themselves.'[13]

Relations between the two socialist sports internationals were hostile right from the start, the RSI accusing its 'reformist' rival of diverting the workers from the class struggle by preaching that sportsmen should be neutral and that sport should be apolitical. RSI further charged it with preventing its members from competing against Soviet and other revolutionary sports bodies (the WSI accused the RSI of the 'militarisation' of sport). Until 1928, the RSI, like the *Comintern*, pursued a policy favouring open competition between sportsmen of the two internationals and joint opposition to all 'bourgeois' sports bodies. The WSI countered that the RSI only wished to undermine it, infiltrate it and take it over, citing the RSI Manifesto *To All Workers of the World*, in which the RSI had called upon the communist parties of 47 countries to form communist cells in workers' sports associations so as to conduct ideological work among worker athletes.[14] This 'subversion' evidently had some success, judging by the disaffiliation of several important sports organisations from the WSI and by the rather tendentious names attached to the newly formed clubs – e.g. a Paris workers' sports organisation became *L'Etoile Rouge* and a Parisian soccer club named itself after Red Sport International President Nikolai Podvoisky.[15] Furthermore, a number of WSI affiliates were defying its ban on contacts with RSI teams, particularly those from the Soviet Union. Soviet sides had played against WSI-affiliated members, such as the *TUL* workers' sports association in Finland and against other affiliates in 1923 in Estonia, Germany, Norway and Sweden. In the same year, the Workers' Sports Federation of France voted by 71 to 14 to switch allegiance from the WSI to the RSI.

Under pressure, in 1925, the leaders of the WSI permitted affiliates to compete with Soviet sportsmen 'as long as they do not exploit the occasion for political purposes'. As a result, the number of international workers' events in which Soviet teams participated

[13] Koz'mina, *Mezhdunarodnoye rabocheye sportivnoye*, p. 171.
[14] Ibid., p. 172.
[15] *Izvestiya sporta*, 1922, No. 8, p. 2.

rose – 6 in 1922, 27 in 1923, 30 in 1924, 38 in 1925, increasing sharply to 77 in 1926 and 87 in 1927; the sports concerned were speed skating, skiing, wrestling, boxing, soccer and athletics.[16] That there were not more contacts was largely due to the vetos of foreign governments on the entry of Soviet athletes into their countries.

This international activity received weighty backing from the Central Committee of the Communist Party: in its first major pronouncement on sport in July 1925, it declared that 'the promotion of physical culture in the USSR is paramount for the international workers' movement, insofar as contacts in sport and gymnastics between Soviet and foreign workers' organisations strengthen the international labour front'.[17]

Open competition was shortlived, however; in 1927, the WSI reproached RSI members with repeatedly violating the 1925 conditions and forthwith sundered all sporting ties. Subsequently, many WSI affiliates expelled all communists from their ranks. Once again, the WSI evidently had cause for complaint: the RSI made no secret of its efforts to infiltrate and take over its rival. In a missive sent to all member organisations in 1926, the RSI insisted that its 'members and supporters should be wherever worker-sportsmen carry on their work, because patient and lengthy propaganda within this international [the WSI] can do much to liberate WSI worker-sportsmen from the fatal influence of their petty bourgeois leaders and win them over to the genuine aims of the workers' sports movement'.[18] The policy of 'infiltration' caused some controversy within the RSI, principally between its president Podvoisky and its secretary Reisner, the former maintaining that the RSI should be on the offensive and use sport as a weapon in the class war. In the flush of revolution and before the 'socialism in one country' doctrine, he had declared, 'The Bolshevik Party and the Second Congress of the *Comintern* see the current period as a stage in the development of world revolution . . . the communist movement is now confronted

[16] F. I. Samoukov (ed.), *Istoriya fizicheskoi kul'tury* (Moscow, 1964), p. 283.
[17] *Izvestiya tsentral'novo komiteta Rossiiskoi Kommunisticheskoi Partii* (b), 20 July 1925, p. 5.
[18] *Krasny sport*, 2 June 1926, p. 1.

by world socialist revolution.'[19] Later, in legitimising the post-Lenin policy, communist historians have repudiated such predictions and the 'erroneous' policies of the RSI and its president, basing themselves on such premises. A Czechoslovak historian, for example, writing in 1967, asserted that, 'In speeches by many delegates at the Third RSI Congress, we find statements to the effect that the world revolution was upon them. Yet that was in direct contradiction to Lenin's views; he had demonstrated the prematurity of such assertions, thereby trying to prevent the Party and its workers' organisations, including the *sportintern*, from taking decisions that were rash and incorrect for the time.'[20]

Meanwhile, following the WSI-sponsored First World Workers' Olympics of 1925, which excluded Soviet athletes,[21] Moscow staged its first great international sporting event in 1928: the First Workers' *Spartakiad* dedicated to the First Five-Year Plan and the tenth anniversary of the Soviet sports movement (see above, Chapter 4, p. 110). The games were intended to demonstrate proletarian internationalism in sport by being a universal workers' Olympics and a counterbalance to the 'bourgeois' Olympic Games being held the same year in Paris. Although the *Spartakiad* was dominated by Soviet athletes, a sizeable foreign contingent arrived – in spite of the WSI ban on its members attending. Some 600 foreign athletes (about 15 per cent of all the participants) from a dozen or more countries are said to have taken part in the games.[22] The programme ranged over 21 sports, approximating to the programme of the 'bourgeois' Olympics. It differed from the latter, however, in that, besides team and individual competitions, the *Spartakiad* contained two innovations

---

[19] Verbatim report of the 2nd *Comintern* Congress (February 1921), read in the Archives of the Central State Institute of Physical Culture, Moscow. (It is not generally available.)

[20] Olga Nalepkova, 'Iz istorii osnovaniya krasnovo internatsionala', *Teoriya i praktika fizicheskoi kul'tury*, 1967, No. 11, p. 76.

[21] The WSI actually invited RSI athletes to compete on condition that the two internationals amalgamated. The RSI refused.

[22] *Pravda*, 13 August 1928, puts the figure at 12 nations: Austria, Britain, Czechoslovakia, Estonia, Finland, France, Germany, Latvia, Norway, Sweden, Switzerland and Uruguay; *Fizkul'tura i sport*, 1928, No. 33, adds Algeria and Argentina.

thought to be appropriate to such a proletarian gathering: first, a variety of pageants and displays, including an elaborate ritual of opening and closing ceremonies, carnivals, mass games, motor car and motorcycle rallies; second, demonstrations of folk games and folk dancing. In addition, there were displays of such team games as were unfamiliar to many of the participants (e.g. rugby, tennis, grass hockey) as well as mock 'battles' between the 'world proletariat' and 'world bourgeoisie'.

Strengthening the USSR as a nation-state: 1929–1939

Shortly after this, the USSR and the *Comintern* undertook a radical change of foreign policy. Concerned at the ebb of the world communist movement and convinced that it was only a matter of time before the capitalist powers renewed attempts to destroy the Soviet régime, the Soviet leaders felt it necessary to build up defence capacity and to try to postpone the coming attack as long as possible so as to permit the consolation and strengthening of Soviet defences through the industrialisation of the country. The growing weight attached to the defensive aspects of Soviet foreign policy was greatly reinforced by the triumph of Stalin's doctrine of 'socialism in one country' first hypothesised in 1924/1925. Trotsky and the other leaders who saw the strengthening of the world revolutionary movement as the only real guarantee of maintaining the gains of October had, by the end of 1927, been driven into the political wilderness; henceforward, there could be no doubt that it was the Russian revolution rather than international revolution which was dominant. Trotsky complained, 'We have today a "theory" which teaches that it is possible to build socialism completely in one country and that the relations of that country with the capitalist world can be established on the basis of "neutralising" the world bourgeoisie [Stalin]. The necessity to call for a [socialist] United States of Europe falls away, or is at least diminished, if this essentially national-reformist and not revolutionary-internationalist point of view is adopted.'[23] But it was adopted and the work of the *Comintern* became defensive in object – the aim being to prevent

[23] Trotsky, *The Age of Permanent Revolution*, p. 147.

or frustrate an anti-Soviet coalition rather than to further and lead revolution.

Not only did Soviet foreign policy alter in relation to bourgeois states; it changed towards the social democrats. Since 1920, Communist parties abroad had been acting under the slogan of a 'United Front' which indicated a readiness, at least in theory, for some sort of cooperation with other parties of the Left. However, it was in the name of this policy that the Chinese Communists had collaborated with the Kuo-min-tang and met with disaster when Chiang Kai-shek had turned on his Communist partners. In Europe, Communist parties had encountered little success in their approaches to social-democratic parties. A new policy in relation to social democrats went into operation after the Sixth World Congress of the Comintern in the summer of 1928. As the British historian, E. H. Carr, describes it: 'The manifesto issued by the Congress, ranging the Social Democrats with the Fascists, denounced them as being "on the side of the exploiters, on the side of the imperialists, on the side of the imperialist robber states and their agents", and called on the workers everywhere to fight "against reformism and Fascism for the proletarian revolution".'[24]

This new policy was, of course, applied in all areas, including sport. It was taken up immediately by the RSI which appealed for a 'relentless fight against the social-fascist leaders'.[25] Subsequent events – economic depression in Europe and the growth of fascist régimes in Italy and Germany – witnessed a great thinning, if not decimation, of the ranks of both the WSI and RSI. By the mid-1930s, their feud had become an anachronism, with the backbone of the WSI (the nearly two million-strong sports association of Germany) broken by Hitler and the RSI virtually confined to the USSR. As late as 1933, the Soviet Foreign Minister, Maxim Litvinov, saw no reason for the USSR to alter its policy towards Germany; he made what Carr has called a 'rather crude avowal of Soviet opportunism':[26] 'We, of course, sympathise with the sufferings of our German comrades, but we Marxists are the last who can be reproached with allowing our feelings to dictate our

24 E. H. Carr, *German–Soviet Relations Between the Two World Wars, 1919–1939*, O.U.P., 1951, p. 99.
25 *Krasny sport*, 12 May 1929.
26 Carr, *German–Soviet Relations*, p. 110.

policy. The whole world knows that we can and do maintain good relations with capitalist states of any brand, including the Fascist. We do not interfere in the internal affairs of Germany, as we do not interfere in those of other countries; and our relations with her are conditioned not by her internal but by her external policy.'[27]

Although no sports ties linked Germany and the Soviet Union during the 1930s, Soviet sportsmen were venturing into contests with bourgeois states. Thus, in the first Soviet chess venture abroad, Mikhail Botvinnik drew with the world champion, the Czechoslovak, Flohr, in 1933; three years later, his tie for first place with the Cuban, Capablanca, at the world championship held in Nottingham merited a picture and full-length article on the front page of *Pravda*.[28] Following the signing of a mutual assistance pact between Soviet Russia and Czechoslovakia in 1935, three soccer matches were played by Prague against Leningrad, Moscow and the Ukraine.

However, following Hitler's announcement in March 1935 of what he called 'the restoration of German sovereignty' and unlimited rearmament, the fear of fascism became very real for the Soviet leadership and foreign policy veered once more toward cooperation between social democrats and communists. In July 1935, a congress of the *Comintern* – the Seventh and last – was summoned for the purpose of generalising the new line. 'In face of the towering menace of Fascism', declared the main resolution, '. . . it is the main and immediate task of the international labour movement in the present phase of history to establish the united fighting front of the working class.'[29] The defence of democracy against fascism was said to be the supreme task of labour. Sport, too, was to play its part in 'safeguarding democracy and constitutional government'.[30]

The Soviet side advocated the unification of the international workers' sports movement – and, although the two sports inter-

---

[27] M. M. Litvinov, *Vneshnyaya politika SSSR* (Moscow, 1937), p. 78.

[28] Fourteen years previously, the then 14 year old Botvinnik had beaten Capablanca in Moscow during an exhibition of simultaneous play by the then reigning world champion.

[29] *Sed'moi vsemirnyi kongress Kommunisticheskovo Internatsionala* (Moscow, 1935), p. 7.

[30] *Fizkul'tura i sport*, 1935, No. 7, p. 3.

nationals could not agree on a Popular Front, they did reach some measure of consensus on certain points: they issued a joint appeal for all sportsmen to boycott the 1936 Olympics (Berlin being the host city); and Soviet sportsmen were permitted to take part in the WSI-sponsored International Workers' Olympics held in Antwerp in 1937. Nevertheless, large areas of discord remained, notably over competition with 'bourgeois' sportsmen: while the WSI leaders were opposed to such 'fraternisation' with the class enemy, Soviet sports leaders pressed for contacts with 'all organisations opposed to the fascist danger'.[31] Soviet leaders saw a difference between the earlier United Front and the current Popular Front in that the latter extended to the anti-fascist bourgeoisie and Soviet leaders played down the class struggle against them. A few months after the outbreak of the Spanish Civil War, a Basque soccer team played nine matches in the Soviet Union during early 1937, winning seven of them. But international events, particularly the gathering of war clouds over Europe, were to bring to an end the period in which the policy of 'popular fronts' was pursued.

Relations with Axis Powers: 1939–1941

It is fundamental to an understanding of Soviet policy in this period that the Soviet leaders seemed to think an aggressive war by Hitler certain, and were determined at all costs to avoid having to face him alone. If the alliance with the West failed, then neutrality in a war between Germany and the West or, at worst, alliance with Hitler, were the only ways out. This consideration followed the signing of the Munich agreement on 29 September 1938 (there had been no prior consultation with the Soviet government), the apparent bankruptcy of the Soviet Union's Western policy and the necessity of coming to terms with Hitler. As Carr comments, 'Once this diagnosis of Western policy had been accepted in Moscow, only one conclusion could be drawn: if the Western alliance could not be achieved, then let Hitler at all costs strike West and let Russia purchase immunity by "non-intervention".'[32] This was the conception embodied in the Molotov–

[31] *Pravda*, 27 June 1938.
[32] Carr, *German–Soviet Relations*, p. 136.

Ribbentrop pact of 23 August 1939, when, in return for 'non-intervention', 'Stalin secured a breathing space of immunity from German attack . . . and German agreement to the existing Soviet frontiers in Eastern Europe.'[33]

The events of the first few months after the signing of the Soviet–German non-aggression treaty – and the subsequent commercial and cultural (including sport) exchanges – provide ample evidence of the ease with which a state of the Soviet type could carry into effect a new policy, whatever the magnitude of the apparent change involved. Internal propaganda conformed to the new line and all anti-fascist expressions vanished.[34] The *Comintern* followed suit and swung into line behind the Soviet–German 'peace offensive'. A *Comintern* announcement on 7 November 1939 condemned both Germany and the Allies for engaging in a war for world domination, but the emphasis in this period was on Allied responsibility for the war. As Beloff has written: 'Communist parties which only yesterday had been the most bellicose advocates of collective resistance to an aggressor fell back into the more congenial atmosphere of revolutionary defeatism.'[35]

This *volte face* found its echo, naturally, in sport. The first-ever sports agreements signed between the Soviet Union and a West European state were those concluded with Germany shortly after the Molotov–Ribbentrop pact. They envisaged a wide exchange of sportsmen: German fencers, swimmers, gymnasts, soccer players, athletes and tennis players came to the Soviet Union, while Soviet gymnasts, swimmers and weightlifters all competed in Germany. In fact, more sports contests took place between Soviet and German sportsmen during 1940 than between the sportsmen of the USSR and all 'bourgeois' states in all the preceding years since 1917 put together: some 250 German sportsmen competed in the USSR and 175 Soviet sportsmen in Germany between September 1939 and the end of 1940.[36] All this, presumably, was intended to reinforce the newly established Soviet–German friendship.

[33] Ibid., p. 136.
[34] Thus, for example, even guards in labour camps were forbidden to call prisoners 'fascists' any longer.
[35] M. Beloff, *The Foreign Policy of Soviet Russia, 1929–1941*, O.U.P., 1947, Vol. II, p. 288.
[36] Romanov, *Mezhdunarodnoye sportivnoye dvizhenie*, p. 192.

Following the German invasion of Norway on 9 April 1940, and the establishment there of the Quisling fascist régime, a Soviet–Norwegian sports agreement was signed; it brought an exchange of skiers to compete in bilateral skiing contests in December 1940.[37]

Sports contacts with the Baltic states followed the Soviet–German division of spheres of interest, the signing of mutual assistance pacts with the three Baltic states[38] and the establishment of Soviet military bases there. In the period between the signing of these pacts in late 1939 and the incorporation of the three Baltic states into the USSR in August 1940,[39] sports agreements resulted in Estonian boxers and wrestlers, Latvian skaters and Lithuanian basketball players competing in the Soviet Union.[40]

The only other foreign sports contacts involving the USSR in the years 1940 and 1941 were two soccer matches played between Moscow *Spartak* and Sofia, first in Sofia and then in Moscow in mid-1940, on the eve of Bulgaria's occupation by the Germans and at a time when the USSR was attempting to conclude non-aggression pacts with Balkan states, including Bulgaria.

This interlude of sports contacts with three states that were shortly to become the USSR's wartime foes and with three border states that were soon to be incorporated into the Soviet Union as Union Republics brings the history of pre-war foreign sports contacts to an end. No foreign sports contacts existed during the period of Soviet involvement in the war (1941–1945).

With the signing of the Soviet–German pact in August 1939 and the subsequent outbreak of World War II, the *Comintern* had gone into eclipse; it was finally dissolved, no doubt to the satisfaction of the leaders of the USSR's wartime allies, on 22 May 1943, giving further support to those who argued that the Soviet Union was 'a State among other States, pursuing

---

[37] Ibid., p. 193.

[38] The pact with Estonia was signed on 29 September, that with Latvia on 5 October and that with Lithuania on 10 October 1939.

[39] On 1 August, a special session of the Supreme Soviet admitted Lithuania as a Soviet Socialist Republic, adding to it certain territories previously part of Belorussia; Latvia was admitted on 5 August and Estonia on 8 August 1940.

[40] Romanov, *Mezhdunarodnoye sportivnoye dvizhenie*, p. 193.

clearly defined ends by the conventional methods of *realpolitik*'.[41]
It is an interesting sidelight on the not always straightforward
relations within *Comintern* organisations that the Red Sport
International is rumoured not to have died immediately after the
Nazi attack on the Soviet Union on 16 June 1941. Although
Moscow is said to have given instructions for its dissolution, some
of its leaders, including the secretary Reisner, are said to have
ignored the order and only halted activities in November 1942.[42]

USSR as a world power: 1945 onwards

Status as a world power

The Soviet Union emerged from the war a victor, its military
power having penetrated into Central and Eastern Europe, thus
altering radically the balance of power in Europe and the world.
Within the space of the four immediate post-war years, ten Soviet-
aligned states came into existence.[43] In the circumstances of international friction ('Cold War') which developed after World
War II, the existence of two 'hostile camps' and rival military
blocs confronting one another in a divided Europe, sport became
an obvious arena for international competition, 'defeating' one's
ideological opponent. In the West, it was initially felt by most
governments valuable and expedient to have sporting contacts
with the Soviet Union, both as an expression of the formal victors'
unity that survived the war and as a relatively harmless means of
keeping certain options open for a more cooperative future (as in
other cultural exchanges). In the USSR, domestic sport was now
thought strong enough to take on the world; victories over
bourgeois states would demonstrate the vitality of the Soviet
system. In a speech to the Party Central Committee in 1946, the
Party spokesman then responsible for ideological and cultural
affairs, Andrei Zhdanov, lauded the supremacy of Soviet culture

[41] Beloff, *The Foreign Policy of Soviet Russia*, p. 390.
[42] The story of the demise of the RSI has never been told officially; this
version was told to me in Moscow by a Soviet sports-historian.
[43] These states were Yugoslavia (1945), Bulgaria (1946), Albania (1946),
Hungary (1946), Rumania (1946), Poland (1947), Czechoslovakia (1948),
North Korea (1948), the German Democratic Republic (1949) and China
(1949).

and urged an offensive against the 'decadent' Western world.[44] In a mood of nationalistic fervour that accompanied a great military victory, Soviet sport, too, an 'inalienable part of the overall culture of society',[45] was therefore to take the offensive and, in the words of a Party resolution on sport, 'win world supremacy in the major sports in the immediate future'.[46] To do this would be to advertise the socialist system: 'The increasing number of successes achieved by Soviet sportsmen in sport has particular political significance today. Each new victory is a victory for the Soviet form of society and the socialist sports system; it provides irrefutable proof of the superiority of socialist culture over the decaying culture of the capitalist states.'[47]

Before the war, apart from the sports exchange between the USSR and Nazi Germany and the Baltic states in 1940, few official representatives of foreign states had visited the Soviet Union for a sporting event, nor had Soviet athletes competed, except (as we have seen) on rare occasions, with athletes other than those belonging to workers' sports associations. Nor had Soviet sports associations joined or been invited to join international federations. Further, since tsarist Russia's participation in the 1912 Games, no Russian or Soviet team had contested the Olympics.[48] That is not to say that standards in Soviet sport were

[44] In an admonition to Soviet writers, Zhdanov had said: 'Is it right for Soviet patriots like us, representatives of progressive Soviet culture, to play the part of admirers of disciples of bourgeois culture? Our literature reflects a society which is on a higher plane than any bourgeois–democratic society, a culture which is obviously superior to bourgeois culture and, therefore, it need hardly be said, has the right to teach others the new, universal morals. Where can one find another people like ours, or a country like ours? Where can one find such wonderful human qualities?' *Pravda*, 6 June 1946, p. 1.

[45] See *Entsiklopedichesky slovar' po fizicheskoi kul'ture i sportu*, Vol. III (Moscow, 1963), p. 226.

[46] *Kul'tura i zhizn'*, 1 November 1949, gives the full text of the resolution 'On the Work of the All-Union Committee on Physical Culture and Sports Affairs in Implementing the Directives of the Party and the Government on the Development of the Mass Sports Movement in the Country and on Improving the Skill of Soviet Athletes'.

[47] Y. D. Kotov and I. I. Yudovich, *Sovetskaya shakhmatnaya shkola* (Moscow, 1951), p. 4.

[48] The International Olympic Committee continued to recognise the old tsarist Russian Olympic Committee for several years after 1917. Such

necessarily inferior to those in the West. It is claimed that, by 1939, 44 Soviet records bettered world records, including 23 in weightlifting, 9 in athletics, 9 in pistol shooting, 2 in swimming and 1 in speed skating.[49] They could not be registered because the Soviet Union was not party to international federations.

In the immediate post-war years, Soviet sports associations affiliated to nearly all the major international sports federations (see Table 19) and Soviet athletes were competing regularly at

TABLE 19   *Affiliation to international federations, by sports: 1946–1973*

Year	Sports federations affiliated to in given year	Cumulative total sports affiliated (no.)
1946	Basketball, soccer, skiing, weightlifting	4
1947	Athletics, chess, speed and ice skating, swimming (including diving and water polo), wrestling	9
1948	Gymnastics, volleyball	11
1949	Boxing	12
1951	(Soviet Olympic Committee formed and affiliated to the IOC)	12
1952	Cycling, canoeing, equestrianism, fencing, ice hockey, modern pentathlon and biathlon, pistol shooting, rifle shooting, rowing, yachting	22
1954	Table tennis	23
1955	*Bandy*	24
1956	Draughts, lawn tennis, motorcycle racing, motor racing	28
1958	Gliding, handball	30
1962	Judo, radio sport	32
1965	Sub-aqua sport	33
1966	Model boatcraft sport	34
1967	Archery, mountaineering, orienteering	37
1969	Motor boat sport	38
1970	Field hockey	39
1971	Tobogganing	40
1973	Trampoline, rugby	42

Sources: A. O. Romanov, *Mezhdunarodnoye sportivnoye dvizhenie* (Moscow, 1973), pp. 236–242; A. O. Romanov, *Mezhdunarodnye sportivnye ob"yedineniya i turistskie organizatsii* (Moscow, 1973), pp. 309–317.

ROC members as General Butovsky, Count Ribopierre, Baron Vilebrandt and Prince Urusov all served on the IOC in the period 1917–1932.

[49] Romanov, *Mezhdunarodnoye sportivnoye dvizhenie*, p. 193.

home and abroad against foreign 'bourgeois' opposition (see Table 20).

TABLE 20 *Foreign sports groups visiting the USSR and Soviet sports groups travelling abroad: selected years, 1948 – 1973*

Year	Foreign sports groups visiting the USSR (no.)	Soviet sports groups travelling abroad (no.)
1948	12	23
1954	131	142
1958	294	330
1959	352	353
1960	407	399
1961	490	455
1965	439	507
1967	699	806
1969	504	533
1971[a]	389	477
1973	617	598

[a] More than two-thirds of the exchange was with other socialist states.
Sources: F. I. Samoukov (ed.), *Istoriya fizicheskoi kul'tury* (Moscow, 1964), pp. 350, 371; V. V. Stolbov and I. G. Chudinov, *Istoriya fizicheskoi kul'tury* (Moscow, 1970), p. 219 (for 1965 data); A. O. Romanov, *Mezhdunarodnoye sportivnoye dvizhenie* (Moscow, 1973), p. 196 (post-1965 data); *Sport v SSSR* (1974), No. 8, p. 1.

Between 1946 and 1958, the USSR joined 30 international federations, and by 1973 – 42, thereby embracing nearly all the major world sports. Moreover, some 200 Soviet officials held posts in international sports organisations in 1975.[50]

Spearheading the assault on the 'bourgeois' fortress was the Moscow *Dinamo* soccer team which, only two months after the war, accepted invitations to visit Sweden, Norway and Britain and played four matches against leading British clubs without defeat (beating Cardiff 10–1, Arsenal 4–3, and drawing with Chelsea 3–3 and Glasgow Rangers 2–2) – and this at a time when British soccer was still considered to be supreme in the world. The tour should be seen as part of the effort to show that, despite the war losses, the USSR was still strong and that conditions were

[50] S. Pavlov, 'Vklad sporta v ukreplenie mezhdunarodnovo sotrudnichestva', *Teoriya i praktika fizicheskoi kul'tury*, 1975, No. 7, p. 4.

reasonably 'normal'. In 1946, Soviet weightlifters came second to the Americans in the world championships. In 1947, Soviet wrestlers competed in the European championships and won three divisions. In 1948, Botvinnik won the world chess title and, in 1949, Ludmilla Rudenko won the women's world chess title (the men's title was retained until 1972, when it was won by Robert Fisher of the USA [the title reverted to the USSR in 1974]; the women's is still [1977] held by the USSR). Also in 1949, the Soviet men's volleyball team became world champions and the women's team, European champions. These were, to say the least, extremely auspicious international débuts.

Despite these early successes, Soviet sportsmen moved cautiously into international competition and, before 1952, tended not to enter an event without reasonable expectation of victory. No Soviet team was sent to the London Olympic Games of 1948; in many Olympic events – notably in athletics and swimming (the 'anchor' sports of the Games) – it was felt that Soviet standards were still insufficiently high for the USSR to do well. Instead, a number of officials attended the Games as observers. Only in May 1951 was a Soviet Olympic Committee formed and accepted by the International Olympic Committee.

The USSR made its Olympic début at the 15th Olympic Games, held in Helsinki, in 1952. The extent of Soviet preparation was evident from the fact that Soviet athletes were to contest all events in the Olympic programme (with the exception of field hockey). Bearing in mind that nearly all the Soviet sportsmen and sportswomen had never competed previously against world-class opposition from outside the USSR, the Soviet performance was remarkable. Although, in the unofficial Olympic table (see Table 21), the USSR gained fewer gold medals than the Americans (22:40), it gained more silver (30:19) and bronze (19:17) and tied with the USA in points allotted for the first six places (according to the system used in the *Olympic Bulletin*).

The USSR took no part in the 1952 Winter Olympics and made its winter début only in 1956 at Cortina d'Ampezzo in Italy. There it amassed most medals and points, winning gold medals in speed skating, skiing and ice hockey. The ice hockey success was particularly creditable since the sport had been taken up in the Soviet Union only after the war; even two years before

TABLE 21 *Soviet performance in the Olympic Games: 1952–1976*

	Summer Games				Nearest rival		Winter Games				Nearest rival	
Year	Gold medals	Medal total[h]	Points[a]	Position	Medals	Points[a]	Gold medals	Medal total	Points[a]	Position	Medals	Points[a]
1952	22	71	494	1	76	494[c]	–[b]	–[b]	–[b]	–[b]	–[b]	–[b]
1956	37	98	624.5	1	74	498[e]	7	16	103	1	11	66.5[d]
1960	43	103	683	1	71	463.5[e]	7	21	146.5	1	7	62.5[e]
1964	30	96	608.3	1	90	581.8[e]	11	25	183	1	15	89.3[f]
1968	29	91	591.5	2	106	709[c]	5	13	92	2	14	103[f]
1972	50	99	665.5	1	93	636.5[c]	8	16	120	1	14	83[g]
1976	47	125	788.5	1	90	636.5[g]	13	27	201	1	19	138[g]

a The points allocation is that used in the *Olympic Bulletin*: awarding seven points for first place, five for second and so on down to one point for sixth place.

b USSR not participating.   c USA.   d Austria.   e Sweden.   f Norway.   g East Germany.

h The comparative British medal totals for the Summer Olympics were: 1952–11, 1956–24, 1960–20, 1964–18, 1968–13, 1972–18, 1976–13.

Sources: K. A. Andrianov et al. (eds.), *Olimpiiskie igry* (Moscow, 1970); *Sovetsky sport*, 16th February 1972, p. 4; *Sportsworld*, September 1972; *Sport v SSSR*, 1976, No. 3, p. i; *The Times*, 2 August 1976, p. 8.

the 1956 Winter Olympics, the Soviet ice hockey team had won the world championships at its first attempt.

At the next Olympics, held in Melbourne in 1956, the USSR sent a team of over 300 athletes. Once again, all events except field hockey were contested, and, this time, the scope of the challenge was much wider; besides gaining more medals and points than any other nation, the Soviet Union reaped the first gold medals in track events (both won by Vladimir Kuts), boxing, soccer, sculling, canoeing and the modern pentathlon.

There was no mistaking the boost that Olympic success gave at the time to many Soviet people's pride in their sportsmen and, by extension, in the country and even the system that had produced such world beaters. Nor were the leaders slow to appreciate the benefit the USSR could reap from its enhanced reputation at home and abroad. By a decree of the Presidium of the Supreme Soviet of the USSR of 27 April 1957, a large group of Soviet athletes, coaches and sports officials were rewarded with some of the country's highest honours.[51]

At the 1960 Olympic Games, held in the winter at Squaw Valley in the USA and in the summer in Rome, the USSR provided by far the most successful performance. In the winter, it won three times as many medals as its nearest rival (Sweden). In the summer events, it gained 103 to the 71 medals of its nearest rival (USA). Victories were recorded in sports comparatively new to the Soviet Union, like cycling, yachting, fencing and show jumping.

In the following Olympic Games, held in the winter at Innsbruck in Austria and in the summer of 1964 in Tokyo, the USSR once more emerged triumphant, winning first gold medals in pairs' figure skating (by Belousova and Protopopov) and in the biathlon in the Winter Olympics, and with Soviet contestants first in 7 of the 23 sports in the summer programme: Graeco-Roman wrestling, weightlifting, boxing, gymnastics, fencing, the

---

[51] *Pravda*, 30 April 1957. Twenty-seven beneficiaries received the supreme accolade, the Order of Lenin, 145 – the Order of the Red Banner of Labour, 367 – the Badge of Honour, 353 – the medal 'For Outstanding Labour' and 75 – the medal 'For Excellent Labour'. Never before – or since – have the leaders honoured so highly the efforts of Soviet sportsmen.

modern pentathlon and, for the first time, men's volleyball. A gold medal was also won for the first time in swimming.

At the 1968 Olympics, however, the Soviet winter and summer contingents showed they were not invincible by being placed second to Norway in the Winter Olympics, held at Grenoble in France, and second to the USA in the Summer Olympics, held in Mexico City.

One conclusion to be drawn from the 1968 Olympics was that other nations, too, were reaping rewards from extensive sports planning. At the summer Olympics, for example, six competing East European nations (excluding the USSR and the non-participant Albania) aggregated 120 medals, including 40 gold (with a total population of 100 million); the six leading West European states accumulated 81 medals, including 25 gold (with an aggregate population of 230 million). Hungary alone, with a population of only 10 million, gained twice as many medals (32) as Britain (53 million and 15 medals). West Germany (with a population of 57 million) won 25 medals, including 5 gold – the same number as East Germany, whose total included 9 gold (with a population of only 17 million). Spain (with a population of 30 million) obtained no medals at all. Mongolia, on the other hand (with a population of just over a million) gained 4 medals. Despite the Soviet setback in not 'winning' the Olympic Games for the first time in its short history of competition, the team's versatility was some indication of the comprehensive planning of the sports movement in the USSR. Not only did Soviet athletes contest 22 of the 23 sports at the Mexico Olympics (the exception, as before, was grass hockey), but they gathered medals in all sports except cycling – by far the most balanced achievement by any nation in the history of the modern Olympics.

In the winter and summer Olympic Games held during 1972 at Sapporo (Japan) and Munich (West Germany), the Soviet Union reclaimed its leading position. In the summer Olympics, the USSR acquired more gold medals and points than any nation had done before – this despite the obvious improvements in world-wide athletic standards, particularly in Eastern Europe and the 'third world'. Soviet success was achieved largely at the expense of the more established sports nations, primarily the USA.

The 'spread' of Soviet performance and success in the Olympics may be seen in Table 22 below which shows the first six team placings in every sport contested at Munich. Grass hockey was, once again, the only sport uncontested by the USSR.

Table 22 confirms that the USSR was the best all-round and most successful nation at the Summer Games, winning 9 of the 23 sports in which it competed, coming second in 6 and third in 2; by comparison, the USA had 4 firsts, 3 seconds and 1 third. Besides being superior overall, the USSR also was the most consistently versatile, being placed in the first six nations in 23 of the 24 sports in the Games (the USA – in 14, East Germany – 12, West Germany – 9). In terms of population-medal balance, the most outstanding nations were East Germany, Cuba and Hungary. Overall, the 11 socialist countries (Bulgaria, Cuba, Czechoslovakia, East Germany, Hungary, Mongolia, North Korea, Poland, Rumania, USSR and Yugoslavia) out of the 121 states represented at the 1972 Summer Olympic Games, accounted for over half the gold medals (100 out of 194) and 47 per cent of the medals. The improvement of the socialist states is noteworthy; when most of them made their Olympic début in 1952, only 3 featured in the top ten nations in the unofficial points table – the USSR (1st), Hungary (3rd) and Czechoslovakia (10th). In 1968, there were 4: USSR (2nd), East Germany (3rd), Hungary (4th) and Poland (8th). At the 1952 Summer Olympics, socialist states won 20 per cent of the total points and 29 per cent of the medals, in 1956 – 33 per cent and 34 per cent, 1960 – 40 per cent and 40 per cent, 1964 – 38 per cent and 38.9 per cent, 1968 – 40.6 per cent and 40.7 per cent and 1972 – 46.4 per cent and 47 per cent respectively. Commenting on the successes of the USSR and the fraternal states in 1972, *Pravda* left no doubt that it saw them as a victory internationally for the socialist system: 'The grand victories of the USSR and the fraternal states convincingly demonstrate that socialism opens up the greatest opportunities for man's physical and spiritual perfection.'[52] In recognition of Soviet success, athletes, coaches and officials who excelled during the 1972 Olympics were rewarded by a decree of the Presidium of the USSR Supreme Soviet (5 October 1972):[53] six persons

[52] *Pravda*, 17 September 1972, p. 1.
[53] *Sovetsky sport*, 6 October 1972, pp. 1–2. 'On Awarding USSR Orders and Medals to Athletes, Trainers and Physical Culture and Sports

TABLE 22 *First six team places in all sports contested at the 20th Summer Olympic Games*

Sport	First	Second	Third	Fourth	Fifth	Sixth
Archery	USA	*USSR*	Poland	Sweden	Finland	Belgium
Athletics	USA	East Germany	*USSR*	West Germany	Kenya	Britain
Basketball	*USSR*	USA	Cuba	Italy	Yugo-slavia	Puerto Rico
Boxing	Cuba	Hungary	Poland	USA	*USSR*	Bulgaria/Kenya
Canoeing	*USSR*	2–3 Hun-gary	/Rumania	4–5 East Germany	/West Germany	Bulgaria
Cycling	*USSR*	Australia	3–5 East Germany	/West Germany	/Poland	France
Diving	USA	Italy	Sweden	East Germany	*USSR*	Czecho-slovakia
Equestrian	West Germany	England	*USSR*	4–5 Italy	/USA	Sweden
Fencing	Hungary	*USSR*	France	Italy	Poland	Rumania
Football	Poland	Hungary	3–4 East Germany	/USSR	–	–
Gymnastics	*USSR*	Japan	East Germany	Hungary	Poland	USA
Handball	Yugo-slavia	Czecho-slovakia	Rumania	East Germany	*USSR*	West Germany
Hockey[a]	West Germany	Pakistan	India	Nether-lands	Australia	Britain
Judo	Japan	*USSR*	Nether-lands	Britain	France	West Germany
Modern pentathlon	*USSR*	Hungary	Finland	4–6 Britain	/Sweden	/USA
Rowing	East Germany	*USSR*	West Germany	4–5 Czech-oslovakia	/New Zealand	USA
Shooting	*USSR*	USA	East Germany	Czecho-slovakia	5–6 Italy	/Poland
Swimming	USA	Australia	East Germany	*USSR*	West Germany	Canada
Volleyball	Japan	*USSR*	East Germany	North Korea	5–6 Bulgaria	/South Korea
Water Polo	*USSR*	Hungary	USA	West Germany	Yugo-slavia	Italy
Weight-lifting	Bulgaria	*USSR*	Hungary	Poland	East Germany	Iran
Wrestling: free-style	*USSR*	USA	Japan	Bulgaria	Hungary	Iran
Graeco-Roman	*USSR*	Bulgaria	Rumania	Hungary	Yugo-slavia	Czecho-slovakia
Yachting	Australia	Sweden	3–4 France	/USA	Britain	*USSR*
Soviet Total 23	9	6	2	2	3	1

Obliques indicate combined award. [a] USSR was a non-participant.
Source: The Times, 12 September 1972, p. 8.

received the Order of Lenin (including Borzov – winner of the 100 m and 200 m sprints, Alexeyev – winner of the super-heavy weightlifting division, and Saneyev – winner of the triple jump for the third Olympics in succession), 20 – the Order of the Red Banner of Labour, 105 – the Badge of Honour, 48 – the medal 'For Outstanding Labour' and 74 – the medal 'For Excellent Labour'. Though high, the number of awards was more modest than that after the 1956 Melbourne Olympics, when the Soviet Union first gained most points in the unofficial table.

That is not to say other high-level contests in the full glare of world publicity are seen as unimportant. Several international contests rank high in prestige value to the winners – e.g. the biennial USA v USSR athletics match, the World Cup in soccer, and the various European and world championships. Outside the Olympics, therefore, the range of Soviet international competition grew steadily after the war. At the beginning of the 1960s, the reaffirmation of the policy of 'peaceful coexistence between countries with different social and political systems' by N. S. Krushchov at the 22nd Party Congress in 1961 found reflection in sport in the shape of rapidly increasing contacts between Soviet and foreign teams in a wide variety of sports. Sportsmen from abroad were invited to many Soviet cities and Soviet people were able, more often than not, to cheer and take pride in successes scored by their own athletes against foreign opposition. In 1961, as many as 490 foreign teams visited the USSR (see Table 20), competing in more than 40 Soviet towns; in the same year, Soviet sports organisations were in contact with 77 countries. The foreign visits were all the more significant since this was the first time most ordinary Soviet people outside Moscow and Leningrad had seen foreigners since World War II. Besides identifying the ordinary Russian or Georgian, Tatar or Latvian with Soviet performance, the matches with foreign teams, particularly with those from economically underdeveloped states, helped to re-establish the international fellowship that had receded into the background during the war and the years of intensive Cold War that followed. It is an interesting observation that few visiting foreign sportsmen found much to criticise in Soviet crowd

Officials in Connection with the Results of the XX Summer Olympic Games.'

behaviour; nor did foreign crowds in the conduct of Soviet athletes. The British diplomat and author, Wright Miller, felt that, 'The old feelings of solidarity, of decent relations between man and man, seem to have prevented any development of the dirty play and ugly crowd behaviour typical of so many countries where sport is a new thing. Soviet international teams have sometimes made a bad impression through being overzealous about national prestige, but I do not think foreigners have ever had to complain of any lack of sportsmanship on the field. When foreign teams or athletes defeat Russians on Russian ground they never meet with unpleasantness from the crowd unless they have been thought unsporting.'[54]

It seemed that few sports were outside the winning range of Soviet sportsmen once they had made their international début. Even old 'aristocratic' sports like yachting, rowing, fencing, lawn tennis, show jumping and horse racing were not out of reach. Soviet yachtsmen gained their first gold medal in yachting at the 1960 Olympics, Soviet rowers visited the Henley Regatta in 1961, winning two cups (including the top prize – the Grand Challenge Cup for Eights), Soviet men and women fencers won their first gold medals at the 1960 Olympics, tennis players entered the Davis Cup world tennis tournament in 1962, show jumpers (attired in the top hat and tails which the sport had inherited from the English country gentry) gained their first gold medal at the 1960 Olympics and Soviet horses and jockeys ventured onto the world's leading flat and steeplechase courses in the early 1960s.

As the 1960s progressed and relatively new sports came to be practised in the Soviet Union, Soviet competitors and teams extended their range of international competition and took part – now often without serious hope of immediate success (e.g. in motor rallies, rugby, badminton and field hockey) – in order to acquire experience. They even competed against foreign professionals in soccer, tennis and ice hockey, though in the complex world of amateur/professional distinctions, there is a number of sports in which the best Soviet competitors never meet the best foreign competitors. This is so in boxing, basketball, cycling and figure skating. In other sports, 'amateurs' and 'professionals' may

[54] Wright Miller, *Russians as People* (London, 1963), p. 148.

compete together – e.g. in soccer, motor racing and motorcycle racing. In yet others, there is a partial distinction – so that, for example, all tennis players may mix in 'open' tournaments, as at Wimbledon, but no 'professionals' may compete in the Davis Cup.

Soviet soccer teams entered nearly all the major international tournaments, winning the European Nations' Cup in 1962 and the European Cup Winners Cup in 1975, though failing to win successive World Cups. Soviet archers made a winning début in the European championships in 1969 and 1971; Soviet motor-cyclists – on dirt, grass and ice – won world titles at the end of the 1960s, and Soviet cars and crews entered the Monte Carlo Rally (1964), the London–to–Sydney Marathon (1968) and the London–to–Mexico Marathon (1970), and won the golden team trophy in the 1971 Tour of Europe Motor Rally; they also entered a number of Grand Prix. In skin-diving, the USSR won the European championships on its international début in 1967, and, the next year, won 20 of the 25 medals in the European championships. In parachuting, a Soviet man and woman won the absolute world individual titles in 1970 and the USSR won the women's team title. Soviet table tennis players won the European League in 1969 and again in 1970. Two Soviet tennis players, Olga Morozova and Alexander Metreveli, collected a major international title in 1971 (the South Australian Open Singles). In draughts, the Soviet team dominated the European championship after 1967. In trampoline sport, Soviet athletes won three of the four titles on their international début in the 1973 European championships. In the not-so-distant future, it is not unrealistic to forecast, the USSR is likely to be a leading power in world badminton, rugby, grass hockey and motor racing, at all of which its sportsmen are practising hard. Nor, one may predict, will it be long before Soviet winter athletes enter (and do well in) such sophisticated sports as the slalom, bobsleigh and tobogganing events – just as they have of late come to dominate figure skating and ice dancing and have won the world ski jumping championship. There are signs at the moment of them taking up golf and squash – even bridge, karate, ladies' soccer and body building are all developing an (unofficial) following.

As an example of thorough preparation for a 'new' sport, the USSR formed a grass hockey federation in 1968 and affiliated to the International Hockey Federation in 1970 – with virtually no popular support for the game at home – with the declared aim of fielding a team in the Munich Olympics in 1972. Almost the entire Soviet world-champion *bandy* team was drafted into grass hockey in order to form the nucleus of the Olympic squad. It made its international début at the European championships in 1970, coming third of four teams in its group; it did not, however, qualify for Munich. Nevertheless, the official campaign to promote hockey resulted in eight teams contesting the first Soviet Hockey Championship in Alma Ata in 1971. The importance to the USSR of hockey is that it is the *only* sport for which the country has so far been unable to field a team at the Olympics.

During the 1960s, the USSR won over twice as many world titles in a wide range of major sports as the USA, and over three times as many European titles as its nearest rival (West Germany). Moreover, of thirteen matches (1958–1975) held between the two world athletics giants, the USA and USSR (also regarded by many as the world representatives of their respective ideologies), the USA won only twice overall; it is noteworthy that Soviet *men* won three times only and Soviet *women* lost once only – that this occurred says much for the part played by women in Soviet sport.

These results and those at the Olympic Games examined earlier suggest that the Soviet Union has gone a considerable way to achieving its aim of world supremacy in sport, but *essentially* in aggregate terms of points over the whole range of amateur Olympic sports taken together. Until the anomalies that keep some amateurs and professionals apart are removed, it is difficult to gain an overall perspective of Soviet performance in relation to human maxima. The USSR appears to be more successful in the amalgam of combat sports (wrestling, weightlifting and judo), artistic expression (gymnastics and figure skating), quasi-military sports (fencing, shooting, archery, biathlon, modern pentathlon, skiing, parachuting and equestrian sports) and cerebral skills (chess and draughts). Harnessed to a purposeful planning system, these skills may have their roots in the physical strength of the Russian peasant and belligerent border peoples like the Cossacks and Transcaucasians (who produce many of the weightlifters, wrestlers and boxers); in the artistic body movements of gymnastics and figure skating by a people keenly appreciative of aesthetic self-expression in ballet and folk music; in the long-established (pre- and post-revolutionary) association between sport and military training; and in the intellectual skill of chess in a society in which intellectual and cultural activities are held in high esteem.[55] It is less successful in swimming and athletics, and 'newer' (for it) sports like grass hockey, rugby, badminton and tennis. The failure to dominate world athletics and swimming may be attributed partly to the climate, partly to the late start in sport of most Soviet children (due to the lack of facilities and instructors and to the high priority given to scholastic work) and partly to the paucity of amenities generally – school playing fields, soccer pitches, tennis courts, indoor stadiums and swimming pools being few and far between even in the 1970s.[56] The international success in, and popular following for, team sports in the USSR may be due to the vigorous official encouragement given to them for the values they are felt to impart; discipline, reliance on others and the merging of the individual in the group have long been valued by the Soviet authorities. It seems not an unreasonable hypothesis that the reasons behind such popularity of team play and international success in it may be sought in a societal environment that stresses collectivism and cooperation over individualism and self-interest.

As we have seen above, the Soviet Union is keenly aware of the advantages that are thought to accrue from international sporting success and, of course, deliberately prepares its athletes for inter-

[55] In the world chess ranking list issued by the International Chess Federation in 1972, Soviet men occupied 7 of the top 10 places, 15 of the top 20 and 52 of the top 100 places; Soviet women filled the top 7 places and 19 of the first 25 places. *Sovetsky sport*, 11 November 1972, p. 3.

[56] It provides some measure of the impact in recent years of sports needs on state thinking to recall that until the year of the Soviet Olympic début, 1952, there were only three indoor swimming pools in the whole of the Soviet Union (i.e. one pool per 61 million people). Even in 1970, the USSR had only 1 pool per 100,000 people (1 per 250,000 in the Russian Federation); in the same year, Britain, despite extensive access to the sea, had 1 indoor swimming pool per 37,000 people. See *Sport v SSSR*, 1971, No. 7, p. 14; *World Sports*, June 1970, p. 43.

national events. A recent statement of sports aims makes the point that, 'The main purpose of our international sports ties is to consolidate the authority of the Soviet Union by ensuring that Soviet athletes play a leading rôle internationally, that their sports skill constantly grows, that the successes of the Soviet people in building communism are made widely known and that physical culture and sport are promoted in our country.'[57] Testimony to the attention devoted to participation in international sport comes (wryly) from an unlikely source: the eminent biochemist, dissenter and now exile, Zhores Medvedev (himself denied an exit visa to address the CIBA Foundation on gerontology) wrote of the high priority given by the Party Secretariat to international sports events: 'I knew of a case of a soccer player who was suddenly required for an international match and was summoned and rushed by air from the resort where he was on holiday, approved by all departments, including the visa section, delivered from Moscow to England, driven straight from the airport to the stadium, and all this within twenty-four hours. He was to play for the Rest of the World against an All-England side. . . But this, of course, was a special case: soccer, sport, the glamour, the prestige! It was not a lecture on gerontology.'[58]

The Soviet Union is not slow to capitalise on international sporting success by using its outstanding sportsmen as 'ambassadors of good-will', not infrequently as a 'try-out' for political initiatives. For example, in 1972, as part of an intensive campaign for a détente with the USA and as a prelude to President Nixon's visit to Moscow, the Soviet leaders sent their leading girl gymnasts (including Olga Korbut and Ludmilla Turishcheva) on a gymnastics display tour of America. Two months later, when the USA–USSR Treaty on Contacts, Exchanges and Cooperation was signed in Moscow, it included a clause (Article XIII) on

---

[57] V. S. Rodichenko (ed.), *Rekordy, sobytiya, lyudi, 1969* (Moscow, 1970), p. 105. To emphasise the international impact of success in sport by socialist states, one writer has referred to 'the interesting fact that 8 per cent of West Germans who advocate recognition of the GDR do so because of the successes of the German socialist state in international sport and, especially, the Olympic Games'. See *Teoriya i praktika fizicheskoi kul'tury*, 1973, No. 8, p. 5.

[58] Z. Medvedev, *The Medvedev Papers* (Macmillan, London, 1971), pp. 160–161.

sports exchanges, on which *Sovetsky sport* commented 'the foreign policy of our Party and government is reflected in international sports relations which must play their part in establishing firm foundations of mutual understanding and friendship between our peoples'.[59] A month after the signing of the new agreement (and at the end of the year's Soviet–American athletics match, in which the USSR had soundly beaten its rival), the new entente was symbolically represented on the track by Soviet and American athletes linking arms, doing a lap of honour together and waving to spectators – a far cry from the atmosphere of the relations between the 'bastions of communism and capitalism' over the prewar and most of the postwar years.

Relations with state-socialist countries

Today, the bulk of Soviet foreign sports competition, like that of foreign trade, is with other socialist states – above all with those of Eastern Europe. During 1969, for example, 825, or some 58 per cent, of the 1,420 international contests in which Soviet athletes were involved were confined to members of the East European bloc; in bilateral and multilateral contests, East Germany and the Soviet Union met 187 times, Bulgaria and the USSR – 151 times, Poland and the USSR – 127 times and Czechoslovakia and the USSR – 74 times.[60] 'Sporting relations with socialist states are central to Soviet foreign sports contacts and every year exceed half the entire Soviet sports exchange. Thus, in 1970, they amounted to 55 per cent and, in 1971, to 67 per cent of the total exchange.'[61]

Insofar as sport is centrally controlled in all these states and fully integrated in the political system, it can be wielded for manifestly functional purposes. 'The overriding principle [of socialist states' international sporting relations] consists in developing relations between fraternal communist and workers' parties which control physical culture and sport and formulate the foreign policy tasks of the national sports organisations.'[62] Sports

---

[59] *Sovetsky sport*, 27 June 1973, p. 4.
[60] Rodichenko, *Rekordy, sobytiya, lyudy, 1969*, p. 106.
[61] Romanov, *Mezhdunarodnoye sportivnoye dvizhenie*, p. 196.
[62] Ibid., pp. 183–184.

contacts 'help to strengthen fraternal cooperation and friendship and develop a sense of patriotism and internationalism among young people of the socialist states'.[63] From the Soviet point of view, this can enable Soviet leaders to use sport to integrate the various socialist societies, to bind them to Soviet institutions and policies and to maintain and reinforce the USSR's 'vanguard' position within the bloc.

Relations have tended to reflect the political tenor within the bloc, with the Soviet Union defending (or imposing) its 'special relationship' as the 'most advanced socialist state', and the other socialist states striving for compensatory supremacies that are denied them elsewhere. In the period 1945 to 1956, most of the other socialist states (with Yugoslavia becoming the notable exception) were more or less obliged to learn from the Soviet model, to form Soviet-type administrative organisations and run physical fitness programmes like the *GTO* – this, despite the long sporting traditions of Hungary, Czechoslovakia (with its *Sokol* gymnastics) and East Germany, all of which had competed successfully in international sport many years before Soviet participation. Since 1956, however, there has been a gradual loosening of the Soviet grip on sport in other socialist states. Albania has, of course, gone its own way, following China, while other states have resurrected certain national sporting traditions and institutions which were submerged during the late Stalin era. Thus, for example, the *Sokol* gymnastics movement now plays a major part, once more, in Czechoslovak sport, and East Germany pioneered the use of sports boarding schools in the early 1960s. In place of Soviet-organised exchanges, new bilateral agreements have been drawn up and negotiated separately between the USSR and other socialist states – and among the members of the bloc. The USSR signed a five-year sports exchange agreement in 1966 with East Germany, in 1969 with Bulgaria, in 1971 with Poland and Hungary, in 1972 with Czechoslovakia and Cuba, and in 1973 with Mongolia, Yugoslavia and Rumania. These last two states pursue the most independent sports policy in Eastern Europe, paralleling their greater autonomy today in other spheres.[64]

[63] Ibid., p. 177.
[64] Rumania has, for example, permitted some athletes and coaches to travel and work abroad with far greater freedom, particularly in regard

Sports contacts between the socialist states embrace a variety of sports and take place at various levels. Their sportsmen come together in such single-sport tournaments as the annual Peace cycling race across Eastern Europe and the Znamensky[65] Memorial athletics meeting (held in Moscow), in such multi-sport tournaments for specific groups and organisations as the Friendship sports tourneys for junior sportsmen,[66] socialist rural games, twinned-city games, the Baltic Sea Week and annual sports meetings between army and security forces' sports clubs. Few opportunities are lost to associate sporting events with a political occasion or to employ sport to cement loyalties within the bloc. Thus, to celebrate the fiftieth anniversary of the formation of the USSR, a mass assault was made on its highest mountain, Peak Communism (formerly Peak Stalin – 7,495 m). In all, 87 climbers reached the summit and planted there the flags of the 15 union republics of the USSR and of eight other socialist states (Bulgaria, Czechoslovakia, East Germany, Hungary, Mongolia, Poland, Rumania and Yugoslavia) as 'a symbol of unshakable friendship and inspired by the ideal of proletarian internationalism, peace and friendship between peoples'.[67] To mark the same anniversary, one outstanding athlete from each socialist state (with the exceptions of Albania, China and North Vietnam, but including Cuba, Mongolia and North Korea) was made a Merited Master of Sport of the USSR.[68]

The sporting ties between army and security forces' clubs are particularly illustrative of the Soviet policy of military integration

to disposing of their foreign income, than athletes from other socialist states (except Yugoslavia). A Rumanian soccer trainer worked (until 1973) for three years with the famous Dutch and European champions *Ajax*: the unrestrained behaviour of the globe-trotting tennis star Ilia Nastase is certainly something the Soviet authorities would not condone among its players

[65] The Znamensky brothers were outstanding Soviet athletes before the war.

[66] The 1973 Friendship junior athletics match took place in the Soviet city of Odessa with teams from Bulgaria, Cuba, Czechoslovakia, East Germany, Hungary, Mongolia, Poland, Rumania and the USSR competing. By convention, no team score is made during these matches. See *Sovetsky sport*, 8 August 1973, p. 2.

[67] *Sport v SSSR*, 1972, No. 9, p. 2.

[68] *Sovetsky sport*, 21 December 1972, p. 1.

– or, at least, the desire to put a friendly face on some of the possibly less popular aspects of the Warsaw Pact. A Sports Committee of Friendly Armies (*SCFA*) was formed in Moscow in 1958, three years after the establishment of the Warsaw Pact. It embraced all members of the Pact plus China, North Korea and North Vietnam. Neither the Pact nor the *SCFA* included Yugoslavia. Cuba joined the *SCFA* in 1969 and the Somali Democratic Republic in 1973; China, Albania and North Vietnam took no part in it after 1960. The declared aims of the *SCFA* are 'to strengthen friendship between the armies, improve the quality of physical fitness and sport among servicemen and popularise the attainments of army sport'.[69] Each year, *SCFA* arranges, on average, 15 army championships in a variety of Olympic and paramilitary sports; by 1972, it was holding some 200 championships in member countries, including two summer multi-sport *SCFA spartakiads* (held in East Germany and the USSR) and three winter *spartakiads* (held twice in Poland and once in Czechoslovakia). The third summer *spartakiad* was held in Czechoslovakia in 1973,[70] and the fourth winter games in Bulgaria in late 1973. Apart from these inter-state army meetings, army clubs compete regularly against one another: thus, during 1972, army clubs met in Bulgaria for a Friendship Sports Week to contest events in weightlifting, the modern pentathlon, boxing, wrestling and shooting – sports with a distinctively military utility. In the same year, in September, a *Dinamo* Soccer Tourney was held in Moscow's *Dinamo* Stadium for junior teams of security forces' clubs from Bulgaria, Czechoslovakia, East Germany, Hungary, North Korea, Poland, Rumania and the USSR.

The improving sports standards in other countries of the bloc are reflected in the changing pattern of sporting aid. During the 1950s and early 1960s, this was mostly a one-way process, coaches, instructors and officials from the USSR going abroad in order to fashion (or refashion) the sports movements in the countries of its

[69] Romanov, *Mezhdunarodnoye sportivnoye dvizhenie*, p. 90.
[70] For the first time at this *SCFA spartakiad*, a team from outside the bloc participated – Horsed, the army team of the Somali Democratic Republic. Although its members won no medals, one athlete received a special prize awarded by the USSR Ministry of Defence. The Republic subsequently became a member of *SCFA*. See *Sovetsky sport*, 23 February 1974, p. 4. Iraq and Yemen joined in 1975.

allies and to help raise standards in individual sports to world levels. The sporting aid given by the Soviet Union and other socialist countries to Cuba was part of the process whereby that country was drawn into the ambit of state-socialist powers after a period of isolation and hesitation. The immediate aim was to help harness and build up Cuban sporting skill in order that Cuba might put up a good showing in sports confrontations with other states on the American continent. In the years 1969–1972, 'more than 50 Soviet coaches helped train Cuban athletes for the Olympic and Pan-American Games'.[71] The subsequent Cuban successes[72] in both tournaments provided ample material for linking sporting successes with the political system and demonstrating through the popular and readily understandable (particularly so in Latin America) medium of sport the advantages of the 'Cuban road to socialism' for other Latin American states: 'More and more Latin American states realise that Cuban victories in international sport are invariably connected with the successes of the Cuban revolution and the country's progressive system.'[73]

In recent years, however, a number of coaches and instructors from socialist states have been assisting Soviet athletes in sports in which the Soviet standard is below world class. In 1972, East Germany was training a Soviet team in bobsleighing (a sport only recently taken up by the USSR); in the same year, the Cuban sprinter Ernesto Figarola was coaching in Odessa and Minsk. Hungarian fencing, swimming and pentathlon coaches have been training Soviet sportsmen in these sports and Czechoslovak ice hockey coaches have been working with Soviet squads. As a number of the USSR's allies build up specialised facilities and sports amenities, they become increasingly in a position to enable other sportsmen from within the bloc to gather together on the eve of important international events for joint training; thus, in recent years, Soviet athletes have attended training camps in East Germany, Poland, Czechoslovakia and Bulgaria. These and other

[71] Romanov, *Mezhdunarodnoye sportivnoye dvizhenie*, p. 178.
[72] Cuba came second, not many points behind the USA, in the 1972 and 1975 Pan-American Games, and progressed from 53rd at the 1960 Olympics to 8th in 1976. Eight Soviet coaches accompanied the Cuban team to the Olympics and 12 to the 1972 Pan-American Games. *Sovetsky sport*, 22 June 1973, p. 3.
[73] *Sovetsky sport*, 30 January 1974, p. 4.

forms of mutual assistance and integration are said to have become an important contributory factor in the sporting successes of socialist states internationally.

Relations with newly independent countries

Since the early 1960s, the Soviet authorities have paid increasing attention to aid to the 'third world' in the field of sport as well as in the economic and in other cultural spheres. This assistance takes the form of sending coaches and instructors abroad, building sports amenities, training foreign sports administrators in the Soviet Union, arranging tours and displays by Soviet athletes and holding Sports Friendship Weeks that often have an unabashedly political character. Much of this aid, including the provision of sports amenities, is said to be given free of charge.[74] Sometimes the sports contact is used as a prelude to political contacts. After all, 'Sporting ties are one way of establishing contacts between states even when diplomatic relations are absent.'[75]

In the five years up to 1971, over 100 Soviet coaches and instructors had worked in 37 Afro-Asian states (i.e. an average of 3 per country), including Algeria, Egypt, Iraq, Lebanon, Syria and Tunisia in the Middle East, Chad, Congo, Ghana, Guinea, Mali, Senegal and Togo in Africa, and Afghanistan, Burma, Cambodia, India, Indonesia and Malaysia in Asia.[76] In late 1972, there were said to be more than 200 such people working in 28 foreign states (i.e. an average of 7 per country).[77] Sports cooperation treaties were signed with Egypt in 1969, Nigeria and the Sudan in 1970, Algeria, Iraq and Syria in 1972 and the Lebanon in 1973 (in which Soviet volleyball, fencing, gymnastics and athletics coaches had been working).[78] That such cooperation is not entirely motivated by altruistic considerations is apparent in a comment on the Nigerian–Soviet Sport Friendship Week held in Nigeria in the autumn of 1972: 'Sporting attainments today have an immense power of influence. It is not at all surprising, there-

[74] See D. Prokhorov, 'Nam nuzhny vashi spetsialisty', *Sport v SSSR*, 1970, No. 11, p. 14.
[75] Romanov, *Mezhdunarodnoye sportivnoye dvizhenie*, p. 182.
[76] Prokhorov, 'Nam nuzhny vashi spetsialisty', p. 15.
[77] *Sport v SSSR*, 1972, No. 12, p. 25.
[78] *Sovetsky sport*, 22 April 1973, p. 4.

fore, that Nigeria should arrange a sports week of friendship dedicated to the fiftieth anniversary of the formation of the USSR.'[79] Nigeria, like Egypt and the Sudan, had held a sports week, with the participation of Soviet athletes, also to mark the Lenin centenary in 1970.

The USSR has built sports centres in Afghanistan, Algeria, Cambodia, Congo, Indonesia, Iraq, Senegal and Togo. By 1970, students from 25 Afro-Asian states had received a Soviet coaching diploma and over 100 persons (from Afghanistan, Cambodia, Egypt, Ethiopia, Ghana, Guinea, Iraq, Malaysia, Mali, Sudan, Syria and Tunisia) had graduated from Soviet institutes of physical culture. Another 50 had completed dissertations in the field of sport and physical education in Soviet colleges.[80]

Judging by the rapidly mounting scale of operations for promoting sport in developing countries, the Soviet leaders obviously regard sport as an important weapon in the 'battle for men's minds'. It is a serious business: 'the authority of sport in the world has grown enormously; there is no longer any place for dilettantism in the politics of sport'.[81] Given the signal Soviet successes in international sport, such sporting aid is seen as an effective means of demonstrating the possibilities of the 'socialist path of development'. In arranging contacts and assistance, much emphasis is placed on the propaganda value of the successes attained in erstwhile backward areas of the Soviet Union: 'In arranging these ties, we attach special importance to the sports organisations of the various republics, to sportsmen from Kazakhstan, Uzbekistan, Azerbaidzhan, Armenia and Georgia, when they visit Africa and Asia, and when the representatives of those countries meet our republican sportsmen at home.'[82] As a prelude to Brezhnev's visit to India in November 1973, an 'Indo-Soviet Friendship Week' took place with the famous ex-soccer player Lev Yashin and the tennis star Alex Metreveli prominent in the Soviet delegation. The leader of the Soviet group was, significantly, the Secretary of the Tadzhikistan *Komsomol*.[83] Prior to that, a Kazakh gym-

[79] *Sport v SSSR*, 1972, No. 12, p. 25.
[80] *Sovetsky sport*, 14 July 1971, p. 4.
[81] *Sport v SSSR*, 1972, No. 12, p. 24.
[82] *Fizkul'tura i sport*, 1971, No. 3, p. 1.
[83] *Sovetsky sport*, 25 November 1973, p. 4.

nastics team had been the first Soviet sports group to visit India under the Indo-Soviet Cultural Agreement;[84] in the same year, another Kazakh group, the *Dorozhnik* volleyball team from Alma Ata, became the first Soviet sports delegation to visit the Malagasy Republic. Naturally enough, the sports emissaries 'told them of sport in Kazakhstan, of its rôle in the life of the family of equal fraternal Soviet republics'.[85]

It is remarkable that, apart from individual visiting sportsmen, Western states have tended to dismiss officially sponsored sporting aid to developing countries. In fact, the pattern has generally been one in which promising 'colonial' athletes are attracted away from their homelands to seek fame and fortune in the teams of metropolitan countries. Such a trend is particularly evident in Italian, French, Spanish and Portuguese soccer and in British cricket and boxing.

One final aspect of Soviet 'aid' to Afro-Asian states has been support for third-world campaigns to exclude from international contests countries believed to be operating racial discrimination in sport. The Soviet Olympic Committee instigated moves in 1962 within the International Olympic Committee to exclude South Africa from the Olympic Games; the moves succeeded, and South Africa has subsequently not been able to compete in the Olympics. The USSR has lent its considerable authority to moves to have South Africa and Rhodesia banned from all international sports tournaments. It is not unusual for Soviet competitors to forfeit matches (in tennis, for example) rather than play against white South Africans and Rhodesians. There is little doubt that such Soviet action wins much sympathy among wide circles in the 'third world', which see in the USSR a champion of their cause.[86] This attitude is reinforced in frequent Soviet references to the multinational nature of Soviet sport: 'The Soviet Olympic delegation of 1972 was a mirror of Soviet multinational sport. . . Patriotism and collectivism, friendship and mutual assistance have become integral to the outlook of our athletes. They there-

[84] *Sovetsky sport*, 2 August 1973, p. 1.
[85] Ibid., p. 4.
[86] The USSR refusal in November 1973 to play its World Cup qualifying soccer match in Chile, following the right-wing coup that brought down President Allende, may be seen in a similar light – as a moral decision that meets with the approval of national liberation movements.

fore look upon racial discrimination in sport as monstrous and inhuman.'[87] 'The internationalist character of socialist sport', the conclusion is drawn, 'has a great effect on the newly liberated ex-colonies.'[88]

Relations with non-state groupings

The USSR promotes sports contacts with pro-Soviet and potentially sympathetic groupings in foreign countries, such as the Finnish Labour Union (*TUL*); it encourages the participation of Soviet and foreign athletes in annual races through Paris and Moscow (sponsored by the French communist newspaper *l'Humanité* and by *Izvestiya* respectively) and it sponsors the World Youth Festival, in whose programme sport plays a prominent part. The 10th World Youth Festival, held in Berlin over 9 days in August 1973 with the participation of 20,000 foreign visitors from more than 120 countries, was described in the Soviet press as 'a festival of unity and solidarity of the international communist and the entire democratic youth and student movement, a vivid demonstration of the solidarity of young people in the fight against imperialism'[89] – and in the British press as 'a massive propaganda effort to demonstrate the virtue, strength and inevitability of Soviet-style communism'.[90]

As a measure of the importance attached by the Soviet Union to sport as a means of demonstrating its vanguard position in the communist youth movement, a 138-strong sports delegation was sent to the 1973 Festival; it included Olympic and world champions Ludmilla Turishcheva (gymnastics), Valery Borzov (sprinting), Faina Mel'nik (discus and shot), Irina Rodnina (figure skating), Mikhail Tahl and Anatoly Karpov (chess). 'The language of sport', it was claimed, 'became the language of friendship.' Ludmilla Turishcheva, after taking part in a symbolic

---

[87] *Sportivnaya zhizn' Rossii*, 1972, No. 11, p. 7; the further point was made that representatives of 26 Soviet nationalities, including some from all 15 union republics, were present at the 1972 Munich Olympics – 'eloquent testimony for all the world to see of the triumph of the Leninist national policy in physical culture and sport'.

[88] *Sport v SSSR*, 1973, No. 2, p. 19.

[89] *Sovetsky sport*, 27 July 1973, p. 1.

[90] *The Times*, 17 August 1973, p. 14.

relay through Berlin ('In Honour of the Peoples of Vietnam, Laos and Cambodia') made the point that 'we took part in this race to demonstrate once again our solidarity with the working people of the whole world, particularly young people'.[91]

The second main type of such contact is with trade and professional associations, such as the International Sports Union of Railwaymen and the International Federation of University Sport.

The International Sports Union of Railwaymen (ISUR) was set up after the war, in 1947, in Austria with the participation of trade unions from Austria, Belgium, Czechoslovakia, Finland, France, Hungary and Italy. Despite the presence of the two East European members, the leadership was predominantly social-democratic until the affiliation of other East European states in 1956 (Bulgaria and Rumania) and 1957 (East Germany, Poland and the USSR). The Union has now expanded to cover virtually all European states and many railwaymen's organisations in other parts of the world. That internal relations are not entirely smooth is testified to by the strict delineation of countries during championships into two independently competing groups – socialist and the remainder, so as to ensure opportunities for athletes from non-socialist states to win events. A compromise has been reached on representation on the ISUR governing body giving six places to non-socialist states (in 1975, Belgium, Finland, France, Holland, Italy and West Germany) and six to socialist (Czechoslovakia, East Germany, Poland, Rumania, USSR and Yugoslavia). At least four individual sports championships are held annually, each sport (of the 19 cultivated) being contested once every four years.[92]

Soviet sports relations with foreign student sports unions have also had their vicissitudes since the end of the war. International university games had been held before the war at two-yearly intervals since 1923, but without Soviet participation. After the war, a new International Union of Students (IUS) was formed in

---

[91] *Sovetsky sport*, 31 July 1973, p. 4.
[92] See Romanov, *Mezhdunarodnoye sportivnoye dvizhenie*, pp. 84–87. The 19 sports are athletics, basketball, bowls, boxing, chess, cross country running, cycling, fishing, soccer, handball, shooting, skiing, swimming, table tennis, tennis, volleyball, water polo, weightlifting and wrestling.

1947; its sports section arranged student games in Paris the same year, in which Soviet students made their international début. The domination of the IUS and its sports section by the students' unions of socialist states and their sympathisers in Western students' unions led to the student games of 1949 and 1951 being given an explicitly political slant by being combined with communist-sponsored World Youth Festivals. A split occurred when several Western students' unions tried to bar their members from taking part in the youth festivals and set up a breakaway organisation – the International Federation of University Sport (FISU) in 1949. Between 1949 and 1958, the two student sports organisations held their games separately; they came together again in 1959 when all the sports organisations of Eastern Europe (with the exceptions of East Germany and Albania) were admitted, on application, to FISU. As mutual compromises, the sports council of the International Union of Students was dissolved and the FISU Games were renamed *Universiad*, or World Student Games. Disagreement again occurred, however, in 1967 when the socialist states boycotted the *Universiad* as a protest against the presence of the Taiwan students as representatives of China. Nonetheless, the socialist states continue to hold their student and youth games within the bounds of the overtly political World Youth Festival, although prime Soviet attention is today concentrated on the *Universiad* which, in 1973, was held in Moscow.[93]

Since the war, therefore, there has been no serious effort to turn either communist or social-democratic sports organisations into alternatives to the existing sports federations, as happened prior to the war. Nor has 'loyalty' to communist sports organisations abroad been permitted to interfere with the Soviet policy of 'peaceful coexistence' and, latterly, détente. A leading Soviet sports journal has editorialised: 'Sport is an essential element in contemporary international relations; it affects their development, their forms of organisation and their content. Sport effectively helps to break down national barriers, create international associations, and strengthen the international sports movement. It is a

---

[93] The Moscow *Universiad* was held on the Olympic model in the following 11 sports: athletics, basketball, diving, fencing, free style and Graeco-Roman wrestling, gymnastics, swimming, tennis volleyball and water polo.

great social force helping to establish and promote international contacts between national sports-associations of countries with different social systems.'[94]

Relations with adjacent states: 1917–1977

The final aspect under which Soviet foreign sports policy may be considered is that in regard to adjacent or geographically close states.[95] For several years after the 1917 revolution, the USSR's ability to bargain with the Great Powers was severely limited by its weakness as well as by the mistrust in which it was held. On the other hand, the Soviet Union was less handicapped in its dealings with its immediate neighbours, all of whom, with the exception of Poland, were extremely weak. The Soviet aim was, as Beloff has written, 'to link these (states) to Russia by treaties embodying the three major principles of "non-intervention", "non-aggression" and "neutrality".'[96] In 1929, the so-called Litvinov Protocol on renunciation of war was signed in Moscow, originally by Estonia, Latvia, Poland and Rumania, then by Danzig, Lithuania, Persia and Turkey. Finland remained the only one of the USSR's neighbours outside the Soviet security system. Sports contacts reflected these strategic considerations.

Right from the outset, Soviet policy was to encourage sports relations with 'bourgeois' (or even 'feudal') states that were adjacent or geographically close to the USSR. Contacts took two forms: between All-Union and foreign national teams (e.g. between the USSR and Turkey, Finland or Sweden), and between local Soviet and local and national foreign teams from just across the border (e.g. between Baku and Iran, Odessa and Turkey, Leningrad and Finnish town clubs).

---

[94] *Teoriya i praktika fizicheskoi kul'tury*, 1971, No. 3, p. 5.

[95] Today, immediate neighbours include six states in Europe (Norway, Finland, Poland, Czechoslovakia, Hungary and Rumania) and six in Asia (Turkey, Iran, Afghanistan, Mongolia, China and North Korea). Countries whose geopolitical situation brings them within the category of strategically important 'neighbours' of the Soviet Union are evidently Sweden and Denmark in the Baltic area, Bulgaria, Albania and Yugoslavia in the Balkans, Egypt, Algeria, Iraq, Syria and the Lebanon in the Middle East, and Japan in the Far East.

[96] Beloff, *The Foreign Policy of Soviet Russia*, p. 5.

Table 23 gives an indication of the pattern of sports contacts on an official level (i.e. not with workers' sports associations) between the USSR and countries that border on or are geographically close to it. Of the pre-war neighbours in Europe, official sporting relations were maintained regularly with Finland, Estonia and Latvia. With Germany, they only began in 1940 after the signing of the non-aggression pact with the Nazis. The notable exceptions are Poland and Rumania, both of whose governments refused sporting and other cultural contacts with the Soviet Union before the war. Of the geographically close European states, relations with Norway, Denmark and Sweden were

TABLE 23   *Official sports contacts between the USSR and nearby states: 1920–1975*

Country	1920–1925	1926–1930	1931–1935	1936–1939	1940–1941	1945–1950	1951–1955	1956–1960	1961–1975
Albania							×	×	
Afghanistan							×	×	×
Bulgaria					×	×	×	×	×
China							×	×	
Czechoslovakia			×			×	×	×	×
Denmark	×	×	×			×	×	×	×
Estonia[a]	×	×	×		×	—	—	—	—
Finland	×	×	×			×	×	×	×
East Germany					×	×	×	×	×
West Germany								×	×
Hungary						×	×	×	×
Iran		×	×			×	×	×	×
Japan							×	×	×
Latvia[a]	×	×	×		×	—	—	—	—
Lithuania[a]			×		×	—	—	—	—
Mongolia									×
Norway	×	×	×		×		×	×	×
North Korea									×
Poland						×	×	×	×
Rumania						×	×	×	×
Sweden	×	×	×			×	×	×	×
Turkey	×	×	×	×		×	×	×	×
Yugoslavia						×			×

[a] Contacts with the pre-war Baltic States (Estonia, Latvia and Lithuania) are shown here up to 1940, when these countries were incorporated into the Soviet Union.

Sources: A. O. Romanov, *Mezhdunarodnoye sportivnoye dvizhenie* (Moscow, 1973); N. Y. Kiselev (ed.), *70 futbol'nykh let* (Lenizdat, 1970); F. I. Samoukov and V. V. Stolbov (eds.), *Ocherki po istorii fizicheskoi kul'tury* (Moscow, 1967).

more or less regular before the war, those with Czechoslovakia spasmodic and sports exchanges were non-existent with Albania, Hungary and Yugoslavia. The first contact with Bulgaria accompanied that with Germany in 1940. In the south, relations with Iran and Turkey were regular, particularly with Turkey, with whom the USSR maintained sporting contact during the latter part of the 1930s at a time when sports contacts with the rest of the world virtually came to a halt due to the tense situation in Europe and the mass repression within the USSR.

Since the end of the last war, the range of contact has corresponded to the international situation and Soviet concepts – first, that of 'two camps' and then, that of 'peaceful coexistence'. Nonetheless, priority in sports relations with non-socialist states has continued to go to the good-neighbourly policy, with particular emphasis on meetings between the USSR's neighbours and adjoining Soviet cross-frontier (often ethnically related) peoples. Thus, a Black Sea regional soccer competition was launched in 1970 which included teams from Odessa, Sevastopol, Novorossiisk and Batumi, on the one hand, and from Turkey, Rumania and Bulgaria, on the other. A similar regional contest has existed for several years in the Baltic basin for Finnish, Swedish, Estonian and Leningrad teams. Similarly, in 1972, a Baltic Cup weightlifting competition was held with participants from Finland, Norway, Sweden, East and West Germany, Poland and the USSR. The first tournament was held in Riga, capital of Latvia. In the summer of 1973, Baku was the venue of a now traditional 2-day athletics match between Iran and Azerbaidzhan.

Although sports ties with Middle Eastern countries might fall into the category of 'seeking support among developing states' (see 'Relations with newly independent countries' above), the fact that the Soviet Union often promotes contacts between their athletes and Soviet Central Asian nationals indicates also that some priority is being given to these contacts for regional, 'strategic' reasons. Bilateral sports meetings with Egyptian, Syrian, Iraqi, Lebanese and Algerian athletes, which have grown since 1969 (in line with heightened Soviet interest in the Middle East), have generally taken place in the Soviet Union within the former Islamic area. Under the terms of the sports cooperation treaty between the USSR and Egypt, signed in 1969, it was agreed to hold annual 'Soviet–Arab Sports Weeks' alternately in the two states; the first such 'Sports Week' was held in Egypt in 1970, when a team of Uzbek, Kirgiz and Kazakh sportsmen was sent. The next year, a group of Egyptian athletes, weightlifters, swimmers and wrestlers competed against Soviet Uzbek opponents in Tashkent, Samarkand and Andizhan. A similar agreement was signed with Iraq, Syria and Algeria in 1972, and with the Lebanon in 1973.[97]

Other countries with whom sports relations might be said to be promoted for 'strategic' reasons are Austria and Japan – the only capitalist states (along with Finland) in which Soviet sports coaches and players were working (up to 1975). Soviet ice hockey coaches and players were (in 1973) employed by the Austrian Atletik-Klub, *KAS* (Klagenfurt), Graz *ATSE* and the Viennese club *WAT-Stadtlau*.[98] A long-term sports exchange agreement was signed with Japan in 1971 and an ice hockey tournament was held in April 1973 in Sapporo between Japanese players from Hokkaido and Soviet players from the Soviet Far East and Siberia.

Contacts with other neighbours have depended on certain other factors; for example, with Afghanistan, Mongolia, China and North Korea they were long inhibited by the backwardness of sport in those countries. Sporting contacts were established with Afghanistan in 1955 and exchanges now take place regularly between Uzbek and Afghan athletes. Exchanges with Mongolia and North Korea commenced in the mid-1960s. With China, sports relations have closely followed the course of the Sino-Soviet dispute: bilateral contacts, which began only in 1955, were abruptly halted in 1961. Thus, for example, the Leningrad *Zenit* soccer team played 11 matches in China in September 1955 (winning ten and drawing one) and the Soviet national soccer team toured China in the spring of 1958. The last recorded Sino-Soviet soccer match was between Peking and Leningrad *Zenit* in

[97] The five-year sports cooperation agreement with Syria covered bilateral and multilateral competitions in both countries, joint training and seminars, exchange of documents and agreements to build sports amenities and manufacture equipment.

[98] *Sovetsky sport*, 27 January 1973, p. 4. The strategic value of Austria is that it acts as a neutral wedge some 500 miles deep between West Germany and Italy, thus splitting the Western bloc in two.

Leningrad (won 3–2 by *Zenit*) on 29 July 1961.[99] The post-cultural revolution resumption of political contacts between China and the West, said to have been presaged by table tennis matches in 1971, has not yet been paralleled by a similar renewal of sports contacts with the USSR (1977).

On balance, the Soviet policy of promoting sporting ties with neighbouring states – a quite deliberate attempt to use sport to cement good-neighbourly relations – has been fairly successful. This policy has been pursued in regard to neighbouring states even when general foreign and sports policies towards other 'bourgeois' countries have been radically at variance with this.

It has to be noted that, in most sports, the USSR's neighbours lag, often considerably, behind the world's foremost sporting nations and have generally been inferior to their Soviet opponents. By encouraging *regional* as often as national contacts, the USSR has avoided completely demoralising or publicly shaming opponents; pitting its strongest teams against them might well have had the opposite effect to the one desired. Pursuit of the goal of demonstrating the progress made by kindred peoples under socialism is in no way vitiated by this. The success of, say, Azerbaidzhanian against Turkish athletes is often cited by Soviet publicists as evidence of the progress made by national minorities under socialism.

Summary

To sum up, the pattern of foreign sports competition involving the USSR has closely followed the course of Soviet foreign policy and displays clearly differentiated contours in regard to the geo-political situation of different countries. With the new balance of power after the last war (the creation of a group of socialist buffer-states, the emergence of newly independent Afro-Asian states and

[99] N. Y. Kiselev (ed.), *70 fulbol'nykh let* (Lenizdat, 1970), pp. 210, 222, 242. Sports ties with Albania followed a similar pattern: the Leningrad Labour Reserves soccer team played matches in Tirana in 1954 and Tirana *Dinamo* played in Moscow and Leningrad in 1956. No matches are recorded after 1960, when Albania withdrew from international competition (except with China). It is noteworthy that, following China's resumption of competition against foreign athletes in 1971, Albania joined the International Weightlifting Federation (in 1972).

a nuclear stalemate), the Soviet leaders have assigned sport such tasks as demonstrating the superiority of and winning support for the communist system, encouraging friendly, commercial and good-neighbourly relations with the USSR and, within the socialist bloc, achieving unity on Soviet terms.

With its control of the sports system, the Soviet leadership has been able to mobilise resources to achieve the maximum efficiency of its sports challenge and, hence, to perform what it believes to be salient political functions. It is hardly possible to measure the impact of international success in sport on the behaviour of individuals or states – to discover whether such success can, in fact, ever affect policies. What is certain is that there can no longer be any belief that success is, as it was in the past, primarily a matter of the physical and moral resources of the individual participant.

The Soviet Union has demonstrated that the highest realisations of human potential can be most effectively achieved through the planned application of societal resources towards that desired end. It has done this in sport (and many other fields of human endeavour and excellence – e.g. musicianship) and it has done this for the conscious (political) demonstration effect which it is supposed, quite plausibly, to have. In general, in the Western world, the whipping up of popular fervour in sport has, consciously or unconsciously, resulted in the sacrifice of the sporting ideal on the altar of national or ethnic chauvinism. In the USSR, thanks partly to its multinational population, this has been largely avoided; it is not some innate ethnic or national superiority which has been seen to triumph but a political system.

That Soviet international sporting contacts are in general subordinate to the general lines of Soviet foreign policy is indisputable, and this has resulted on occasion in the grossest political opportunism. But it is equally true that this has also resulted on occasion in giving sport a pre-eminent rôle in moral leadership in world political terms, as exemplified by the apartheid issue. The increasing political isolation of South Africa in world affairs must be due in no small measure to the catalytic rôle played by the now very extensive boycott of sporting contacts with that country and to which the Soviet Union has made a notable, even leading, contribution.

Conclusions

In the light of our historical account of Soviet sport, which has revealed the main features of the course of events and of policies and their results relating to sport, we are now in a position to draw some general conclusions about the place of sport in Soviet society.

The practice of Soviet sport

In practical policy, the Soviet leaders, from about 1928 on, would seem to have opted for the following:

(1) the organisation of working people in their leisure time to the maximum possible extent within the framework of a tidy hierarchical and functional structure;

(2) the cultivation of *competitive* sport (a leisure time analogue of the competition between people at work designed to raise work tempos) with – again, as at work – material rewards for victors, the more effectively to improve people's readiness for work and to pre-train soldiers for the Soviet nation-state;

(3) using sport, specifically, as a means of obtaining the fit, obedient and disciplined work force needed for achieving economic and military strength and efficiency – in particular, in order:

(a) to raise physical and social health standards – and the latter meant not simply educating people in the virtues of bodily hygiene, regular exercise and sound nutrition, but also combating unhealthy deviant, anti-social (and therefore, anti-Soviet) behaviour: drunkenness, delinquency, prostitution and even religiosity and intellectual dissidence;

(b) to develop general physical dexterity, motor skills and other physical qualities useful for 'labour and defence';

(c) to socialise the population into the new establishment system of values; character training, advanced (so the Soviet leaders seem to have believed) by sport, in such values as loyalty, conformity, team spirit, cooperation and discipline, may well have encouraged compliance and cooperation in both work and politics – including of course, the development of an uncynical attitude towards political leaders;

(d) to encourage a population, in transition from a rural to an urban way of life, to identify themselves with wider communities – all-embracing social units such as the workplace, the neighbourhood, the town, the district, the region, the republic and, ultimately, the whole country. By associating sport (like other amenities) organisationally with the workplace, the Party leadership and its agencies could, moreover, better supervise, control and 'rationalise' the leisure time activities of employees;

(4) linking sport ideologically and even organisationally with military preparedness; the reasons for this 'militarisation' of sport have already been examined (see above pp. 294–295).

Of course, despite the form into which recreation was cast, workers and peasants could still derive satisfaction from it (both that of simple play and for some the derivative benefits of a competitive system). These satisfactions may be said to include the following:

(1) in the society of the USSR, in which work, for much of the Soviet period, has been physically and mentally exhausting, in which the lack of varied popular entertainment has been marked, in which cramped homes have been more places to sleep in than to live in, in which the mass media have tended to be more instructional and work-oriented than entertaining and in which the psychic pressures on the individual have sometimes been overwhelming, both participant and spectator sport have offered a particularly rewarding area of relaxation and recreation – a sphere of action providing genuinely pleasurable excitements through playful and unthreatening competition;

(2) in an environment, like that of the historical Soviet Union, in which personal choices about work and home have been

extremely limited, association based upon shared sporting interests may have been both particularly necessary and particularly satisfying to members of various groups of people – especially those uprooted geographically and socially from traditional patterns of culture;

(3) in a society going through periods of crisis and disorientingly rapid change, sports seem to play a particularly valuable rôle for individuals both as a 'safety valve', providing more or less harmless outlets for the release of accumulated emotional tensions, and as a compensatory device, offering satisfactions denied elsewhere in society; sport constitutes a socially acceptable area of self-expression and even creativity. Sports pageants and Olympic-style festivals, for example, contain all the trappings of communal ritual and provide, for some, a cathartic experience not dissimilar in function to that of a religious service. Both religion and sport have been described as 'opiates of the masses', serving in many societies to dull the senses, to mystify fundamentally unequal social relationships and to exact conformism;[1]

(4) in a society in which the 'politicisation' of so much of life and the consequent dependence of personal prestige and membership of society's élite groups on one's political record and reliability made it difficult to gain access to certain privileges by non-political means, sport – though set in a political context – constituted one such rather rare means – the most accessible to the rank-and-file – of acquiring prestige and material rewards by relatively non-political means.

Similarities and dissimilarities in Western and Soviet sport

As Western urban-industrial society developed, a wide range of sports was gradually created (or adapted from the sports of the nobility) for play, largely in an urban setting, by the 'middle classes', imbued with their values and designed initially for their

[1] Sport and religion were, of course, not alone in offering outlets or escapes from the work centred and highly disciplined aspects of Soviet life: harsh working and living conditions and other frustrations certainly encouraged escape into the oblivion of drunkenness; excessive demands for stoicism and discipline may well have stimulated the taste for grotesque counterparts such as the circus and (more dangerously) satire.

training and entertainment. With economic change, rising living standards and the beginnings of leisure for wider sections of the community, many sports were extended to the urban masses, a few being taken over almost completely by them and some new ones even being invented by members of the populace. In the course of these changes, many sports became commercialised and adapted for mass consumption and diversion, dominated by the profit motive and emasculated by the needs of a 'sports industry'. In recent years, with the increasing 'political' importance of international sports competition and 'success' (particularly against socialist states), Western governments, aided by commercial sponsorship, have intervened in the organisation of some sports and provided amenities for pursuing them.

In the development of Soviet society, sport has always been state-controlled, encouraged and shaped by specific utilitarian and ideological designs – primarily for labour and military training and the all-round education of an ideal citizen. Sport was proclaimed an essential ingredient of the way of life of *all* citizens. This state-centralised control of sport prevented commercial exploitation of mass spectator sports for private profit and the playing of particular sports in which actual or simulated violence predominated, and inhibited the extremes of hooliganism, corruption and commercialism associated with a number of sports in the West.

In spite of these dissimilarities, there are today features of organised sport strikingly common to both Soviet and Western societies. There are, of course, the very *sports themselves* – sports that were, in the main, organised by 'middle-class' groups in the course of Western industrial development. Together with these sports goes an elaborate system of government sports departments, giant amphitheatres, officials, trainers, semi- and full-time professional players, sports journalists, and so on – even gambling establishments. A similar sports ideology in East and West cultivates irrational loyalties and ascribes similar prominence to the winning of victories, the setting of records and the collection of trophies, and surrounds these created 'events' with an aura characterised by what can only be termed 'ballyhoo'. All this constitutes a fetishism of sport in both worlds – though the motives for this in the two societies may differ.

Whereas in Western society, the fetishism of sport was a consequence of this field of human action (like almost all others), offering the possibilities of profit-making – and turning out, characteristically without any conscious purposive intent, to be a highly appropriate means of distracting the masses from class-conscious politicisation, in Soviet society, it characteristically resulted from centralised planning and administration designed to subordinate areas of social life such as sport to the political and economic tasks of building a strong state. The distinction is important in terms of the potential dynamics of the two systems.

Today, the inheritors of the sports system evolved during the Stalin years find themselves in a quandary: To what extent should or must they break with the past? How sharply and through what new forms should necessary change be brought about? In the field of culture, and specifically of recreation, how could they dismantle the various by now well-entrenched fetishised institutions and values? The task is circumscribed partly by the fact that, today, sport is evidently regarded as an important weapon in the rivalry between what Soviet leaders may see as the two diametrically opposed world systems – capitalism and Soviet socialism. The international situation is just one of a number of objective constraints (that also include domestic, economic, cultural and political factors) on leaders attempting to realise their desires – which are likely to be by no means uniform or clearly perceived. Whatever course of action is pursued, the *subjective will* of the leaders is bound to be constrained by the *objective possibilities* of the situation.

It is hardly surprising, then, that the actions of the leadership should appear contradictory: on the one hand, it reinforces the fetishism of sport by its increasing stress on international success in sport and on the training of ever faster, stronger and more skilful full-time sportsmen (e.g. through sports boarding schools) in an ever-growing range of highly organised and institutionalised sports, while it cultivates among the mass of people an obsession with mass-produced, media-oriented spectator sports. On the other hand, the leadership is increasing the amount of free time available to people, is providing an ever-wider range of amenities and equipment for people to pursue recreational activities of their choice, is encouraging people to be active participants rather than passive spectators and is increasing opportunities for individuals to enjoy recreational activities in a non-institutional setting (fishing, hiking, rock climbing, boating, potholing, water skiing, horse riding, skin diving).

The public's positive gains

Whatever the interpretation of past events or the perspectives for future development, there can certainly, however, be no doubt about the absolute positive material gains of the population of the old Russian Empire in the sphere of recreation since 1917. It is also in many ways better off in this respect than the public in Western countries. Most of the urban population can today pursue the sport of their choice, using facilities largely free of charge through their trade union sports society. Sports are not, as they were before the Revolution, in the hands of foreigners, commercial promoters, circus entrepreneurs or private clubs with restricted entrance. Unlike some Western sports clubs, Soviet sports societies do not discriminate in regard to membership on the basis of sex, nationality, income or social background. Even sports involving expensive equipment are open to anyone who shows natural ability and inclination.

The Soviet Union could hardly have become what it is today – the world's leading all-round competitive sporting power – without a genuinely wide base – virtually universal access to the means of practising sports. Lastly, there has been, too, an undeniable consistent aspiration and effort in the USSR to make sport culturally uplifting, aesthetically satisfying and morally reputable which, given all necessary qualifications, has set a tone of altruism and devotion in its sport in which there is much which cannot but be admired.

Appendix I
Sports leaders and the *Nomenklatura*: biographies and comment

As part of the mechanism of its overall control of sport, the CPSU leadership places reliable Party cadres in positions of authority in the sports movement. Through its *nomenklatura* (list of Party appointments) the Party can control the personnel at every level of the sporting, like every other, hierarchy. Decisions on the appointment of top sports leaders (for example, the chairman of the central sports body) are made directly by the Party Secretariat, whereas those on the appointment of principals of institutes of physical culture, heads of scientific institutes concerned with sport, chairmen of voluntary sports societies and suchlike are the responsibility of the appropriate departments of the Party Central Committee; Regional Party Committees supervise lower-level appointments.

In choosing officials, political reliability and past successes at lower levels appear to be more important than technical knowledge of a particular field and its organisation. This is the principle in sport as in most other fields. The major characteristics desired in Party officials appears to be trustworthiness, rather than technical training. Nonetheless, changes have occurred over time that have inevitably affected the 'generalists' v 'specialists' status in Soviet institutions. With the increasingly technical nature of sport and the availability of enough good specialists to fill technical posts, leading positions in the sports hierarchy have, since the war, been full-time appointments. No longer does a leading Party member combine several top posts, as happened in the 1920s and 1930s. All the same, the Party leadership continues to place reliable Party cadres in the chairmanship of the central sports body, refusing to relinquish the post to a full-time specialist with previous experience in sport and physical culture. The pattern is apparent if we examine the biographies of the dozen people who have been the top sports leaders.

NIKOLAI PODVOISKY (1880–1948), Chairman of the Supreme Council of Physical Culture attached to *Vsevobuch*, 1920–1923 and of the Red Sport International. He had been a Party member since 1901 and was chairman of the Military Revolutionary Committee in Petrograd during the October 1917 revolution. Despite the fact that he had had no previous background in sport, he did write a number of booklets on the subject, including *Kakaya fizicheskaya kul'tura nuzhna proletariatu SSSR i kem ona dolzhna sozdavat'sya (What Physical Culture the USSR Proletariat Needs and Who Should Provide It)* (1923) and *O mezhdunarodnom krasnom sportivnom dvizhenii i yevo ocherednykh zadachakh (On the International Red Sports Movement and its Immediate Tasks)* (1924). Although, unlike many old Bolsheviks, he escaped arrest and execution during the purge years, he was deprived of all influence after the mid-1930s.

NIKOLAI SEMASHKO (1874–1949), Chairman of the Supreme Council of Physical Culture, 1923–1931, while concurrently People's Commissar of Health of the RSFSR (1918–1930). He had been a Party member since 1893, had worked as a doctor after graduating in medicine from Kazan' University in 1901, was secretary of the Foreign Bureau of the Central Committee of the Bolshevik Party, 1908–1910, and took part in the October insurrection in 1917. His medical qualifications found reflection in the 'hygienist' bias of sport and physical culture during the 1920s; he is, in fact, regarded as 'the founder of Marxist social hygiene'. After 1930, he worked in various (relatively minor) administrative posts within the health service, surviving the purges. His writings include *Ocherki po teorii organizatsii zdravookhraneniya (Essays on the Theory of Health Protection)* (1947) and *Puti sovetskoi fizicheskoi kul'tury (Paths of Soviet Physical Culture)* (1926).

NIKOLAI ANTIPOV (1894–1941), Chairman of the All-Union Council of Physical Culture, March 1931–1933. He had been a Party member since 1912 and was a deputy to the Petrograd Soviet in 1917. He served as Chairman of the Petrograd Extraordinary Commission *(Cheka)* 1917–1919, was a member of the Presidium of the All-Union Central Council of Trade Unions after 1920, acted as People's Commissar for Posts and Telegraph, 1928–1931, was a Party Central Committee member from 1924 to 1934 and a Deputy-Chairman of the USSR Council of People's Commissars, 1931–1936. He had had no previous experience of sport prior to taking up the chairmanship of the All-Union Council of Physical Culture. In 1936, he was arrested and charged with being a 'right oppositionist' and an accomplice of Bukharin; he is reported as having been shot in 1941.

VASILY MANTSEV (1889–1939), Chairman of the All-Union Council of Physical Culture, 1933–1936. He, too, was an Old Bolshevik and had occupied a high post in the *Cheka* since 1919. He had, in fact, been a founder of *Dinamo* Sports Society and one of its first organisers during the 1920s. Like many other Party officials, he had to be versatile enough to occupy several different posts, some concurrently. One of these was sport, after which he briefly became a Deputy-Chairman of the RSFSR Supreme Court (1936–1937). His fate was to be arrested, charged as a 'left oppositionist' and executed in 1939. Ironically, he had been called as a witness in the trial of his 'right oppositionist' predecessor, Antipov, in the so-called Right Opposition Trial of 1938.

IVAN KHARCHENKO (1906–1939), Chairman of the All-Union Committee on Physical Culture and Sport Affairs, June 1936–August 1937. He (like the present chairman, Sergei Pavlov) had risen through the ranks of the *Komsomol* and had supervised its department concerned with physical culture – therefore he did have some prior experience of sports administration. He acceded to the post of Chairman at the relatively young age of 30 but was the third successive sports chairman to be purged at a time when the sports administration was caught up in the general campaign of vilification and denunciation of leaders in all walks of life (except, of course, the Leader himself – Stalin) as 'enemies of the people'. He is reported to have died in a labour camp in 1939.

E. L. KNOPOVA, Chairwoman of the All-Union Committee on Physical Culture and Sport Affairs for a brief period of three months, August–October 1937. She was the only woman ever to have held the top sports post, but she stood down to become Deputy-Chairman very soon after her accession. Although far fewer women than men were purged – hence the possible reason for her appointment – her sex did not save her from arrest in September 1938. Her fate has not been disclosed.

ALEXANDER ZELIKOV, Chairman of the All-Union Committee on Physical Culture and Sports Affairs, October 1937–September 1938. He had the misfortune to take over the reins of the sports movement at a time when the sports administration had come under constant attack in the press for harbouring numerous 'enemies of the people', including Trotskyists, whose alleged intention was to sabotage an organisation regarded as vital to the defence of the USSR. Zelikov was accused of being 'non-Bolshevik' and removed from office along with all his deputy-chairpersons in September 1938. No information is available on their ultimate fate.

VASILY SNEGOV, Chairman of the All-Union Committee on Physical Culture and Sport Affairs and, subsequently, *Vsevobuch*, January

1939–1945, saw the sports movement through the war years. Being a military man – a colonel and previously an official in the People's Commissariat of Defence – he was evidently thought to be eminently suited to adapt physical culture to military training and the needs of war.

NIKOLAI ROMANOV, Chairman of the All-Union Committee on Physical Culture and Sport Affairs, 1945–May 1948, Deputy-Chairman, 1948–1953 and again Chairman, 1953–1962. He had come up through the *Komsomol* ranks to gain the sports chairmanship, then moved on to become the Secretary of the All-Union Central Council of Trade Unions.

NIKOLAI APPOLONOV, Chairman of the All-Union Committee on Physical Culture and Sport Affairs, May 1948–1953. He had been commander of the MVD Border Guards immediately after the war; it has been suggested that this was a qualification which the leadership believed could bring better discipline and organisation to the sports movement at a time when Soviet athletes were venturing into the international arena. However, he was removed from his post following the fall of Beria in July 1953.

YURI MASHIN, Chairman of the Union of Sports Societies and Organisations of the USSR, 1962–1968. He, too, had had little or no experience in sport, was a relatively young Party official seconded to the post, and he survived the general reorganisation after the fall of Khrushchov in October 1964.

SERGEI PAVLOV, Chairman of the All-Union Committee on Physical Culture and Sport Affairs since 1968 (the present incumbent). Significantly, he studied for two years at the Moscow Institute of Physical Culture (1950–1952) after completing a course in farm management at a *tekhnikum*. But his career has been solely in Party-appointed posts. He was accepted into the Party in 1954 (at the age of 25) while Secretary of the Krasnogvardeisky District (Moscow) *Komsomol* Committee (1952–1955). Subsequently, he became a Second Secretary, then First Secretary of the Moscow *Komsomol* Committee (1957–1959) prior to becoming Second and then First Secretary of the Central Committee of the *Komsomol* (1959–1968). Concurrently, he was a Deputy to the RSFSR Supreme Soviet (1959 convocation) and to the USSR Supreme Soviet (1962 convocation), during which time he was also a member of the Foreign Affairs Commission of the Soviet of the Union. He gained trust and experience from several trips abroad, heading delegations to Austria, Guinea, Cuba, Finland, Bulgaria and East Germany in the period 1959–1963. He was therefore well-qualified to take over the sports administration in 1968.

Comments

(1) The leadership has changed frequently – 13 times in the space of just over half a century, and ten times since 1930; this turnover was, of course, particularly accelerated by the purges. As with other positions of responsibility in the Soviet Union, leaders have tended to rise and fall with the success or failure of their charge; thus, Yury Mashin lost his post after the 'failure' of Soviet athletes to 'win' the 1968 Olympic Games either in winter or in summer. But, at high levels, there is an even greater tendency to fall with one's patron (Bukharin – Beria), which does not seem to have happened since 1954 in sport – perhaps because sport is seen as more technical nowadays.

(2) Political experience and reliability appear to be more important than knowledge of or experience in sport. None of the chairmen (with the possible exception of Pavlov) are recorded as ever having been active in sport or even to have had any administrative training in it. These *nomenklatura* personnel received a 'generalist' training in Party schools whose purpose is ideological education rather than training in functional skills (the courses normally include such subjects as History of the CPSU, History of the Working-Class Movement, Marxist–Leninist Philosophy, Political Economy, and Propaganda and Agitation). Like military colleges, they tend to assure their graduates of successful promotion in an administrative hierarchy. Hence, capable administrators with an interest and background in sport tend to be overlooked in favour of a reliable Party man because the former may well not have attended a Party school.

(3) Despite the importance of women to the international success of Soviet sport and the large number of active sportswomen and women coaches, there has been only one chairwoman of the sports movement – and she for only three months. This reflects the position of women in top administrative positions in other sectors of society – particularly in regard to important Party appointments. Thus, in 1976, only 23 per cent of Party members were women and there was no women in the Politbureau of 20.[1] the *nomenklatura* is certainly an area in which Soviet women do not take advantage of the equal rights with men guaranteed them by the Constitution.

---

[1] The proportion of women in the highest positions in state and Party is relatively low in general: in Union-Republican Councils of Ministers, it was (in 1972) five per cent, and in the USSR Council of Ministers, it was one per cent; in the Party Central Committee and Central Auditing Commission, it was four per cent. See G. R. Barker, 'Women, Sex Rôles and Soviet Society' (paper delivered at Pendrell Hall Conference, 30 June 1972), p. 29.

Appendix II

Dates of first championships

Sport	Year	
	Men	Women
Speed skating	1918	1928
Skiing	1919	1921
Athletics	1920	1922
Chess	1920	1927
Swimming	1921	1922
Soccer	1922	–
Weightlifting	1922	–
Cycling (track)	1923	1924
Diving	1923	1925
Basketball	1924	1923[a]
Tennis	1924	1924
Figure skating	1924	1928
Russian draughts[b]	1924	1936
Yachting	1924	1945
Pistol shooting	1924	1951
Graeco-Roman wrestling	1924	–
Ski jumping	1926	–
Cycling (road) ⎫ Fencing ⎪ Rowing ⎬ Sculling ⎭	1928	1928
Gymnastics	1928	1932
Rifle shooting	1928	1949
Bandy ⎫ Water polo ⎭	1928	–
Volleyball	1933	1933
Equestrian sport	1938	1938
Motor boat racing	1938	–
Acrobatics	1939	1940
Sambo	1939	

Sport	Year	
	Men	Women
Free-style wrestling	1945	–
Motorcycling	1946	1946
Ice hockey	1947	–
Calisthenics	–	1949[a]
Table tennis	1951	1951
Canoeing ⎱	1953	–
Pentathlon ⎰		
Draughts	1954	–
Handball	1956	1956
Sub-aqua sport	1958	1958
Badminton	1963	1963
Archery	1964	1964
Rugby	1968	–
Field hockey	1971	1935[a]
Orienteering	1972	1972

[a] Women first.
[b] Russian draughts are played on a 64-square (not 100-square) board.
Sources: N. A. Makartsev, *Stranitsy istorii sovetskovo sporta* (Moscow, 1967), pp. 40, 43; *Sport v SSSR* (1968), No. 5, p. 17; *Sport v SSSR* (1968), No. 9, p. 6; *Sovetsky sport*, 17 September 1972, p. 3.

Appendix III
Administrative Structure of trade union Voluntary Sports societies (*VSS*)

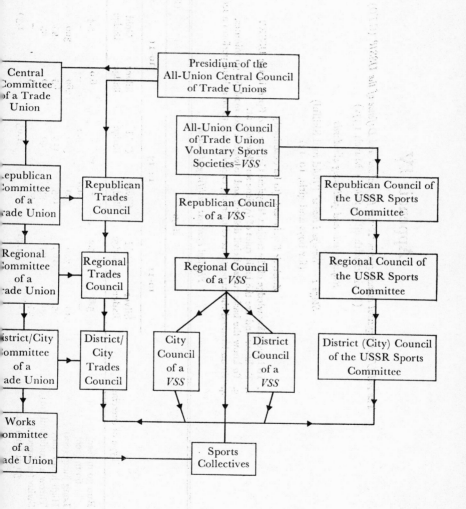

Appendix IV

The All-Union physical culture system 'Ready for Labour and Defence of the USSR' (GTO)
(Revised with effect from 1 March 1972)

Requirements and qualifying standards

Stage 1 – 'Smelye i lovkie' ('Bold and Skilful')
(for boys and girls, 10–13)

Academic Requirements (to be examined)

1. To have a knowledge of the subject 'Physical Culture and Sport in the USSR'.
2. To know and use the basic rules of hygiene and keeping fit.
3. To know the basic rules of civil defence and to wear a gas mask for 30 minutes.
4. To understand the importance of morning exercises and to be able to perform a set of exercises.

Physical exercises: qualifying standards

| | Boys | | | | Girls | | | |
| | 10–11 | | 12–13 | | 10–11 | | 12–13 | |
Type of exercise	Silver Badge	Gold Badge	Silver Badge	Gold Badge	Silver Badge	Gold Badge	Silver Badge	Gold Badge
1. Run 30 m (sec)	5.8	5.2	–	–	6.0	5.4	–	–
60 m (sec)	–	–	10.0	9.2	–	–	10.2	9.6
2. Long jump (cm)	310	340	340	380	260	300	300	350
3. High jump (cm)	95	105	105	115	85	95	100	110
4. Throw a tennis ball (m)	30	35	35	40	20	23	23	26
5. Swim (untimed, m)	25	–	50	–	25	–	50	–
50 m (min sec)	–	1.20	–	1.05	–	1.30	–	1.15

6. Ski 1 km (min sec)	8.00	7.30	–	–	8.30	8.00	–	–
Ski 2 km (min sec)	–	–	14.00	13.00	–	–	16.30	15.30
In snow-free regions:								
Cycle 5 km (min) or	16	15	15	14	19	18	18	17
Run cross country (m)	500	1,000	1,000	1,500	300	500	500	1,000
7. Pull-ups	3	5	5	7	–	–	–	–
Climb a rope using one's legs (m cm)	–	–	–	–	2.50	2.80	2.80	3.50

Note: For the Gold Badge, one must attain not less than five qualifying standards at Gold Badge level plus two standards at Silver Badge level.

Events to be selected by Gold Badge candidates
(any two events for 10–11's, any three for 12–13's)

1. Obstacle course 80 m	–	4 obts.	–	5 obts.	–	3 obts.	–	4 obts.
2. Gymnastics	–	3 exs.	–	4 exs.	–	2 exs.	–	3 exs.
3. Tourist hike with test of tourist knowledge	–	5–6 km	–	Fulfil requirements for the 'Young Tourist' badge	–	–	–	Fulfil requirements for the 'Young Tourist' badge
4. Shooting	–	–	–	Fulfil requirements for the 'Young Marksman' badge	–	–	–	Fulfil requirements for the 'Young Marksman' badge
5. Speed skating 100 m (sec)	–	20	–	18	–	22	–	20
6. Take part in team game competitions	–	5	–	8	–	5	–	8

Note: To obtain a Gold Badge, in addition to obtaining the five qualifying standards at Gold Badge level and two at Silver Badge level, one must pass in two or three of the above events.

Stage 2 – '*Sportivnaya smena*' ('Sporting Reserve')
(for boys and girls 14–15)

Academic requirements (to be examined)

1. To have a knowledge of the subject 'Physical Culture and Sport in the USSR'.
2. To know and carry out the rules for personal and public hygiene.
3. To know the basic rules of civil defence and to wear a gas mask for 30 minutes.
4. To be able to explain the importance of and perform a set of morning exercises.

Physical exercises: qualifying standards

	Boys		Girls	
Type of exercise	Silver Badge	Gold Badge	Silver Badge	Gold Badge
1. Run 60 m (sec)	9.2	8.4	10.0	9.4
2. Run 500 m (min sec)	–	–	1.00	0.55
500 m (min sec)	1.45	1.30	–	–
or				
Skate 300 m (min sec)	0.58	0.50	1.05	1.00
3. Long jump (cm)	390	450	310	360
or high jump (cm)	120	130	105	110
4. Throw a tennis ball (m)	38	46	25	30
5. Ski 2 km (min)	–	–	15	14
3 km (min sec)	17.30	16.30	–	–
In snow-free regions:				
Run cross country				
1 km (min sec)	–	–	5.20	5.00
2 km (min sec)	10	9	–	–
or				
Cycle 5 km	28	26	–	–
10 km	28	26	–	–
6. Swim 50 m (min sec)	1.00	0.50	1.10	1.00
7. Do pull-ups or press-ups	–	–	8	10
8. Tourist hike with test of tourist knowledge (km)	12	16	12	16
9. Obtain a sports ranking (in any sport)	–	Junior II–III	–	Junior II–III

Note: For the Gold Badge, one must attain not less than six qualifying standards at Gold Badge level plus two standards at Silver Badge level (except item 9).

Stage 3 – '*Sila i muzhestvo*' ('Strength and Courage')
(for boys and girls 16–18)

Academic requirements (to be examined)

1. To have a knowledge of the subject 'Physical Culture and Sport in the USSR'.
2. To know and carry out the rules for personal and public hygiene.
3. To master the programme for initial military training (including the section on protection from weapons of mass destruction) and to wear a gas mask for 1 hour, or undergo specialist training in a *DOSAAF* organisation, or obtain an applied technical speciality (for boys). Girls should know the basic rules of civil defence and wear a gas mask for one hour.
4. To be able to explain the importance of and perform a set of morning exercises.

Physical exercises: qualifying standards

	Boys		Girls	
Type of exercise	Silver Badge	Gold Badge	Silver Badge	Gold Badge
1. Run 100 m (sec)	14.2	13.5	16.2	15.4
2. Run 500 m (min sec)	–	–	2.00	1.50
1,000 m (min sec)	3.30	3.20	–	–
or				
Skate 500 m (min sec)	1.25	1.15	1.30	1.20
3. Long jump (cm)	440	480	340	375
or				
High jump (cm)	125	135	105	115
4. Hurl a hand-grenade of				
500 gm (m)	–	–	21	25
700 gm (m)	35	40	–	–
or putt the shot of				
4 kg (m cm)	–	–	6.00	6.80
5 kg (m)	8	10	–	–
5. Ski 3 km (min)	–	–	20	18
5 km (min)	27	25	–	–
or 10 km (min)	57	52	–	–
In snow-free regions:				
Run cross country 3 km (min)	–	–	20	18
6 km (min)	35	32	–	–
or cycle cross country				
10 km (min)	–	–	30	27
20 km (min)	50	46	–	–
6. Swim 100 m (min sec)	2.00	1.45	2.15	2.00
7. Press-ups	8	12	–	–
Pull-ups			10	12

	Boys		Girls	
Type of exercise	Silver Badge	Gold Badge	Silver Badge	Gold Badge
8. Fire a small-bore rifle at 25 m (points)	33	40	30	37
or at 50 m (points)	30	37	27	34
or				
Fire a heavy weapon – according to the initial military training programme	Satis-factory	Well	Satis-factory	Well
9. Tourist hike with test of tourist knowledge and orienteering	1 hike of 20 km or 2 hikes of 12 km	1 hike of 25 km or 2 hikes of 15 km	1 hike of 20 km or 2 hikes of 12 km	1 hike of 25 km or 2 hikes of 15 km
10. Obtain a sports ranking in:				
(a) motor car, motor boat, motorcycle, gliding, parachuting, aeroplane, helicopter, sub-aqua or water sports, biathlon, pentathlon, pistol shooting, radio sport, orienteering, wrestling or boxing;	–	III	–	III
(b) any other sport	–	II	–	II

Note: For the Gold Badge, one must complete not less than 7 qualifying standards at Gold Badge level and 2 standards at Silver Badge level (except item 10). Girls who have completed a first-aid training course may forego item 10 for their Gold Badge.

Stage 5* – '*Bodrost' i zdorov'ye*' ('Fitness and Health')
(for men 40–60, women 35–55)

Academic requirements (to be examined)

1. To have a knowledge of the subject 'Physical Culture and Sport in the USSR'.
2. To know and carry out the rules for personal and public hygiene.
3. To know the basic rules of civil defence and to wear a gas mask for 30 minutes.
4. To be able to explain the importance of and to perform a set of morning exercises.

* For Stage 4, see pp. 222–223 above.

Physical exercises: qualifying standards

	Men		Women	
Type of exercise	40–49 Gold Badge	50–60 Gold Badge	35–44 Gold Badge	45–55 Gold Badge
1. Run 60 m (sec)	12.0	–	12.8	–
Jogging 200 m (min sec)	–	–	–	1.20
400 m (min sec)	–	2.50	–	–
2. Run 300 m (min sec)	–	–	1.25	–
800 m (min sec)	3.15	–	–	–
or Jogging (min)	20	15	10	8
3. Standard long jump (cm)	190	170	150	130
4. Hurl a hand grenade of				
500 gm (m)	–	–	18	–
700 gm (m)	32	–	–	–
or putt the shot of				
4 kg (m cm)	–	–	5.50	–
7.257 kg (m cm)	6.20	–	–	–
Throw a medicine ball of				
2 kg (m)	–	8	–	6
5. Ski 2 km (min)	–	–	18	Without time-check
5 km (min)	35	Without time-check	–	–
In snow-free regions:				
Jogging 3 km (min)	–	–	25	Without time-check
5 km (min)	40	Without time-check	–	–
or Cycle 5 km (min)	–	–	20	–
10 km (min)	40	–	–	–
6. Swim, time-free (m)	100	50	100	50
7. Press-ups	10	8	6	4
8. Fire from a small-bore rifle at 25 m (points)	34	–	–	–
9. Tourist hike (km)	20	10	20	10

Note: Gold Badge only (no Silver) is awarded; candidates must complete all exercises at the standards indicated.

Appendix V

Syllabus for undergraduate teacher-coaches at the State Central Institute of Physical Culture: 1975

	Total number of:		Distribution of disciplines by year of course			
Discipline	exams	tests	I	II	III	IV
History of the Communist Party of the Soviet Union	2	–	+			
Marxist–Leninist Philosophy	4	–		+		
Scientific Atheism	7	–				+
Political Economy	6	–			+	
Scientific Communism	–	8				+
Foreign Language	7	4	+	+		+
Introduction to Specialism	–	–	+			
Biochemistry and Sports Biochemistry	3	2	+	+		
Human Anatomy	2	–	+			
Sports Morphology	–	3		+		
Biomechanics with Fundamentals of Sports Techniques	–	4		+		
Physiology and Sports Physiology	5	3		+	+	
Hygiene and Sports Hygiene	6	6			+	
Sports Medicine (medical control, sports pathology)	8	6			+	+
Sports Massage	–	4		+		
Psychology and Sports Psychology	4	4		+		
Education and History of Education	2	–	+			
Theory and Method of PE	5	4		+	+	
Sports Coaching	6	–			+	
Biometrics	–	8				+
Statistics	–	2	+			

History of Sport	1	–	+			
Organisation, Economics and Management of Sport	7	7				+
Sports Amenities	–	1	+			
Film and Photography	–	2	+			
Chosen Sport and Method of Teaching it	8	7	+	+	+	+
Additional Sports:						
Athletics	2	2	+			
Gymnastics	3	3	+	+		
Swimming	3	3	+			
Team Sports	6	5		+	+	
Skiing	1	1	+			
Weightlifting	–	1	+			
Optional courses*	7	8		+	+	
Civil Defence	–	8				+
Remedial physical education (for women)	8	7		+	+	+

* These include political education in sport, organisation of sports work, organisation of the international Olympic movement, forecasting sports talent, rehabilitation of work capacity, etc.

In addition to their lectures and seminars, students are required to go on organised visits to museums, exhibitions, and places of revolutionary, war and labour glory. They must prepare dissertations, take part in readings from Lenin, make reports and become acquainted with the working conditions and everyday lives of factory workers. They must also themselves work on state farms and construction sites.

By way of financial support, students receive a state grant of 40 rubles a month in their first three years, and 45 rubles a month in their final year. Students who obtain 'excellent' marks in their tests and take an active part in the social life of the Institute may receive a 15 per cent increment to the ordinary grant – i.e. 50 rubles in the first three years and 56 rubles in the final year. The best students in Year III may be sent abroad to other socialist states for their practical work.

The Final Examination for students who have completed all academic and other requirements is in two subjects: Scientific Communism and Physiology. In addition, students must defend their dissertation. Successful students are then awarded the diploma of 'Teacher of Physical Education and Coach in (a particular sport)'. A government commission gives each student a placement in a particular area of the country where he or she has to work according to his or her speciality for a minimum of three years.

Source: Notes for the Guidance of Students at the State Central Order of Lenin Institute of Physical Culture (in Russian) (Moscow, 1975), p. 43.

Appendix VI

Voluntary Sports Societies (VSS)[a], *by membership and distinctions: 1966*

				Including	
Club	Constituency	Sports collectives	Sportsmen	First-rank sportsmen	Masters of Sport
I. All voluntary societies	USSR population	...	...	...	...
of total I:					
A. Republican	Population at large	77,086	21,098,330	145,913	13,651
of total A:					
a. *Trud*	RSFSR, urban areas	9,727	5,188,342	72,972	6,984
b. *Urozhai*	RSFSR, rural areas	26,668	5,506,328	9,870	447
c. *Avangard*	Ukraine, urban area	3,749	2,004,167	21,505	1.911
d. *Kolgospnic*	Ukraine, rural areas	12,697	3,338,481	4,235	164
e. *Krasnoye Znamya*	Belorussia, urban	369	219,705	3,409	330
f. *Urozhai*	Belorussia, rural	3,931	658,246	686	46
g. *Enbek*	Kazakhstan, urban	556	308,499	3,456	241
h. *Kairat*	Kazakhstan, rural	2,988	659,872	1,567	82
i. *Daugava*	Latvia, urban	435	182,880	3,093	444
j. *Varpa*	Latvia, rural	1,286	134,183	1,039	62
k. *Jalgiris*	Lithuania, urban	369	162,272	4,040	521
l. *Nemunas*	Lithuania, rural	2,123	194,838	765	35
m. *Kalev*	Estonia, urban	418	133,978	2,194	523
n. *Eiud*	Estonia, rural	660	72,617	724	114
o. *Gantiadi*	Georgia, urban	747	149,147	2,825	344
p. *Kolmeurne*	Georgia, rural	1,853	263,418	1,583	240
q. *Ashkhatank*	Armenia, urban	217	53,309	920	122
r. *Sevan*	Armenia, rural	1,107	115,308	661	50
s. *Neftyanik*	Azerbaidzhan, urban	332	91,760	1,912	187
t. *Mekhsul*	Azerbaidzhan, rural	1,718	235,400	423	5
u. *Mekhnat*	Uzbekistan, urban	323	138,089	2,223	147
v. *Pakhtakor*	Uzbekistan, rural	1,720	418,967	848	28
w. *Tadzhikistan*	Tadzhikistan, urban	272	91,998	724	82
x. *Khosilot*	Tadzhikistan, rural	411	94,353	128	23

Club	Constituency	Sports collectives	Sportsmen	Including: First-rank sportsmen	Masters of Sport
y. *Alga*	Kirgizia, urban	144	51,604	478	63
z. *Kolkhozchu*	Kirgizia, rural	469	102,789	62	9
aa. *Zakhmet*	Turkmenia, urban	270	81,635	1,025	102
bb. *Kolkhozchy*	Turkmenia, rural	472	98,439	191	10
cc. *Moldova*	Moldavia, urban	331	108,795	1,959	293
dd. *Kolkhoznikul*	Moldavia, rural	724	238,831	396	42
of total A:					
1. urban	USSR pop., urban	18,259	8,966,180	122,735	12,294
2. rural	USSR pop., rural	58,827	12,132,150	23,178	1,357
B. All-Union	Categories listed below:	...	...	...	...
of total B:					
a. *Burevestnik*	Students	663	1,280,777	41,767	5,854
b. *Dinamo*	Security forces and Border Guards	...	...	...	...
c. *Trudovye rezervy*	Vocation school pupils	...	...	...	...
d. *Lokomotiv*	Railway employees	6,737	1,363,400	15,395	1,755
e. *Spartak*	Employees in communications, road transport, health, administration, trade, food, culture, building, education and local industry	...	4,540,900	33,000	4,000
f. *Vodnik*	Sea, river and canal transport employees	1,090	189,000	4,191	397
of total I:					
α Trade Union	T.U. members	...[b]	16,340,257	217,088	24,300
β Other	Pupils, security forces, peasants	...	...	...	...

[a] All the urban Republican and the All-Union societies, with the exception of *Dinamo* and *Trudovye rezervy* (Labour Reserves), are run by the trade unions; *Spartak* came under trade union auspices in 1960. The major sports organisations other than *VSS* comprise the Soviet Army clubs, *DOSAAF*, the Ministry of Education *Detsko-yunosheskie sportivnye shkoly* (Children's and Young People's Sports Schools) and the *Obshchestvo okhotnikov* (Hunters' Society).

[b] The figure 26,749 excludes *Spartak*.

Sources: A. Dobrov, *God sportivny* (Moscow, 1968), p. 143; N. A. Makartsev, P. A. Sobolev (eds.), *Govoryat tsifry i fakty* (Moscow, 1968), pp. 9–10; N. A. Makartsev, *Stranitsy istorii sovetskovo sporta* (Moscow, 1967), pp. 13–14; *Entsiklopedichesky slovar' po fizicheskoi kul'ture i sportu*, Vol. I (Moscow, 1964), pp. 267–270.

Bibliography

This bibliography is compiled largely of the major works on sport and physical education published in the USSR between 1960 and 1975. It does not include dissertations or the more popular books on particular personalities or sports published in the West.

Western publications

Morton, H. W. *Soviet Sport*, Collier, New York, 1963
Richards, D. J. *Soviet Chess: Chess and Communism in the USSR*, OUP, 1965
Riordan, J. W. *Sport and Physical Education in the Soviet Union: an Outline*, SCR, London, 1975

Soviet publications

Area studies

Absalyamov, G. Sh. *Natsional'nye vidy sporta nenetskovo naroda. Dissertatsiya* (*National sports of the Nenets people. Dissertation*), Moscow, 1963
Nachkebiya, K. G. *Gruzinskie narodnye konnye igry* (*Georgian folk equestrian games*), Tbilisi, 1964
Narusova, I. *Salavat vykhodit na start* (*Salavat lines up for the start – Bashkir games*), Moscow, 1966
Natalov, G. G. *Evolyutsiya fizicheskikh uprazhnenii. Materialy XXI nauchnoi konferentsii Kazakhskovo GIFK* (*Evolution of physical exercises. Material of the 11th scientific conference of the Kazakh State Institute of Physical Culture*), Alma Ata, 1966
Steponaitis, V. I. *Nekotorye obshchie cherty fizicheskoi kul'tury litovskovo i drugikh narodov* (*Certain common features of physical culture among the Lithuanians and other peoples*), Kaunas, 1960
Tanikeyev, M. *Razvitie kazakhskikh natsional'nykh vidov sporta i igr s perioda prisoedineniya Kazakhstana k Rossi do Velikoi*

Oktyabr'skoi sotsialisticheskoi revolyutsii. Dissertatsiya (Development of Kazakh national sports and games from the time of Kazakhstan's attachment to Russia to the October Socialist Revolution. Dissertation), Leningrad, 1961

Vakhaniya, O. V. *Fizicheskoe vospitanie i sport v Abkhazii. Dissertasiya (Physical education and sport in Abkhazia. Dissertation)*, Moscow, 1961

Facts and figures

Dobrov, A. (ed), *God sportivny (Sporting year)*, Moscow, 1968
 Vsyo o sporte. Spravochnik (All about sport. Handbook), Moscow, 1972

Makartsev, N. and Sobolev, P. A. *Govoryat tsifry i fakty (Facts and figures speak)*, Moscow, 1968

Makartsev, N. and Rybolovlev, V. G. *Govoryat tsifry i fakty (Facts and figures speak)*, Moscow, 1969

Miroshnikov, V. F. (ed.), *Rekordy, sobytiya, lyudy, 1970 (Records, events, personalities, 1970)*, Moscow, 1971

Panorama sportivnovo goda, 1973 (Panorama of the 1973 sports year), Moscow, 1974

Rekordy, sobytiya, lyudy, 1968 (Records, events, personalities, 1968), Moscow, 1969

Rodichenko, V. S. (ed.), *Rekordy, sobytiya, lyudy, 1969 (Records, events, personalities, 1969)*, Moscow, 1970

Rubin, L. *Lyudy, sobytiya, rekordy − sport v tsifrakh i faktakh (People, events, records − sport in facts and figures)*, Moscow, 1966

Schmidt, N. E. and Polyev, A. S. *Sportivnye sooruzheniya v SSSR (Sporting amenities in USSR)*, Moscow, 1970

General

Entsiklopedichesky slovar' po fizicheskoi kul'ture i sportu v 3 tomakh (Encyclopedia on physical culture and sport in 3 volumes), Moscow, Vol. I (1961); Vol. II (1962); Vol. III (1963)

Fizicheskaya kul'tura, sport i turizm (Physical culture, sport and tourism), 2nd edn. Moscow, 1965

Galitsky, A. and Perepletchikov, L. *Puteshestvie v stranu igr (Journey into the land of games)*, Moscow, 1971

Ivonin, V. A. (ed.), *Velenie vremeni (Command of the times)*, Moscow, 1971
 Sputnik fizkul'turnovo rabotnika (Companion of the physical culture official), Moscow, 1972

Nemeshaev, N. A. (ed.), *Glavny rekord – zdorov'e* (*The main record is health*), Moscow, 1972
Shishigin, M. *Sport. Informatsiya. . . Informatsiya* (*Sport. Information, information*), Moscow, 1974
Yurmin, G. *Kakaya ty, Sportlandiya? Ot A do Ya po strane sporta* (*What are you, Sportland? From A to Z in the land of sport*), Moscow, 1970

Health, physiology and training

Biryukova, Z. I. *Vysshaya nervnaya deyatel'nost' sportsmenov* (*Higher nervous activity of sportsmen*), Moscow, 1961
Biryukova, Z. I. *Nervnaya sistema i sport* (*Nervous system and sport*), Moscow, 1968
Dobrovol'sky, V. K. *Fizicheskaya kul'tura i zdorov'e* (*Physical culture and health*), Moscow, 1967
D'yachkov, V. M. *Fizicheskaya podgotovka sportsmena* (*Physical preparation of a sportsman*), Moscow, 1967
Farfel', V. S. *Fiziologiya sporta* (*Physiology of sport*), Moscow, 1960
Farfel', V. S. and Kots, Ya. M. *Fiziologiya cheloveka* (*Physiology of man*), Moscow, 1970
Filin, V. P. (ed.), *Novoe v metodike vospitaniya fizicheskikh kachestv u yunykh sportsmenov* (*New factors in the methods of developing the physical qualities of young sportsmen*), Moscow, 1969
Gandel'sman, A. and Smirnov, K. *Sport i zdorov'e* (*Sport and health*), Moscow, 1963
Letunov, S. P. and Motylyanskaya, P. E. *Sport i serdtse* (*Sport and the heart*), Moscow, 1966
Psikhologicheskie voprosy sportivnoi trenirovki (*Psychological questions of sports coaching*), Moscow, 1968
Tambian, N. B. *Samokontrol' sportsmena* (*Self-control of the sportsman*), Moscow, 1967
Ter-Ovanesyan, A. A. *Sport, obuchenie, trenirovka, vospitanie* (*Sport. Teaching, coaching, educating*), Moscow, 1967
Tsivilizatsiya, sport i serdtse (*Civilisation, sport and the heart*), Moscow, 1968
Vaitsekhovsky, S. M. (ed.), *Fizicheskaya podgotovka sportsmenov vysshevo klassa* (*Physical preparation of top-class sportsmen*), Moscow, 1969
Yakolev, N. N. *Pitanie sportsmena* (*Diet of the sportsman*), Moscow, 1967
Yakolev, N. N., Korobkov, A. V. and Yananis, S. V. *Fiziologicheskie i biokhimicheskie osnovy teorii i metodiki sportivnoi trenirovki* (*Physiological and biochemical fundamentals of the theory and method of sports training*), Moscow, 1960

Zatsiorsky, V. M. *Kibernetika, matematika, sport* (*Cybernetics, mathematics and sport*), Moscow, 1969

History

Chudinov, I. D. (ed.), *Osnovnye postanovleniya, prikazy i instruktsii po voprosam fizicheskoi kul'tury i sporta, 1917–1957 gg.* (*Major resolutions, orders and instructions on issues concerning physical culture and sport, 1917–1957*), Moscow, 1959

Demeter, G. S. *Lenin ob okhrane zdorov'e trudyashchikhsya i fizicheskoi kul'ture* (*Lenin on safeguarding the health of working people and physical culture*), Moscow, 1969

Ekonomov, L. *Strastny uchitel'. Povestvovanie o P.F.Lesgafte* (*Enthusiastic teacher. Story of P.F. Lesgaft*), Moscow, 1969

Il'in, E. and Sokolov, I. *Nash Fizkul'tparad* (*Our physical culture parade*), Moscow, 1968

Istoriya i organizatsiya fizicheskoi kul'tury (*History and organisation of physical culture*), Yerevan, 1971

Kiselev, N.Ya. (ed.), *70 futbol'nykh let* (*70 years of football – in St Petersburg and Leningrad*), Leningrad, 1970

Korshak, Yu. *Stary, stary futbol* (*Old, old football*), Moscow, 1975

Lanshchikov, A. (ed.), *Sportsmeny. Seriya biografiy* (*Sportsmen. Biography series*), Moscow, 1973

Makartsev, N. A. *Stranitsy istorii sovetskovo sporta* (*Pages from the history of Soviet sport*), Moscow, 1967

Materialy pervoi vsesoyuznoi nauchno-metodicheskoi konferentsii po istorii i organizatsii fizicheskoi kul'tury. 1963 (*Material of the first All-Union research and methodological conference on the history and organisation of physical culture, 1963*), Moscow, 1964

Moskalev, V. M. and Spassky, O. D. (eds.), *Sport i vek* (*Sport and the age*), Moscow, 1967

Ocherki po istorii fizicheskoi kul'tury (*Studies in the history of physical culture*), Moscow, 1964

Orlov, L. P. (ed.), *Pyat'desyat shagov sportivnoi Rossii* (*Fifty steps of sporting Russia*), Moscow, 1967

Samoukov, F. I. (ed.), *Istoriya fizicheskoi kul'tury* (*History of physical culture*), Moscow, 1964

Samoukov, F. I. and Stolbov, V. V. (eds.), *Ocherki po istorii fizicheskoi kul'tury* (*Studies in the history of physical culture*), Moscow, 1967

Shatunov, G. *Leninsky vsevobuch* (*Leninist vsevobuch*), Moscow, 1970

Starovoitova, Z. *Polpred zdorov'ya* (*Ambassador of health – biography of N. Podvoisky*), Moscow, 1969
Stolbov, V. V. and Chudinov, I. D. *Istoriya fizicheskoi kul'tury* (*History of physical culture*), Moscow, 1970 (new edition 1976)
Tarasov, E. P. *Nikolai Il'ich Podvoisky. Ocherki voennoi deyatel'nosti* (*Nikolai Ilyich Podvoisky. Studies of military activity*), Moscow, 1964
Yesenin, K. *Moskovsky futbol* (*Moscow football – a history*), Moscow, 1974
Yusin, A. *Vek sportivny* (*Sporting age*), Moscow, 1971
Zholdak, V. I. (ed.), *Stranitsy moskovskovo sporta* (*Pages of Moscow sport*), Moscow, 1969

Important biographies and autobiographies

Baklanov, G. *Tochka opory* (*Point of support – gymnast's autobiography*), Moscow, 1971
Belousova, L. E. and Protopopov, O. A. *Zolotye kon'ki s brilliantami* (*Golden skates with diamonds – figure skaters' autobiography*), Moscow, 1971
Brumel', V. *Vysota* (*Height – autobiography of the high jumper*), Moscow, 1971
Latynina, L. *Ravnovesie* (*Balance – gymnast's autobiography*), Moscow, 1970
Starostin, A. *Povest' o futbole* (*Story of football*), Moscow, 1973
Zhukov, D. A. *Ivan Poddubny* (*Ivan Poddubny – a biography*), Moscow, 1975

International sport

Andrianov, K. A. (ed.), *Olimpiyskie igry* (*Olympic Games*), Moscow, 1970
Grigor'ev, A. N. *Luchnik protiv atleta* (*Archer against the athlete – criticism of some aspects of West German – 'militaristic' sport*), Moscow, 1971
Koval', V. I. *Sport – posol mira* (*Sport – an envoy of peace*), Moscow, 1974
Lyubomirov, N. and Sobolev, R. *Na pyati kontinentakh* (*On the five continents*), Moscow, 1967
Marinov, I. A. *Bunt' chernykh obeliskov'* (*Black obelisk band – critical remarks on some West German sport*), Moscow, 1970
Novoskol'tsev, V. *Sport puteshestvuet bez viz* (*Sports travels without visas*), Moscow, 1969
Pechersky, N. V. *Sport na strazhe mira* (*Sport on guard of peace*), Moscow, 1970

Romanov, A. O. *Mezhdunarodnoye sportivnoye dvizhenie* (*International sports movement*), Moscow, 1973
Mezhdunarodnye sportivnye ob"yedineniya i turistskie organizatsii (*International sports associations and tourist organisations*), Moscow, 1973

Labour and sport

Belinovich, V. V. *Kak organizovat' proizvodstvennuyu gimnastiku* (*How to organise production gymnastics*), Moscow, 1966
Fizkul'tura i podgotovka molodyozhi k trudu (*Physical culture and preparing young people for work*), Moscow, 1963
Grinenko, M. and Sanoyan, G. *Trud, zdorov'e, fizicheskaya kul'tura* (*Work, health and physical culture*), Moscow, 1974
Khairova, Yu. A. *Proizvodstvennaya gimnastika shakhtera* (*Production gymnastics for the miner*), Moscow, 1966
Muravev, I., Sitnikov, A. D. and Pomerantsev, Yu. *Proizvodstvennaya gimnastika dlya rabochikh shveinoi promyshlennosti* (*Production gymnastics for workers in the clothing industry*), Moscow, 1966
Nifontova, L. N. *Proizvodstvennaya gimnastika dlya rabotnikov umstvennovo truda* (*Production gymnastics for white-collar workers*), Moscow, 1969
Puchkov, K. P. *Sportivny zaporozhstal'* (*Sporting zaporozhstal*), Moscow, 1965
Zholdak, V. *Sport – pomoshchnik v trude* (*Sport – an aid in work*), Moscow, 1971

Organisation

Bunchuk, M. F. *Organizatsiya fizicheskoi kul'tury* (*Organisation of physical culture*), Moscow, 1972
Dupkov, A. D. (ed.), *Fizicheskoe vospitanie trudyashchikhsya* (*Physical education of working people*), Khar'kov, 1962
Fizicheskaya kul'tura, sport, turizm. Sbornik rukovodyashchikh materialov (*Physical culture, sport and tourism. Collection of material for guidance*), Moscow, 1965
Korotkov, I. and Kaleshnichenko, I. *Fizicheskaya kul'tura i sport v rabote kluba* (*Physical culture and sport in the work of a club*), Moscow, 1967
Makartsev, N. A. *Organizatsiya raboty fizkul'turnovo kollektiva* (*Organisation of the work of the physical culture collective*), Moscow, 1964
Mironenko, I. *Instruktoru fizkul'tury* (*To the physical culture instructor*), Moscow, 1966

Nikiforov, I. I. and Pol'shansky, V. S. (eds.), *Organizatsiya fizicheskoi kul'tury (Organisation of physical culture)*, Moscow, 1965

Pastukhov, E. *Kollektiv fizkul'tury na predpriyatii (Collective of physical culture at the factory)*, Moscow, 1967

Sereda, A. (ed.), *Ty – sportorganizator (You – sports-organiser)*, Moscow, 1975

Sto sovetov po fizicheskoi kul'ture i sportu (Hundred pieces of advice on physical culture and sport), Moscow, 1971

Vaitsekhovsky, S. M. *Kniga trenera (Book for the coach)*, Moscow, 1971

Volodin, P. and Makartsev, N. A. *Rozhdenie sportivnovo kollektiva (Birth of a sports collective)*, Moscow, 1965

Yedinaya vsesoyuznaya sportivnaya klassifikatsiya na 1969–1972 gg. (Uniform All-Union sports classification for 1969–1972), Moscow, 1969

Physical education, young people and sport

Bulgakova, N. Z. *Plavanie v pionerskom lagere (Swimming in a pioneer camp)*, Moscow, 1970

Fridman, M. G. *Uchebnoye posobie po kursu fizicheskovo vospitaniya (Study aid for the physical education course – for the physical education instructor at a Pioneer camp)*, Moscow, 1974

Kachashkin, V. M. *Metodika fizicheskovo vospitaniya (Methods of physical education)*, Moscow, 1972

Kayurov, V. S. (ed.), *Kniga uchitelya fizicheskoi kul'tury (Book for the teacher of physical culture)*, Moscow, 1973

Khotimsky, E. N. *V nashei sportshkole (In our sports school)*, Moscow, 1970

Kuznetsova, Z. I. (ed.), *Fizicheskaya kul'tura v shkole, Metodika urokov v 4–8 klassakh (Physical culture in school. Methodology of lessons for classes 4–8)*, Moscow, 1972

Materialy vtoroi nauchnoi konferentsii po fizicheskomu vospitaniyu detei shkolnovo vozrasta (Material of the second scientific conference on physical education of school-age children), Moscow, 1964

Materialy tret'ei nauchnoi konferentsii po fizicheskomu vospitaniyu detei i podrostkov (Material of the third scientific conference on the physical education of children and young people), Moscow, 1966

Orlov, S. V. *Vospitatel'naya rabota na urokakh fizicheskoi kul'tury v V–VIII klassakh (Educational work in the physical education lessons of classes 5–8)*, Moscow, 1966

Starikov, V. A. *Shkol'nikam o sporte (For schoolchildren about sport)*, Moscow, 1968

Voprosy yunosheskovo sporta (*Questions of young people's sport*), Moscow, 1967

Vasil'eva, T. N. et al., *Fizicheskaya kul'tura v V–VIII klassakh* (*Physical culture in classes 5–8*), Moscow, 1967

Yakovlev, V. G. *Fizicheskoye vospitanie detei v sem'e* (*Physical education of children in the family*), Moscow, 1971

Zaitsev, N. A. (ed.), *Voprosy fizicheskovo vospitaniya studentov* (*Questions of the physical education of students*), Leningrad, 1965

Sociology of sport

Borisov, Yu. V. (ed.), *Planirovanie razvitiya fizicheskoi kul'tury i sporta sredi sel'skovo naseleniya* (*Planning the development of physical culture and sport among the rural population*), Moscow, 1974

Borisov, Yu. V. and Pereverzin, I. I. (eds.), *Problemy upravleniya fizkul'turnym dvizheniem* (*Problems in administering the physical culture movement*), Moscow, 1973

Fizicheskaya kul'tura v sem'e (*Physical culture in the family*), Moscow, 1966, 2nd edn. 1969

Frenkin, A. A. *Estetika fizicheskoi kul'tury* (*Aesthetics of physical culture*), Moscow, 1963

Frenkin, A. A. (ed.), *Kritika burzhuaznoi 'sotsiologii sporta'* (*Criticism of bourgeois 'sociology of sport'*), Moscow, 1965

Kukushkin, G. I., Pereverzin, I. I. and Borisov, Yu. V. (eds.), *Planirovanie razvitiya fizicheskoi kul'tury i sporta* (*Planning the development of physical culture and sport*), Moscow, 1974

Materialy pervoi vsesoyuznoi konferentsii po sotsiologicheskim problemam fizicheskoi kul'tury i sporta (*Material of the first All-Union conference on sociological problems of physical culture and sport*), Leningrad, 1966

Materialy vsesoyuznoi konferentsii po rezul'tatam konkretnykh sotsiologicheskikh i sotsial'nykh issledovanii po fizicheskoi kul'ture i sportu (*Material of the All-Union conference on the results of concrete sociological and social research into physical culture and sport*), Moscow, 1966

Nikolaev, V. *V dvizhenii – zhizn'* (*Life in movement*), Moscow, 1970

Pereverzin, I. I. *Prognozirovanie i planirovanie fizicheskoi kul'tury* (*Forecasting and planning of physical culture*), Moscow, 1972

Ponomaryov, N. I. *Vozniknovenie i pervonachal'noe razvitie fizicheskovo vospitaniya* (*Origin and initial development of physical education*), Moscow, 1970

Rudik, P. A. (ed.), *Psikhologicheskie voprosy trenirovki i gotovnosti sportsmenov k sorevnovaniyu* (*Psychological questions concerning the coaching and preparation of sportsmen for competition*), Moscow, 1969
Stepanidin, G. (ed.), *Sport i lichnost'* (*Sport and personality*), Moscow, 1974
Stepovoi, P. S. *Sport i obshchestvo* (*Sport and society*), Tartu, 1972
Tezisy dokladov nauchno-metodicheskoi konferentsii po sotsiologicheskim voprosam fizicheskoi kul'tury (*Theses of reports at the scientific methodology conference on sociological questions of physical culture*), Minsk, 1966
Zholdak, V. I. (ed.), *Fizicheskaya kul'tura i svobodnoye vremya trudyashchikhsya i uchashcheisya molodyozhi* (*Physical culture and free time of working people and young students*), Moscow, 1972

Sport and the military

Gavrilin, V. *Sportsmen of the Soviet Army*, Moscow, 1973
Gavrilin, V. (ed.), *S emblemoi TsSKA* (*With the emblem of the Central Sports Club of the Army*), Moscow, 1973
Korol'kov, N. P. *Sport i zashchita rodiny* (*Sport and defence of the homeland*), Moscow, 1969
Tul'po, V. L. *Voenno-sportivny kompleks* (*Military sport programme*), Moscow, 1969
Vinokurov, V. and Kucherenko, O. *Dinamo Moskva* (*Moscow Dinamo*), Moscow, 1973

Theory, role and functions

Belorusova, V. V. (ed.), *Pedagogika. Uchebnoye posobie dlya institutov fizicheskoi kul'tury* (*Pedagogics. Study aid for physical culture institutes*), Moscow, 1972
Kharabuga, G. D. (ed.), *Teoriya i metodika fizicheskovo vospitaniya* (*Theory and methods of physical education*), Moscow, 1969
Kharabuga, G. D. *Sovetskaya sistema fizicheskovo vospitaniya* (*Soviet system of physical education*), Leningrad, 1970
Koryakovsky, I. M. (ed.), *Teoriya fizicheskovo vospitaniya* (*Theory of physical education*), Moscow, 1961
Mikhailov, V. *Sovetskaya sistema fizicheskoi kul'tury i sporta na novom etape* (*Soviet system of physical culture and sport at a new stage*), Moscow, 1967

Novikov, A. D. and Matveev, L. P. (eds.), *Teoriya i metodika fizicheskovo vospitaniya* (*Theory and methods of physical education*), Moscow, 1967

Orobinsky, M. D. *O zakonakh i zakonomernostyakh v fizicheskom vospitanii* (*On Laws and law-governed processes in physical education*), Volgograd, 1963

Petukhov, I. N. (ed.), *Nauchnye osnovy fizicheskovo vospitaniya i sporta. Referativny sbornik dissertatsii* (*Scientific basis of physical education and sport. Reference book of dissertations*), Moscow, 1971

Shishigin, M. V. *Propaganda fizicheskoi kul'tury i sporta* (*Propaganda of Physical Culture and Sport*), Moscow, 1975

Tourism

Alekseyenko, V. and Mamaev, F. *Mototsikletny turism* (*Motorcycle tourism*), Moscow, 1972

Korotkov, I. and Kolesnichenko, I. *Zony otdykha – fizkul'turnye zdravnitsy* (*Recreation zones – physical culture health resorts*), Moscow, 1969

Mikhailov, A. N. *Nasha rodina zimoi* (*Our country in winter*), Leningrad, 1969

Rakhmanov, P. A. *Posobie organizatoru turizma: osnovnye marshruty, konsultatsii, 1970* (*Aid for the tourism organiser: principal routes and advice, 1970*), Moscow, 1970

Smirnov, N. P. (ed.), *Russkaya okhota* (*Russian hunting*), Moscow, 1972

Vasil'ev, I. *V pomoshch' instruktoru turizma* (*Assistance for the instructor of tourism*), Moscow, 1966

Bibliographies

Kulinkovich, K. A. (ed.), *Upravlenie istorii sotsiologii fizkul'turnovo dvizheniya* (*History of sociology of sport movement* – 74 papers), Minsk, 1975

Mil'shtein, O. A. *Sotsiologiya fizicheskoi kul'tury i sporta v SSSR. Obzor osnovnykh napravleniy i annotirovanny ukazatel' literatury (1918–1974 gg.)* (*Sociology of physical culture and sport in USSR. Review of main trends and annotated guide to literature [1918–1974]*), Moscow, 1974

Index

CARROLL COLLEGE LIBRARY
Sport in Soviet society
GV623.R56

2 5052 00098993 1

DATE DUE

FE 2 '79			
MY 11 '79			
FE 6 '80			
MR 24 '80			

DEMCO 38-297

WITHDRAWN
CARROLL UNIVERSITY LIBRARY